D1741295

1 MONTH OF
FREE
READING

at

www.ForgottenBooks.com

By purchasing this book you are eligible for one month membership to ForgottenBooks.com, giving you unlimited access to our entire collection of over 1,000,000 titles via our web site and mobile apps.

To claim your free month visit:

www.forgottenbooks.com/free205580

ISBN 978-0-332-42191-9
PIBN 10205580

This book is a reproduction of an important historical work. Forgotten Books uses
state-of-the-art technology to digitally reconstruct the work, preserving the original format
whilst repairing imperfections present in the aged copy. In rare cases, an imperfection in
the original, such as a blemish or missing page, may be replicated in our edition. We do,
however, repair the vast majority of imperfections successfully; any imperfections that
remain are intentionally left to preserve the state of such historical works.

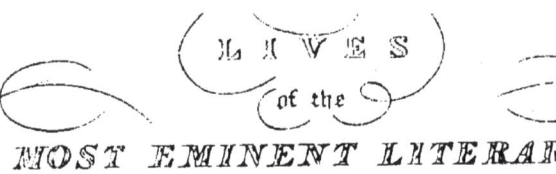

LIVES
of the
MOST EMINENT LITERARY
AND
SCIENTIFIC MEN
OF
GREAT BRITAIN.
English Poets.

By Robert Bell, Esq. Author of a History of Russia

VOL. II.

T. Creswell, del.   E. Finden. s

TABLE,

ANALYTICAL AND CHRONOLOGICAL,

TO THE SECOND VOLUME OF

LIVES OF
EMINENT LITERARY AND SCIENTIFIC MEN.

ENGLISH POETS.

JOHN DRYDEN.
1611—1700.

TWO CENTURIES OF MINOR POETS.

THOMAS SACKVILLE, EARL OF DORSET.

1527—1608.

JOHN BROWNSWERD.

15 [—]—1589.

JASPER HEYWOOD.

1535—1598.

THOMAS WATSON.

a 4

ALEXANDER POPE.

1688—1744.

b

EDWARD YOUNG.

1681—1765.

MARK AKENSIDE.

1721—1770.

LIVES

OF

EMINENT

LITERARY AND SCIENTIFIC MEN.

ENGLISH POETS.

JOHN DRYDEN.

1631—1700.

Of all our English poets, there is not one who, during his life, occupied so large a share of attention, or who sustained his reputation at its height through so long a period, and against such a clamour of jealousy and vituperation, as John Dryden. In whatever aspect we regard him — whether as a dramatist, a poet, a satirist, or a critic — the influence he exercised upon his age will be found deep and permanent. He tried nearly every form of poetry, originated some, revived others from the languages of antiquity, and was equally successful in all. Some of his contemporaries may have excelled him in particular styles, but none of them rivalled him in versatility of genius, fecundity of invention, and rapidity of production. A man who possessed such vigour of understanding, powers so various and flexible, and whose restless constitution sc peculiarly adapted him to a time of action and transition, might be expected not only to impart an energetic impulse to the arts he cultivated, but to become intimately mixed up with the transactions of his times. The expectation is realized in the narrative of his career. He gave a new direction to the public mind, and his life is the history of the literature with which it was blended.

Dryden opened an important era in English poetry. Spurning the refinements of Fairfax and his courtly imitator, he was the first who, in a comprehensive spirit, demonstrated and illustrated the poetical capacity of our language. He created our English school of poetry, alike removed from the tinsel imported by the Restoration, and the clouded metaphysics of erudite triflers at home. The boldness of his innovations, the originality of his labours, and, perhaps, the impetuosity of his temper, involved him in endless warfare with the writers of the day ; and thus, by the necessity of defending himself as a poet, he insensibly became an expounder of poetry. It would be difficult to decide in which character he contributed more essentially to elevate the standard of judgment ; but it is certain that his great merits cannot be fully appreciated without surveying him in both.

Yet, notwithstanding the prominent position he occupied, his biography was suffered to remain a blank in our literature, until it was undertaken by Dr. Johnson, whose means of obtaining the requisite materials appear to have been extremely limited. He complains, indeed, that he was compelled to collect his information from such sources as " casual mention or uncertain tradition supplied ;" but Malone, who was still later in the field, discovered a number of facts that had wholly escaped the researches of his predecessor, correcting, at the same time, a variety of mistakes into which he had fallen. Dr. Johnson seems to have contented himself in this biography with such particulars as happened to be immediately at hand, and to have atoned for circumstantial deficiencies by the weight and precision of his critical dissertations. A slight biography of Dryden, written by Derrick, who edited an edition of the poet's miscellanies in 1760 *, furnished the groundwork of Dr. Johnson's scanty narrative ; but its deficiencies and errors in matters of fact, are abundantly compensated by its splendid criticisms on Dryden's poetry. It was reserved for the patient industry of Malone to rescue from oblivion the life of Dryden, as Johnson had thus rescued his works ; and nothing more appeared necessary to the justification of his fame, than a biography that should combine the features of both, a labour which has been executed with masterly ability by sir Walter Scott. Since the publication of the life by Scott, another life of the poet has been written by the Rev. Mr. Mitford, which, although it adds nothing to our stock of information, may be consulted with advantage as a clear and accurate epitome. Dryden, therefore, after a long period of neglect, may be said to have been singularly lucky in his biographers at last. It is hardly to be hoped that the most sedulous investigation can increase the amount of actual details already ascertained and collected ; but a few side lights may nevertheless be derived from contemporary memoirs and correspondence, and from other sources not embraced in previous inquiries, by which the biography, without being enlarged in bulk, may be rendered more lucid and complete. Isolated and sometimes important illustrations are often derived from quarters where we least expect to find them ; and a discursive examination of the literature of the reign of Charles II., and of subsequent criticisms upon its history, and its influence. may suggest a few points of sight from which the life and productions of Dryden have not hitherto been viewed. It may also be observed, that the whole period abounds in interest of a kind which is not likely to be exhausted in the biographies of its poets.

---

* This edition was published by the Tonsons. It was got up with care and elegance, but had a very limited sale.

The family name of Dryden was originally spelt Driden. The substitution of the *y* for the *i* is said to have been adopted by the poet, and to have given serious offence to some of his friends, who, upon graver topics than this, were in the habit of confounding the letter and the spirit. Wood spells the name Dreyden, and in other places it is spelt Dreydon, so that the innovation was not without precedent. The genealogy is traced back to the great-great-grandfather of the poet, who it appears was married to a lady of the name of Nicholson, and who settled somewhere in Cumberland. His son John married the daughter of sir John Cope, of Canons-Ashby, in Northamptonshire, by which alliance he obtained a tolerable estate, that led him to fix his residence in that county. John is said to have been a schoolmaster*, a statement which is questioned by sir Walter Scott, on the ground that it was not likely an individual who married the heiress of a man of knightly rank could have followed such a profession. The doubt —whatever it may be worth in the estimation of those who regard schoolmasters with contempt—is of no weight in comparison with the assertion of Wood, who lived close to the time, and knew some of the poet's relatives and friends. Wood also tells us, that John Driden was honoured with the friendship of the great Erasmus, who, he says, stood godfather for one of his sons. If this circumstance were true, it would afford us a sort of collateral evidence in support of John's useful avocation, as it was much more probable that Erasmus would have conferred his friendship on a schoolmaster than on the son-in-law of a knight; but unfortunately the detection of some anachronisms in this tradition renders it impossible to rely upon a statement which would have formed a very pleasant article of poetical faith.†

* See Wood — Fasti Oxoniensis.
† It is remarkable that Wood, who is generally very accurate in his dates, and who is entitled to great credit for the diligence of his inquiries, should have overlooked the extraordinary discrepancy contained in his own account of this episode in the family history. He informs us in the Fasti,

. The eldest son of this John Driden, called after his grandfather, succeeded to the estate, was high sheriff of the county under Elizabeth, was knighted by king James, and was married to the second daughter and co-heiress of William Wilkes, of Hodwell, in Warwick-shire. By this marriage he had three sons, all of whom seem to have been estated gentlemen—sir John Driden, who inherited the patrimony of Canons-Ashby, William, who succeeded to the estate of Farndon, in North-amptonshire, and Erasmus, of Tichmarsh, in the same county, the father of John Dryden the poet. Of Eras-mus, we learn that he was married to the daughter of the Rev. Mr. Pickering, a puritan pastor, youngest son of sir Gilbert Pickering, whose family were noted for their opposition to the Catholics, and marked for victims at the time of the gunpowder plot. The discovery of that frantic design, however, saved the family from destruction, by consigning the conspirators to the block, one of their own relations amongst the number; but it does not appear that the overthrow of their enemies had any effect in moderating their religious rancour. On the contrary, the pious fury of this estimable family was only the more heated by their triumph over the papists, and the race of the Pickerings continued zealous persecutors to the end of the chapter.

Erasmus Driden was probably dependent to a certain extent upon his wife's relations, for we find that he resided, at least at one period, in the parsonage-house of Oldwinkle, All-Saints, of which the Rev. Mr. Picker-

that Erasmus Driden, the son of John Driden, took his degree as bachelor of arts at Oxford, on June 17. 1577. Now Erasmus of Rotterdam who, according to Wood, was his godfather, died in 1536, so that Erasmus Driden must have been at least forty-one years of age when he took his degree. This very improbable circumstance is completely set aside*by the ascer-tained fact that Erasmus Driden was born in 1553, and therefore could not have enjoyed the sponsorial honour assigned to him by old Anthony, who, in the face of these difficulties, very quietly observes, that the name con-tinned to descend amongst the family, " many of whom," he adds, " have gloried in it in my hearing." Baker thinks that Erasmus Driden was called after Erasmus, the eldest son of sir John Cope, his mother's bro·ther, who might perhaps have derived it direct from the famous writer. Malone is inclined to adopt this conjecture.

ing was rector, and where John Dryden, the poet, was
born, about the 9th of August 1631. That his estate,
or property, of Tichmarsh yielded him a respectable
income, may be inferred from the fact that he held a
commission of the peace under Cromwell, to which, no
doubt, he was strongly recommended by the puritanical tendency of his principles. But Erasmus, whatever his means might have been, had more than enough
to do with them. His wife brought him fourteen children—ten daughters and four sons. Of this numerous
issue every one seems to have reached maturity; and
the indefatigable inquiries of Mr. Malone enable us to
add, that one of the daughters, Rose, married a doctor
of divinity in Huntingdon; another, Lucy, married a
merchant of London: two others, Agnes and Martha,
made respectable matches in the country; another married a bookseller in Little Britain; and the youngest,
Frances, became the wife of a tobacconist in Newgate
Street, where, however fortune may have otherwise dealt
with her, she enjoyed a remarkably vigorous constitution, surviving to the great age of ninety, and out-
living the poet by nearly thirty years. She died in
1730. Of the sons, we learn that the second, Erasmus,
was engaged in some description of trade in King Street,
Westminster, which he abandoned on the death of sir
John Driden, when he succeeded to the estate of
Canons-Ashby, where he died. He left one daughter
and five grandsons. The next son, Henry, died in
Jamaica, leaving a son, Richard; and the fourth son,
James, who was a tobacconist, died in London, leaving
two daughters. The remainder of the family of Erasmus Driden have not been traced by the industrious
investigator to whom we are indebted for these particulars.

Some of Dryden's literary opponents accused his
family of being anabaptists, but sir Walter Scott,
anxious to claim for the church the honour of the poet's
maternity, is of opinion that the accusation was altogether unfounded, although he forgets to favour us

with the evidence by which he arrives at that conclusion. It would be a sad waste of time to dispute the importance of an inquiry to determine whether Dryden really was christened; but, however laudable the curiosity by which it might be prompted, we do not unfortunately possess the means of satisfying it. The register of the parish church of Oldwinkle, All-Saints, in which the ceremony is presumed to have taken place, has long since ceased to exist, and the entry does not appear in any other. If Dryden, therefore, ever was baptised, the fact cannot now be ascertained. It is certain that some of his contemporaries, including the duke of Buckingham, suspected that he was not.*

That he received the rudiments of his education at Tichmarsh is attested by an inscription on a monument erected in the church to his memory.† From Tichmarsh he was removed to Westminster, where he was admitted as a king's scholar under the famous Dr. Busby. Between this erudite person and the future poet a warm friendship rapidly sprang up, which every year of their subsequent lives contributed to augment. Into whatever mood the controversies and labours, in which he afterwards became engaged, happened to plunge the poet — however he may have been galled by the world at one moment, or flattered by it the next, he always manifested towards Dr. Busby the same sentiments of unmixed esteem and veneration. His earliest exercises in English verse, especially the translation of the third satire of Persius, which he produced as a Thursday night's task, remained in the hands of Dr. Busby when he left Westminster, and have never been

---

* In the "Poetical Reflections," published by the duke of Buckingham in 1681, he thus alludes to this point : —

> " And though no wit can royal blood infuse,.
> No more than melt a mother to a muse,
> Yet much a certain poet undertook,
> That men and manners deals in without book ;
> And might not more to gospel-truth belong,
> Than he (*if christened*) does by name of John."

† This monument was built by Elizabeth Creed. The inscription runs thus : —" We boast that he was bred and had his first learning here."

recovered. The only Westminster poem of Dryden's which survives, is an elegy upon the death of lord Hastings*, written in his eighteenth year, and published in 1650, in a volume entitled " Lachrymæ Musarum," which contained no less than ninety-eight elegies on this same subject. It is not a little curious that one of Milton's earliest compositions — the monody to the memory of Lycidas — was written and printed under similar circumstances.

A popular tradition assigns to Dryden, as a school exercise during the period of his residence at Westminster, the celebrated epigram on the miracle of turning the water into wine,

" Lympha pudica Deum vidit et erubuit:"

but the merit of this beautiful line belongs to Crashaw. †

On the 11th May, 1650, Dryden entered Trinity College, Cambridge, under the Rev. John Templer, M. A., a theological and controversial writer, who figured in the crowd by which Hobbes was so violently assailed in his own day. Very little is known of his career in college. Shadwell — whose lampoons must not be implicitly relied upon, and who, in common charity, might be excused if he exaggerated Dryden's faults — says that he was obliged to run away from college for traducing a nobleman : and Mr. Malone quotes an order from the books of the college, in which Dryden was commanded to be put out of commons for a fortnight at least, during which time he was not to go out of the college except to sermons, without express leave from the master or vice-master ; and that at the end of the fortnight he was to read a confession of his

---

* Of this poem Dr. Johnson gives the following ridiculous but just account : — " Lord Hastings died of the smallpox ; and his poet has made of the pustules, first rosebuds, and then gems ; at last exalts them into stars ; and says,

' No comet need foretell his change drew on,
Whose corpse might seem a constellation.' "

† See Lives of the English Poets, vol. L p. 58.

crime in the hall, at dinner-time, at the table of the fellows.. The offence thus summarily punished was disobedience to the vice-master; and the scurrility alluded to by Shadwell, was no doubt one of those flashes of satire which it was neither within his inclination nor his power to repress. Shadwell's words are—

> " At Cambridge first your scurrilous vein began,
> Where saucily you traduced a nobleman;
> Who, for that crime, rebuked you on the head,
> And you had been expelled had you not fled."

The scurrility is likely enough, but the flight from college is an embellishment which must be referred to the active fancy of a writer who was just then smarting under the terrible inflictions of Dryden's ridicule. Dryden may have embroiled himself with a nobleman at college, but there is no doubt that he regularly took the degree of bachelor of arts in January 1653-4, and that he afterwards, by dispensation from the archbishop of Canterbury, received the degree of master. It is to be observed, however, that he never became a fellow of the university, although, as Malone observes, he resided there three years beyond the usual period. It is known, also, that he always entertained a strong aversion for Cambridge; he compares it to Thebes, and Oxford to Athens, and upon all occasions not only elevates the latter above the former, but even expresses feelings of uneasiness and ill will about " his now mother university," which cannot otherwise be accounted for except upon the supposition that it was the scene of some disagreeable and perhaps painful recollections.

Dryden's residence at Cambridge was interrupted for a short period by the death of his father in 1654, which obliged him to leave the university for the purpose of taking possession of two thirds of a trifling patrimony near Blakesley, in Northamptonshire, his share of which was valued at sixty pounds per annum. The remainder was vested in his mother during her lifetime, and fell to the poet on her death. Having arranged his affairs, he resumed his studies, and remained at the University three years longer. During all this time he appears to have been chiefly employed in the formation of his future literary plans, and the cultivation of his taste, rather than in the active exercise of his powers. He wrote very little, and the few pieces he did produce were sadly deformed by conceits and crudities derived from that very school of poetry which he afterwards effectually extinguished. That Dryden, who waged open war all his life against the metaphysicians, should have commenced his career by imitating them, is a curious fact, highly suggestive of the progress of a powerful mind. The glitter of the phrases, the dexterous and epigramatic turn of the verse, the pageantry of the images, and the apparently logical and profound tone of the treatment, were calculated to fascinate him in his youth, just as children are engrossed by the enchantments of romance ; but he soon outgrew these puerilities, and looked back with wonder upon the ingenious subtleties by which he had been so early captivated, and then set himself in right earnest to expose and repudiate them. Dryden's juvenile ecstasies, after the manner of Donne, in his copy of love verses to his beautiful cousin Honor*, are not more unlike his later

* Honor was an heiress as well as a beauty, and the poet is said to have been really in love with her, and to have been rejected. It would be some consolation to know that she had bestowed her wealth and her charms on some one else, but the legend does not furnish us with so agreeable a catastrophe. She never married. It is supposed that the name of Honoria in *The Rival·Ladies*, one of his early plays, was adopted as a testimony of his attachment to his fair cousin. A letter is extant from Dryden to the beautiful Honor, in which he acknowledges the receipt of a silver ink-stand, with which she thoughtfully presented him while he was at college. This letter is full of conceits, and a passage from it will exhibit the vitiated style with which the writer commenced his career. Madame Honor was at first all flushed with vexation at the obscure student's suit; but when he became an eminent poet, she was so proud of the compliments he had formerly paid her, that she used to carry this letter about with her, and show it to all her friends. Perhaps with a view to make it appear a more recent address, or unwilling to let it betray her age, she obliterated the two latter figures, which are here however restored : —

" To the faire hands of Madame Honor Dryden these crave admittance.
" Madame,   ·   " Camb. May 23. 16[55].
" If you have received the lines I sent by the reverend Levite, I doubt not but they have exceedingly wrought upon you : for beeing so longe in

productions, than the modest youth in his quaint "uniform clothing of Norwich drugget," which he is said never to have changed until he became a man of celebrity, is unlike the poet in brocade regulating the laws of taste at the court of Charles II. It is much, however, to Dryden's honour, that while be abandoned the sober livery of his youth, and put his body into a gayer garb, in conformity with the fashions of the day, his mind rose superior to the fopperies of that brief term of boy-

---

a clergy-man's pocket, assuredly they have acquired more sanctity than theire authour meant them. Alasse, madame! for ought I know, they may become a sermon ere they could arrive at you ; and beleive it, haveing you for the text, it could scarcely proove bad, if it light upon one that could handle it indifferently. But I am so miserable a preacher, that, though I have so sweet and copious a subject, I still fall short in my expressions; and, instead of an use of thanksgiving, I am allways makeing one of comfort, that I may one day againe have the happinesse to kisse your faire hand ; but that is a message I would not so willingly do by letter, as by word of mouth.

"This is a point, I must confesse, I could willingly dwell longer on ; and in this case, whatever I say you may confidently take for gospell. But I must hasten. And indeed, madame, (beloved I had almost sayd,) hee had need hasten who treats of you ; for to speake fully to every part of your excellencyes, requires a longer honre then most persons have allotted them. But, in a word, yourselfe hath been the best expositor upon the text of your own worth, in that admirable comment you wrote upon it ; I mean youre incomparable letter. By all that's good (and you, madame, are a great part of my oath,) it hath put mee so farre besides myselfe, that I have scarce patience to write prose, and my pen is stealing into verse every time I kisse your letter. I am sure the poor paper smarts for my idolatry : which by wearing it continually near my brest, will at last be burned and martyrd in those flames of adoration which it hath kindled in mee. But I forgett, madame, what rarityes your letter came fraught with, besides words. You are such a deity that commands worship by provideing the sacrifice. You are pleased, madame, to force me to write by sending me materialls, and compell me to my greatest happinesse. Yet, though I highly value your magnificent presente, pardon mee, if I must tell the world they are imperfect emblems of your beauty ; for the white and red of wax and paper are but shadowes of that vermillion and snow in your lips and forehead ; and the silver of the ink-horn, if it presume to vie in whitenesse with your purer skinne, must confesse itselfe blacker than the liquor it contains. What then do I more then retreive your own guifts, and present you with that paper, adulterated with blotts, which you gave spotlesse ? "

He concludes with a snatch of rhymes which are really so execrable, that one is glad to let this specimen of embroidered prose stand alone without such a foil. The seal of this letter, which is described by Malone as having a piece of blue riband under it, is a crest of a demi-lion on a wreath, holding in his paws an armillary sphere at the end of a stand. From all that can now be gathered concerning Honor Driden, it seems highly probable that she repented her coldness when it was too late, and that she would willingly have recalled the passion she had thus foolishly spurned, but that more elevated views had, in the mean time, given a different direction to the poet's feelings.

hood in which he betrayed the common indiscretion of
a misplaced devotion.

The inheritance of the young scholar being too small
to support him according to the habits of his kinsmen,
he took shelter under the wing of his cousin-german, sir
Gilbert Pickering, upon leaving the university. It is
not known in what capacity he entered the family.
Shadwell, with his usual humorous malice, says that he
was sir Gilbert's clerk, which is not improbable. But
the relationship subsisting between them sufficiently ex-
plains the nature of their connection, without requiring
us to expend much ingenuity in fruitless conjectures.
Sir Gilbert was bound to foster and protect his young
friend by double ties of blood, for his father was married
to Dryden's aunt, and his sister was married to Dryden's
father, so that the claims of consanguinity were of two
fold force. In addition to this, sir Gilbert was a man
of considerable weight in the parliament and the privy
council, a rigid puritan, a sequestrator and committee
man, and one who, from his position and the responsibilities it entailed, must have stood in need of such assistance as his cousin from the university could render
him. This man seems to have been regarded as a prominent and remarkable character in his time, and, in
consequence of the extravagant excesses of temper into
which he was accustomed to fall, he was generally called
the " Fiery Pickering." One of Dryden's biographers
has taken the trouble to collect two or three passages
concerning him from the writings of his contemporaries,
by which it appears that he was one of the council of the
protector, with a salary of 1000*l.* per annum, and that
he was also high steward of Westminster and lord chamberlain of the protector's household or court. He is
described to have been as finical and spruce as an old
courtier, to have been as corrupt in his practices as he
was jesuitical in his manners, and is justly reproached
for having accepted honours at the hands of Cromwell,
against which he had, all throughout the struggle with
the king, exhibited the most violent and implacable hos-

tility. In short, sir Gilbert Pickering appears to have been one of those men who are always ready to commit themselves to the worst crimes for the advancement of their party, and then to take advantage of the consequences for their own benefit. That odd compound of fanaticism and knavery, which was the monstrous birth of the national convulsion, was very felicitously represented in the person of sir Gilbert.

It was under the protection of this rich unprincipled puritan that John Dryden first entered the world. The influence of the experiences to which he was thus early exposed, although at first it sensibly affected his imagination, ultimately converted his reason to the opposite side. The ghostly meetings of these solemn ministers of a mighty transition, their strange forms of speech and behaviour, and the singular union which they presented of worldly abasement and spiritual pride, touched the poetical faculty just as long as the novelty lasted ; but the restoration had no sooner dissolved the fantastic dreams of the party than Dryden renounced them. The circumstances under which this conversion took place naturally surrounded it with suspicion, and it must be frankly allowed that Dryden's life is not so distinguished by purity as to warrant us in attributing to him the most conscientious motives, except in cases where no self-interest happened to be involved. The close connection of his friends with Cromwell's party — the notorious elevation of sir Gilbert Pickering to a seat in that spurious house of lords, which threw into ridicule the whole theory of the commonwealth — and the confidence which was reposed by the protector in his uncle, sir John Driden, one of the most zealous puritans of the times, afforded him, at the outset of his life, such prospects of advancement as few young men, recently liberated from a collegiate course, and starting with a narrow income, could be fairly expected to resist. He embarked at once on the same side with these powerful friends, and whether he espoused the " old cause," as it was designated, in a hearty spirit, or merely because it happened

to be in the ascendant, it is equally certain that while
he continued to support it he did not scruple to avow
himself openly.   He is even said to have held an appointment in one of the sequestration commissions * ; but
the statement rests solely on the authority of a lampoon,
and is hardly entitled to credit.   The publication of a
poem on the death of Cromwell, however, fixes beyond
all doubt the early bias of his mind.   That his attachment to either party was not considered a matter of
conscience, but rather of policy, with him, may be
gathered from the flying satires of the day.   Thus, one
of his adversaries reminds him of his devotion to the
protector after he had become a servant to the king,
taunts him with having learned his loyalty at the court of
Cromwell, and concludes with suggesting, that if Cromwell could again displace the monarch, Dryden would
again be found in his train : —

> " Your loyalty you learned in Cromwell's court,
>   When first your muse did make her great effort;
>   On him you first show'd your poetick strain,
>   And praised *his opening the basilick vein;*
>   And were it possible to come again,
>   Thou on that side would draw thy slavish pen. "

In another piece of scandal he is charged with having
taken office in the committees : —

> " He honest kept as long as e'er he could,
>   But glittering guineas cannot be withstood,
>   And *Bayes* was of *committee-man's flesh and blood.* "

The facility with which Dryden turned from Cromwell to Charles, and the fervour with which he applied
terms of equal, and, as far as the circumstances would
allow, similar panegyric to each, cannot be selected from

---

* These commissions were appointed by parliament, and dispersed over
the country for the purpose of detecting and punishing all persons, lay
and clerical, who professed allegiance to the house of Stuart.   The
offenders were called malignants, and the punishments usually inflicted
upon them were imprisonment and sequestration.   Very few instances occurred in which they escaped with only one of these penalties.

the history of the times as a very remarkable occurrence ; nor is it indeed likely that it provoked much private animadversion. Waller acted in precisely the same way ; and Dryden was a younger man, less skilled in courts and poetry, and having fewer pledges in the past to repent and violate. His heroic stanzas on the late lord protector were hardly before the public when they were succeeded by *Astrea Redux,* a poem on the happy restoration and return of his most sacred majesty king Charles. So fast did his loyalty to the king follow upon his lamentation for the protector, that it may be said to have tripped up its heels. His heroic stanzas seem to have made scarcely any impression at the moment. The first copies were hastily bought up, and then they were reprinted with those of Sprat and Waller, and fell into oblivion, from which they would probably never have been rescued (certainly not by the author), had it not been for one of Dryden's opponents, who revived them some years afterwards in a fit of spleen and vengeance, "to show the loyalty and integrity of the poet." The people were too much occupied at the time to trouble themselves with the tergiversation of a young writer, who as yet had accomplished no distinction. Besides, the nation was literally turning round to the monarchy itself, for as Cromwell had upon some vital points grievously disappointed the hopes and resisted the councils of his friends — in the encreasing forms of sovereignty that he suffered to grow up around him, for example, and the ill-advised Spanish expedition — the general sympathies of the country began gradually to revert to the royal family, who, throughout the whole period of their banishment, were never at a loss for means to keep alive the fidelity of their adherents. The enthusiasm which was inseparable from the mighty movement that agitated all classes in the community, drowned the offences of individuals. A sort of amnesty seemed to be extended to men of letters, and even to their immediate connections. Milton, the most courageous and powerful of the friends of the commonwealth, was spared after a brief interval of terror but not without having been subjected to the cruel and superfluous torture of intimidation and suspense. Waller, the kinsman and once the confidential counsellor of Cromwell, was received into the intimate friendship of the king; (it is true he had long before expiated his attachment to one party by dedicating the remnant of his fortune to the service of the other;) and even sir Gilbert Pickering, who actually signed the instrument for proclaiming Richard Cromwell, contrived to escape with the negative punishment of being rendered incapable of holding any office under the crown. It must not, of course, be inferred that the restoration was a tranquil and bloodless movement; but it so chanced, against the grain of its general character, that some of those who had most prominently distinguished themselves in opposition, not only obtained an indemnity for their offences, but were suddenly and unexpectedly taken into favour.

In his poem to the memory of Cromwell, Dryden is believed to have distinctly defended the death of Charles I., in the following passage where he is comparing Cromwell with his predecessors: —

    " War, our consumption, was their gainful trade ;
        We inward bled, whilst they prolonged our pain ;
        He fought to end our fighting, and essay'd
        To staunch the blood by breathing of the vein. "

Sir Walter Scott thinks that these lines " plainly apply to the civil war in general ; " but the criticism merely represents the desire of the writer to relieve Dryden from the odium of having applauded the regicide. The meaning of the passage is clear enough. Dryden regarded the sacrifice to be essential to the peace of the kingdom, and refers to it as a proof of Cromwell's anxiety to terminate an unnatural strife, which was so injurious to the national prosperity. Dryden found it convenient to alter his views ; but that he entertained this opinion when he wrote his stanzas on the protector can no more be denied than the fulsome and slavish praise with which he welcomed the return of Charles with whom, he says, —

> " The officious muses came along,
> A gay, harmonious quire, like angels ever young."

The muses that came along with Charles were French muses, — a train of twinkling, meretricious, and lascivious nymphs, who went nigh to destroy the purity and freshness of our literature, by their artificial and conceited airs, and who would have effected a complete revolution in it, but for the strenuous labours of the very panegyrist who thus pretended to fall in love with their harmony and their angelic youth.

The critic, it is true, had not yet become visible in Dryden. He was as yet merely practising his fancy in versification, and following in the footsteps of those writers who had filled the air around him with florid images and extravagant turns of expression. He had not yet begun to think and act for himself. He was like an ardent youth cast into a headlong crowd, and eagerly urging his way along with it. That sedate period — close as it was at hand — had not yet arrived when he was to turn away from the multitude, and strike out a new and glorious path for himself.

Cowley was the master spirit of the time. He had long struggled against fortune ; but now that his friends were restored to power, he looked to the world for the recognition of his genius as the only compensation left to him for his sufferings and his wrongs. Nor was he in this respect disappointed, although his private friends fell from him one by one, and left him to expire in solitude. His poetry gave the tone to the age. Milton had not yet risen upon the world with his magnificent and unapproachable epic ; and the startling paradoxes and mystical involutions of Cowley's pindarics inspired a host of imitators, who occupied the whole field of literature. The light and trivial style which was introduced by the followers of king Charles, instead of putting these wild metaphysical rhapsodies out of fashion, only had the effect, at first, of giving them a higher elevation by the force of contrast. When Dryden turned his thoughts to the cultivation of poetry as a profession, compelled by the necessities of his fortune to become an author, and by the necessities of his genius to trample upon the lifeless forms which engrossed the worship of his con-temporaries, he found half a dozen cavalier versifiers, with Wild, the poetical disciple and imitator of Cleveland at their head, in full possession of the public mind. Waller must not be included in this enumeration, for his day was nearly run out, — Cowley was vanishing from the scene, — Milton was in retirement, meditating the noble structure of the " Paradise Lost," — and the race of the Sedleys, Ethereges, and Rochesters had not yet commenced.

The immediate effect of the restoration on poetry was to give a temporary currency to the most extravagant description of verse that has ever at any time been written in the English language. But one subject — " His Glorious Majesty, and his Happy Return" — appears to have occupied the genius of the most popular writers; and but one mode of treating it — hyperbole heaped upon hyperbole, and fairly running riot with the most preposterous panegyrics — appears to have been considered appropriate to the enthusiasm of the times. Indeed, to such length was this intoxicating topic carried, that the poets were not content with exhausting their wit upon it in a thousand forms of the most fantastic eulogy, but they contrived to bring it in upon all occasions, by some dexterous allusion or simile which gave a court air to their labours, and showed that the versifier, whatever he might have been in other respects, was, at all events, a devoted royalist. The king's countenance was stamped as legibly upon the current productions of the day, as upon the current coin ; and as long as the rage lasted, a new and, it must be ad-mitted, a very uncommon class of poetry was thus strangely called into existence.

Dryden, in his early panegyrical poems, fell into the

most obvious vices of that class. His conceits were as numerous, and quite as strained, as any of his contemporaries, and he ransacked all departments of nature and art in search of the most remote and uncommon images. It is not surprising, therefore, that his hostile critics should have recurred to these pieces in after years for the means of charging upon Dryden the commission of those heresies in taste which he was so prompt to detect and condemn in others. But, in some instances, their spleen did injustice to their judgment. In a poem on the king, for example, the following lines attracted reprehension from several quarters : —

> " An horrid stillness first invades the ear,
> And in that stillness we the tempest fear."

A world of small criticism was launched against this couplet for the purpose of showing that stillness, being passive, could not commit an act of invasion. Even Dr. Johnson has thought it necessary to defend Dryden, by referring to the popular use which is made of darkness and cold, which, although passive, like silence, are both said to invade us. " Death," he adds, " is also a privation ; yet who has made any difficulty of assigning to Death a dart, and the power of striking ? " But this figure is not so happy as the other. Death is a privation only in one sense, and it would be more accurate still to call it a de-privation. The active power of Death is quite as palpable as its abnegation of life ; but stillness presents no image of active power whatever, and its existence is known only by, and consists solely of, the absence of sound. The subject, however, is hardly worth discussion, and may be considered as finally disposed of in the universal right of poetry to apostrophise such images through any types she pleases. Captain Ratcliffe, in his " News from Hell," censures it after this fashion : —

> " Invade ! and so 't might well, 'tis clear ;
> But what did it invade ?—an ear."

The point of the ridicule is not so apparent in this as in the following couplet from the " Dialogue in Bedlam," in which the writer makes the " horrid silence " invade his eye, so that his voice becomes invisible !

> " A horrid silence does invade my eye,
>   While not one sound of voice from you I spy."

Such wretched humourists as these Dryden might justly despise.

The commencement of Dryden's literary career in London was darkened by very discouraging circumstances. His patrimony was too small to sustain the unavoidable expenses of a residence in the metropolis, while his change of parties may be supposed to have destroyed all hope of any further assistance from his puritanical relatives. The consequence was, that he worked in indigence and obscurity, until he found a patron in Sir Robert Howard, a poet, a man of rank, and a devoted royalist. Shadwell pretends to give Dryden's own authority for an accurate account of his mode of living during this period. " At first," he makes Dryden say, " I struggled with a great deal of persecution, took up with a lodging which had a window no bigger than a pocket looking-glass, dined at a three-penny ordinary, enough to starve a vacation tailor, kept little company, went clad in homely drugget, and drunk wine as seldom as a Rechabite, or the grand seignior's confessor." The "persecution" here alluded to can have reference only to family matters, and arose, probably, from the offence which his political apostasy must have given to the fiery Pickerings. It is not unlikely that his patrimony, which was drawn from the same source from whence his mother derived her income, was reduced in value through their agency, and that the difficulties described by Shadwell really had a foundation in fact, although they were no doubt exaggerated in the relation.

His first employment was that of a literary drudge to Herringman, the bookseller, who was one of the principal publishers of poetry and plays, and from whose shop, in the New Exchange, nearly all the eulogistic verses on the restoration were issued. Dryden's occupation consisted in the preparation of dedications and prefaces, and such occasional pieces as might be required in the multifarious business carried on by Herringman.*

The custom of the times created a vast demand for flattering addresses in prose and verse, which were always rewarded by a gratuity from the patron to whom they were inscribed. The king received such a multitude of these special thanksgivings and congratulations, every one of which his majesty was expected to acknowledge with a handsome present, that it at last became a very expensive proceeding, and he is said to have consulted Rochester upon the best means of putting an end to it. The expression of the national delight was not confined to odes and epistles, but took almost every shape which the ingenuity or the resources of the panegyrists could devise. Some sent his majesty a picture or a bust, some a new invention in machinery, others an extraordinary fruit or flower; and the palace was literally besieged with candidates for the honour of presentation, in all of whom the actuating motive was the expectation of a munificent gift. His majesty, if the tradition may be relied upon, received from one person a turnip of such enormous dimensions as to excite the general admiration of the court. Being a lover of all monstrous growths and productions, the king ordered a gift of one hundred pounds to be sent to the fortunate grower of the turnip. This piece of generosity no sooner became known, than it gave a fresh

* The circumstance is thus recorded by his inveterate satirist in " The Medal of John Bayes "

> " He turn'd a journeyman to a bookseller;
> Writ prefaces to books for meat and drink,
> And as he paid, he would both write and think :
> Then, by the assistance of a noble knight,
> Thou had'st plenty, ease, and liberty to write;
> First like a gentleman he made thee live,
> And on his bounty thou did'st amply thrive."

incentive to the cupidity of the flatterers, one of whom immediately sent a magnificent blood horse to his majesty, arguing to himself, that if a turnip was rewarded by a hundred pounds, his blood horse ought to bring at least a title and an estate. But upon this occasion his majesty began to think it was full time to cool the enthusiasm of these time-servers, and he accordingly consulted Rochester as to how he ought to deal with the man who sent the horse. "Send him the turnip, by all means," replied the wit ; "it cost your majesty a hundred pounds."

The acquaintance with sir Robert Howard was formed at the house of Herringman, who was sir Robert's publisher. Dryden was largely indebted to the kindness of this gentleman, who fully appreciated the merits of his *protégé,* took him into his house to reside with his family, and was ultimately the means of introducing his works to the notice of the fashionable world. Dryden says, that sir Robert Howard was not only "careful of his fortune, which was the effect of his nobleness, but solicitous of his reputation, which was that of his kindness." His productions at this time, however, do not appear to have been either numerous or important. It is not unlikely that many of them were published anonymously, or under the names of other writers, or were absorbed and lost in miscellaneous anthologies. An encomiastic poem, presented to the lord chancellor Clarendon in 1662, some lines prefixed to Dr. Charleton's account of Stonehenge, a short satire upon the Dutch, written about the same time, and some occasional verses on the duke of York's victory, celebrated also by Waller, are the principal pieces he composed previously to the appearance of the *Annus Mirabilis,* a work by which he at once achieved a high reputation. The slowness with which he emerged out of obscurity has not escaped the notice even of his most enthusiastic admirers.

> " Great Dryden did not early great appear,
> Faintly distinguished in his thirtieth year."

Throughout all the pieces above enumerated, the indecision of the poet's mind, on its way to the formation of an original style, may be clearly traced. Sometimes they exhibit the intricate subtleties of Donne and Cowley — sometimes the exquisite polish and embroidery of Waller and Suckling—and sometimes the rough vigour and elaborate energy of Davenant, whose " Gondibert " had, about this period, opened a new world of poetry. In the *Annus Mirabilis* Dryden indicated his approach towards that refinement and simplicity of expression, and strength of thought, which became more and more manifest as he advanced, and which was finally to emancipate himself and his successors from that meritricious and inflated jargon which had so long held possession of the public taste.

The form of the *Annus Mirabilis* was favourable to the poetical reformation of which it was the herald. The measure is heroic quatrains, and is the same which was employed with so much success by Davenant in the " Gondibert," which, indeed, seems to have suggested the idea of the work, and which is unquestionably entitled to the distinguished honour of having been the first regular performance of its peculiar kind in our language. A stanza of alternate rhymes was more likely to render the altered spirit of the style acceptable to readers who had been accustomed to ·the laborious trifling of the metaphysicians, than if Dryden had at once attempted the heroic couplet, which he afterwards brought to perfection ; and it may be doubted whether the latter form of verse would have answered his purpose so well in other points of view. The object of the poem was to describe the remarkable events of the year 1667— the year of wonders : and as he had to deal with heroes and victories, sieges, and providential incidents, he required some such machinery in the structure of the work as would enable him to adapt the " elocution," for which he claims especial credit in the dedication, to the fluctuations of his subject. He alludes to the difficulties of the stanza, as if he feared he had not

quite vanquished them, and he evidently bestowed extraordinary pains upon the mechanism of his lines. Dr.
Johnson observes, that the poem may be esteemed as one
of his most elaborate performances ; and a later critic,
whose opinion seems to have been still more carefully
formed, observes, " Variety is its chief want, as dignity
is its greatest excellence ; but in spite of this defect, and
of much bad taste, we doubt whether so continued a
strain of poetry could at that time be found in the
language."* The want of variety is the fault of the
stanza chosen by the poet, who nevertheless stoutly
defends his choice, and calls in to his support the authority of Davenant, who considered the respite and pause
afforded by the quatrain to be of great advantage, alike
to the author and the reader, adding, " nor doth alternate rhyme, by any lowliness of cadence, make the sound
less heroic, but rather adapt it to a plain and stately
composing of music."† Dryden declared that he considered the alternate rhyme to be more noble, and of
greater dignity both for sound and number, than any
form of verse then in use. He certainly illustrated its
dignity with unparalleled success ; and but for the nature
of his subject, which even a greater genius could not
have elevated above the interest of a chronicle, he
might possibly have shown that it was susceptible of
greater variety than his commentators suspected. But
variety was not the object contemplated in this production. Dryden disclaimed all the vulgar artifices for
securing an audience, and bestowed his chief attention
throughout upon the accuracy and stately march of the
rhythm. It was here that the great reform was to be
worked. The dull uniformity of these cadences assisted
him in his design, by banishing from his page the ordinary temptations to verbal excesses, with which the
irregular form of popular poetry abounded ; and, con-
fining himself almost exclusively to the attainment of
elegance and strength of diction, he effectually achieved
a sober triumph of judgment, from which the decline

* Hallam.   † See preface to " Gondibert."

of what he contemptuously called " wit-writing" may be dated.

But this pursuit of chaste modes of poetry — this war upon brilliant fancies and fantastical conceits — did not yield a sufficient harvest of profit to justify Dryden in limiting himself to a task otherwise so agreeable to his taste. He was forced to cultivate more advantageous paths of literary distinction, and he turned to the theatre as the richest and most accessible, although he never was altogether content with his vocation, and always seemed to follow it like one who was toiling against his will.

The stage, which had gradually declined after the accession of James I., and was wholly extinguished during the commonwealth, was suddenly and enthusiastically revived on the restoration. It might be expected that so long a slumber of theatrical entertainments would have begot indifference towards them on the part of the public, and that the return of the relish for such amusements would have been slow and gradual; but, instead of recovering their popularity by degrees, they regained it all at once, and were received with even greater éclat than ever. The reason of this was, that it became a mark, and in some sort a test, of loyalty to sustain the stage, and the cavalier party rallied in support of the theatre with as much zeal as they would have rallied round the standard of the king. The stage, therefore, opened at this juncture such prospects to a poet so fertile and adaptive as Dryden, that it may be easily understood how, even at some sacrifice of his own desires, he felt them to be irresistible. He embraced it, in the first instance, from motives of necessity, and continued to cultivate it because he found it profitable. His career as a dramatic writer was eminently successful, although, like other monarchs in periods of revolution, he held possession of the throne through an uninterrupted war with critics and rivals.

He at first meditated a play on the history of the *Duke of Guise*, of which he gives the following account : " Iu the year of his majesty's happy restoration, the first play I undertook was the *Duke of Guise,* as the fairest way which the Act of Indemnity had then left us of setting forth the rise of the late rebellion, and by exploding the villanies of it upon the stage, to precaution posterity against the like errours." But the plan of this essay was not considered sufficiently skilful to insure success, and it was abandoned for some years. It was succeeded by a comedy, *The Wild Gallant,* which (apparently because it was first represented) he calls his first attempt in dramatic poetry. This piece is conjectured to have been represented in February 1662-3, by the king's company in Vere Street, previously to their removal to Drury Lane. The rage for novelty seemed to have superseded at that time all desire for those profound studies of human nature with which Shakspeare and his contemporaries had familiarised the public; in fact, the poets who delighted and instructed the age of Elizabeth were totally set aside during the reign of Charles II. A new species of comedy, derived chiefly from the example of such masters of intricate and intriguing action as Lopez de Vega, had begun to set in; and he who wrote for patronage was compelled to adapt himself to the prevailing tone. The court, fresh from the frivolities of the French capital, and reeking with licentiousness, inspired and sustained this extravagant taste; and Charles authenticated the fashion himself, by commanding sir Samuel Tuke and Crowne to translate two comedies from the Spanish for his especial entertainment. These pieces, *The Adventures of Five Hours,* and *Sir Courtly Nice,* are celebrated amongst the earliest specimens of this class of English comedy. The latter, it is but just to observe, is distinguished by some discriminating touches of character, for which Crowne claimed the credit in his own person, and apart from his original.

Such was the temper of the stage for which Dryden wrote his *Wild Gallant.* Its principal, if not indeed its only merit, consisted in the involution of the incidents, and the gladiatorial word-catching of the dialogue. Its reception was very equivocal, and it would probably have failed altogether, but for the countenance of the beautiful countess of Castlemaine, afterwards duchess of Cleaveland, whose favourable notice on this occasion was acknowledged by the author in a copy of fulsome verses. The whole affair, comedy, verses, and duchess were mercilessly ridiculed a few years afterwards in the " Session of the Poets."

" Dryden who, one would have thought, had more wit,
   The censure of every man did disdain ;
   Pleading some pitiful lines he had writ
   In praise of the countess of Castlemaine."*

Dryden's failure in this instance discouraged him in the further pursuit of comedy, and, perhaps because he failed, he declared that " comedy was the most difficult part of dramatic poetry." Of the truth of that axiom, however, there can be no reasonable doubt, since not only so few writers have cultivated comedy with success, but so few specimens are extant, in which the highest qualities of comedy are developed. His next production was the *Rival Ladies*, a tragi-comedy, the heroic part written in rhyme, and those parts which are of a lighter cast in blank verse. He considered it necessary to defend the practice of rhyme in an elaborate dedication to the earl of Orrery ; but the utmost ingenuity cannot establish the propriety of a style which the utmost skill cannot reconcile to nature. As there is no notice of the way in which this piece was received, it is presumed to have found some favour from the audience, who were then accustomed to the stilted tragedies of the French school.

Rhyming plays were rendered popular on the revival of theatricals by the example of such persons as the

---

* Pepys went to see the " Wild Gallant," and says that it was " ill-acted." He tells us, that " the king did not seem pleased at all the whole play, nor any body else ;" but he adds, as some compensation for those who were disappointed with the performance, " My lady Castlemaine was all worth seeing to-night, and little Steward."

earl of Orrery and sir Robert Howard, and Dryden felt
little inclination to disturb a practice which was illustrated by men to whom he was under great personal
obligations. In 1663 or 1664, we find him associated
with sir Robert Howard in the authorship of the *Indian
Queen;* but what share he had in that piece is not
known. He claims a part of it in his preface to the
Indian Emperor, which immediately followed, and
which presents a continuation of the same history, followed out in the subsequent fortunes of the successors of
the same set of characters.* It is conjectured that Dryden
corrected the versification of the *Indian Queen* throughout, which is not unlikely, as it is more melodious than
any other production ascribed to sir Robert.

The *Indian Emperor* raised Dryden nearly to the
height of that reputation which he afterwards maintained against a host of adversaries. It was brought out
with extraordinary splendour, and its scenic attractions
were increased by aerial music, flying demons, ghosts,
and a trap-door ascent. Evelyn, with his usual simplicity and air of wonder, declares that it was the
most gorgeous spectacle ever witnessed; and the duchess
of Monmouth, one of the most influential women of her
time, was so enraptured by the costly exhibition, that
she immediately extended her patronage and protection
to the author, permitting him to dedicate the work to
her as an earnest of her future favours.† How much
the play was indebted for its success to the combination of
the arts it embraced, or to its intrinsic merits as a dra-

---

* Of this connection between the two plays, due notice was given to the
audience by printed bills distributed at the doors of the theatre, an expedient ridiculed in the " Rehearsal," where Bayes relates how many reams
of paper he had printed to enable the spectators to understand his plot.
  † This play was afterwards presented at court, and the duchess appears
to have taken a part in the performance with distinguished success. Pepys
gives the following account of it, under the date of the 14th January, 1667-8.
" Thence by coach to Mr. Pierce's, where my wife is ; and there they fell
to discourse of the last night's work at court, where the ladies, and the duke
of Monmouth and others, acted the ' Indian Emperour,' wherein they told
me these things most remarkable : — That not any woman but the duchesse
of Monmouth and Mrs. Cornwallis did any thing but like fools and stocks,
but that these two did do most extraordinary well : that not any man did
any thing well but captain Olrigran, who spoke and did well, but above all
things did dance most incomparably."

matic poem, may be determined by the gradual decline
of its popularity in later years. When other plays of
Dryden's continued to hold possession of the stage, the
Indian Emperor was forgotten ; romantic dresses and
brilliant scenery could not impart that vitality which
belongs to the loftiest forms of tragedy alone. But,
probably, had it been a finer production, it might not
have been so efficacious as a means of drawing out the
powers of the author. Dryden needed such a stimulus
as the great success of this piece held out to him.

The plague and the conflagration which at this period
afflicted London, suspended the performances at the theatres from May, 1665, to Christmas, 1666, during which
interval Dryden retired to the country, and is supposed
to have resided at Charlton, the seat of the earl of
Berkshire, sir Robert Howard's father. It was here he
composed his celebrated *Essay on Dramatic Poesy*,
which, with the exception of some strictures on English
versification,— of which Gascoigne's and Webbe's were
the most important, — must be regarded as the first regular piece of criticism in our language. Here, too, he
met the lady Elizabeth Howard, to whom he was married before he returned to town. The circumstances
connected with this marriage have not been very clearly
ascertained, and certain lampoons which reflected am-
biguously on the honour of the lady were suffered to take
effect without any formal contradiction.* There is, on the
one hand, no evidence to prove the truth of the insinuations circulated by Dryden's assailants ; nor, on the other,
any evidence of an attempt to expose their mendacity,
which we have a right to look for, considering the rank
and celebrity of the parties implicated, and the notoriety
of the charge. Of the incidental levities of Dryden's
life about this time, there are not wanting some vague
notices ; but it may be fairly doubted whether such circumstances justify us in concluding that he carried the
spirit of licentious gallantry so far as to dishonour the
hospitality and patronage of his intimate friend, sir

* The satire in which the charge originated is imputed to lord Somers.

Robert Howard. A popular author constantly frequent-
ing the green-rooms of the theatres, especially one who
is said to have been distinguished by the favours of the
fair sex, could hardly be expected to escape pure from
the temptations which beset a path so brilliant and so
dangerous. That Dryden did fall into some of the
vices of the town is proved by his connection with
Mrs. Reeves, the actress, who performed in several of
his plays, and for whom he is believed to have written
some of his characters. But this *liaison*, and others that
are obscurely alluded to in the fleeting literature of the
day, did not take place until he had become infected
with the tone of fashionable society, and had in some
sort gone out of his original character in the flurry and
excitement of a new and prosperous career. One of
his contemporaries appears to indicate as much in the
following slight reminiscence. " I remember plain John
Dryden, before he paid his court to the great, in one
uniform clothing of Norwich drugget. I have eat tarts
with him and Madame Reeve at the Mulberry-garden,
when our author advanced to a sword and a Chadreux
wig."*   This change is the symbol of the change from
the puritans to the cavaliers — from severe simplicity
to open levity : it represents the spirit of the times, and
the dramatic poet floating unresistingly along with the
current : and, whether it assisted him to win or to dishonour the lady Elizabeth Howard, cannot now be determined. His biographers, according to the cast of
their tempers, take different views of the doubt, Dr.
Johnson appearing to favour the darker side, and sir
Walter Scott, with a generosity characteristic of his
nature, leaning strongly the other way.

The marriage does not appear to have been very fortunate for either in its results. Whether their disappointment may be referred to the fact that the portion
of the lady was incommensurate with her station and
her habits, or that a laborious literary life was ill-suited
to her tastes, or whether both these causes may not have

* Correspondent of the Gentleman's Magazine, 1745.

combined to render their intercourse mutually sullen, it is certain that their union was not productive of much happiness. " It is difficult," observes sir Walter Scott, " for a woman of a violent temper and weak intellects — and such the lady seems to have been — to endure the apparently causeless fluctuations of spirits incidental to one doomed to labour incessantly in the feverish exercise of the imagination. Unintentional neglect, and the inevitable relaxation, or rather sinking of spirit, which follows violent mental exertion, are easily misconstrued into capricious rudeness, or intentional offence; and life is embittered by mutual accusation, not the less intolerable because reciprocally just. The wife of one who is to gain his livelihood by poetry, or by any labour (if any there be) equally exhausting, must either have taste enough to relish her husband's performances, or goodnature sufficient to pardon his infirmities." Lady Elizabeth, there is reason to believe, had neither; and probably this was the true solution of their discontent. Dryden took his revenge in his own way, by launching sarcasms against marriage wherever a seasonable opportunity occurred to him in the progress of his literary labours, and often made a pretext to go out of his way to satirise unsympathising wives. But it was a grievous error of the understanding to impute to an institution the faults of an individual.

In the *Essay on Dramatic Poetry*, Dryden resumed his defence of rhyming tragedies. The argument is conducted in the form of a dialogue (a form adopted probably as being peculiarly appropriate to the inquiry), and the lord Buckhurst, sir Robert Howard, sir Charles Sedley, and the author himself, are made to espouse the several views, *pour et contre*, under feigned names. In this dialogue the unsuccessful advocacy of blank verse is assigned to sir Robert Howard, who had previously ventured into the lists to combat indirectly Dryden's former defence of rhyme. The publication of this piece drew a rejoinder from sir Robert, who, in the preface to the *Duke of Modena*, which appeared in 1668, reasserted his opinion in a tone of contemptuous superiority that betrayed how deeply he was offended by the liberty Dryden had taken with him. Perhaps there lurked under all this some unacknowledged feeling of private resentment; nor is it improbable that the incidents connected with the marriage, and its results, may have influenced them both even more than the subject over which they disputed with so much asperity. Dryden, roused for the first time by an antagonist whose position in the world rendered him formidable, replied in a tract entitled the *Défence of the Essay of Dramatic Poetry*, in which he poured out the most unsparing irony upon his opponents. This pamphlet, and the ridicule it provoked upon all sides amongst the shallow wits of the day, for a long time divorced the friends, who were reconciled only after a long interval of years, and not until the *Défence of the Essay*, which had originated the quarrel, was called in, and, as far as such an act of amnesty at such a distance of time could be effectual, suppressed.

The high reputation of Dryden now pointed him out as the fittest person to succeed Davenant as poet-laureat. This honour was conferred upon him by letters patent in 1670, two years after Davenant's death; but as the grant had a retrospective effect covering the whole of that period, it is not unlikely that he enjoyed the distinction from 1668, and that the patent was delayed by accident. The emoluments accruing from this office, and from that of historiographer royal, which was also bestowed upon him at the same time, were 200*l*. a-year, to be paid quarterly, and one butt of canary annually from his majesty's cellars at Whitehall. That his talents were highly estimated may be inferred from the terms of the grant, which refer to him as a man of learning and eminent abilities, and of " great skill and elegant style both in verse and prose."

With the increase of fame came an increase of labour and profit. Confiding in the fertility of his powers, he entered into an engagement with the king's company of players to provide for the theatre three plays yearly, in consideration of which he was to hold one share and a quarter, fluctuating in value annually between 300*l.* and 400*l.* But this bargain was hastily acceded to on both sides. Dryden either was unable to fulfil his undertaking, or repented, on other grounds, of having entered into it; and during the first three years he produced only seven plays, in two of which he was aided by other writers. It does not appear, however, that the agreement was cancelled in consequence: the players were anxious to monopolise him upon any terms, and, although he failed in his bond, he continued to derive the stipulated profits from the house. In these transactions Dryden was treated with great kindness and generosity by the players, notwithstanding that he not only failed to fulfil his contract, but violated it still more reprehensibly by giving a play, in the authorship of which he was concerned with Lee, to the Duke's company. A curious document, which had long been preserved in the Killigrew family, and which was first published by Mr. Malone, sets forth the particulars in the form of a memorial from the players to the lord chamberlain. In this memorial the complainants state, after reciting the terms of the agreement, that "though he [Dryden] received the moneys, we [the memorialists] received not the playes, not one in a yeere." In consequence of the burning and rebuilding of the theatre, debts were contracted, and the value of the shares diminished, upon which Dryden remonstrated with the company upon the decline of his profit, and they, continues the memorial, were "so kind to him, that they not only did not presse him for the playes which he so engaged to write for them, and for which he was paid beforehand, but they did also, at his earnest request, give him a third day for his last new play, *All for Love*, and at the receipts of the money of the said third day, he acknowledged it as a guift, and a particular kindnesse of the company. Yet, notwithstanding this kind procceding, Mr. Dryden has now, jointly with

Mr. Lee, (who was in pension with us to the last day of our playing, and shall continue,) written a play called *Œdipus*, and given it to the Duke's company, contrary to his said agreement, his promise, and all gratitude, to the great prejudice and almost undoing of the company, they being the only poets remaining to us." It must be allowed that the whole narrative is unfavourable to the dramatist, whose conduct, contrasted with the good faith and forbearance of the players, is not very creditable either to his feelings or his integrity.

But even at the rate of five plays in three years, not to speak of the two in which he assisted, Dryden wrote too fast for his fame. He mistook rapidity for power, and believed that he was inventing when he was frequently only imitating others, or repeating himself. A dramatic composition, such as he aimed at producing in the form if not in the substance, cannot be so hastily minted off. The conception may be quick; but the execution, if it embody living passion and present a true image of nature, must be slow and thoughtful. Nothing short of inspiration—or a genius such as Shakspeare's, which confounds all our notions and experience of genius—could have elaborated such a number of plays in so short a space, in a shape equal to the pretensions asserted by Dryden. The consequence was, that all these pieces betrayed marks of haste, cumbrous metaphors, dialogues prolonged to weakness, extravagant flights of turgid poetry, and broad scenic effects, under which the soul of the life within was crushed and annihilated. One of these remarkable performances was an alteration of *The Tempest*, in which, by an unaccountable perversity of taste, Dryden engrafted some deformities of so monstrous a kind upon that exquisite poem, as, in a better instructed age, would have exposed him to the summary condemnation even of the most vulgar part of his audience. He fitted Miranda with a sister, and contracted her with a hero who had never seen a woman, giving, to complete the literary profanation, a companion female to the monster Caliban. The interplay of these doubles delighted the public as much as they seem to have pleased the author, who describes with incredible simplicity, in his preface, the ecstasy with which he invented them. Nor did he stop even here. He embroidered the language of Shakspeare with revolting pruriences, adapted no doubt to his own age, but in the last degree inconsistent with the purity of the text. We might marvel how the spectators could have endured these anomalous grossnesses ; but an audience who could patiently hear Prospero ask his daughter —

" Miranda, where's your sister ?"

might readily be excused for enduring the coarsest breaches of decorum. The want of refinement is hardly less indicated by the one than the other. Happily we have survived this sacrilege, and lived to see Shakspeare restored to the stage in his original form.

The names of these pieces were — *The Maiden Queen* * — a tragi-comedy ; — *The Tempest* — a Shakspearean desecration; — *Sir Martin Mar-all* — an adaptation of the Duke of Newcastle's translation of Molière's *L'Etourdi,* which owed its popularity chiefly to the performance of a celebrated comedian † ; — *The Mock Astrologer* — a composition from the *Dépit Amoureux* of Molière, and *Le Feint Astrologus* of Corneille, itself founded on El Astrologo Fingido of Calderon, and remarkable only for the bustle of the incidents and the

---

* This piece Pepys tells us was "mightily commended for the regularity, and the strain and wit ; and the truth is," he adds, " there is a comical part done by Nell [Gwynne], which is Florimell, that I never can hope ever to see the like done again by man or woman. The king and the duke of York were at the play. [The date of this entry is March 2. 1666-7.] But so great performance of a comical part was never, I believe, in the world before as Nell do this, both as a mad girle, then most and best of all when she comes in like a young gallant, and bath the motions and carriage of a spark, the most that ever I saw any man have. It makes me, I confess, admire her." It appears that Nell, who was so successful in comedy, utterly failed, in Pepy's opinion, when she attempted tragedy. Speaking of her acting in Dryden's *Indian Emperour,* he says, " I was most infinitely displeased with her being put to act the emperour's daughter, which is a great and serious part, which she does most basely."
† See Cibber's graphic description of the comic humour of Nokes in the character of Sir Martin Mar-all.

licentiousness of the characters and dialogue * ; — *Ty-rannick Love*—an heroic tragedy, abounding in turgid verse, relieved at long intervals by passages of tenderness and sublimity; and the first and second parts of *The Conquest of Granada* — two plays, in which the false grandeur of a theoretical chivalry and the passionate excesses of romantic love are carried to their height. Dr. Johnson has disposed of these productions in a criticism as just as it is striking. " The scenes," he observes, " exhibit a kind of illustrious depravity and majestic madness, such as, if it is sometimes despised, is often reverenced, and in which the ridiculous is often mingled with the astonishing."

To all these plays Dryden prefixed elaborate essays and dedications, the main object of which was to defend the plan of each, and to exalt himself not only over his contemporaries, but even over his predecessors. Thus, in reply to some one, who accused him (with more truth than discretion) of plagiarism, he says " he only desired that they who accuse me of thefts would steal plays like mine;" and speaking of the great fathers of the English drama, he charges Shakspeare with having taken his jests out of the hundred novels of Cinthio, and Beaumont and Fletcher with having derived theirs from Spanish stories, and says that Jonson alone made them for himself ; as if the invention of the story, and not the delineation of human character and passion through the developement of the action, were the great business and glory of the dramatist. But, apart from this consideration, it is not true that Jonson was the only one of the elder poets who invented his plots, as Shirley's plays, without a single exception, are his own creation, plot, distribution, and dialogue. Notwithstanding these faults —which belonged to his temperament rather than to any prejudices of judgment—Dryden's introductions

---

* Evelyn says of this piece, " A foolish plot, and very profane ; it affected me to see how much the stage was degenerated and polluted by the licentious times." And Pepys tells us, on the authority of Herringman, the bookseller, that Dryden himself considered it only a fifth-rate play.

to his plays, apparently written to increase their saleable value, are full of accurate and profound criticisms upon almost every form of dramatic poetry. This kind of literature was then strange to the public, especially coming in a shape so tangible and apposite, and it had the effect of rapidly elevating and improving the taste of the audience. Indeed, Dryden complained to Swift, that one result of these dissertations was, that they soon made his readers too skilful to be easily satisfied.

It is impossible to examine the structure and composition of Dryden's heroic tragedies — which he now completely succeeded in bringing into vogue — without being struck by the extraordinary anomaly which his judgment as a critic exhibits with his practice as a dramatist. It is true that he laboured very ingeniously to defend this bombastic class of plays, and that he even ventured to lay down rules for their conduct, in which, with marvellous but unconscious candour, he exposes all their most glaring faults. He maintained that tragedy ought to deal only with the highest and most exalted personages (exactly as if he thought that there was no grief or pathos, heroism or tenderness, lower down in the scale of humanity), and that, in order to express the sufferings and fortitude of such lofty characters with a becoming sublimity, they ought to speak a language unknown in common life, that they ought to be for ever on a superhuman stretch of diction, and that blank verse, being too humble for them, they ought to deliver themselves in rhyme. "The plot," he observes, "the characters, the wit, the passions, the descriptions, are all exalted above the level of common converse, as high as the imagination of the poet can carry them, with proportion to verisimility. Tragedy, we know, is wont to image to us the minds and fortunes of noble persons, and to portray them exactly; heroic rhyme is nearest to nature, as being the noblest kind of modern verse.

' Indignatur enim privatis et prope socco
Dignis carminibus narrari cœna Thyestæ,'

says Horace : and in another place,

' Effutire leves indigna tragœdia versus.'

Blank verse is acknowledged to be too low for a poem,
nay, more, for a paper of verses ; but if too low for an
ordinary sonnet, how much more for tragedy, which is
by Aristotle, in the dispute betwixt the epic poesy and
the dramatic, for many reasons he there alleges, ranked
above it." That such a critisism should have appeared
. in the same age that produced the *Paradise Lost,* is a memorable evidence of the unsettled state of literature, and
the want of popular instruction in the higher departments of poetry. If any further proof of this were
needed, it is furnished in the neglect with which Milton's immortal epic was treated by his contemporaries,
while the rhyming tragedies of Dryden, which Scott
happily describes as metrical romances of chivalry in
the form of a drama, were received with such universal
applause, that, for a time, they effectually superseded
even Shakspeare and Ben Jonson. But this was the
only one important point on which Dryden committed
a grievous error of judgment, and perhaps it would be
only just to attribute the energy with which he defended
it to that pertinacity which he always displayed in
vindicating himself against rivalry and accusation. He
seems to have considered it necessary to protect any
usage he sanctioned, however irreconcilable it might
be with nature or common sense, by endeavouring
to build up elaborate arguments to prove that it was
justified by some pedantic rules of art ; and the more'
an error was assailed, the more he persisted in its defence, under an impression that the propriety of a practice he continued to adopt could not long continue to be
doubted by the multitude. Upon nearly all other
questions connected with dramatic poetry, his criticisms
will always be consulted with advantage. The clearness

of his views, the minuteness with which he analyses the
essential elements of a play, the truth, accuracy, and
force he exhibits in tracing the various requisites that
enter into action and character, and the extensive
knowledge, not drawn merely from books, but from
human nature, which enriches his diversified commentaries, confer upon them an interest that will be fresh
amongst readers of all classes when his dramas shall
have been wholly forgotten.

Dryden's great success, and the flattering associations
to which it introduced him, contributed, in a large measure, to encourage that vanity and vain-glory which
breaks out so frequently in his prefaces and dedications,
the latter of which were generally as servile and eulogistic as the former were caustic and satirical. Amongst
his friends and patrons might be included such men as
the dukes of Monmouth, Ormond, and Newcastle, lords
Clifford, Dorset, Buckhurst, and Rochester, sir Charles
Sedley, and the rest of the court wits and poets ; while
the most distinguished men of genius of the time,
Waller, Denham, Davenant, and even Cowley, crowded
round the fashionable and elated author. His income
from the theatre, from his laureateship, and other sources,
at this period, has been estimated at 600*l.* or 700*l.* per
annum ; so that from this point he must be regarded as
occupying a distinguished and influential place amongst
his contemporaries.

But the height and publicity of his position only
rendered him the surer mark for the envy of small
wits, and the ridicule of the critics, who were never at
a loss for excuses enough in his hurried productions to
justify their assaults upon his reputation. One of those
who earliest fell off from him was Rochester, a man whose
enmity was perhaps as dangerous as his friendship was
worthless. At first the enthusiastic admirer of Dryden, he soon became his most inveterate opponent,
libelling him in scurrilous verses, and even openly
patronising his literary antagonists. But the first effective attack made upon Dryden's reputation was in the

witty poem of *The Rehearsal,* projected by Villiers, duke
of Buckingham. The history of this production is a cu-
rions episode in dramatic literature. The original object
proposed was merely to ridicule the rhyming tragedies
of Sir William Davenant; but as this description of
drama increased in popularity, the scope of the design
was enlarged, until it embraced the whole body of
rhyming authors. The hero was consequently changed
from time to time to hit the reigning favourite. Originally Davenant is supposed to have been intended for
the principal part, then Howard, and lastly Dryden,
upon whom the entire force of the satire fell in the
figure of Bayes. To prevent the possibility of mistaking
the purpose and aim of the piece, not only was the name
of Bayes adopted to indicate the laureate, but Lacy, the
actor, who played the part, was instructed to imitate him
in dress and manner: while well-known passages from
his various plays were humorously parodied through
the scenes. The composition of the *Rehearsal* is ascribed to a knot of wits, who from the mixed motives of
a desire to restore the elder drama, and to gratify their
jealousy of Dryden, willingly engaged in an undertaking which promised them such brilliant means of
achieving both ends. Butler, Clifford, and Sprat, are
said to have assisted the duke of Buckingham in its
production, but what portions are to be assigned to each
cannot be determined. From such a coalition of talents great results might have been expected; yet it is
tolerably certain that ten years were consumed in the
progress of this long meditated satire. Probably it was
occasionally laid aside altogether, and then revived in a
whim, and laid aside again in caprice. Personal consi-.
derations may also, at intervals, have delayed its accom-
plishment; for it appears that even after it was
produced upon the stage, nearly a year elapsed before
it was printed, which Prior attributes to an apprehension on the part of the duke of Buckingham that the
the earl of Dorset, whose satirical powers were dreaded

by all his contemporaries, would "rehearse on him again."

The success of the *Rehearsal* was unprecedented. A strong party was made against it, but the ridicule was irresistible, and the laughter of the audience drowned the opposition of the mortified authors who crowded to the theatre with their adherents. The skill with which the prominent peculiarities of the rhyming plays were parodied; the happy choice of their striking passages, which were familiar to the public at large; and the exquisite humour thrown into the acting, by which Dryden's personal and well-known eccentricities of manner were closely mimicked—his testiness, pomp, and affectation—must have wounded the vanity of the poet deeply; but he had sufficient prudence to conceal his chagrin, and even endeavoured to turn off the point of the satire by joining in the general commendation of its sparkling wit. It was, of course, expected that it would elicit some rejoinder, but he never took any notice of it; and some years afterwards, in his preface to *Juvenal*, he assigned as a reason for not answering it, that he knew "the author sat to himself when he drew the picture, and was the very Bayes of his own farce." Notwithstanding, however, this apparent indifference to a satire, which for the time turned the current against him, he subsequently revenged himself upon the duke of Buckingham in the poem of *Absalom and Achitophel**—to which we shall come in the order of its production. †

---

* The character of Buckingham is drawn in the celebrated lines beginning —

> " Some of their chiefs were princes of the land ;
> In the first rank of these did Zimri stand,
> A man so various that he seem'd to be
> Not one, but all mankind's epitome," &c.

† Spence relates an anecdote, on the authority of Dr. Lockier, dean of Peterborough, which shows the aversion in which the duke of Buckingham held Dryden's plays. Happening to be in the theatre on one occasion, when a tragedy of Dryden's was performed, he effectually succeeded in turning the whole piece into ridicule, by seizing upon a particular line, and giving it a ludicrous turn. When the actress had to speak the line, she assumed

The *Rehearsal* did not banish heroic plays from the stage with such complete effect as might have been anticipated from its great success, for they continued to linger several years afterwards ; but Dryden yielded to the clamour it produced, and in the following year, 1672, he brought forward two comedies, *Marriage à la Mode*, and *The Assignation, or Love in a Nunnery*. These pieces were severally dedicated to Rochester (who had not yet deserted the poet) and Sedley; the former appears to have been received with applause*; but we have Dryden's own testimony of the unequivocal

---

a moving and affecting tone, which she considered appropriate to the sentiment, then slowly repeated —

" My wound is great, because it is so small! "

and paused with a terrible look of distress ; upon which the duke of Buckingham, rising from his seat, added in a loud mimicking voice—

" Then 't would be greater were it none at all! "

The effect was electrical. The actress was hissed off the stage, and the play was never performed again, which, as it was only the second representation, caused Dryden to lose his benefit night. — See *Anecdotes.*

* Connected with the Comedy of *Marriage à la Mode*, there appear to be some perplexities respecting the date of its production, and its reception on the stage. The *Rehearsal* was acted in 1671, and the *Marriage à la Mode* was not acted, according to Mr. Malone, until the following year ; yet the allusions to it in the *Rehearsal* are so clear, that they cannot be mistaken. Sir Walter Scott gets rid of the difficulty, by assuming that Dryden had suffered the plan of the piece to transpire in the circle which Buckingham frequented, who might thus have made it the subject of satire by anticipation. This, I confess, seems to me very improbable. Dryden wrote too fast, and too much, and was pressed too hard by the necessity of getting out his productions as quickly as he could, to keep a play upwards of a year on his hands for the private entertainment of his friends. But allowing this to be so, is it likely that he would have submitted this very play to the public so soon after it had been parodied and ridiculed in Buckingham's triumphant satire ? The whole circumstances of the case appear to favour the supposition that *Marriage à la Mode* was produced before the *Rehearsal*, and a passing notice in Pepys's Diary, of a comedy by Dryden, bearing nearly the same name, which he saw in 1668, tends greatly to strengthen, if it do not actually confirm, that view. It will be remembered that Mr. Malone had never seen Pepys's Diary, which was not published until 1825, and that, therefore, he relied wholly upon evidence of a different nature. According to Pepys, the play was performed on September 15. 1668, and, instead of being attended with great success, it failed somewhat ludicrously on the second representation. " To the king's playhouse to see a new play, acted but yesterday, a translation from the French by Dryden, called *The Lady's à la Mode*, so mean a thing as, when they came to say it would be acted again to-morrow, both he that said it (Beeson) and the pit fell a-laughing." There is no other play of Dryden's at this period to which the description can refer, and the coincidence of the name is at least equally remarkable.

failure of the latter. In the next year he ventured upon a tragedy, called *Amboyna*, which · he wrote in a month for the temporary purpose of feeding the national antipathy against the Dutch, with whom we were then at war; but in this piece he carefully avoided the ponderous and inflated style in which he had previously indulged, and took care to inform the public that the " subject was barren, the persons low, and the writing not heightened with many laboured scenes." These faults, however, were not found out by the audience, or perhaps were not considered by them as faults, and the tragedy was acted with as much success as the most gorgeous of its stilted predecessors.

Dryden now appears to have suspended his dramatic labours for an interval, during which he was employed in the composition of a species of lyrical poem in the dramatic form, but evidently not designed nor calculated for representation. The original title of this piece was *The Fall of Angels, and of Man in Innocence,* by which title it was registered at Stationers' Hall ; but it was afterwards altered to *The State of Innocence.* The subject of this poem is nearly the same, although differently treated, as that of the *Paradise Lost,* to which work the author gratefully acknowledged his obligations, bearing honourable testimony at the same time to the transcendent excellence of that noble production.* That the *Paradise Lost* considerably modified Dryden's opinions on the subject of rhyme is strongly indicated by an observation he is said to have made to a country gentleman, who, conversing with him concerning that poem, remarked, in reply to Dryden's lofty praises of it, that it was not in rhyme. "No!" said Dryden,

* " I cannot, without injury to the deceased author of *Paradise Lost,* but acknowledge that this poem has received its entire foundation, part of the design, and many of the ornaments from him. What I have borrowed will be so easily discerned from my mean productions, that I shall not need to point the reader to the places. And truly I should be sorry, for my own sake, that any one should take the pains to compare them together, the original being undoubtedly one of the greatest, most noble, and sublime poems, which either this age or nation has produced." — *Preface to The State of Innocence.*

" nor would I have done my Virgil in rhyme, if I was to begin it again."* According to Aubrey, the State of Innocence was undertaken with a view to turn the Paradise Lost into rhyme, recasting it in a dramatic shape. It is not easy to conceive how a poet of Dryden's great capacity and clear judgment could ever have entertained such a project; but Aubrey, if he may be relied upon, actually communicated the plan to Milton with a view to obtain his consent, and Milton contemptuously answered, " Ay, you may *tag* my verses if you will."†

The tragedy of Aureng-Zebe followed in 1675, and is chiefly remarkable as the last of Dryden's heroic plays. With this piece he renounced his favourite rhyme, and fairly admitted in the prologue that he had become at last convinced of its unsuitableness for the drama.

> " Passions too fierce to be in fetters bound,
> And nature flies him like enchanted ground."

It is only surprising that he did not make this discovery sooner.

With this salutary change in Dryden's taste came a change in his fortunes and his literary position. The burning of the king's theatre, already alluded to, had greatly diminished his resources; and the questions which now began to be debated on all sides arising out of the boldness of his critical essays, surrounded him with a host of opponents, who omitted no opportunity of assailing his reputation. His life, therefore, became emphatically a succession of contests. No doubt all the troubles in which he was involved might either be traced in the first instance to his own jealous and irritable disposition, or were greatly increased by the spirit in which he encountered the criticisms of his contempora-

---

* Richardson.
† Meretricious as this design was, it found admirers. Lee, the dramatic poet, in a copy of verses addressed to Dryden on this occasion, compliments him upon having refined the ore of Milton.

ríes. He was so suspicious of rivals, and so much afraid of acknowledging living merit, lest it might undermine his popularity, that he often acted with the strangest inconsistency and want of candour. Old Jacob Tonson related of him, that he would compliment Crowne, the dramatist, whenever a play of his happened to fail, but that he always treated him with coldness and apathy when he succeeded. Of Crowne he used to say, that he thought he had some genius ; but then he would add, in a sinister way, that " his father and Crowne's brother were very well acquainted."* Such a temper was sure to bring him into quarrels perpetually, and to bring him out of them discreditably.

Various attacks from different quarters now accumulated upon Dryden, some originating in feelings of personal ill-well, others dictated by an ambition to pluck down his laurels, and not a few to arrest the progress of the literary heresies he illustrated in verse and defended in prose. These controversies, with scarcely a single exception, began upon some point of criticism, and finally degenerated into mere scurrility and abuse. Martin Clifford was one of the first who assailed him, in the shape of notes upon his poems, in which he dissected verbal quibbles with microscopic ingenuity, and poured out a volley of angry denunciations, conceived in the coarsest and most opprobrious language. Dryden never condescended to answer him, which Clifford exultingly assumed as a proof that his charge was unanswerable. Ravenscroft, an obscure scribbler, who patched up some plays for the theatres from Shakspeare and Molière, had the audacity to sneer at Dryden's tragedies in the prologue to one of his motley productions. Dryden, with more irritation than the circumstance was worth, retorted upon him in another prologue; and thus a petty warfare was commenced between the greatest poet of the day and one of the most wretched of the tribe of play-wrights.

* Spence's Anecdotes.

Numerous pamphlets, levelled at Dryden's pieces, especially at *The Conquest of Granada*, appeared from time to time. In one of these Dryden was charged with having lampooned living characters in his comedies, a charge which is no where else brought against him, and which, unquestionably, has more malice than truth in it. As it was impossible to answer all these attacks singly, he adopted the plan of replying to them *en masse* in his prologues, dedications, and prefaces. The sweeping invectives in which he indulged on these occasions, had the effect of widening the field of battle, and giving fresh excuses for renewed and extended conflicts.

Of all these, the controversy with Elkanah Settle was the most remarkable and the most prolonged. The origin of this quarrel is to be referred partly to Dryden's jealousy of the favour in which Settle was held at court, and partly to the animosity of Rochester, who supported Settle in his attacks upon his formidable rival.

It appears that Rochester was first excited against Dryden in consequence of the patronage which was extended to him by Sheffield earl of Mulgrave, afterwards duke of Buckingham. In one of his reckless sallies, Rochester had given personal offence to Mulgrave, for which that nobleman considered it necessary to call him to account; but Rochester, according to the statement made at the time by his antagonist, behaved with so much pusillanimity on the ground, that he was branded as a coward, and of course never forgave the man by whom he was thus humiliated. Afraid to encounter Mulgrave openly, he availed himself of every opportunity that offered to annoy him through indirect channels; and finding that he had taken Dryden under his protection, he immediately set up Elkanah Settle — a person of inferior abilities, and arrogant presumption — as a rival to his opponent's *protégé*, although, only a short time before, he had accepted a dedication from Dryden full of the most slavish panegyrics, and had rewarded him for it with a munificent donation. But such sudden transitions and inconsistencies surprised nobody who was acquainted with the character of the inconstant, the capricious, and the profligate Rochester. Settle first came into notice by the success of a play called *Cambyses, King of Persia*, which afforded Rochester a sufficient excuse to make him known to his majesty. Introduced at court, and distinguished by the favour of so celebrated a wit, Settle's next production, *The Empress of Morocco*, was received with tumultuous applause, and continued to be acted with unabated success for an entire month. It was fairly carried through by the influence of fashion, without possessing a single particle of real merit. Rochester, to crown the triumphs of the poetaster, wrote a prologue for the piece, and contrived to get it acted at Whitehall by the lords and ladies of the court, on which brilliant occasion his own lines were spoken by the beautiful lady Elizabeth Howard. *

Intoxicated by such extraordinary success, and wound up to the highest pitch of vanity by the compliments lavished upon him at court, Settle at once assumed the airs of an established favourite, and in the dedication of his play to the Earl of Norwich, he attacked Dryden in a way that did not admit of being misunderstood or evaded. Nor was this all : his play was published with engravings, sold at the advanced price of two shillings, and announced as the production of Elkanah Settle, servant to his majesty.† It would have well become Dryden to have passed over all their insulting circumstances with silent contempt ; but he was too irritable to bear such assaults from so mean a quarter with patience. Accordingly, assisted by Shadwell and Crowne, who were equally jealous of Settle's

---

* It is not a little curious that the prologue which was spoken on the first representation of Settle's play at Whitehall was written by Mulgrave, Rochester's opponent, the prologue by Rochester having been spoken only on the second representation, and written probably for the purpose of superseding the former. This fact escaped the attention of Dryden's biographers until it was noticed by Scott. Both prologues were spoken by lady Elizabeth Howard.

† Sir Walter Scott had a copy of this rare edition, which he gave to Mr. Kemble. He says that the engravings were sufficiently paltry, and that even in his day it would have been dear at two shillings.

rising representation, he answered him in a pamphlet full of vulgar and angry ridicule, alike unworthy of his own fame and so pitiful a subject. Settle, glad of any occasion that drew him into a controversy with such a distinguished opponent, replied in a similar strain of vituperation, and there the matter rested until a fresh cause of animosity renewed the strife.*

Rochester, with his usual infidelity to his friends, had no sooner brought Settle into this quarrel, than he left him to fight his way out of it, and deserting him for Crowne, he used his interest to get that dramatist employed to write a masque for the court. This was even a more direct affront to Dryden than his patronage of Settle, as it was a part of the poet-laureate's business to furnish entertainments of that description. Compelled however to submit to the production of Crowne's masque of *Calisto*, Dryden endeavoured to conceal his discomfiture, by tendering his services in the shape of an epilogue; but Rochester interposed, and the epilogue was rejected. *Calisto* ran for nearly thirty nights; but scarcely was its triumph complete, than Crowne was discarded for Otway, whose tragedy of *Don Carlos* had just appeared, and was universally pronounced to be one of the very best of the heroic plays. Rochester, distrusting Crowne's talents as an antagonist to Dryden, or wishing, perhaps, to harass the latter still farther by increasing the number and virulence of his enemies, took Otway by the hand, and recommended him to the patronage of the court, which had been so recently lavished upon Settle and Crowne. These favours were duly acknowledged in the preface to Don Carlos, where the poet thanked his patron in the usual language of adulation, and, to enhance the expression of his gratitude, sneered contemptuously at Dryden. But all Otway gained by this was a niche in Rochester's

---

* The reader who is curious to see how this very unequal contest was conducted, and who may not have access to the original works, will find extracts from both sides in Dr. Johnson's " Life of Dryden."

Session of the Poets, where his name was held up to public scorn and ridicule by the man who fostered him for a brief season, and then cast him off to a doom of poverty and despair.

The perseverance with which Rochester prosecuted his enmity against Dryden is perhaps wholly unparalleled in the history of literary warfare. He assailed him through every channel his station and influence could command, laboured assiduously to destroy him at court, and at last even stooped to the degrading act of hiring bravoes to waylay and beat him. The immediate cause of this piece of derogatory violence was the publication of a poem entitled an *Essay upon Satire*, which was written by Mulgrave, and carefully revised, at his lordship's desire, by Dryden. The satire evidently received no further assistance from the hands of Dryden than might be necessary to improve the music of its numbers, and even in this respect he left it imperfect, and in many places rugged. But there was ground enough for Rochester's venom in the rumour which associated Dryden in the authorship, or which, at all events, involved him in the responsibility, more or less, of participating in a publication which reflected severely on that dissolute and unprincipled courtier. The passage in which Rochester is referred to may probably have been heightened by Dryden, but certainly never could have been written by so accomplished a master of poetry. But apart from the internal evidence of the work, its baldness, flatness, and monotonous style, a candid and discerning opponent must have acquitted Dryden of the authorship, in consequence of the scurrility with which it attacked the king. Of all things it was most unlikely that the laureate would satirize his royal master, upon whose countenance his fortunes in a great degree depended. Notwithstanding, however, all these improbabilities, Rochester did not hesitate to accuse Dryden of having actually written the poem. In a note upon a copy of the satire which he sent to his friend Henry Saville, he observed, " I have sent you herewith a libel, in which my own share is not the least. The king, having perused it, is no way dissatisfied with his. The author is apparently Mr. Dr., his patron, Lord M., having a panegyric in the midst." Proceeding upon this assumption, he declared, in a private letter to another correspondent, that "if he [Dryden] falls upon me at the blunt, which is his very good weapon in wit, I will forgive him if you please; and leave the repartee to black Will with a cudgel." He fulfilled his threat; and on the night of the 18th of December, 1679, Dryden was attacked by some hired ruffians, who sprang upon him in the dark, in Rose Street, Covent Garden, as he was returning home from Will's coffee-house. A reward of fifty pounds was offered in the public papers for the discovery of the perpetrators, but, of course, screened by the nobleman who hired them, they evaded detection.*

This Will's coffee-house was the favourite resort of the wits of the day, and owed its popularity entirely to Dryden. It was afterwards frequented by Addison, who transferred the patronage of the literary people to the house of Bullar, a servant of his, who lived on the opposite side of the way, in Russell Street, Covent Garden. As all such localities are objects of public interest, it may be added that Will's coffee-house was No. 23., and was situated on the north side. at the end of Bow Street. Here, observes Malone, Dryden had his armed chair, which in winter had a prescriptive place by the fire, and in the summer was placed in the balcony. These two places he used to call his winter and his summer seats. He was the appellate jurisdiction of the room in all cases of literary dispute. The company always assembled in · the first floor (hence the

balcony), and sat dispersed at different tables; and Ward
tells us, that the young beaux and wits, who seldom
ventured to sit at the principal table, thought it a great
honour to obtain a pinch of snuff from Dryden's box.

In connection with this peep into the interior of the
coffee-house, it will not be out of place to observe that
Dryden was remarkable amongst his contemporaries
for his abstemious habits. In the last ten years of his
life he spent a great deal of time with Addison, and
was tempted by him to fall into intemperance, probably
to an excess, according to Dennis, that may have
hastened his end.* He lived in Gerrard Street†, the
fifth house from Little Newport Street. His apartments at the back looked into the gardens of Leicester
House, and he used to write in the ground-room next
the street.‡ His mode of occupying his time appears to
have been regular and unvaried : he wrote in the
mornings, dined *en famille,* and then went to Will's,
which he generally retired from at an early hour.§ Upon
the same authority we are informed, that he " was not
a very genteel man, *he was intimate with none but
poetical men.* He was said to be a very good man, by
all that knew him ; he was as plump as Mr. Pitt ; of a
fresh colour, and a down look, and not very conver-
sible." These are the words of Pope, who saw Dryden
only in his decline. One may almost instinctively
discern the finical and artificial spirit of the author of
The Rape of the Lock, in the intimation that Dryden
was not "a very *genteel* man," that he was "*intimate
with none but poetical men.*" Yet Pope, in spite of
this conventional and uneasy feeling, had a deep reverence
for Dryden's genius, at least as deep a reverence as his
nature was capable of entertaining. He felt his superiority, and made him his model, after he had done

* Spence's Anecdotes.
† This street is also memorable as having been the residence of Edmund
Burke, whose house is now a boarding-house.
‡ Pope — Spence's Anecdotes. § Ibid.

admiring Waller.* He said to Mr. Spence, " I saw
Mr. Dryden when I was about twelve years of age:
this bust is like him. I remember his face well, for
I looked upon him, even then, with the greatest
veneration, and observed him very particularly."† Great
as was his veneration for Dryden, he rated him at this
very time, as he acknowledges in another place, below
Waller and Spenser, placing the former first of the
three.

Passing from these episodical illustrations, we resume
the narrative of Dryden's productions. We have seen
that he indicated a disposition to abandon his opinions
concerning the fitness of rhyme for tragedy, and now
it would appear that he began to grow wearied of the
theatre altogether, fairly confessing that he was excelled
by many of his predecessors in all kinds of dramatic
composition, and even by some of his contemporaries in
comedy. Perhaps the disputes with Settle, Crowne,
and Otway, helped not a little to confirm this lurking
distaste for the drama, aided, no doubt, by the failure
of *The Assignation,* and one or two other pieces.
But before he acted upon this shapeless and indistinct
distrust of himself and his powers (if, indeed, he dis-
trusted either), he produced the tragedy of *All for
Love,* which he says was the only play he ever wrote
for himself — the rest were given to the people. The
subject of this piece is the story of Anthony and Cleo-
patra, which had been already treated by Shakspeare,
with infinitely greater truth, but with less regularity of
structure. Perhaps Dryden contemplated something
like a rivalry to Shakspeare, or desired to contrast his
own elaborate versification with the bolder periods of
his great predecessor ; but whatever may have been his

---

* He said that he " learned versification wholly from Dryden's Works,
who had improved it much beyond any of our former poets, and would
probably have brought it to its perfection, had not he been unhappily
obliged to write so often in haste. He always used proper language :
lively, natural, and fitted to the subject. It is scarce ever too high, or too
low ; never, perhaps, except in his plays.' — *Spence.*

† Spence's Anecdotes.

real object in the selection of the plot, it may be affirmed that he would have succeeded better had not those resemblances existed which rendered such a comparison inevitable. The play is allowed on all hands to be more free from bombast than any of his heroic dramas, probably because, treading in the wake of Shakspeare, he considered it incumbent upon him to write with more than ordinary circumspection.

The comedy of *Limberham* followed, and was condemned on the third night in consequence of its indelicacy, which must have been extravagantly gross to have offended the public in the licentious age of Charles II. But the real cause of its failure was not so much its immorality, as the unskilfulness of the treatment. The fate of this comedy ought to be a warning to all dramatists who aim at satirising the vices of the day. Dryden informs us, that the object of the piece was to expose " the crying sin of keeping;" and he adds that it failed, because it " expressed too much of the vices it decried." The most profligate audience will endure a well-directed satire against their favourite sins, but will resent the exhibition of them as an affront. Whoever, therefore, proposes to correct vice, must be careful not to fall into the error of parading its image openly through a procession of subordinate virtues.

This play was acted at Dorset-Gardens, for Dryden's contract with the king's company appears to have been dissolved about this time: partly, it may be presumed, from the dissatisfaction of the players, and partly from Dryden's disinclination to fulfil his undertaking. He meditated, also, an epic poem, which evidently diverted his thoughts from the stage; and all he required to enable him to proceed with its execution was some solid encouragement from his patrons. In a letter to lord Mulgrave he mentions that he had submitted the design of his projected work to his majesty and his royal highness, who approved of it, and encouraged it by their commands ; " but," he adds, " the unsettledness of my condition has hitherto put a stop to my thoughts concerning it." The subject of this poem was to have been thoroughly English, either the story of Arthur or of Edward the Black Prince, and he proposed to make the king and his brother its heroes. It is not a little remarkable that Milton had long conceived a similar intention of writing a poem on king Arthur and his knights.* Neither of them ever carried out a speenlation for which both, in different ways, were eminently qualified.

The tragedy of *Œdipus*†, written in conjunction with Lee, was next produced at Dorset-Gardens, and was succeeded by an adaptation of *Troilus and Cressida*, under the name of *Truth found too late*. Prefixed to this latter piece, which was published in 1679, are some remarks on the grounds of criticism in tragedy, in which the writer renounces, not formally but substantially, the error he had formerly maintained with so much pertinacity. He even indulges so far in the confession of his faults, as to furnish an example from one of his own pieces, in which a hero pursued by his enemies was made to describe his dilemma in a long and intricate trope, utterly out of keeping with the exigencies of his situation. The principles of dramatic construction laid down in this Essay are lucid, incontrovertible, and comprehensive. They comprise nearly all the rules essential to the natural and dignified conduct of the tragic drama.

Dryden had now evidently relinquished the heterogeneons comedy of intrigue and confusion which had been adopted in his time from the Spanish theatre, and which he had himself contributed to bring into vogue; but he still contended for that description of mixed play in which humour and pathos are so ingeniously interwoven as to preserve a constant alternation of comic and tragic scenes. Whoever, he observed, cannot perform both parts, is but half a writer for the stage. His *Spanish*

---

* See Lives of the Poets, vol. i. p. 158.
† Dryden wrote the first and third acts, and arranged the plan of the whole.

Friar, acted in 1681, is a very perfect specimen of the class. Dr. Johnson remarks that it is eminent for the happy coincidence and coalition of the two plots; and certainly a more felicitous combination of opposite elements, in so far as the mechanism of the play is involved, can hardly be found. But it may be doubted whether the same praise can be given to the style of the composition. The tragic portion is, for the most part, inflated, and the comic is often coarse and inelegant, if not in its ultimate tendency immoral.

The Spanish Friar was brought out at the moment when the country was agitated by the discovery of what has been called the popish plot, and the main purpose of the play was to satirize the Roman catholic religion, a design which the author believed would be acceptable to the public. Dryden avowed his intention in the dedication to lord Haughton, where he emphatically describes the piece to be a protestant play inscribed to a protestant patron. This proceeding is the more remarkable, as the duke of York, who had hitherto been his friend, had embraced that religion, and could not, therefore, be supposed to regard the play otherwise than as an indignity to himself and his friends. His royal highness subsequently exhibited his displeasure when he acceded to the crown, by prohibiting the performance of *The Spanish Friar*, which was the only play he considered it necessary to interdict. To whatever cause Dryden's conduct may be attributed, it is impossible to give him credit for conscientious motives, unless we are also to believe that his religious impressions were singularly light and fleeting; for not very long afterwards he became a convert to the religion he thus stigmatised, and even went exorbitant lengths in its defence. Perhaps the true motive was revenge upon the duke of York for having failed to bestow upon him the encouragement he required in the prosecution of his epic poem; although such a means of revenge, it must be confessed, was neither prudently nor skilfully chosen. But Dryden's most effectual weapon was the stage, and he might have deceived himself into the expectation that the horror of the catholics which prevailed through England at that time would have seized upon this occasion to show itself in an open demonstration of hostility to his royal highness. The theatre was the great arena for the display of popular sentiment, and *The Spanish Friar* may be considered as a desperate attempt to turn it to a profitable account. Dryden's declining circumstances furnish apparently a clue to this rash speculation. His pension as laureate had latterly been very irregularly paid, and, according to one of his biographers, it was stopped altogether : his contract with the players was at an end ; and the most successful of his dramas did not yield him more than 100*l.* ; this, too, while Southern had received for one tragedy as much as 700*l.* Thus reduced in his resources, and depending wholly upon the most precarious of all literary occupations, he seems to have adopted this mode of reproaching his court friends, by throwing himself into the ranks of their opponents.

The very next phase of Dryden's life exhibits him in defence of the monarchy. After having assailed the catholic religion, to vex the court, he now turned round to assail the whigs in defence of the court. The occasion was unquestionably one of great interest, and the agitated state of the country could hardly allow so distinguished a writer to remain inactive. The duke of York required his help against the growing popularity of Monmouth, and whatever anger he felt towards Dryden in reference to *The Spanish Friar,* was easily propitiated by a graceful prologue spoken at the theatre upon his return from Scotland. Dryden's situation, no doubt, exposed him to the temptations which were thus thrown in his way, and we must not be surprised that he who could alternately flatter and revile his friends and patrons under the influence of an irritable temper, should be found no less capricious by every party whose cause he happened to espouse. The truth is, that Dryden was a man of impulse, and seems never to have been regulated in' any of his acts by fixed principles. The greater part of his life presents an almost unbroken series of peenniary vicissitudes. He seemed to be always writing for bread, and ready to devote his talent to the most lucrative tasks. There was no moral dignity in his character. He wrote like one who was engaged in a perpetual slavish struggle for subsistence, a melancholy truth which the loftiness of his powers only rendered the more conspicuous. The man who could so far debase his genius as to compare the patron of the hour to a god, could not be expected to exhibit much independence as a politician.

The justly celebrated satire of *Absalom and Achitophel* was the first fruit of Dryden's accession to the party of the king. In this splendid and masterly performance he attacked the whole of the whig party with such caustic severity, that the effect is described to have been overwhelming. It was rapidly circulated through all parts of the kingdom, and it may be reasonably doubted whether his majesty could have devised any mode of bringing his opponents into contempt so likely to produce the desired result. Shaftesbury, and Buckingham, were the chief objects of the poet's searing anathema; and, in proportion as he held them up to public scorn and detestation, he eulogised the virtues and the talents of such men as Ormond, Halifax, and Hyde, earl of Rochester. Considered merely as a work of art, apart from its personal application, this poem must be pronounced a model in his kind. The principal figures are drawn with consummate ability, the diction is apt, various, and energetic; and the versification is exquisitely finished. Dr. Johnson objects to the imperfections of the plan, but sir Walter Scott has shown that they could not have been avoided.

The great success of this satire led to the immediate production of another upon the acquittal of lord Shaftesbury. The release of that nobleman from the Tower was celebrated by his adherents in a variety of ways; and, amongst other contrivances adopted to testify their exultation, a medal was struck in commemoration of the event. This circumstance furnished the subject of the poem, which was called *The Medal*, a satire against sedition, and which is said to have been suggested to Dryden by the king one day, as they were walking together in the Mall. " If I were a poet," said the king, " and I think I am poor enough to be one, I would write a poem on such a subject in the following manner," and so his majesty went on laying down the plan of the work. Dryden was not slow to appreciate such a suggestion from such a quarter, and when the satire was finished, he hastened to present it to his royal master, who was so pleased with the execution, that he presented the author with 100 broad pieces.* In this poem Shaftesbury was assailed with even greater force than in the former, his whole life was traced, his political inconsistencies laid bare, the ribald licentiousness of his habits exposed, and all the anomalies and deformities of his political and private character unsparingly chastised ; the beauty of the poetry, as an acute critic observes, adding grace to the severity of the satire.

A multitude of antagonists immediately started into the field to repel those attacks upon their party. All the old animosities against Dryden were revived with increased venom, and amongst the puny whipsters who now rose to combat him, was his ancient and implacable rival, Elkanah Settle. The whole humour of Settle's response was its parody of the Jewish names adopted by Dryden, but there ended the sting. He had caught up the garments of the Hebrews, but lacked the vital energy to fill them with the requisite vigour. Of all his opponents, the duke of Buckingham, who quivered under the wounds inflicted upon him in *Absalom and Achitophel*, was the most distinguished ; but, as if his sprightly genius quailed before the solemn march of Dryden's stately and masculine lines, his answer was altogether unworthy of the wit to whom is assigned the credit of the principal share in *The Rehearsal.* Samuel Pordage, one of the petty rhymers of the day, who ventured into the lists, was crushed by one of those fatal epithets, which Dryden, in his higher moods of indignation, hurled against his enemies.* A non-conformist clergyman attacked him in a couple of ridiculons lampoons, called *A Whip for the Fool's Back,* and *A Key,* with the *Whip,* &c.; and one Hickeringill, a scurrilous fanatic, attempted to retort upon him in a fantastic preposterous poem, called *The Mushroom,* which, because it happened to be sent to press on the same day on which the medal appeared, he attributed to divine inspiration. A great diversity of similar pamphlets, and frantic satires, poured out day after day, attacking Dryden upon all points—his marriage —his poverty—his early association with the puritans —his rencontre with the cudgel-men in Rose Alley, and every part and fragment of his life, which was susceptible of ridicule or calumny. None of these attacks, however, seem to have affected him very keenly, not even the nicknames of Bayes and Poet Squab, which were bandied about in the streets and coffee-houses; and the only occurrence of this personal and literary war that seriously moved him were the renewed hostility of Settle, and the defection of his quondam friend, Shadwell, who now came out in the ranks of his assailants.

The way in which the dramatists of that age chiefly kept up their feuds was through their prologues and epilogues. Thus Settle assailed Dryden in the prologue to *The Emperor of Morocco,* employing language that never could be forgotten or forgiven. He did not omit, amongst the rest of his abuse, to remind the audience that Dryden was a changeling and a stipendiary poet:

" And poets, we all know, can change like you,
    And are alone to their own interest true;

---

* Dryden dismissed this presumptuous scribbler, by branding him as Lame Mephibosheth, the wizard's son.

Can write against all sense, nay, even their own :
The vehicle called *pension* makes it down.
No fear of cudgels, where there's hope of bread,
A well-filled paunch forgets a *broken head.*"

To all such assaults—and they were numerous and
unmerciful, and all the more bitter because there were
some unpalatable truths mixed up in them—Dryden
replied in a powerful satire entitled, " *Mac-Flecknoe,* or
a Satire on the True Blue Protestant Poet, T. S., by
the Author of Absalom and Achitophel." This was
rapidly followed by a second part to *Absalom and Achitophel,* which was composed by Nahum Tate, under the
superintendence and revision of Dryden, who supplied
in the body of the poem some of its most vigorous and
effective lines. Nahum Tate was, on this occasion, as
upon many others, employed as a hack. He merely
versified Dryden's ideas, and appears to have possessed
that sort of mechanical facility which admirably adapted
him for such useful but inglorious labours. Shadwell
was the hero of the *Mac-Flecknoe,* and the effect
was so tremendous, that although he floundered and
blustered a great deal, and even attempted to revenge
himself in sundry lampoons, he never recovered from
the disgrace with which it overwhelmed him. From
the time of its publication Shadwell rapidly fell into
contempt, until at last, notwithstanding the favours conferred on him at the Revolution, he came to be remembered only as the annihilated antagonist of Dryden.
Poor Settle experienced, if possible, a still worse fate.
He who was once the flattered poet of Whitehall, who
was patronised by the king, and whose plays were acted
by the ladies of the Court, sunk down into a show-
man at Bartholomew Fair, where he was reduced to
the miserable expedient of acting on the stage amongst
the wooden puppets, and finally died in the Charter-
house.

The circumstances which drew Dryden into these
controversies discovered in him a new talent, which rendered him more formidable than ever to his opponents,

and more useful to his friends.. His satires turned the tide of poetry into fresh channels, and as his preliminary essays to his published dramas originated a species of criticism previously unknown in England, the *Absalom and Achitophel*, and *Mac-Flecknoe*, may be said to have created in our language that form of satire which was afterwards so successfully imitated by Pope, Roscommon, Gifford, and Byron. The *Religio Laici* followed, a poem, the professed object of which was to defend the church of England against her assailants. But the undertaking was evidently little better than an act of policy on the part of the poet. His mind, at the very time when he wrote this piece, was in a state of such incertitude about religion, that it may be doubted whether he really believed in Christianity, and whether he was not struggling between infidelity and the church of Rome. Considered as a defence of the church of England, the *Religio Laici* betrays the scruples of an advocate who is pleading against his conviction, or at least trying to make out arguments in favour of a cause the justice of which he distrusts. His subsequent conversion to the church of Rome undoubtedly assists us to a clearer view of these indications of scepticism; but an attentive examination of the poem, even without this aid from circumstantial illustration, must satisfy the reader, that while Dryden was writing in favour of Protestantism, his opinions were undergoing a revolution that weakened his resolution at every step.

The tragedy of the *Duke of Guise*, acted by the united company of players, who had at length brought their disputes to a termination, and sealed the pacification by joining their force, was the next production of our prolific poet, and was represented for the first time on the 30th December, 1682. It was planned by Dryden, who wrote nearly the half of it, the rest being contributed by Lee. The play had all throughout a political tendency: the puritans were delineated in the leaguers, and the story of the unfortunate Monmouth was exhibited in that of the rash and impetuous Guise.

Its success was such as might have been expected from a piece favourable to one side and obnoxious to another. The Tories applauded it, the Whigs hissed it, and, although it was repeatedly acted amidst a clamour of contention, it never became popular.

The *Duke of Guise* was attacked by Shadwell in verse and prose, and by one Thomas Hunt, a barrister. Dryden considered it necessary to vindicate the play against its critics, but his vindication consisted rather of the expression of sovereign contempt for his enemies, than a serious justification of his political principles. We next find him engaged in an edition of *Plutarch's Lives,* to which he contributed a biographical preface, and a translation of Maimbourg's *History of the League,* which he undertook at the express command of the king. The finances of the writer were at this time so low, in consequence it would appear of those labours in the royal cause, which compelled him, as he stated, to neglect his " beneficial studies," that he was obliged to memorialise Rochester for half a year's pension " for his necessities," and to ask, after a glance at his services, for some " small employment to render his condition easy." To such an extremity of distress did the merry monarch and his courtiers permit their ablest champion to sink, even at the very moment when his best energies were most successfully dedicated to their cause ! The memorial to Rochester presents a humiliating picture of the adversities of genius. The following passage is too striking and affecting to be omitted.

" I have three sons growing to man's estate. I breed them all up to learning, beyond my fortune ; but they are too hopeful to be neglected, though I want. Be pleased to look on me with an eye of compassion : some small employment would render my condition easy. The king is not unsatisfied of me ; the duke has often promised me his assistance ; and your lordship is the conduit through which their favours pass. Either in the customs, or in the appeals of the excise, or some other way, means cannot be wanting, if you please to

have the will. 'Tis enough for one age to have ne-
gleeted Mr. Cowley, and starved Mr. Butler ; but
neither of them had the happiness to live till your
lordship's ministry."

To these names might have been added that of Milton, who, on the opposite side, was equally neglected
by the age. But the appeal was useless. Dryden
could not obtain the pitiful place he asked for, and soon
afterwards the death of the king extinguished all hope.
As an expedient for present relief, he made a collection
of miscellaneous poems, including translations from
Ovid, Horace, Virgil, and Theocritus, which were published by Jacob Tonson ; and upon the death of his
majesty, although he had so little reason to be grateful,
he paid an honourable tribute to his memory in the
Threnodia Augustalis, which closed with an apostrophe
to his successor James II. This was followed by the
opera of *Albion and Albanius,* originally designed as a
prelude to *King Arthur,* and now completed as a separate allegory, in which the whole progress of the restoration, the Popish plot, and the downfall of the Whigs,.
were gorgeously exhibited. The scenery is described to
have been unusually splendid, embracing, amongst other
grand pictorial designs, a celestial phenomenon of three
suns, with two demi-rainbows enclosed within one whole
rainbow, which captain Gunman, of the navy, saw, as he
lay off Calais pier, in March, 1683. The sixth representation of this opera was interrupted by the announcement
of Monmouth's invasion, the news of which reached the
theatre during the performance, and threw the audience
into consternation. The piece was never repeated.

Soon after this Dryden embraced the Roman Catholic religion. He had been visibly vibrating between
scepticism and the church of Rome for some time, and
his doubts now terminated in the open avowal of tenets
which, at the commencement of his career, he held in
abhorrence. There is nothing very remarkable in this circumstance, although every one of Dryden's biographers
have founded dissertations upon it. One would sup-

pose that a man's religion is always to be regarded with
suspicion, unless he continues to think invariably as he·
was taught to think in his childhood, since the moment
he ventures to think for himself he is liable to be accus‑
ed of corrupt intentions. Agreeably to this view of the
subject, the purest religionist is the man who never
thinks at all, but who, strictly following the course
originally laid down for him, transmits the family
creed to his successors exactly as he inherited it from·
his fathers. When any individual diverges from the
regular line, he must be prepared to submit to imputa-
tions of the worst kind. If, from strong convictions, he
abandons one form of Christianity and embraces another,
he early discovers that, under such circumstances, the·
only way to preserve his reputation is to conceal his conscientiousness, and that, in order to appear honest, he
must act like a hypocrite. It is rarely taken into consideration, that the question is not one that can be settled
here ; that it rests exclusively between the Creator and
the creature ; that no man can penetrate the motives of
another; and that, if he could, he has neither the power·
nor the right to decide upon them. A man may surely
be allowed to assert his own feelings in matters that con‑
cern his eternal happiness, without being exposed to
doubts of his integrity in temporal affairs. It is possible
to profess tradition and the Bible, and be an honest man ;
and equally possible to repudiate tradition, and be a
rogue. If we are to shape our confidence in men by
our reliance on their religious professions, it is tolerably
clear that one half of Christendom must regard the
other half with sensations not unlike those of settlers in
savage lands, who live in a state of constant alarm,
amidst sentries and watchfires, lest they should be de-
voured by the wild beasts, whose howl at a distance
fills them with terror.

Dr. Johnson observes, that " that conversion will
always be suspected that apparently concurs with interest :" but he thinks that " truth and interest are not
by any fatal necessity at variance, and that one may, by

accident, introduce the other;" and, believing that
Dryden "wanted skill to discover the right, rather than
virtue to maintain it," he gives up the inquiry by leaving the convert to his Judge. That Dryden should
have wanted the requisite skill to discover the right, is
not less marvellous than that Dr. Johnson should have
pronounced the discovery of the right to be dependent
upon skill of any kind.

Sir Walter Scott enters at great length into the circumstances of Dryden's conversion, with a view to
justify his own impression that it was not guided by
base motives. He says that Dryden maintained his
new faith with firmness through evil report and good
report, and that his adherence to a falling sect may be
regarded as an evidence of his sincerity. But in the
next sentence he tells us, that "the conversion of Dryden did not long remain unrewarded, nor was his pen
suffered to be idle in the cause which he had adopted."
It is plain, therefore, that although Dryden embraced
a falling sect, he did not fall by it himself, and that
Scott believed him to be sincere in spite of his good
fortune.

The clearest reason might become bewildered in these
refined attempts to vindicate or excuse the conduct of Dryden in doing that which he had an unimpeachable right
to do, and which no critic or biographer can otherwise
exhibit than as an act which he is neither required to
defend, nor qualified to explain. Dryden's conversion
was speedily followed by an increase in his pension of
100l. per annum, and by ample employment as the
advocate of the Roman church against Stillingfleet and
the Protestant divines. From these facts, it has been
concluded by some commentators that he was actuated
by mercenary motives; and unquestionably such motives may have influenced him to a certain extent: his
life unfortunately is not so pure in reference to matters
of doctrine and opinion as to justify us in giving him
the benefit of the doubt. But whatever may have originally induced him to renounce Protestantism, there is no

room for suspecting him of any indecision on religious subjects afterwards. He embraced the Roman Catholic faith publicly, and maintained it zealously to the end of his life. He who was first an *élève* of the puritans —next, a hot-headed establishment man — then a sceptic— now became an energetic defender of the church of Rome. His controversy with Stillingfleet, however, is memorable rather for asperity and boldness, than for polemical learning. Stillingfleet attempted to answer him in his own scornful and abusive tone, but he handled such weapons so awkwardly, that he more frequently exposed himself to wounds than succeeded in inflicting them. *The Hind and the Panther* was the issue of this furious dispute — a poem in which Dryden exhibits the two churches — draws them out, with all the sectaries, into an open feud — and ends by leaving them implacable and irreconcilable enemies. The church of Rome in this allegory is represented by the milk white hind, and the church of England by the spotted panther.

A greater clamour was excited by this publication than even by *Absalom and Achitophel.* Two young men, Prior and Montagu, who were just rising into fame, answered it in a pert parody, called *The Town and Country Mouse.* Prior had by far the larger share of this work, although Montagu alone reaped any advantage from it.* The effect upon the public was instantaneous and complete, and Dryden's humiliation is said to have been so overwhelming that he shed tears at the ingratitude of the youthful authors, to whom he had shown some marks of favour —probably amongst the frequenters of Will's coffee-house.

Dryden of course was accused of inconsistency and infidelity to his former opinions. The *Religio Laici*

---

* Dorset is said to have presented Montague to king William, observing, at the same time, " I have brought a *mouse* to wait on your majesty." " I will make a *man* of him," was the reply, and a pension of 500*l. per annum* was immediately settled on the lucky satirist. Prior afterwards complained of neglect, expostulating,

" That one mouse eats while t'others starved."

was contrasted with *The Hind and the Panther:* and
the dramatist who attacked the catholics in *The Spanish
Friar* was exhibited in juxtaposition with the contro-
versialist who now assailed the protestants. There were
enough of materials in his earlier works to enable his
opponents to convict him in detail of what they called
apostacy. It could not be denied that he had fairly
turned round and opposed all the principles he had
ever before maintained; but the last principles we
espouse are generally held with greater vigour than those
they displace, for the same process that has convinced
us of their truth has also convinced us that all other
principles are false. In youth we only submit: in manhood we investigate and adopt. Dryden exemplified
the force of this universal condition of mind by the zeal
with which he defended himself, and laboured to dis-
seminate the doctrines he had embraced. He commenced the translation of Varilla's *History of Heresies,*
which, however, for some reason, he afterwards aban-
doued, but only to give to the world a translation of
the life of St. Francis Xavier, whose miraculous performances were just at that time regarded with wonder
by the whole of catholic Europe. He is said also to
have translated about the same period Bossuet's *Expo-
sition of the Catholic Doctrine:* but the authority on
which this statement rests is not very clear or satisfactory. Yet although his thoughts were so busily
occupied in the advocacy of his new views of religion,
Dryden did not abandon the art he loved. His faith
in the beauty and wisdom of poetry was too deep to be'
shaken; and in the midst of his graver pursuits he
found leisure to produce such exquisite things as the
Ode to the Memory of Mr. Killigrew, and the translation of the *Te Deum,* the *Veni, Creator Spiritus,* and
the *Hymn for St. John's Eve.* The poetical part of
his gorgeous religion particularly affected his feelings;
and those noble hymns which form so important a feature in the catholic ritual were amongst the first objects

of his enthusiastic admiration. Indeed, it might suggest an inquiry of some interest to ascertain whether
Dryden's judgment was not wooed and won through
his imagination. Genius is easily converted if that approach be once secured.

The moment was now at hand when all Dryden's
glory was destined to be quenched in an event that for
ever destroyed his prospects at court, and cast him at
once upon the last resources of his pen. This event
was the Revolution, which altered Dryden's destiny in
no less a degree than it changed the whole aspect of
public affairs. It was impossible that the prince of
Orange, on the throne of England, could permit the
catholic poet to hold the office of laureate. Dryden's
dismissal from that situation, although he was the
fittest man living to fill it, was, therefore unavoidable.
But, however he might have reconciled his pride and
shaped his necessities to this misfortune, he could not
brook the appointment of his ancient opponent, Shadwell, to be his successor. Had the nomination been
guided by a distinct determination to wound and oppress
him, it could not have struck home more deeply: and
it is difficult not to avoid the suspicion, for which there is
no other ground than the strangeness of the coincidence,
that Shadwell was really appointed for the express purpose of making the downfal of Dryden the more humiliating and complete. To enhance the mortification,
Shadwell was presented to the king by Dorset, not as
the best poet, but as the most honest man amongst the
candidates, and was inducted into the two offices held
by Dryden, laureate and historiographer, with a salary of
300*l.* per annum. Shadwell, elated by his triumph, did
not omit to celebrate it in some verses, which are not
very creditable to his generosity or his taste.

Dryden's only resource was the theatre ; and here,
before he had time to prepare a new piece, he was destined to witness the revival of his own *Spanish Friar,*
in which he had only a short time before so bitterly
satirized the religion for which he was now enduring

the sufferings of a martyr. He resolved, however, to
rise superior to these reverses and sarcasms, and in his
tragedy of *Don Sebastian*, produced in 1690, he exhibited a genius so lofty and commanding, that it ex-
torted applause even from his greatest enemies. He
admits that he bestowed great pains upon this play, and
the result justified the labour it cost. The piece was
not very successful at first, and was curtailed and altered
before it attained that height in public favour which it
afterwards reached and kept. It is justly regarded as
the most perfect of Dryden's dramatic productions. In
the same year the comedy of *Amphitryon* was acted
with great applause ; and was followed by the opera of
King Arthur, which, with Purcell's music, was emi-
uently successful.

The rapidity with which the two following plays —
Cleomenes and *Love Triumphant*—were produced, may,
in some degree, account for their total failure on the
stage. Dryden was ill, probably depressed in spirits,
and obliged to invoke the assistance of his friend
Southerne to enable him to finish the labours he had
commenced. Under such circumstances, no other result could have been looked for than that which actually
took place. The audience, although they may be supposed to have felt some friendly disposition towards one
who had so frequently entertained them, yet did not
hold Dryden in such favour as to tolerate his dulness
for the sake of serving him in his necessities. The
play of *Cleomenes*, which was nearly prohibited altogether on political grounds *, was too lethargic for
the patience of the public, and *Love Triumphant* was
condemned, because it mixed up with the buffoon-
eries of farce some of the darkest and most revolting
features of that species of tragedy which has since become popular in Germany, but which has at all times
been ill received in England. Dryden was so deeply

---

* Dryden's enemies caused it to be rumoured, before its production, that
Cleomenes was a Jacobite play; but this assertion was disproved by its
publication.

offended by the decision of the audiences on these plays, that, after an angry vindication of the fables and characters he had depicted, in which he attempted to show that it was the judgment of the spectators and not his own that was at fault, he took his leave of the stage for ever. Thus he ended as he began with an unsuccesful play.

During this long career as a dramatic author, Dryden produced twenty-seven pieces. They were variously received. Some of them failed utterly,—others had a sort of doubtful success,—a few were triumphant,— none kept long possession of the stage. There is no óther poet, of equal reputation and pretensions, whose progress in reference to dramatic literature, so forcibly illustrates the uncertainty that darkens the fortunes of him whose subsistence is even partially dependant on the theatre.

It may be proper in this place to say something of Dryden as a writer of plays, although the verdict of universal opinion renders minute criticism unnecessary. Not one of his pieces has survived to the present day, and perhaps we should be justified in adding that, with the single exception of *Sebastian*, not one of them outlived his own age. When we discover such an anomaly as this in the history of one, whose fame in other forms of poetry is so pre-eminent, we may be assured that there is some solid and unanswerable reason for it. The reason is simply this—that Dryden's plays have not a particle of nature in them. They do not bring men and women before us, but sphinxes, colossal monsters, baboons, sprites, and unnatural hybrids. His characters are not personifications either of individuals, or of passions, or of a composition of human elements —they are stuffed figures, made to speak by machinery, and ready with the same hard limbs and features to make love or commit murder, to laugh, weep, gasp, dance, or fight, according to the whim or necessities of the occasion. In his comedies, Dryden creates a new world of his own—a place in which we are surrounded

by faces that appear to be undergoing the penalty of
perpetual contortions, where love degenerates into bru-
tality, and hope is wrought by fierce enjoyment into
a sentiment of defiance — where intrigue, and bustle,
and sensuality, and riot, appear to be necessary to
the state of existence to which these strange creatures
are destined — where there is no sympathy, no honour,
no sense of degradation, no motive for integrity — where
the gratification of the coarsest appetites supply the
materials of action, and the images, associations, and
inventions of a depraved imagination furnish the language and expedients of intercourse. The people in
these comedies are exactly fitted to this extraordinary
condition of things. The gallants are all rogues, bullies,
slanderers, and profligates ; their lives exhibit an unvaried round of fighting, drinking, gambling, and intriguing :— there is no rest, no pause, no compunction,
and they carry on their affairs with a sleepless energy
that would wear out their bodies, if they had any, and
that could not with propriety be assigned to any figures
intended to imitate humanity. The women are cast in
a similar mould — fiery, rampant, vulgar, and insensible
to shame : they eat and drink like cannibals, swear their
lovers out of countenance, and themselves into a rage ;
talk the language of the stews, which is as familiar to
them as cheating at cards, quarrelling over their dice, or
fencing in the Park in man's attire ; they bestow their
favours on one man to revenge themselves on another ;
set themselves up to the grossest bidder before marriage,
and marry merely that they may make their own election afterwards. It is not merely that all these characters
are unredeemed by any atoning virtues, that their baseness never receives a solitary reproof from some subduing
quality of tenderness or remorse ; but that they exhibit
a combination of antagonist vices which could not be reconciled to each other in one nature, which could not
subsist together in a human shape, and which the common exigencies and ordinary influences of society would
either obliterate or modify.

Dryden's tragedies are equally remarkable for their remoteness from humanity; but here the figures are wholly different, more marvellous, and less offensive. In the tragedies every thing is on a grand scale; we no longer witness the developement of mean, demoralising passions; we no longer see lewd satyrs grinning at us, and sensuous women leaping over the stage; all is elevated, vast, exaggerated, and magniloquent. The heroes are demigods, expanding until they fill the horizon, and speaking amidst the clouds — the heroines are beings so spiritualised and independent of human motives and desires — so entranced in lofty thoughts and aspirations — so steeped in conventions that are unintelligible in this nether sphere, that we expect to see wings growing out of their shoulders to carry them at once up to heaven, or at the least that they shall be turned into marble on the spot, and canonised. So far as the portraiture of character is concerned, we must be content with declamation. Grandeur, not consistency of action, is the aim of the poet; if he can strike by gigantic excesses, he is indifferent to propriety or vraisemblance. If the conduct he assigns to the persons of this monstrous drama be absurd or impossible in reference to humanity, it yet may not be absurd or impossible in reference to his super-humanity, or if it be, there is no one competent to decide. As there is nothing too low for the comedies, there is nothing too high for the tragedies; for neither is it possible to conceive any thing too extravagant or unnatural.

But whatever may be said of these classes, separately considered, the tragi-comedy, in which their peculiar characteristics are united, transcends them both. Here Dryden produced one of those extraordinary births of fancy which we are at a loss to describe by a reference to any known existences, and which cannot be otherwise delineated than by grouping into one portrait a set of features taken at random from men, women, wild beasts, birds, fishes, and reptiles. The most opposite scenes are made to follow and interleave each other : — the vagrant, licentious prose of comedy, flouncing up to the stately, rhetorical, heroic rhyme of tragedy ; — cupboard lovers and debauchees scandalising the solemn presence of ineffable virgins and grave commanders ; — the profane ribaldry of the night-house filling some antique temple with shouts and screams ; — a tawdry company and lascivious revel side by side with a chamber of death and mourners ; — scandal, malice, and millinery spite ; — oracles, big drums, trumpets, and chariots ; — mincing and mouthing ; — teapots and the pyramids. Of such elements and incongruities were the tragi-comedies composed. They are to be censured, not only because the figures to which they introduce us are extravagant, but because they are not human ; — not only because the mixture of passions they contain is heterogeneous, but because the passions themselves are impossible. We look in vain throughout nature for resemblances to these deformities and hyperboles — there is nothing within the range of our experience from which they could have been derived — they seem to have been created like the fantastical outlines in the kaleidoscope, by taking a fragment of every part of humanity, and reflecting them just as they happened to fall together. But as the odd results produced by accidental combinations of broken spars, bits of feathers, glass, and foil, are altogether unlike any thing else upon earth, although we detect in them colours and shapes with which we are acquainted, so the pictures that are formed out of this jumble of metaphysical chips have no analogy whatever with any known realities, although they bear a sort of grotesque and evasive likeness to a world we have visited in dreams.

In accordance with his resolution to abandon the stage, we find Dryden in 1692 issuing a translation of Persius and Juvenal, which he was enabled to complete by the assistance of his two sons, Congreve, Creech, Tate (his man of all work), and others. This publication, together with an *Essay on Satire* prefixed to it, was inscribed to the earl of Dorset, who, although he had

deprived Dryden of his office of laureate, was not unwilling to be his patron, and is even said to have accompanied that harsh, but perhaps unavoidable, measure,
by a private donation.   Indeed, Dorset appears to have
befriended the poet on many occasions, and to have
conferred benefactions upon him unasked, and, at times,
when they could hardly have been looked for.*

With the exception of this essay, which contains
some valuable criticisms, and a few translations and
occasional poems inserted in Tonson's Third and
Fourth Miscellanies, Dryden seems now to have laid
up all his power for his meditated English Version
of Virgil.   To this great undertaking, his attention
appears to have been directed in the first instance by the
success that attended his translations from Juvenal and
Persius, and from Ovid and Homer in the Miscellanies.
But, by whatever motive he was originally impelled, he
determined to forsake all other occupations for the
purpose of accomplishing with credit a work which was
of a nature to task his powers to the utmost.   It was
no sooner known that he was engaged in this labour,
than copies of the various editions were forwarded to
him.   Mr. Chetwood furnished a life of Virgil, and a
preface to the Pastorals, and Addison contributed the
arguments to the several books, and an essay on the
Georgics.   Thus encouraged, he proceeded steadily in
his task, and in about three years the work was concluded.   The interval was not passed, however, in the
enjoyment of that literary ease which is so essential to
the due execution of such a continuous performance.
Sometimes Dryden was exposed to humiliating controversies with Jacob Tonson, who had, on former occasions, especially in reference to the Miscellanies, exhibited a mercantile spirit that was very offensive to the
pride of the poet.   Tonson, it appears, entered into

* There is a tradition that Dryden and Tom Brown being invited to dine
with his lordship, found themselves very unexpectedly in possession, the
one of 100l., the other of 50l., which their liberal host had caused to be
placed under their covers.   This method of conveying such a present might
in those days have been considered delicate, degrading as it would be in our
times.

some calculations concerning the number of lines furnished by Dryden, and endeavoured to show that he had not supplied an equivalent for the sum he had received ; thus measuring the intellectual produce by the ell and yard in a coarse, trading, and unappreciating spirit, which was naturally rebuked with scorn and contempt by the irritated author. At another time, Tonson attempted some manœuvre respecting the subscribers to the translation of Virgil, which produced a fresh feud, afterwards inflamed to its height by the economy of the bookseller, who refused to allow Dryden any additional emolument for the notes.* These petty details, in the last degree vexatious to a man whose mind was absorbed in an occupation that left him no leisure for quarrelling with the world, made, for the time, a deep impression on Dryden. He acquired, at last, a sort of morbid dread of Tonson. Lord Bolingbroke was one day with him, when a person was heard to enter the house. " This is Tonson," said Dryden ; " you will take care not to depart before he goes away ; for I have not completed the sheet which I promised him ; and if you leave me unprotected, I shall suffer all the rudeness to which his resentment can prompt his tongue." In all such contests, it is necessary to hear both sides. If booksellers are often grasping and unjust in their estimates of literary exertion, and their appropriation of its fruits, authors are not less frequently *exigeant* in their demands, and indifferent to the punctual discharge of their engagements. It must be remembered, also, that they view the same objects from opposite points of sight. The bookseller is ambitious of that which will please the public — the author of that which will please himself. The bookseller thinks only of what

* A triplet on Tonson, written by Dryden, is extant, in which, probably during their quarrels, he indicates the commencement of a satire which Tonson, it may be presumed, was cunning enough to avert by some seasonable act of submission.

    " With leering looks, bull-faced, and freckled fair.
    With two left legs, and Judas-colour'd hair,
    And frowzy pores, that taint the ambient air."

" Tell the dog," said the poet, " that he who wrote these can write more."

he hopes will sell — the author only of what he hopes will be read. Tonson would not pay for notes on Virgil — Dryden held them to be essential to its completeness. Tonson was rude and violent to the poet — the poet had not finished the sheet he had promised. These are antagonist elements that cannot be blended, although they may be rendered, in their separate and mutual influences, to act usefully upon each other and the world. It is as impossible to inspire a publisher with the feelings of an author, as to impress upon an author a correct notion of the risks and anxieties of a publisher.   ●

The translation of Virgil — " the most noble and spirited," exclaims Pope, " which 1 know of in any language," — appeared in July, 1697. It was brought out by subscription *, and Dryden realised by the issue about 1200*l.* †, a large sum for that period, although much less than Pope afterwards received for the Iliad.‡ The appearance of such a work from such a hand excited a sensation equal to the novelty of the undertaking, and the power expended in its execution. So impatient were the public to possess a production to which they had so long looked forward with eager anticipation, that the first edition was sold in a few months, and a second prepared early in the following year. The book requited the universal curiosity ; even the most bitter of Dryden's enemies acknowledged its great merits. Yet there were not wanting some malicious critics, who affected to consider it a failure. Swift ridiculed it in *The Tale of a Tub*, and Milbourne attempted to exhibit its faults in a formal criticism ; but Swift had a personal cause of offence against Dryden§,

---

* There were two classes of subscribers : the first, 101 in number, paid five guineas, and were to have embellished copies, each engraving being emblazoned with the arms of a subscriber ; the second, of whom there were 250, paid two guineas each. Dryden, in an angry letter to Tonson, accused him of attempting to cheat him of the profits of this second class.

† Dryden cleared every way about 1200*l.* by his Virgil, and had sixpence each line for his Fables.— *Pope.— Spence's Anecdotes.*

‡ Pope cleared between 5000*l.* and 6000*l.* by the iliad.

§ Swift, who was related to Dryden, while he was yet a young man, sub-·

and Milbourne wanted to displace Dryden's translation, that he might make room for his own.*

With the exception of a prose version of Fresnoy's *Art of Painting*, which was published in 1695, and a life of Lucian, undertaken for the purpose of being prefixed to a translation by Moyle, Shere, and others, Dryden produced no other work during the time he was engaged upon Virgil; but immediately afterwards appeared the immortal *Ode to St. Cecilia*, familiarly known by the title of *Alexander's Feast.* This splendid lyric, which Pope vainly attempted to emulate, was written at the urgent request of the musical meeting, which had for several years met to celebrate the feast of their patron saint. Dryden seems to have written it under an impression that he was not to derive any benefit from it, but the society subsequently paid him 40*l.* as a slight acknowledgment of the delight it diffused amongst them. Some difference exists concerning the history of this composition, which has been considered worth the arbitration of Scott. Dryden, in one of his letters, speaks of the Ode as a troublesome task in which he was engaged — a task which, according to Dr. Birch, occupied him a fortnight; and lord Bolingbroke, on the other hand, states that, paying a morning visit to Dryden, he found him in a state of unusual agitation, and upon inquiring the cause, was informed that, having been requested to write an ode for St. Cecilia's feast, he

---

mitted to the poet several of his early compositions—odes, in which he carried the Pindaric fashion of the time to the height of absurdity. "Cousin Swift," said Dryden, "you will never be a poet." The dean of St. Patrick never forgave this observation, and insulted and ridiculed Dryden wherever he could find any excuse for introducing his name in his works. See especially, the *Rhapsody*, the *Battle of the Books*, and the introduction to the *Tale of a Tub.*

* This Milbourne was a clergyman, and in the publication above referred to he had the courage to introduce some translations of his own in juxtaposition with specimens from Dryden's, to show how Virgil ought to be rendered, and how he was spoiled. This was honest, certainly, but not very wise. Dryden afterwards settled his accounts with him in his celebrated Epistle, where he disposes of him and Blackmore, under the name of Maurus, together: —

" Wouldst thou be soon despatched, and perish whole,
      Trust Maurus with thy life, and Milbourne with thy soul."

was so struck by the subject that he could not leave it till he had completed it; that he had sat up the whole night, and so finished it at a sitting. Scott reconciles these apparent contradictions by suggesting that "it was possible Dryden might have completed the whole ode at one sitting, and yet have employed a fortnight, or much more, in correction." The solution of the difficulty is simple enough, and certainly could not have been derived from a more competent authority. There never was, perhaps, an author who possessed such marvellous facility in composition as Scott, or who corrected his labours (in the proof sheets) to such an extent, not so much to improve as to enlarge what he had written. His imagination seemed to know no bounds when it was recalled to the subject he had already disposed of, and every time he went over the same ground he created fresh materials to increase its value.

But apart from the reasonableness of the supposition that a theme which had made so vivid an impression on Dryden's mind was struck out at a single heat, there are enough of evidences in the poem to show that its design, at least, was not the work of elaboration and repeated effort. It is one grand conception—sudden and complete. It could hardly have been composed by piecemeal. An able critic, speaking of its extraordinary popularity amongst all classes of readers, says, that it does not owe its superiority to its language, or to any great merit in its lines, taken separately: "it must be," he adds, "the rapid transition, the mastery of language, the springiness of the whole, which hurries us away." * These are not the characteristics of tedious labour, but rather of conscious power, in a felicitous moment of inspiration, throwing off its exuberant fancies with ease and rapidity. Sir Walter Scott confirms this view of our magnificent English ode. "There is strong internal evidence," he observes, "to show that the poem was, speaking with reference to its general

* Hallam.

structure, wrought off at once. A halt or pause, even of a day, would perhaps have injured that continuous flow of poetical language and description which argue the whole scene to have arisen at once upon the author's imagination."

The music designed for the Ode at the festival was composed by one of the stewards, Jeremiah Clarke, who was celebrated rather for the pathos than the strength or variety of his productions, and whose life terminated in a catastrophe as melancholy as his music.* Clarke's composition not being considered worthy of the ode, it was afterwards set to music by Hughes, and finally by Handel, whose genius crowned in an imperishable strain the triumph of the noblest lyric in our language. Dryden did not hesitate to say that he regarded this piece as the best of all his poems. " I thought so," he said in a letter to Tonson, " when I wrote it; but, being old, I mistrusted my own judgment." Mr. Malone tells us, also, that Mr. Marlay, the father of the lord justice Marlay, then a templar, happening to sit next Dryden at Will's coffee-house, congratulated him on having produced the finest ode in any language. " You are right, young gentleman," replied the poet; " a nobler ode never *was* produced, nor ever *will*." This burst of enthusiasm must up to this day be allowed to have been prophetic.

Dryden, now declining in years and health, was called upon for increased literary exertions to sustain the costs of his family. Two of his sons were studying at Rome, and one of them had met an accident which rendered additional expenditure unavoidable. With a painful consciousness of his growing responsibilities he persevered, and even under these depressing circumstances he contemplated an undertaking still more laborious than any he had yet attempted — the translation of Homer. It was believed that he proposed to render the immortal Grecian in blank verse, but his great

* He committed suicide in a fit of despair arising from an unfortunate attachment.

command of his favourite form of versification tempted him to abandon the design, if, indeed, he ever seriously entertained it. Whatever may have been his doubts or wishes, it is certain that he never commenced the grand work, but that, on the contrary, he rendered into rhyme the first book of Homer, and never went further. But he had yet to encounter fresh attacks from new enemies, who, unable to appreciate, or unwilling to acknowledge, the important services he had conferred upon our literature in his latter productions, assailed him in his decline for the errors of his earlier labours. One of these was sir Richard Blackmore, a court physician residing in Cheapside, who published a feeble and monotonous epic called *Prince Arthur*, in the preface to which he complained of the licentiousness of the stage, and announced his intention of endeavouring to draw the muses into purer and pleasanter paths. This epic was followed by another called *King Arthur*, and succeeded by a flippant satire in which Dryden was openly vituperated. The patience of the old bard could bear no more from such ignoble hands, and in an epistle to his kinsman, Mr. John Driden of Chatterton, he took his revenge in a spirit so powerful, that it must have crushed or shamed into silence any man less ponderous or insensible than the dull persevering author of a dozen leaden epics. Blackmore was followed by a formidable assailant in Jeremy Collier, a man of unequalled talents for controversy, who, seizing upon the immoralities of the stage as his theme, and having moreover the best of the argument on his side, continued the siege through a period of twenty years, until at length he forced his opponents to capitulate and retire. Dryden treated Collier with some distinction, admitted the justice of his charges in the main, but remonstrated against the malice with which he had endeavoured, in many instances, to extract evil meanings from passages in themselves innocuous and blameless.

The translations, or paraphrases, of Boccacio and Chaucer, and *The Fables*, were the next and almost the last of Dryden's labours. These pieces have been so universally commended for the beauty of their versification, and the richness of their treatment throughout, and are so familiar to all readers of English poetry, that it is superfluous to describe the effect they produced upon the cultivation of poetry. It may with the severest truth be said of Dryden, that however he incidentally deviated, or occasionally fell, from his own high standard of excellence, he went on gradually improving to the end — that his course was a course of certain, although irregular, progression — and that in these final productions he reached the height of that excellence which he had all along aimed at ultimately accomplishing. "In his old age," to employ the nervous language of Campbell, "he renewed his youth, like the eagle; or rather his genius acquired stronger wings than it had ever spread." *

It is gratifying to find that these publications brought rewards of a kind which were now more than ever needed by Dryden. His relative, Mr. John Driden, is reported to have sent him a present of 500*l.* for the dedication of the epistle, and an equal sum was transmitted from the duchess of Ormond in acknowledgment of the beautiful introduction to *The Fables,* in which her charms and accomplishments were apostrophised in lines that have rarely been exceeded in grace and spirit.

The close of Dryden's life was now visibly drawing nigh. His last effort was the production of a secular mask for Vanbrugh's adaptation of Fletcher's comedy of *The Pilgrim,* together with the prologue and the epilogue, which were written within twenty days of his death. The prologue was mainly directed against the ridiculous Blackmore, and the epilogue against Collier ; and Dryden may thus be said to have died in the struggle with his inveterate enemies. Reduced in physical strength, while his mind seemed to have acquired increased vigour, of a plethoric habit, and, after tedious sufferings from gout and gravel, erysipelas at last ap-

* Specimens of the British Poets, vol. i.

peared in one of his legs. Beginning with slight inflam-
mation, a gangrene became developed in his toe, and an
eminent surgeon who attended him, Mr. Hobbes, proposed the amputation of the limb to prevent mortification.   But Dryden would not consent to the oper-
ation : he thought that he could not live long by course
of nature, being an old man, and therefore did not care
to part with one limb, at such an age, to preserve an
uncomfortable life on the rest.*   As had been anticipated, the fatal consequences rapidly set in ; and he died
at his house in Gerard Street on Wednesday morning,
May 1. 1700.   His last hours are stated to have been
tranquil.   He retained his senses nearly to the end, and
died in the profession of the Roman catholic faith.

As it has too often happened with men of genius,
the tributes that ought to have been rendered to Dryden
in his life to mitigate his misfortunes, were reserved for
his grave.   It was no sooner known that he was dead,
and that his family were preparing, as well as their very
limited resources would permit, to bestow the last tenderness upon his remains, than a public subscription was
got up by lord Jefferies, and other persons of quality,
for the purpose of marking the estimation in which he
was held by a funeral worthy of his fame.   In order to
enable them to carry this object into effect, the body
was embalmed at the College of Physicians, and kept in
state for ten days, whence it was removed for interment
to Westminster Abbey.   The procession consisted of a
hearse, drawn by six horses, and an attendance of nearly
fifty carriages of the nobility, preceded by a band of
music.   Dr. Garth pronounced a Latin oration over the
grave of his friend, and Dryden's remains were deposited, with an appropriate feeling of the place he occupied amongst the poets of his country, between the
graves of Chaucer and Cowley.   The spot where he
was buried long remained undistinguished, until it was.
marked by a tablet erected by the duke of Buckingham,
simply inscribed with his name.   Dryden required no
other epitaph.

* Ward — London Spy.

A ridiculous story respecting the circumstances of this funeral was written thirty years afterwards by an unfortunate woman, Mrs. Thomas, the Corinna of Pope, then a prisoner for debt in the Fleet. It appears that this person was tempted to invent the monstrous fiction for a pecuniary consideration, and that she founded her narrative upon a humorous letter of Farquhar's, in which, with his usual tendency to the ridiculous, he distorted the incidents of the mournful scene merely to amuse a female correspondent. Farquhar, who died with a melancholy jest upon his lips, was at best an indifferent authority; but Mrs. Thomas improved upon his burlesque, and entered into a statement so minute and circumstantial, that even Dr. Johnson, although he knew not how to credit it, was so far imposed upon by the plausibility of its tone as to give it a place in his biography of the poet. For seventy years this story continued to be received without question, but with much wonder, until Mr. Malone, after a careful investigation, was enabled to refute it in detail. According to Mrs. Thomas, the lord Jefferies, who really set the subscription on foot, is described as having interrupted the procession in a drunken frolic, and broken into lady Elizabeth Dryden's bed-room with seventy-two gentlemen; Dr. Garth is said to have fallen into a beer vault while he was delivering the oration; two singing-boys are described chanting one of Horace's odes in the Abbey; and Mr. Charles Dryden is finally stated to have demanded reparation for these insults in vain from lord Jefferies, whom he sought after to the end of his life, but never could meet. Mr. Malone has proved that these ingenious details are " merely the ' nimble shapes' and lively effusions of Corinna's forgetive imagination."

Dryden's character as a man has been drawn affectingly by Congreve, who knew and loved him; and, although the hand of friendship is visible in the sketch, the internal evidences of its fidelity are not less obvious and striking. Congreve describes him to have been of an exceedingly humane and compassionate nature, easily forgiving injuries, and capable of a prompt and sincere reconciliation with those who offended him. His friend-ship went beyond his professions, and he frequently performed acts of generosity which his income could ill sustain. In conversation he was remarkably modest, frank in the communication of knowledge, and wholly free from pedantry and dogmatism. This part of his character affords a curious contrast to the severity of his writings, since it appears that he who went beyond all the men of his age in the employment of unsparing satire, was of all men the most easily put out of confi-dence in himself by any appearance of reserve or opposition in the ordinary intercourse of society. A passage from Congreve's delineation of the poet will sufficiently illustrate this remarkable trait.

" He was extreme ready and gentle in his correction of the errors of any writer, who thought fit to consult him ; and full as ready and patient to admit of the reprehension of others, in respect of his own oversight or mistakes. He was of very easy, I may say of very pleasing, access ; but something slow, and, as it were, diffident in his advances to others. He had something in his nature that abhorred intrusion into any society whatsoever. Indeed, it is to be regretted, that he was rather blameable in the other extreme ; for, by that means, he was personally less known, and, consequently, his character might become liable both to misappre-hensions and misrepresentations.

" To the best of my knowledge and observation, he was, of all the men that ever I knew, one of the most modest, and the most easily to be discountenanced in his approaches either to his superiors or his equals."

Notwithstanding this credible testimony of his retiring habits, there can be no doubt that he knew how to value his own powers, and that he did not use any ceremony in letting the world understand the estimate he put upon them. His dedications, essays, prefaces, and controversial writings, are full of indignant vindications of his labours, and scornful contempt for his opponents, frequently amounting to a measure of self-approbation wholly inconsistent with the modesty of his personal bearing. But he had two natures, which are not uncommon to men of letters : the one was the nature of the author, teeming with vivid conceptions, energetic, passionate, and impetuous ; the other was the nature of a man mixing timidly with the world, incapable of entering into its noisy pleasures, quiet, slow, and hesitating. He was one of those persons described by Dr. Johnson as " men whose powers operate only at leisure and in retirement, and whose intellectual vigour deserts them in conversation ; whom merriment confuses, and objection disconcerts ; whose bashfulness restrains their exertion, and suffers them not to speak until the time of speaking is past ; or, whose attention to their own character makes them unwilling to utter at hazard what has not been considered, and cannot be recalled." In conversation he was as sluggish as he was fluent in writing. It is said of him that, in the order of composition, his thoughts flowed in upon him so fast, that his only care was which to choose, and which to reject : and he is made to declare of himself that in society he was dull and silent, —

" Nor wine nor love could ever see me gay,
    To writing bred, I knew not what to say."*

Yet for all this there was so much weight in his observations, that those who could appreciate the solid in preference to the brilliant, were charmed by his society. One of his contemporaries thus characterises his conversation : — " Silence and chat are distant enough to have a convenient discourse come between them ; and thus far I agree with you, that the company of the author of *Absalom* and *Achitophel* is more valuable, though

* Dryden appears to have been a bad reader as well as a slow and difficult speaker. Colley Cibber says, that when Dryden read his play of *Am-
phytrion* for the actors, " though he delivered the plain sense of every
period, yet the whole was in so cold, so flat, and unaffecting a manner, that
I am afraid of not being believed if I should express it."

not so talkative, than that of the modern men of *banter;*
for what he says is like what he writes, much to the
purpose, and full of mighty sense ; and if the town were
for any thing desirable, it were for the conversation of
him, and one or two more men of the same character." *
There are many instances of great writers who were
indifferent or reluctant talkers. In our times Hazlitt
was a remarkable example, who, except when he was
strongly excited,—and then his eloquence was wondrous,
— rarely discovered in conversation those felicitous and
varied powers by which his works are so pre-eminently
distinguished.

Of Dryden's moral character it may be asserted, that
if in the early part of his life he participated in the common levities of the town, the whole of his later years, his
manhood, and his decline, were exempt even from the
frivolities of the day. Amongst all the charges that
were brought against him by his enemies — who were
numerous, vindictive, and unscrupulous — that of immorality, except in his plays, is not to be found. They
accused him of being a puritan, an apostate, and an
egotist; they libelled him alike for his successes and his
penury ; they attempted to defame the honour of his
wife ; and they even violated the sanctity of his domestic
retirement to show how thriftily and meanly he lived; but
throughout all these assaults they did not venture upon
an accusation reflecting on his morality.   In one point,
doubtless, he was vulnerable.   The servility and syco-
phancy of his dedications betrayed the paltry necessities
that compelled him to sue for those rewards which his
genius ought to have commanded ; and this vice of
egregious flattery and hypocritical adulation might
have fairly exposed him to a charge of insincerity and
falsehood.   But it was not more the vice of Dryden than
it was the vice of the age ; and the only reason why he
became more distinguished in its practice than others,
was because he was more distinguished than others in

* The Humours and Conversation of the Town exposed, in Two Dia.
logues. 1693.

every thing else. He merely did what all his contemporaries did, and the only difference between them was
that he did it better, and that, owing to the rapidity of
his productions, he did it oftener. That the slavish
spirit of his addresses to the great is not to be excused
must be allowed on all hands; but, if we would decide
impartially on a subject of this nature, we must make a
large allowance for the exigencies that generated such
hollow panegyrics, and the fashion of the times by which
they were sanctioned.

The grand claim of Dryden upon the regards and
admiration of posterity is summed up in the grandeur,
the variety, and the strength of his versification. It
stands out prominently from all other English poetry,
and is as fresh and as vigorous at this day as at the
moment when it was minted from his rich and inexhaustible mind. He not only infused a new spirit into
our poetical literature, but he developed new forms
and new resources. He was not merely an improver
but a creator. He banished the meretricious and affected styles 'that enjoyed unbounded popularity in his
youth, and substituted truth and sense in their place.
If he had less refinement and delicacy than Pope, he infinitely surpassed him in originality of expression, in
powers of reflection, in general knowledge of mankind,
and in acuteness of observation. Pope, too, came after
him, and had all the advantages of his example. There
was no littleness in Dryden; he never descended to petty
details; he seized a whole topic at once, and what he
wrote had a living reality in it which was never spoiled
by artificial finery, by terse points, and exquisite trifling.
His thoughts seemed to be always occupied by the object to which they were addressed, and never to be frit-
tered away in consideration about the manner in which
it was to be treated — although the manner into which he
naturally fell was always the best suited to the occasion.

As a satirist, Dryden discovered powers that have
never been equalled. The force of his invective was
overwhelming — his vehemence did not wound, it crushed

his opponents. Pope exceeded him in the keenness of
ridicule, a weapon which was too fragile for the grasp
of Dryden, and which required the petulance and uneasiness of Pope to keep its edge constantly sharp. In
addition to this, Dryden's power of reasoning, of inves-
tigating, and of analysing, gave him such a command
of his topics, as to render him indifferent to the artifices
of premeditated sarcasm — the " tierce and carte" of
polished wit.

In his dramas alone Dryden adopted the corruptions
which his judgment renounced. Yet even here he displayed wonderful versatility, surprising invention, and
energy of language. But his dramas may be forgiven
for the sake of those masterly criticisms — the first specimens of criticism in our language — of which they
were the parents. The very faults he committed in his
plays made the criticisms in some sort necessary to his
fame. His prose, as bold and masculine as his satires,
possesses in the highest perfection all those qualities of
clearness, appropriateness, and unflagging vigour, which
are essential to excellence. His canons must not, of
course, be always received without examination, because
he frequently defended himself when he knew he was
wrong, and endeavoured to vindicate errors he had sanctioned in practice, by setting up fresh errors in theory,
to give them an air of authority. But in his later
critical essays he emancipated himself from these wa-
vering and accommodating doctrines, and paid reveren-
tial homage to the drama of poetry and nature, which
circumstances, rather than his taste, led him originally
to forsake. In all the characters he filled, Dryden
exhibited splendid abilities ; and if, under inequalities
of temperament, and the pressure of the events that
agitated his life, he sometimes failed, it must be remembered that his failures are rendered conspicuous by
his triumphs, and that, in the combination of great and
varied powers, he stands unrivalled in our literature.

TWO CENTURIES OF MINOR POETS.

It is greatly to be regretted that no writer competent
to undertake the task has favoured the lovers of literature with a history of English poetry since the time of
Elizabeth. To the labours of the ingenious Warton
.we are indebted for an elaborate account of the progress of poetry from the earliest periods to the reign
of Elizabeth; and, if we must occasionally dissent from
his critical opinions, too much praise cannot be awarded
to his diligence and integrity. The researches of Percy,
Ellis, Hallam, and others, equally erudite and zealous,
have further contributed to illustrate the remoter annals
of our poetical literature; and, although a vast quantity
of rich materials, in reference to those ages, yet remains
to be developed, it may be allowed that future investigation would be applied with greater utility to later times,
which have not yet been chronicled and reviewed with
sufficient accuracy or fulness. The principal poets of the
reigns of the Stuarts are, no doubt, sufficiently familiar to
the reading public ; and the general character of the great
bulk of our poetry, from the reign of James I. to the
Revolution, has been frequently sketched in various scattered publications. But what is wanted is a history which
should trace the art with regularity and completeness
throughout all its fluctuations and improvements, and
which should render to the literature of the last three
hundred years a service similar to that which Warton
rendered to the literature of the antecedent centuries.

In a work which is not only biographical in form,
but limited in extent, it is impossible to do more than
furnish some slight materials, by way of contribution to
this desiderated record. These materials are also necessarily disproportioned to the interest of the general subject, since they are confined to personal details, and

cannot be expanded into critical outlines without a viola-
tion of the plan on which these volumes are composed.
But it is hoped that even such short notices as we are
enabled to embrace of the minor poets who flourished
in the sixteenth and seventeenth centuries, and who
have hitherto been consigned to comparative oblivion in
the pages of ponderous works of reference, will not be
entirely destitute of instruction and entertainment.

· These notices have been collected with some pains
from a great variety cf sources; so numerous, indeed,
that I have avoided encumbering the miniature biographies with notes of reference, which could answer no
better purpose than that of sending the reader to explore
a multitude of volumes, from which he could glean no
more information than he will find here collected and
condensed to his hand.‐ Many of the works drawn
upon are accessible only in the public libraries ; others
are rare ; and the majority are voluminous and expensive. The collections of Fuller, Wood, Walpole, and
Nicholls, the *Censura Literaria*, the *Biographia Britannica*, Bayle's *Biographical Dictionary*, the *Bibliotheca
Curiosa*, the *Censura Temporum*, the *Historia Literaria*,
the biographical accumulations of Chalmers, Aikin,
Wrangham, and other writers, and the fragments of
Spence, Evelyn, Pepys, and others, have been consulted
in the progress of these minute inquiries ; and, wherever
such authorities existed, individual biographies have
been referred to for the purpose of confirming or enlarg-
ing, as far as possible, the statements contained in the
more miscellaneous publications. It is hardly necessary
to observe that the poets included in these sketches
present only such a selection as may be considered
sufficient to exhibit a general view of the period they
embrace.

In the following brief notices, occasional specimens
of the works of the minor poets are introduced. These
specimens were sometimes chosen, because the originals
have long been out of print ; sometimes because they
exemplify peculiarities of style that rendered their ad-

mission desirable ; and frequently because, even if they were more easily attainable by the reader, they would not be very likely to be sought for; but, in every instance, I have been guided by some reason which, at the time, appeared satisfactory.

It will be perceived that these outlines extend back to the commencement of the sixteenth century, and onwards to the close of the seventeenth, while the lives of some of the more distinguished poets, who flourished in the interval, have already been given in their proper order. As it would have been, however, in the last degree inconvenient to intercept the longer memoirs of individuals who occupied a conspicuous place in their generation by the insertion of such brief notices, merely for the sake of preserving chronological regularity, it was considered advisable to present the whole series of minor poets in one unbroken view. By this means, the course of that under-current of poetry, which has hitherto been too much neglected, is shown without interruption, while those writers whose celebrity demanded independent places, are treated separately at a length commensurate to their importance.

THOMAS SACKVILLE, EARL OF DORSET.

1527—1608.

THOMAS SACKVILLE, the grandson of Anne Boleyn, sister of Thomas Boleyn, earl of Wiltshire, distinguished alike as a poet and a politician, was the son of sir Richard Sackville, by Winifred, daughter of sir John Brydes, lord mayor of London, and afterwards marchioness of Winchester. He was born at Buckhurst, in the parish of Withyam, in Sussex, in 1527 *, received his education at Oxford, graduated as M.A. at Cambridge, and was called to the Bar from the Middle

* This is the date given by Wood. According to other authorities, he was born in 1536.

Temple, not with a view to follow the law as a profession, but to qualify himself for parliament.

In his youth he cultivated poetry, which he seems to
have abandoned almost immediately after his entrance
into public life. Towards the close of the reign of
queen Mary, he obtained a seat in the house of commons,
and in the first parliament of Elizabeth he was elected
knight of the shire for the county of Sussex, his father
being chosen at the same time for Kent; and in the
following parliament he was chosen for Buckingham-
shire, his father taking the representation of Sussex.
Previously to the acquisition of these flattering distinctions, he gave his first poem to the world, called
Induction to a Mirror of Magistrates. This work
was highly and deservedly praised, and Warton declares
that, in his opinion, it "approaches nearer to the *Faery
Queen* in the richness of allegoric description, than any
previous or succeeding poem." The design of this
piece, which was intended to exhibit examples of bad
men in high stations, whose crimes were terminated in
misery or disgrace, was afterwards carried on by Bald-
wyne and Ferrars, who invited Churchyard, Phayer,
and others to their assistance, and published a continuation of the work in 1559, under the title of *A
Myrroure for Magistrates, &c.*

This production was followed, in 1561, by a tragedy
called *Ferrex and Porrex,* which title was changed, in
1590, to *Gordubuc,* the name by which it is now generally known. In this performance he is said to have
been assisted by Thomas Norton, (the associate in the
labours of that inimitable pair, Hopkins and Sternhold,)
who, according to Wood, wrote the first three acts.
However that may be, and it is at best a doubtful
statement, the play is generally allowed to be the first
specimen of regular tragedy in our language, although
prior claims to that honour have been recently asserted
for another tragedy. Considering the state of literature
in England at that period, it is a work of high merit,
and well worthy of the praise bestowed upon it by

Sir Philip Sydney, who, with the qualification that "it is very defectious in the circumstances," says, that "*Gordubuc* is full of stately speeches and well sounding phrases, climbing to the height of Seneca's style, and as full of notable morality, which it doth most delightfully teach, and thereby obtains the very end of poetry." So highly was it esteemed by Pope, that he, in conjunction with Spence, prevailed upon the manager of Drury Lane to bring it upon the stage in 1736, when it was received with considerable applause. In the same year Spence further testified his admiration of it, by undertaking its republication.

Soon after his election for Buckingham, Sackville went to travel into France and Italy; but falling into some imprudences in his expenditure, he was detained at Rome, where it would appear he was imprisoned for debt. The news of his father's death reached him while he was in this difficulty in 1556 *; and, procuring his release, which the change in his circumstances now enabled him to do, he returned home to the enjoyment of a rich patrimonial inheritance. He now rapidly rose in favour with the queen, who, in 1567, conferred the honour of knighthood upon him by the hands of the duke of Norfolk, and afterwards raised him to the peerage with the title of lord Buckhurst. His extravagance, however, kept pace with his increasing resources, and at last exceeded them, and he was compelled to raise money at usurious interest to enable him to support his sumptuous expenditure. A fortunate incident luckily reclaimed him. Calling one day upon an alderman of London who had advanced him large sums, he was kept so long waiting the leisure of his arrogant creditor, that his pride was deeply offended, and he resolved from that hour never to expose himself again to a similar insult. The result was a resolution to economise, which he strictly acted upon for the rest of his life.

* Wood's date is 1566, — corrected as above by Bliss.

He was now called to the service of the queen in a
succession of diplomatic appointments. The first was
as ambassador to Charles IX. of France, in 1571, to
congratulate that monarch on his nuptials. In 1586,
he was nominated one of the commissioners for the
trial of Mary, queen of Scotland; it does not appear,
however, that he sat on that occasion. But when the
parliament had confirmed the sentence of death upon
that princess, he was the peer deputed, with the clerk of
the council, to inform her of the result of the proceedings. In 1588 he was sent as ambassador to the Low
Countries to conciliate the provinces, which had been
disgusted with the earl of Leicester; and, discharging his
duty with more regard to public than to personal interests, he accused the favourite of misconduct, which
so displeased the imperious Elizabeth, that she confined
him for upwards of nine months to his house, from
which obloquy he was not redeemed until the death of
Leicester; when the queen, to make atonement for her
capricious severity, conferred upon him, without solicitation, the order of the Garter. This favour was followed
by his election to the chancellorship of Oxford upon her
majesty's express recommendation, an honour which
was enhanced by a royal visit to the university, where
Elizabeth for many days partook of the banquets and
entertainments provided for her by the new chancellor.
His next service was the negotiation of the peace with
Spain, which he undertook in conjunction with lord
Burghley, and succeeded in obtaining terms highly advantageous to England, and also negotiated, shortly
afterwards, an alliance with Denmark. Upon the death
of lord Burghley, in 1598, he succeeded to the place of
lord high treasurer, and, at the trial of Essex, he was
constituted lord high steward. The office of earl
marshal, having become vacant by the execution of the
unfortunate Essex, was put in commission, and he was
appointed one of the lords commissioners for the discharge of its duties. From this time, either singly, or
in connection with sir Robert Cecil, he had nearly the

entire management of public affairs to the end of the reign of Elizabeth, and subsequently until the 4th year of the following reign.

The death of Elizabeth effected only a temporary suspension of his offices, for, having signed the recognition and proclamation of James, he was rewarded by the renewal of his patent of lord treasurer for life, the office of earl marshal, and the title of earl of Dorset. By James he was consulted on the formation of the new ministry, and in the negotiation of a peace between Spain and Holland, in which he is said to have secretly encouraged the Dutch to insist as a preliminary upon the recognition of their independence. He continued to enjoy his " blushing honours," and to discharge the duties of his offices to the general satisfaction, till the 19th of April, 1608, when he expired suddenly at the council board. The manner of his death, and the suspicious circumstances which pointed out certain needy Scotch favourites, who swarmed about the court, as having been concerned in it, led to some doubts as to whether he was not the victim of a political conspiracy ; but a *post mortem* examination discovered that his mortal disease was dropsy of the brain. Until within a year of his death he had enjoyed unimpaired health; but about that time his strength began to give way under the fatigues of office, and the king was so solicitons about him, that he sent him a gold ring set with diamonds, accompanied by the hope that his life would last as long as the diamonds of that ring should endure. He was first buried at Westminster ; but his body was afterwards removed, according to the directions of his own will, to the chapel at Withyam. The funeral sermon was preached by Dr. Abbott, afterwards archbishop of Canterbury, who was lavish in his praise. Few of the statesmen of that age have left so fair a reputation as the earl of Dorset, a fact which may not be the less credited because it is testified by Walpole.

This nobleman held a very high rank among his literary contemporaries. From his earliest youth he was a lover of poetry. While he was at Oxford he wrote Latin and English poems, and afterwards, when public affairs drew him away from the cultivation of the art, he became a liberal patron of its professors. Time has made sad havock with his compositions. His sonnets, which have been celebrated as " sweetly saufte," are supposed to be all lost. Of his tragedies, for he is said to have written several, in the composition of which Wood tells us " he had an excellent faculty," and " was esteemed the best of his time for that part of the stage," only one remains. Indeed, all that is left of his works occupies but a small compass. His best and longest poem, *The Induction,* consists of only eighty-two stanzas.

Lord Dorset is described as having been so choice in his style, that his secretaries found it very difficult to please him, a fastidiousness natural to one who had abandoned the practice of composition, but who still retained his taste, improved and probably rendered more severe by reflection. In private life, he was distinguished alike by the exercise of the domestic virtues, and by unbounded hospitality. For the last twenty years of his life, he entertained 100 persons from motives of charity, and afforded extensive relief to the poor out of doors. From this distinguished nobleman — celebrated alike for ability as a statesman, genius as a poet, and integrity in his private relations—the present noble family of the Sackvilles are descended.

JOHN BROWNSWERD.

15——1589.

JOHN BROWNSWERD, or Brunswerdus, as he pedantically subscribed himself, was celebrated amongst the distinguished Latinists of his age. He was born somewhere in Cheshire, received the early part of his education in Oxford, but finished his studies in Cambridge, where it is supposed he graduated. After leaving the university, he settled at Macclesfield, in his native county, in the humble but useful office of master to the free school. It was here that he produced those works which acquired for him the reputation of being one of the best Latin poets of the reign of queen Elizabeth. His principal publication is entitled *Progmunsmata aliquot Poemata.* He also wrote several other things which have not been preserved. He died on the 15th of April, 1589, and was buried in the chancel of the church of Macclesfield, where a tablet was erected to his memory on the south by Thomas Newton[*], a hearty admirer of his genius ; with an inscription, in which Brownswerd is styled " Vir pius et doctus," which concludes with the following lines : —

> " Alpha poetarum, Coryphæus Grammaticorum,
> Flos pædagogum hae sepelitur numo. "

Newton, who, in his youth, had been one of Brownswerd's scholars, further testified his respect for the talents of his friend by the following distich in his book called *Encomias,* which contained panegyrics upon certain illustrious men of England : —

> " Rhetora, Grammaticum, Polyhistora, teque poetam,
> Qui negat ; islippus, luscus, obesus, iners. "

Notices of Brownswerd are to be found in the *Athenæ Oxoniensis,* and the *Censura Literaria.*

JASPER HEYWOOD.

1535—1598.

JASPER HEYWOOD was the son of the celebrated epigrammatist. He was a native of London, where he was born in 1535. At twelve years of age he was sent to

---

. [*] Born about 1540—died 1607. Amongst other labours he translated the third tragedy of Seneca, published 1581.

Oxford, distinguished himself in grammar and logic, took a degree in arts in 1533, and became a probationary fellow of Merton College. He remained at the university during a period of five years ; but he fell into such wild and disreputable courses, that the warden and society of Merton were obliged to admonish him three several times 'for various misdemeanors. Having reason to fear that expulsion would inevitably follow, he prudently resigned his fellowship on the 4th April, 1558. His brother, Ellis, is described to have been equally intemperate ; and these graceless sons appear to have embittered the life, and given rather a melancholy tinge to the choice epigrams of their father. But Jasper made a strong effort to recover from his disgrace ; and in the June ensuing we find him taking out the degree of Master, and in the following November he was elected a fellow of All Soul's College. The collegiate life, however, did not suit his taste, and he shortly after threw it up in a fit of ill humour with the world.

He had already acquired some reputation as a poet by the publication of several small pieces, many of which were printed in the *Paradise of Dainty Devizes*, 1573. He translated also three tragedies of Seneca — *Thyestes*, 1560 ; *Hercules Furens*, 1561 ; and *Troas*, 1559, which was specially dedicated to queen Elizabeth. These translations were afterwards collected, along with others, into a quarto volume, entitled *Seneca his Tenne Tragedies, translated into English.*

In 1561 Heywood left England, and became a Roman catholic priest in 1562. Being then at Rome, he entered the society of Jesus on the 21st of May, and took up his residence at the house of the Jesuits in that city. After spending two years amongst them in the study of divinity, he was sent to Diling, in Switzerland, where he remained about seventeen years; and obtained so much distinction in the controversies which were then raging in the valleys of the Alps, between the reformers

* Some account of this work will be found in the first volume of the *Censura Literaria*.

and the Roman catholics, that he was promoted to the honour of D.D., and the "four vows." • At length, with several others, he was sent in 1581 upon a mission into England; where, from his extravagant manner of living, it was remarked of him that his style was more like that of a baron than a priest. He was afterwards ordered to France, respecting public matters connected with his order; but, just as he came in sight of the coast of Normandy, he was driven back by contrary winds on the English shore: here he was seized and examined; but as nothing was proved against him, he with nineteen other priests was transhipped, and landed in France in February, 1584. It is related of him that while he was in prison in England, the earl of Warwick generously offered to relieve his necessities; an act of liberality which he acknowledged in a copy of doggrels, terminating with the following miserable pun : —

> " Thanks to that lord that wills me good,
> For I want all things saving Hay and Wood."

We find him located next in the city of Dole, where, says Wood, he was troubled much with witches; thence he went to Rome; and at length fixed in the city of Naples, where he became known to the zealous John Pitseus, who has recorded a very honourable testimony to his merits. According to the *Neapolitan Register*, Jasper Heywood died on the 9th of January, 1598, and was buried in the college of the Jesuits. He left behind a variety of compositions in prose and verse, some of which are still extant in manuscript.

Heywood had the reputation of being an admirable Hebrew scholar, and of discovering a short method of acquiring a knowledge of that language. He exercised the office of Christmas prince, or lord of misrule, in his college (Merton); and among the MSS. in the Ashmolean museum, there is an oration praising his admirable execution of its functions, written by David de la Hyde.

Heywood is also supposed to have been the author of

H 2

some lines prefixed to *Kyffin's Blessednes of Brytaine,*
1588 ; as well as *Greene's Epitaph, discoursed dialogue-
wise between Life and Death,* a very curious production.
The following lines, from his *Thyestes,* 1560, will
afford a fair specimen of his skill as a translator : —

> " What furye fell enforceth me
> to flee th' unhappie seate,
> That gape and gaspe w^t greedy iawe
> the flecying foode to eate ?
> What god to Tantalus the bowres,
> where brethyng bodies dwell,
> Doth show agayne ? Is ought found worse
> then burning thurst of hell
> In lake alowe ? Or yet worse plague
> then hunger, is there one
> In vayne that euer gapes for foode ?
> shall Sisyphus his stone
> That slypper restles rollyng payse,
> vpon my backe be borne ?
> Or shall my lymms with swyfter swynge
> of whirlwyng wheele be torne ? "

In the translation of Seneca's *Troas* Heywood made
" sundrye additions;" and as we derive from these passages a more direct view of his style than we can obtain from his translations, a few stanzas from the argument prefixed to the tragedy may be added.

> " The ten years siege of Troy, who list to heare,
> And of the affayres that there befell in fight ;
> Reade ye the workes that long since written were,
> Of th' assaultes, and of that latest night,
> · When turrets toppes in Troy they blased bright ;
> Good clerkes they were that have it written well,
> As for this worke, no word thereof doth tell.

> " But Dares Phrygian well can all report,
> With Dictis eke of Crete in Greekish tonng ;
> And Homer telles, to Troye the Greekes resort
> In scanned verse, and Maro hath it song ;
> Ech one in writ hath pen'd a stoary long,
> Who doubtes of ought, and casteth care to knowe
> These antique authors, shal the story showe.   ·   ·

" The ruines twayne of Troye, the cause of each,
    The glittering helmes, in fieldes the banners spread,
Achilles' yres, and Hector's frightes they teach ;
  · There may the iestes of many a knight be read,
    Patroclus, Pyrrhus, Aiax, Diomed,
With Troylus, Parys, many other more,
That day by day there fought in field full sore."

The rhythm of these liues is sufficiently melodious
to sustain the reputation of a writer who was accounted
a poet of no mean pretensions, at a period when poetry
was popular amongst all classes of the people.

THOMAS WATSON.

———1591-2.

THOMAS WATSON was born in London, but the date
of his birth has not been ascertained. He is noted
amongst those who acquired distinction at Oxford
in the "smooth and pleasant studies of poetry and romance," having evidently distinguished himself in those
"faculties." He afterwards settled in the metropolis,
studied the common law at riper years, and published
several works, of which the following are the principal: — *Melibæus Thomæ Watsoni, sive Ecloga in obi-
tum honoratiss. viri Dom. Francisci Walsingham Eq.
aur. ;* written in Latin, and dedicated to the incomparable Mary, countess of Pembroke, who was his
patroness. In the · same year, 1590, he translated
and published this piece in English. — The *Eka-
tomuaoia, or Passionate Centurie of Love.* There is a
fine copy of this work in the Bodleian. · It formerly
belonged to Thomas Hearnes, and came to the public
library amongst Dr. Rawlinson's MSS. — Watson also
translated the *Antigone* of Sophocles into Latin, 1581.
This translation has been erroneously attributed to
Watson, bishop of Lincoln. — *Decastichon ad Oclandum,
de Eulogiis serenissimæ nostræ Elizabethæ post Anglo-*
H 3

rum prælia cantatis, 1582.— *Colathi Thebani-Helenæ raptus, paraphraste Tho. Watsoni, Londinensi;* dedicated to the Earl of Northumberland, 1586.— *The first Set of Italian Madrigalls Englished, not to the Sense of the original Dittie, but after the Affection of the Noate,* 1590.— *A Gratification unto Mr. John Case for his learned Book lately made in the praise of Music.* Three of Watson's poems are inserted in the *Phœnix Nest,* 1593; five in *England's Helicon,* 1600 and 1612; and others in *Davidson's Poetical Rapsodie,* 1611.

Very copious specimens of *Watson's Centurie of Love* will be found in *Ellis's Specimens of Early English Poets,* in the *British Bibliographer,* and in the *European Magazine.* Watson died in 1591 or 1592.

ULPIAN FULWELL.

1546 — ———.

ULPIAN, or, according to the fashion of an age when the pure Saxon was constantly Latinized to give it an air of grandeur, ULPIANNÓ FULWELL, was descended from a respectable family, and born in Somersetshire in 1546. At thirty-two years of age he became a commoner of St. Mary's Hall, Oxford; but it is not known whether he took any degree. During his residence at the university, he partly wrote *The Eighth Liberal Science, called Arsadulandi, or the Art of Flattery;* printed in 1579. This was followed by a pleasant interlude, entitled *Like Will to Like, quoth the Devil to the Collier,* 1587. He was also the author of a strange work in prose and verse respecting a duel which took place between Hamilton and Newton, arising out of some insulting expressions which passed between them, defamatory of the English monarch, and which each endeavoured to fasten upon the other. This duel was decided in favour of Newton, in the presence of lord Grey.

The quaint manner of writing partly in rhyme and partly in prose, all glittering over with conceits, was carried to the height of extravagance by Fulwell in a publication called *The Flower of Fame.** This melange of history and legend was compiled by Fulwell, assisted by Master Edmunde Harman, and dedicated to sir William Cecil, baron of Binghley, whose arms, impaling those of Beaufoy, were engraved on the back of the title page. Fulwell bespeaks favour for his "crabbed metres" in propitiatory prose to the full as crabbed as his verse. He tells us that " he has not the gifte of flowing eloquence, neyther can he interlace his phrase with Italian termes, nor powder his style with the Frenche, Englyshe, or inkhorne rhetoricke, nor cowche his matter under a cloake of curious inventions, to feede the daintie cares of delicate youkers." The whole work is a continuous praise of the "noble vertues" of king Henry, exhibited in the various forms of a chronicle, interspersed with poetical panegyrics. Fulwell cannot of course be regarded as an historian, but merely as a rhyming flatterer of the Tudors. He praises them all in the most indiscriminate vein of adulation. Such verses as the following, forming a part of an epitaph on Anne Bullen, were calculated to obtain extensive popularity in the reign of Elizabeth : —

" Yf wayling woes might win thy lyfe
To lodge in corpes agayne, ·
Thy bodie should, O noble Queene !
Not thus in grave remayne.

" For if that death might lyfe redeeme,
And lyfe were bought with death,
Ten thousand to restore your lyfe,
Would render vytall breath.

* The full title of this work is curious : — *The Flower of Fame. Containing the bright Renowne and moste fortunate Raigne of King Henry the VIII. Wherein is mentioned of Matters, by the rest of our Chronographers over-passed. Compyled by Ulpian Fulwell, &c. &c. 1575.*

" But sith that may in no wise bee,
    For death woulde worke his spight ;
With yernefull voyce and dolefull domps,
    We shall expell delight.

" And shew our greefes with secret sighes,
    And languor of the breste ;
The flodds of teares shed for thy sake,
    Declares our hearts unreste."

Let us now contrast this, which is at least distinguished by kindly and generous sentiments, with the
subjoined lines from the epitaph on Henry VIII. It
would appear surprising that the same poet should have
thus lavished his tears upon Anne Bullen and the king,
were it not that he wrote in the reign of their daughter
Elizabeth.

" Awake ye worthies nyne,
    That long in graves haue rest !
Poure out your plaints with wayling teares,
    Let langor be your geast.

" Do off your shrowding sheetes,
    That clads you in the claye ;
And deck your selues with black attyre,
    Your mourning to displaye.

" Bedewe with saltie teares,
    Your manly faces stowte ;
Laye downe those weapons that were wont
    To quell the raging rowte.

" For nowe that pierlesse prince
    That neuer yet tooke foyle,
The eythth King Henry, hath resynde
    His body to the soyle.

" Recorde your dolefull tunes,
    Ye noble peeres, eche one,
Let gryping greefes gnawe on your breastes,
    To shewe your pensiue moane.

" With bryndie blubbered teares,
　　Ye commons all, lament ;
Sende forth your sobbes from boyling breaste,
　　Let trynkling teares be spent.

" For our Achilles nowe
　　Hath left vs in the fielde,
That wonted was, with valiant force,
　　From foes our lyues to shylde."

The poet who could thus descant upon the merits of king Henry could not have been a man of much moral worth ; yet Fulwell was a clergyman, and held a rectory at Naunton, in Gloucestershire. His poems, especially the historical legends, which are not wanting in a certain flavour of the sweetness of the old ballads, were much esteemed in his own time.

RICHARD STANYHURST.

1547—1618.

RICHARD STANYHURST was one of those singular characters whose multifarious pursuits and acquirements, extensive erudition, versatile abilities, and unequal fortunes render them remarkable among their fellows, without securing them any honourable or permanent preeminence ; illustrating in rather a melancholy way the wide difference between notoriety and fame. His life conveys a moral of universal application, showing the fatal consequences of neglecting in youth those golden opportunities which few possess, and still fewer know how to value until it is too late to redeem them.

His father, James Stanyhurst, was recorder of Dublin and speaker of the Irish house of commons; and in that capacity had " done the state some service" of no ordinary character.* Had Richard made a sagacious use of

---

* He managed to pass the Act of Uniformity, by taking advantage of the absence of the members who would have opposed it.

the advantages which these circumstances threw open to
him, and of the natural endowments of his own mind,
there was no secondary office in the state to which he
might not have aspired with a fair prospect of success.
But he became a man of letters, a philosopher, and a
poet, and suffered the usual penalty of such indiscretion.
For the greater part of his life he was condemned to
endure all the privations to which the followers of those
romantic professions are generally compelled to submit ;
and was glad to eke out a subsistence for his latter days
as a chaplain in Austria, instead of being, as he might
have been, lord chancellor of Ireland.

He was born in Dublin in 1547, and became a commoner of University College, Oxford, in 1563. So
great and rapid was his proficiency in classical literature,
that, before two years had elapsed, he wrote commentaries on Porphyry, which were considered extremely
clever, and worthy of men of greater maturity in learning. Having taken the degree of A.B., he retired to
London, and became a student, first in Furnival's, and
afterwards in Lincoln's Inn. He now devoted himself
for a short time to the study of the common law ; but
wearying of a pursuit, which was evidently averse to
his taste, he returned to Ireland, where he embraced the
Roman catholic religion. This step determined his
ruin, and shut him out for ever from all the prospects
which his birth and station held out.

From the period of his conversion his movements
cannot be traced with much accuracy, in consequence of
the obscurity into which he fell, and the strange expedients he was forced to adopt in the pursuit of a livelihood. He married Genet, a daughter of sir Christopher Barnewall. She died in childbirth in 1579, at the
age of 19, and was buried in Chelsea. For many years
subsequently Stanyhurst travelled on the Continent with
chequered fortunes ; sometimes struggling with penury,
and rarely securing with regularity the means of subsistence. At Antwerp he appeared as an alchemist; but
finding that occupation unprofitable, he went to Spain,

and practised as a physician.* He subsequently became a clergyman; and finally was appointed chaplain to the arch-duke of Austria, whose munificent liberality enabled him to spend the remainder of his days in learned leisure, and in great happiness.† He died at Brussels in 1618.

His attainments, as a scholar, have been much celebrated. As a theologian, philosopher, historian, and orator, he held a foremost place amongst his contemporaries. His rank as an English poet is low enough; although in Latin composition we are told that he was "so rare a poet, that he and Gabriel Harvey were the best for iambics of their age." ‡ Of his works, the principal are some volumes relative to Irish history; some on religious subjects; a collection of epitaphs and *poetical conceits*, some written in Latin and some in English; and a translation of the first four books of the *Æneid* into heroic blank verse. This was considered a very tolerable performance for that age, though it did not escape the censure of contemporary criticism. The work is so rare, and the execution so perfectly *outrè*, that the following specimens are quite irresistible. Thus Stanyhurst translates the "*arma virumque cano*" of the first book : —

"Now manhood and garboils I chaunt and martial horror.
I blaze thee, captaine, first from Troy cittie repairing,
Lyke wandring pilgrim to famosed Italie trudging."

In translating Neptune's address to the winds in the same book, he exhibits his Lincoln's Inn education.

"Dare ye, lo, curst baretours, in this my seignorie regal,
Too raise such racks iacks on seas and danger unorder'd?"

Æneas, in the beginning of the second book, says,

"You bid me, princesse, too scarrifie a festered old soare."

Dido threatens Æneas in the following terms:—'

" I wil, as hobgoblin, foloe thee; thou shalt be soare handled;
I shal heare, I doubt not, thy pangs in lymbo related."

Of the Trojans leaving Carthage, we are informed
that

" Al they the like poste haste did make, with Scarboro
   scrabbling."

This is the style in which the four books are executed, and which drew the comment from a contemporary, that " Mr. Stanyhurst (though otherwise learned)
trod on foul lumbring boisterous wallowing measures
in his translation of Virgil." *   In another place the
same writer says, " Fortune, the mistress of change,
with a pitying compassion respecting Mr. Stanyhurst's
prayse, would that Phayer should fall, that he might
ryse ; whose heroical poetry infired, I should say inspired, with an hexameter furye, recalled to life whatever hissed barbarism hath been buried this hundred
yeare; and revived by his ragged guile such carterlie
varietie, as no hedge plowman in a countrie but would
have held as the extremetie of clownerie: a patterne
whereof I will propound to your judgement, as near as
I can, being part of one of his descriptions of a tempest, which is thus : —

    ' Then did he make heaven's vault to rebound
        With rounce robble bobble,
      Of ruffe raffe roaring,
        With thicke thwacke thurly bouncing.'

Which strange language of the firmament, never subject
before to our common phrase, makes us, that are not
used to terminate heavens moving in the accents of
any voice, esteem of their triobulaire interpreter as of
some thrasonical huffe-snuffe ; for so terrible was his
style to all mylde eares, as would have affrighted our

* Thomas Nashe, in *The Apology of Pierce Penniless.* Lond. 1593.

peaceable poets from intermeddling hereafter with that quarrelling kind of verse."* This description is not infelicitous; and coming from a contemporary who was acquainted with the translation by Phayer and Twyne, which was then in vogue, and highly thought of, it shows in what sort of estimation Stanyhurst was held by those who were capable of forming a correct judgment of his labours. Warton heaps more fire upon the unfortunate translator's head, wonders what could have tempted him to undertake such a work, and adds that in the choice of his measure he is more unfortunate than his predecessors, and that in other respects he succeeded worse. Notwithstanding all this, however, Warton admits that Stanyhurst was a scholar, and then goes on to furnish some instances of the strange liberties he takes with his original. " In this translation," says Warton, " he calls Choraebus, one of the Trojan chiefs, a *Bedlamite;* he says, that old Priam girded on his sword *Morglay,*—the name of a sword in the Gothic romances ; that Dido would have been glad to have been brought to bed even of a *Cockney,* or *Dandiprat-hop-thumb ;* and that Jupiter, in kissing his daughter, *bust his pretty prating parrot.*"† The truth seems to be, that Stanyhurst, having cut himself off from all intercourse with the literary men of the day, was utterly indifferent to their praise or censure; and that he took a sort of malicious pleasure in indulging the utmost freedom of manner, even to the employment of the vulgarest phrases, as if he really meant to turn the dignity of the epic into ridicule. With all his faults, however, he was a man of such solid learning as to extort from Camden the designation, " Eruditissimus ille nobilis Richardus Stainhurstus."

* Nash's Preface to *Greene's Arcadia.*
† Warton, *History of Poetry.*

THOMAS STORER.

15— —1664.

THOMAS STORER was one of the numerous contri-
butors to *England's Helicon* and *England's Parnassus*, and
is on that account chiefly entitled to a niche amongst
the poets.   He also wrote a work in verse, called *The
Life and Death of Thomas Wolsey, Cardinal,* which is
the most elaborate of his productions, and which was
highly applauded for its poetical elegance and historical
fidelity.   All that is known about his personal history
is, that he was born in London; was admitted a student
of Christ Church, Oxford, in 1587 ; took the degrees in
arts, — that of M. A. in 1594, when he was in great repute for his poetry in the university ; and that he died
in November, 1604, in the parish of St. Michael, Basing
haugh, within the city of London, where it is presumed
he was buried.

THOMAS CHURCHYARD.

1520—1604.

THOMAS CHURCHYARD was born in the ancient borough
of Shrewsbury, somewhere about 1520.   Discovering
an irrepressible passion for letters while he was yet only
a child, his father resolved to cultivate it; and accordingly bestowed a careful education upon him, relaxing his
severer studies by instruction on the lute.   But the
term of his youthful studies had hardly expired, when
this indulgent parent thought it was time for his precocious son to see the world; and giving'him a sufficient
sum of money, sent him to please his own fancy at
seventeen years of age to the metropolis.   Young
Churchyard, finding himself free at this unripe age in

a new world of enjoyments, threw aside his books, went to court, and lived like a roysterer until his finances were exhausted. Then, suddenly reduced to necessity, he entered the service of Henry Howard, earl of Surrey, with whom he lived for four years towards the latter end of the reign of Henry VIII. Surrey was not slow to encourage the genius of his dependant; and while Churchyard continued in his household, he applied himself closely to study, and produced several poems ; but the death of the earl again cast him into difficulties. It is certain that although he was constantly about the court, he held no employment there, and that with the death of his patron all his hopes in that quarter were at an end. From that time his career presents a continual succession of troubles, wanderings, and adventures. He entered the army as a private soldier, and there acquired an intimate acquaintance with military discipline ; then, having learned all he could, he left that employment, and travelled on the Continent for the purpose of acquiring a knowledge of modern languages ; returned home ; was received for a time at Oxford ; but being indisposed to resume his studies after so much rambling abroad, rejoined the army ; served in Ireland and Scotland ; was there taken prisoner ; but, upon a peace being made, was released, and came back to London very poor, sickly, and dispirited. Being then thirty years of age, he went to Shrewsbury to raise recruits; and after many fluctuations of fortune, was at last taken under the protection of the earl of Leicester, chancellor of the university of Oxford. He had become too unquiet, however, for a situation so tranquil and obscure ; that "unrest" of the mind which often fills the void of action had taken possession of him, and he fancied himself in love with a rich widow. But the lady received his advances with so much coldness that poor Churchyard became sorely troubled at heart, and to alleviate his grief joined the army in Flanders, where he had a command, was wounded, and taken prisoner ; but showing himself to be brave and of gentle breeding, he

was well treated by the enemy, and, perhaps through a
skilful use of his poetical talents, he made such an impression upon a lady of quality that she interested
herself strongly on his behalf, and ultimately assisted
him in making his escape. He afterwards walked
sixty miles to join his friends; recruited; was again
taken prisoner; committed to close custody; condemned
to death as a spy; and again ' y the powerful intercession
of another noble lady (for all throughout his wayward
career he seems to have addressed himself with singular
success to the fair sex), he was reprieved, relieved, and
sent away. He then returned to England, and seems to
have employed himself chiefly in publishing his poems;
from which, however, he derived more applause than
profit. The time of his death has been variously stated,
but finally decided by the register of St. Margaret's,
Westminster, where he was buried on the 4th April,
1604, close to the grave of Skelton.

Churchyard was one of the most voluminous writers
of his day. Wood gives a list of no less than twenty-
three separate publications, consisting of tragedies,
poems, discourses, translations; and informs us at the
same time that a great many more have been lost. Of
the pieces that have been preserved, the names of some
of them will bear external evidence to the quaintness of
the soul within:—*Dame Dicar's Dreame; A Praise of
the Bowe; A Feast full of sad Cheer; The fortunate
Farewell to the most forward and noble Earl of Essex;
A Rebuke to Rebellion; A Book of a sumptuous Shew
in Shrovetide,* &c. One of his fancies was to insinuate
his own name into the titles of his productions; as, *A
Musicall Consort of Heavenly Harmonie (compounded of
manie parts of Musicke), called Churchyard's Charitie;
The Lamentation of Churchyard's Fryndshipp; Churchyard's Choice; Churchyard's Challenge,* &c. It appears
that the opinions of his contemporaries differed very
materially as to his merits, some accounting him an excellent poet, and others despising him as a poor court poet,
which of all kinds of poverty in poetry must be regarded

as the worst. Wood speaks of him with contempt. Th re is no doubt that the vast quantity of rhyme produced by Churchyard, the unfavourable circumstances under which nearly the whole of it was written (as it is obvious that he could have had but few opportunities, after his golden youth was over, of consulting books, or even re-considering his verses), and the haste enforced upon him by his necessities, contributed to render his works comparatively valueless. But there are sufficient gleams of genuine feeling and cultivated taste here and there, to justify a more kindly estimate of his genius than has generally been put upon it. If, on the one hand, he rarely reached the height of his subject, and frequently committed the worst sins of doggrel, his versatility, fecundity, and copiousness, cannot be denied to him on the other. His *Legend of Jane Shore,* which sir Egerton Brydges marks out especially for admiration, contains many lines of singular beauty, and is on the whole a poem of very considerable merit. As Churchyard's productions are so extremely rare as to be out of the reach of general readers, a passage or two from this legend will appropriately terminate the notice of its luckless and restless author: —

" This wandryng worlde bewitched me with wyles,
And wonne my wyttes wyth wanton sugred joyes,
In Fortunes frekes who trustes her when she smyles,
Shal fynde her false, and full of fickle toyes;
Her tryumphes al but fyl our eares wyth noyse,
Her flatteryng gyftes are pleasures myxt with payne:
Yea al her wordes are thunders threatnyng raine.

" The fond desire that we in glory set,
Doth thirle our hartes to hope in slipper happe:
A blast of pompe is al the fruyt we get,
And under that lies hydde a sodayne clappe:
In seeking rest, unwares we fal in trappe;
In groping flowers, with nettles stong we are;
In labouring long, we reape the crop of care.

" Of noble bloud I cannot boast my byrth,.
For I was made out of the meanest molde,
Myne heritage but seven foote of the earth ;
Fortune ne gave to me the gyftes of golde ;
But I could brag of nature, if I would,
Who fyld my face with favour freshe and fayer,
Where beauty shone like Phœbus in the ayer.

" My shape, some sayd, was seemly to eche syght,
My countenance did shew a sober grace ;
Myne eyes in looks were never proved lyght,
My tongue in wordes were chaste in every case,
Myne eares were deafe, and would no lovers place,
Save that, alas ! a prince did blot my browe ;
Soe, then the strong did make the weak to bowe.

" The majestie that kynges to people beare,
The stately porte, the awful chere they showe,
Will make the meane to shrynke and couche for feare,
Like as the hound, that doth his maister knowe ;
What then, since I was made unto the bowe ;
There is no cloake, can serve to hide my fault,
For I agreed the fort he should assault.

" The egle's force subdues eche bird that flyes ;
What metal may resist the flaming fyre ?
Doth not the sonne dasile the clearest eyes,
And melt the ise, and make the frost retire ?
Who can withstand a puissant kynge's desyre ?
The stiffest stones are pierced through with tooles :
The wisest are with princes made but fooles."

The author of these stanzas, which form but a small
part of a poem which sustains the same excellence all
throughout, possessed all the capabilities for a great
poet, had fortune better assisted the development of his
genius ; and it is pleasant to know that he was also a
man of unstained reputation. Strype, in his life of
Grindal, says that Churchyard was " an excellent soldier, and a man of honest principles."

Thomas Newton.

—— —1607. ·

Thomas Newton was the eldest son of Edward Newton, of Butley, in the parish of Presbury in Cheshire, where he was born. He was sent, when only thirteen years of age, to Trinity College, Oxford, but after a short stay there removed to Queen's College, Cambridge, where, according to Wood, he " became so much renowned for his Latin poetry, that he was numbered by scholars of his time among the most noted poets in that language." Having, after a few years, returned to Oxford, and remained there for some time, he at length settled at or near Macclesfield, where he taught school and practised physic with success. He appears to have been patronised by the earl of Essex; and in 1583 obtained from Elizabeth the rectory of Little Ilford in Essex. There also he kept a school, by which, and his writings and rectory, we are told that he had " gotten a considerable estate" at the period of his death, in 1607. He compiled *A notable History of the Saracens*, a medical tract, and some other prose works of little note or importance; translated the *Thebais* of Seneca, a few books of Cicero, and some religious essays; and wrote a funeral tribute to the memory of Elizabeth, entitled *Atropoion Delion, or the Death of Delia, with the Tears of her Funeral. A poetic excursive Discourse of our late Eliza.* This was published in 1603, but does not appear to have attracted or deserved much attention. He wrote commendatory lines on several works published in his day. Such of his compositions in Latin metre as have been preserved to us possess little merit, and show that he was merely an adept in stringing hexameters and pentameters together with correctness and fluency. There

are no other particulars recorded of his life beside these
we have mentioned. · He died at Little Ilford, in May,
1607, leaving behind him 'a son named Abel, and was
buried in the church belonging to that village.

WILLIAM WARNER.

—— —1608-9.

WILLIAM WARNER was one of that crowd of poets who
contributed to *England's Parnassus;* but he is worthy
of being noted for other and more ambitious labours.
He was born in Warwickshire, and educated at Oxford,
chiefly at Magdalen Hall, where he early exhibited his
preference for poetry over logic and philosophy. Leaving
the university without taking a degree, he went to
London, where he wrote many pieces of poetry which
obtained him a tolerable reputation amongst the poetasters of the day. As he grew older, however, he
seems to have grown wiser, and to have applied himself
to more serious studies. His most important work is
Albion's England, a sort of rhythmical history from the
earliest times to which he added a prose epitome. It
was first published in 1586, and acquired such celebrity
that in a short time it ran through several editions.
Warner is said also to have translated the *Menæchmi,*
and other comedies of Plautus. By these productions
he came at last to be distinguished amongst the refiners
of the English tongue ; but the value of such praise in
that day is very doubtful, since we find Wehbe speaking
of Lilly the euphuist, as a " wonderful improver of our
language *," and even Oldys describing him as a man
of " uncommon eloquence." Wood is more judicious
in his estimate of Warner, who, he says, was not to be
classed with Sydney, Drayton, or Daniel, yet was not
inferior to Gascoigne, Turberville, Churchyard, Con-
stable, or sir Edward Dyer. It is but fair to balance

* Discourse on Poetry.

this opinion by that of Nash, who, after speaking of
Spenser and the rest of the early poets, says, "as poetry
hath beene honoured in those her fore-named professors,
so it hath not been any whit disparaged by William
Warner's *Albion;*" to which general panegyric Drayton
frankly subscribed.

Warner is stated to have died suddenly in his bed
in Hertfordshire, without any previous illness, on the·
9th of March 1608–9.   He was buried under a stone
in the church there.

In *England's Parnassus**, Warner's verses are associated with selections from Drayton, Fairfax, Shakspeare, Lodge, Chapman, Spenser, Marlow, Jonson,
Middleton, Peele, and others, who were esteemed the
first poets of their time.   His admission, however, into
that goodly company, is by no means decisive of his
merits, as we find others admitted who were of a very
inferior grade, and who could not be lifted out of obscurity even by Parnassus itself.   Amongst these poor
rhymers may be enumerated Weever, Hudson, Roydon,
Fraunce, Fitz-Geffrey.   Of Warner's verses the following is a fair specimen :—

MIND.

" Nor is it but our minds that make our native homes our grave,
　As we to ours, others to theirs, like partial fancy have ;
　Transmute we but our minds, and then all one an alien is,
　As if a native, once resolv'd, makes every country his."

---

* A full description of *England's Parnassus* is given by Oldys, in his preface to *Hayward's British Muse*, where he justly censures its faults of taste.
The following is the title of the work as given in the *Censura Literaria :*
"*England's Parnassus; or the Choysest Flowers of our Moderne Poets, with
their Poeticall Comparisons. Descriptions of Bewties, Personayes, Castles,
Pallaces, Mountaines, Groves, Seas, Springs, Rivers, &c. Whereunto are
annexed other various Discourses both pleasant and profitable. Imprinted
at London for N. L., C. B., and T. H.* 1600. With the device of a ling en-
tangled in the branches of a honeysuckle. Pp. 510, besides dedication, &c.
Small 8vo, or duodecimo.*"

THOMAS LEYSON.

15— — ——.

THOMAS LEYSON, equally celebrated in his own time as a poet and physician, was born at Neath in Glamorganshire, and educated in the famous school of William Wykeham. He was admitted perpetual fellow · of New College, Oxford, in 1569, took the degrees in Arts soon after, and was proctor of the university in. 1583, when, as Wood informs us, "he showed himself, an exact disputant before Alb Alaskie, prince of Sirad, when he was entertained by the Oxonian Muses." About that time he settled in Bath as a physician, where, according to Wood, "he became as much noted for his happy success in the practice of physic as before he was for his Latin poetry in the university." He practised at Bath to his death, and was buried there in St. James's Church. It is not known when he died, neither is there any account of the year of his birth, or of his parentage, marriage, or family. That he was married, however, there is no doubt, as we are suggestively told that he " was buried by the side of his wife."

Of his merits as a poet it is now difficult, if not impossible, to speak. Wood says that he wrote, in Latin, " a poem describing the site and beauty of St. Donat's Castle in Glamorganshire, which poem coming to the sight of Dr. John David Rhese, his worthy acquaintance, who styles it *venustum poema*, he turned it into Welsh, and gave the author of it this character, —' *Vir cùm rei medicæ tùm poetices meritissimus.*'" Wood does not speak with much enthusiasm of the merit of the pieces which had fallen under his own notice, contenting himself with observing that he had seen much of Leyson's poetry in several books, "which, if gathered together, might make a *pretty manual.*" He was much respected for his learning by the celebrated sir John Harrington and others of his contemporaries

THOMAS BASTARD.

15——1618.

THOMAS BASTARD, who had the genius and the ill-luck of a poet, was a native of Blandford in Dorsetshire, and a pupil of the celebrated Wykeham. He was admitted to a perpetual fellowship in New College, Oxford, in 1588 ; but, indulging a humour for satire and epigram, or, as Wood says, " being much guilty of the vices belonging to poets and given to libelling," he was compelled to resign his fellowship in 1591. He was, however, made chaplain, soon after, to the earl of Suffolk, and, through his influence, vicar of Beer-Regis and rector of Hamer in Dorsetshire. He was a man of extensive acquirements in classical literature, and of such agreeable manners that his company was always eagerly desired. His epigrams contain much shrewd satire and polished wit. Wood says that in his elder years he was "a quaint preacher." He was three times married. He married his second wife, as he himself tells us in one of his epigrams *, on account of her wealth. Notwithstanding this accession of fortune, however, his vicarage, rectory, poetry, and preaching, he appears to have been always complaining of his poverty, and having become " crazed" in his latter days, he fell into debt, was thrown into the prison of Allhallows parish in Dorchester, died there " very ob-

---

* This epigram is in Latin, and is deserving of a place here.

" Terna mihi ducta est variis ætatibus uxor,
   Hæc juveni, illa viro, tertia nupta seni,
  Prima est propter opus teneris mihi juncta sub annis,
   Altera propter opes, tertia propter opem."

This has been attributed by Wood to Bastard ; but it has been also, with a few slight alterations, attributed by some foreigners to Stephen Pasquier. who is said to have written it on Beza.

scurely and in a mean condition," and was buried in the parish churchyard on the 19th of April 1618.

That he was in good repute as a poet, may be inferred from the friendship of sir John Harrington, who addressed two of his epigrams to him, and from the praises of Sheppard and Heath, the latter of whom complimented him in the following couplet : —

AD THO. BASTARDUM EPIGRAMMATISTAM.

" Thy epigrams are of no bastard race,
For they dare gaze the world's eye in the face."

Warton accords to him the credit of being an elegant classical scholar, and better qualified for that species of occasional pointed Latin epigram established by his fellow collegian, John Owen, than for any sort of English versification. His principal poetical performances are *Chrestolaros*, consisting of seven books of epigrams, &c.; *Magna Britannia*, a Latin poem in three books. There is another poem of his in the king's library, entitled *Jacobo Regi I. Carmen Gratulorium ;* and Wood mentions his libels, two of which he had met in a collection of lampoons written by several Oxford students in the reign of queen Elizabeth. It was for one of these, *Marprelatis Bastardini*, in which he reflects upon all persons of note in Oxford who were suspected of licentiousness, that he was expelled the university. Bastard also published two collections of sermons.

The Oxford lampoon is remarkable for no better quality than coarseness, and whoever may be curious to examine the stuff of which it is composed, may see a specimen of it in the *Censura Literaria.** Bastard seems to have generally had some good moral in view in his epigrams, and to have been ordinarily influenced by excellent intentions. Here is one of his epigrams, extracted from *England's Parnassus :* —

* Vol. iii. p. 410. second edition, 1815.

VIRTUE.

" Virtue dies not; her tomb we need not raise ;
Let them trust tombs, which have outlived their praise."

The following will afford a fair example of his
political feeling and the quaint character of his style :—

AD THOMAM STRANGWAIES.

" Strangwaies ! leave London and her sweet contents,
   Or bring them down to me, to make me glad,
And give one month to country merriments ;
   Give me a few days, for the years I had.
The poet's songs and sports we will read over,
   Which in their golden quire they have resounded ;
And spill our readings one upon another,
   And read our spillings, sweetly so confounded.
Nulam shall lend us light in midst of day,
   When to the even valley we repair;
When we delight ourselves with talk or play
   Sweet, with the infant grass and virgin air :
These in the heat ; but in the even, later,
We 'll walk the meads, and read trouts in the water."

George Turberville.

1530— ——.

George Turberville was chiefly celebrated as a
sonnetteer, and as a translator from the Latin and
Italian languages. His epigrams, songs, and sonnets
are numerously scattered amongst the anthologies of the
period. He was the younger son of Nicholas Turberville, of Whitchurch in Dorsetshire, where he was born
about 1530. He was educated at Wykeham's school,
and became perpetual fellow of New College, Oxford,
in 1561, but left it in the following year, before he had
taken out a degree, and went to reside at one of the
inns of court. Throughout this period he applied himself laboriously to the study of the classics and modern
languages, and independently of poetry, he appears to

have applied himself with effect to more useful and
practical accomplishments. He afterwards became secretary to Thomas Randolph, Esq., when that gentleman
was appointed on a mission from queen Elizabeth to the
emperor of Russia. While he was abroad he wrote
three poetical epistles to three friends, descriptive of the
manners of the Russians. These pieces were published
in *Hacklyt's Voyages*. On his return he was much
courted as an accomplished scholar, and a man of refined
manners ; and published in 1567 the first edition of his
Songs and Sonnets, which was followed by a second
edition in 1570, in which year he also published his
Epitaphs, Epigrams, Songs, and Sonnets. He translated
the epistles of Ovid, and the *Eclogues of Virgil,* and
some *Tragical Tales* from the Italian, adding to each
an argument and l'envoye. There being two other
persons of the same name, who were also natives of
Dorsetshire, and nearly contemporaries, some doubt
exists as to whether the poet was the author of a *Booke
of Fallconry and Hawking,* bearing the name of
G. Turberville ; but the editor of *Phillip's Theatrum* is
of opinion that his authorship is determined by some
commendatory verses attached to the work by Gascoigne.
A better evidence, perhaps, is found in the numerous
allusions Turberville makes in his poetry to those amusements, from which he frequently derives his images and
metaphors. The time of his death is not recorded ; but
as Wood says he was certainly living in 1594, the
suspicion that identified him with a certain Mr. Turberville
who was murdered by one John Morgan in 1579, and
whose violent death was celebrated in a doleful " dittie,"
mentioned by Herbert in his antiquities, cannot be
correct.

Turberville's excellence lay exclusively in his translations, which are highly praised by Meres, and in his
songs and sonnets. Pultenham speaks in his commendation as a poet of good renown, and Harrington wrote
an epitaph upon him, beginning with the following
'curious stanza :—

" When times were yet but rude, thy pen endeavoured
 To polish barbarism with purer style,
When times were grown most old, thy heart persevered,
Sincere and just, unstained with gifts or guile," &c.

Turberville does not appear to have entertained a very
high opinion of his original powers, and perhaps the
best account of his poetry is that which he gives of it
himself in the following quatrains from his epilogue to
the *Tragical Tales.*

" I write but of familiar stuffe,
 Because my stile is lowe ;
I feare to wade in weighty works,
 Or past my reach to rowe.

" Yet meaner muses must not lurke ;
 But each in his degree,
That meaneth well, and doth his best,
Must well regarded be."

SIR EDWARD DYER.

1540 —— ——.

SIR EDWARD DYER is chiefly celebrated as the author
of a poem called *A Description of Friendship,* and as a
contributor of some pastoral odes and madrigals (then a
favourite form of poetry) to the *English Helicon.* He
was descended from an ancient family in Somersetshire,
where, it is conjectured, he was born about 1540; was
educated at Oxford, either in Baliol College or Broadgate's Hall, but left it without a degree, and went
abroad. He early discovered a taste for polite literature,
and on his return from the continent, being already
ranked amongst the poets, he was taken into the service
of the court. Queen Elizabeth entertained so high
an opinion of his abilities that she employed him on
several embassies, especially to Denmark, in 1589 ; and
in 1596, her majesty knighted him, and conferred upon
him the chancellorship of the garter, vacant by the

death of sir John Walley.   But sir Edward Dyer was
not exempt from the usual fate of Elizabeth's favourites.
He occasionally fell into disgrace, and on one occasion
is said to have regained her goodwill by affecting to be
on the point of death in consequence of her displeasure.
He died some years after the accession of king James,
and was succeeded in his office by sir John Herbert
principal secretary of state.

Dyer, in his advanced age, devoted himself to the study
of chemistry and astrology, and was said to have been a
Rosicrucian.   He was certainly duped into the belief
that the celebrated Dr. Dee and Edward Kelly, whose
disciple he had been induced to become, had discovered
the grand secret of the elixir, and he has left upon record, that in Bohemia he once saw them put base metal
into a crucible, and, after stirring it with a stick of
wood, take it out nearly all pure gold.   This species of
credulity was common to that age, and prevailed in later
and better instructed times, even amongst men who were
distinguished for their philosophical acquirements.   Sir
Edward Dyer may be pardoned for his easy faith in such
wonders, when we know that sir Kenelm Digby believed in sympathetic powers, and in the validity of the
test of murder, by which the body of a corpse was expected to bleed afresh on the approach of the murderer;
— that Bacon respectfully doubted witchcraft, in which
sir Thomas Brown conscientiously believed;— and that
Dryden, the poet, used to cast the nativities of his children. *

In a very rare and curious book, entitled *The Arte of
English Poesie contrived into three Bookes*, published in.
1589, sir Edward Dyer is included in an enumeration
of the poets who shed lustre upon the reign of Elizabeth;
" and in her Majesties time," observes the writer, "that
nowe is, are spronge vp an other crewe of courtlie makers,

---

* A strange story is told about Dryden's son Charles, whose melancholy
death is said to have fulfilled the prediction cast by his father at his birth.
It is preserved by Mr. Ryan in his amusing *Anecdotes of Poetry and Poets;*
but the authority is not quoted, and the narrative cannot be relied upon.

noblemen and gentlemen of her Majesties own servants, who have written excellently well, as it would appeare if their doings could be found out and made publicke with the reste [alluding to the practice which pre-vailed of circulating poems in manuscript long before they were printed]: of which number is first that noble gentleman, Edward earl of Oxford, Thomas lord Buckhurst, when he was young, Henry lord Paget, sir Philip Sydney, sir Walter Rawleigh, maister Edward Dyer, maister Fulke Grevell [afterwards lord Brooke]. Gascon, Britton, Turberville, and a great many other learned gentlemen, whose names I do not omit for enuie, but to auoyde tediousnesse, and who huae deserued no little commendation." In another place, describing the particular characteristics of each poet, he celebrates " maister Edward Dyer for elegie most sweete, so-lempne, and of high conceit." The justice of this pane-gyric is confirmed by the applauses of Spenser, who was the personal friend of the chancellor of the garter. The fortunes of Dyer were more prosperous than those of the majority of his poetical contemporaries. He is said to have enjoyed an income of 4000*l.* per annum, and to have inherited a legacy of 80,000*l.* ; but the chronicle adds that, with the usual improvidence of literary habits, he squandered both.

FULKE GREVILE, LORD BROOKE.

1554—1628.

FULKE GREVILE is one of those characters whose claims to be ranked among the poets are rather equivocal, who seem to have been included in the muster roll by an accident, and who have been allowed to remain there by the indifference rather than the sanction of the world.

Descended from an ancient and honourable family living at Milcot in Warwickshire, where he was born in 1554, Fulke Grevile was entered at Cambridge,

from whence he afterwards removed to Oxford, where
he continued to prosecute his studies, until the time
arrived when it was necessary to finish his education
by a course of travels. On his return to England he
was introduced at court by his uncle, Robert Grevile,
who held some office under Elizabeth. This happy in-
eident was the foundation of his subsequent fortunes.
His accomplishments as a scholar and a man of the world
procured him so much admiration and applause, that he
was speedily elevated to a post of honour about the person of the queen, — a delicate trust, which he discharged
with so much discretion, that he had the longest lease
of the queen's favour, and the smoothest time at court, of
any of those who were exposed by their offices to her
majesty's domestic caprices.   In 1588 be was made a
master of arts at Oxford, together with several others,
in compliment to the earl of Essex. On the coronation
of James I. he was created a knight of the bath, and
shortly afterwards he received a grant of the castle of
Warwick. In the twelfth year of James's reign, he
was made a privy councillor, under treasurer and chancellor of the exchequer ; and after enjoying these offices
for six years, he resigned the chancellorship of the exchequer on being appointed one of the gentlemen of the
king's bedchamber, when he was raised to the dignity
of a baron, by the title of lord Brooke of Beauchamps-
court. Upon the accession of Charles I. he was recalled
to a place in the administration, — a distinction which he
did not live long to enjoy. A tragical circumstance drew
his life and his honours to a sudden and melancholy
conclusion. Throughout the greater part of his career
he had a faithful servant of the name of Haywood, who,
having spent many years in his household with diligence
and integrity, and believing himself to be ill-requited,
had frequently remonstrated with his master on the
subject. Perhaps lord Brooke thought his demands
unreasonable, or, probably, as has been suspected, Haywood was afflicted with mental derangement; but, however that may have been, it happened that as they were

alone one day in lord Brooke's bedchamber, at his house in Holborn, Haywood renewed his demands, when, receiving only a very sharp rebuke in reply, he was suddenly seized with such a violent fit of passion, that he stabbed his master in the back, and then, running into another room, killed himself with his own sword. Of that wound lord Brooke died on the 30th of September, 1628, and was buried in a vault on the north side of the collegiate church at Warwick. He is described in his epitaph as, " servant to queen Elizabeth, counsellor to king James, and friend to sir Philip Sydney." In addition to these particulars it may be observed that, although he was chargeable with the usual gallantries of the age, his lordship remained a bachelor through life.

His intimacy with sir Philip Sydney appears to have engrossed the whole period of his youth, and to have cherished in his mind those tendencies which flowered into verse at that ripe season, but of which no further traces are to be found at a later date. From the time he entered the service of the court he abandoned the service of the Muses, nor did he even care to let the world know that he had ever indulged in such light enjoyments, for his poems were not published until 1633, five years after his death, and were never reprinted.* Upon the title-page, they are described as having been " written in his youth, and familiar exercise with sir Philip Sydney." It is not a little curious that in all the copies of these poems that have been recovered, twenty-two pages are wanting, and it has been conjectured that they were cancelled on account of something which was considered censurable in their contents. His remains, consisting of *Poems of Monarchy and Religion*, were published in 1670. . In the advertisement to these pieces, the publisher states that lord Brooke had bequeathed them to an aged gentleman, in whom he confided, Mr. Michael

---

* Some specimens of them are given in Mr. Southey's *Select Works of the British Poets.*

Malet, with a view to their publication, but that on the death of Mr. Malet the trust devolved on sir J. M. M[alet], by whom he was permitted to print them. The former poems consisted of *Cælica*, a collection of 109 sonnets, three tragedies, *A Treatie of Humane Learning, A Treatie of Warres,* and *An Inquisition upon Fame and Honour.* In addition to these, lord Brooke was the author of *A Letter of Travels, A short Account of the Maxims and Policies used by Qu. Elizabeth in her Government,* and a *Life of Sir Philip Sydney ;* for a beautiful edition of which last work, printed at the Press Priory in 1816, English literature is indebted to sir Egerton Brydges.

Lord Brooke was not celebrated as a poet in his own time; for, although some of his pieces were freely circulated in manuscript, they were not of a kind likely to engage the popular attention. He was known rather as a man of learning and distinction than as an author. One who is generally profuse and almost indiscriminate in his eulogies dismisses him with simply observing, that " as a gentleman of noble birth and great estate he was most excellent in his time." *   Another writer, who seems to have examined his works with considerable care, gives the following very accurate account of them : — " Perhaps few men that dealt in poetry had more learning or real wisdom than this nobleman, and yet his style is sometimes so dark and mysterious, that one would imagine he chose rather to conceal than illustrate his meaning ; at other times his wit breaks out again with an uncommon brightness, and shines, I had almost said, without an equal. It is the same thing with his poetry: sometimes so harsh and uncouth, as if he had no ear for music ; at others, so smooth and harmonious, as if he was master of all its powers." †   Upon this Mr. Southey observes, " Lord Brooke is certainly the most difficult of all our poets ; but no writer, whether in prose or verse,

* Wood.   † Mrs. Cooper.

in this or any other country, appears to have reflected more deeply on momentous subjects; and his writings have an additional value, if (as may be believed) they represent the feelings and opinions of sir Philip Sidney as well as his own." I am afraid the conclusion is hardly warranted by the fact. That lord Brooke's poems should represent sir Philip Sidney's feelings and opinions, because lord Brooke enjoyed in his youth the friend-ship of sir Philip Sidney, is by no means a satisfactory reason for putting a factitious value upon them. Nor is it very likely that sir Philip Sidney entertained exactly the same principles that are avowed by lord Brooke. He may have approved of his discretion and good sense, but could hardly have extended his approval to a po-litical creed, which, whatever he may have thought of the form in which it was enunciated, must have been too cold and despotic for a spirit so ardent and generous.

Considered merely as a poet, lord Brooke's pretensions are very doubtful. His verses may be read with some interest for their practical axioms upon human nature, religion, and civil government, although even these have ceased to be " caviare to the multitude;" but it is im-possible to derive much pleasure from them as poems. His "treaties" on monarchy, warres, and learning, are literally essays logically conducted, and put into rhyme, and as slightly relieved even by poetical diction as the nature of versification would allow. In subject and treatment they are purely prosaic, and their rhythmical structure has hardly any other effect than that of cramp-ing their expression, and giving them a still more formal and dogmatic tone. As these works are not familiar to the public, and not very likely to become so, a single passage may be acceptable in illustration of the general character of the whole. The following argument is de-signed to show the excellence of a monarchy over a de-mocracy, the author having demonstrated ir a previous section the superiority of that form of government over an aristocracy.

" Now, if the best and choicest government
Of many heads, be in her nature this;
How can the democratical content,
Where that blind multitude chief master is?
    And where, besides all these forespoken fates,
    The most, and worst sort govern all estates?

" Since, as those persons usually do haunt
The market-places, which at home have least;
So here those spirits most intrude and vaunt
To do the business of this common beast,
    That have no other means to vent their ill,
    Than by transforming real things to will.

" Besides, this equal, stil'd democracy,
Lets fall men's minds, and makes their manners base;
Learning and all arts of civility,
Which add both unto nature and to place,
    It doth eclipse, as death to that estate,
    Wherein not worth, but idle wealth gives fate.

" Nay, where religion, God, and humane laws,
· No other use, or honour, can expect
Than to serve idle liberties applause,
As painted toys, which multitudes affect,
    Who judging all things, while they nothing know, .·
    Lawless and godless are, and would live so.

" Therefore, if any to protect this state,
Alledge imperial Rome grew great by it;
And Athens likewise far more fortunate,
As raising types up both of worth and wit;
    Such as no monarchy can parallel,
    In the rare ways of greatness doing well;

" Or if again, to make good this position,
Any averr that Rome's first monarchy,
For lack of courage, soon chang'd her condition
Of union, into multiplicity;
    Whence Germans over France, and Goths in Spain,
    In Afric Saracens, and Turks in Asia raign;.

" I answer, first, that those subduing prides
(Whereof the people boast) were to the hand
Form'd by the three preceding monarch tides,
And what succeeded (if exactly scan'd)
　　But imitation was of their brave deeds,
　　Who, but their own worth, no example needs."

This passage affords a fair specimen of lord Brooke's
manner of reasoning in rhyme, and of the colour of his
political opinions : as a specimen of the general character
of his versification it is rather favourable, for he seldom
sustains so long an argument with so much perspicuity
of language and melody of numbers.

GEORGE WITHER.

1588—1667

GEORGE WITHER was born on the 11th of June, 1588,
at Bentworth, near Alton, in Hampshire, and was of
the family of the Withers of Manydowne, near Wotton
St. Laurence, in the same county. He received · the
rudiments of his education under John Greaves, a schoolmaster of some note, and was sent to Magdalen College,
Oxford, about the year 1604, where he was put under
the tuition of John Warner, afterwards bishop of Rochester. His inclination, however, diverting his thoughts
into other channels, he made so small a proficiency in
the studies to which his attention was directed, that after
an interval of three years he was taken home by his
friends, and sent to learn the law ; first in one of the
inns of Chancery Lane, and afterwards in Lincoln's Inn.
But nature had made him a poet, and frustrated all these
well-meant designs.   While he was nominally studying
the law, he wrote several pieces, which, being circulated
among his friends, soon acquired him a flattering reputation.   These were called his Juvenilia.   They were
afterwards lost.   In 1612 he published two pieces relative to the death of prince Henry ; and in 1613 his
K 2

*Abuses Stript and Whipt, or Satyrical Essays, in Two Books.** For this poem, which reflected severely on the royalists, he was committed to the Marshalsea, and imprisoned there for several months. This temporary martyrdom established his fame with his own party, and he thenceforth became the great poetic and pamphleteering oracle of the puritans, the more ignorant portion of whom looked upon him as a prophet, and fancied that they saw many things taking place as he was supposed to predict them. Possessing an intimate knowledge of human nature, and remarkable penetration and foresight, he frequently made allusion to " coming events " with so much sagacity, that the vulgar readily attributed his ratiocinations to divine inspiration, especially when they appeared to be so exactly fulfilled. From 1613 he continned to pour out his thoughts, in prose and verse, on all passing political and popular subjects with extraordinary fecundity. Wither was in verse as fertile, as courageous, and as indomitable as Prynne was in prose, and, although he did not fill so large a space in the public mind, he became equally obnoxious to his antagonists. They were both continually writing in open defiance of threats and punishments. Prynne had his ears cut off, and Wither was several times imprisoned. But these penalties did not abate his zeal for " the cause." He tells us, in his *Britannia's Remembrancer,* published in 1628, that he had been imprisoned three times already, but that he felt called upon to speak his mind ; that all he had suffered was only calculated to " prepare him for this worke ;" and that

—— " Therefore neither all the graces
Of kings, nor gifts, nor honourable places,
Should stop my mouth ; nor would I smother this,
Though twenty kings had sworne that I should kiss
The gallows for it : lest my conscience sbould
Torment me more than all men living could ;

* Mr. Dalrymple conjectures that there was an edition of this so early as 1611.

For I had rather in a dungeon dwell
Five years, than in my soul to feel a hell
Five minutes."

His career was as fiery and reckless as his poetry. In 1639 he joined the expedition against the Scots, in which he held the rank of captain of horse and quartermaster-general of a regiment. The progress of public events now put his puritanical zeal to the test, and in 1642 he became so enthusiastic that he sold his estate, and raising a troop of horse with the purchase-money, he joined the camp of the Parliamentarians. The motto on his colours was *Pro Rege, Lege, Grege.* He was immediately made a captain, and soon after a major; and conducted himself with so much credit that the parliament gave him sir John Denham's estate at Egham, in Surrey. Being afterwards taken prisoner by the cavaliers, sir John Denham is reported to have implored the king not to hang him, for this very singular reason — " because so long as Wither lived, he, Denham, would not be accounted the worst poet in England." He was soon after released.

In 1643 Wither published some numbers of the *Mercurius Rusticus,* written in imitation of the weekly "intelligences" of that day. About that period he was made by the Long Parliament a justice of the peace in *quorum* for Hampshire, Surrey, and Essex. In 1646 he published a pamphlet entitled *Justiciarius Justificatus,* in which he made some reflections on sir Richard Onslow, a member of the commons. The subject having been brought under the notice of the house, a debate arose, and it was at length voted that Wither should pay sir Richard 500*l.* for the damages, and that the book should be burnt by the hands of the common hangman. Though he was then imprisoned for a year, he continued to write with unabated zeal and vigour. In 1655, he published *The Protector, a Poem, briefly illustrating the Supremacy of that Dignity, and rationally demonstrating that the Title of Protector providentially conferred, &c.*

About that time he was made major-general of all the
forces in the county of Surrey, in which employment he
rendered himself very obnoxious to the royalists.   He
also obtained a full proportion of the confiscated properties.   The Restoration, however, made a complete revolution of his wheel of fortune.   He lost his employments, and was deprived of all the estates that had been
conferred on him by the ruling party, or that were purchased by his own money.   He was looked upon as a
person dangerous to the new order of things, and, in
March, 1661, was committed to the Tower for a libel on
the commons, of which he was said to have been the
author, but which he denied; at the end of nine months
he was discharged.

It might have been expected that these accumulated
misfortunes, and the hopelessness of his circumstances,
would have now subdued his spirit; but he persevered
in his professional occupation of poet and pamphleteer to
the day of his death, which took place in London on the
2d of May, 1667.   He was buried within the east door
of the Savoy church in the Strand.   In what condition
he lived prior to his death, or in what particular part of
London he died, it is now perhaps impossible to discover;
but if we combine what Wood and Aubrey say with re-
peet to him, it may be inferred that he died in the Savoy
hospital.   The former says he was buried in the " church
belonging to the Savoy hospital," and the latter, that he
was buried " within the east door of the Savoy church,
where he died."

Wither's character as a poet has been variously described, according to the predilections, political or reli-
gions, that mingled in the decision.   The royalists
affected to treat his works with the utmost scorn and
contempt, and even went so far as to assert that he was
crazed; while the puritans, on the other hand, elevated
him to the highest rank amongst English writers.   It
may be fairly assumed that there must have been some
merit in a versifier who was thought to be of sufficient
consequence for so much exaggeration on both sides.

Wither's talents, if not of a lofty order, were, at least, admirably adapted to the purposes to which they were applied. He was the poet of a fanatical, superstitious, and intolerant party, and he reflected in his poems, with instinctive fidelity, their crafty, coarse, and vindictive qualities. Like them, he was fearless, confident in the final triumph of his cause, unrestrained by considerations of person or place, violent, steady, and persevering: he gloried in his punishments, which only acted as pro-·vocations to fresh offences, and the more he was op-'pressed the more he endeavoured to furnish his oppressors with new bills of indictment against himself. * All this was irrational ; but it was the distemper of the times and the sect to which he belonged. He seems to have had an extraordinary facility in versification, which is abundantly testified by the enormous quantity he produced, and the easy flow of his numbers, which was in that age rather a noticeable merit. It is said of him, that: he could make verses as fast as he could write them ; and it may be. suspected, from occasional evidences of hurry, that his invention not unfrequently outstripped his fingers. His wife, who was the daughter of H. Emerson, esq. of South Lambeth, in Surrey, was also a poet, wit, and versifier, and may perhaps have helped him in his productions. Of his classical attainments we have a satisfactory voucher, in his translation of the Greek tract by Nemesius. on the Nature of Man, while his poem of the *Shepheard's Hunting,* consisting of eclogues which he wrote while he was in prison on account of the *Satire upon Abuses,* proves that he was a close and practical observer of nature. The general tone and temper of his productions, and the fugitive interest of the topics to which the majority of them are addressed, have long had the effect of banishing Wither from our national anthologies. Like Churchyard, he wrote too much

* As an instance of his invincible resolution in carrying his objects into effect, it is related of him, that when he had finished his *Britannia's Re-membrancer,* the longest and most valuable of his poems, finding that he could not obtain a licence to print it, although there was nothing either immoral or seditious in the work, he printed it with his own hands.

and too heedlessly, and apparently never troubled him-self with a solitary thought about posterity.   Yet there are some of his pieces so full of sweet and natural grace, so melodious, simple, and affecting, that it would be difficult to point out amongst his minor contemporaries a poet from whose remains so much pure poetry could be extracted.   Sir Egerton Brydges, whose devotion to the old English poets was manifested in many munificent acts of justice to their memory, valued Wither, thus expurgated, so highly, that he republished his *Shepheard's Hunting*, his *Fidelia*, and his *Hymns and Songs of the Church.*

As the reprints of Wither's poems are now very rare, especially his *Satires*, a few passages to illustrate the manner of this rapid versifier may be desirable.   The following is the opening of an appeal to the king, called *A Satyre*, written while he was a prisoner in the Marshalsea : —

Quid tu, si pereo ?
What once the poet said, I may avow ;
'T is a hard thing not to write satyres now,
Since what we speak, abuse reigns so in all,
Spite of our hearts, will be satirical.
Let it not therefore now be deemed strange,
My unsmooth'd lines their rudeness do not change ;
Nor be distasteful to my gracious king,
That in the cage my old harsh notes I sing,
And rudely make a satyre here unfold,
What others would in neater terms have told.
And why ? my friends and means in court are scant :
Knowledge of curious phrase and form I want.
I cannot bear to run myself in debt,
To hire the groom, to bid the page intreat
Some favour'd follower to vouchsafe his word
To get me a cold comfort from his lord :
I cannot soothe, tho' it my life might save,
Each favourite, nor crouch to every knave :
I cannot brook delays, as some men do,
With scoffs and scorns, and tak't in kindness too.

The following description of the plague is worthy of a later age.   It was written in the midst of the scenes

It describes; for Wither remained in London during the year 1627 to observe and record the progress of that calamity, exposing himself fearlessly to infection, under a persuasion that it was his duty to be at his post, and to warn the nation of its danger: —

On some this plague doth steal insensibly,
Their muddy nature stirring secretly
To their destruction.   Some, it striketh so
As if a mortall hand had with a blow
Arrested them, and on their flesh hath seene
A palme's impression to appearance beene.
One man is faint, weake, sickly, full of feare,
And drawes his breath where strong infections are,
Yet 'scapes with life.   Another man is young,
Light-hearted, healthy, stout, well-temper'd, strong,
And lives in wholesome ayre, yet gets a fit
Of this land-calenture, and dies of it.
Some are tormented by it, till we see
Their veines and sinewes almost broken be,
The very soul distracted, sense bereft,
And scarce the smallest hope of scaping left,
Yet soone recover.   Other some, againe,
Fall suddenly, or feele so little paine
When they are seized, that they breathless lie,
Ere any dying symptomes we espy.
On some, an endless drowsinesse doth creepe;
Some others cannot get one winke of sleep.
This useth, ev'ry day, preservatives,
Yet dies; another taketh none, yet lives.
Ev'n thus uncertainly this sicknesse playes;
Spares, wounds, and killeth, many sev'rall wayes.

The regularity of the measure, and the propriety of the diction in these lines — which are not selected from the most poetical of his productions, — justly entitle Wither to a higher place amongst the poets than he has hitherto obtained.

WILLIAM BROWNE.

1590—1645.

WILLIAM BROWNE, the intimate friend of Wither, is distinguished as the pastoral poet of an age when the

public were little disposed to encourage compositions of
so simple a character. He was born at Tavistock, in Devonshire, in 1590, was educated at Exeter College, Oxford, and from thence removed to the Inner Temple,
London, to study the law. But a profession so harsh
and crabbed was wholly unsuited to his taste, and, at
the time when he was nominally dedicated to its dry
and repulsive details, he was really engaged in the composition of the work which entitles him to a place of
honour amongst the poets. At the age of twenty-three
he published the first part of his *Britannia's Pastorals,*
which was received with so much approbation that it
was followed in the ensuing year by his *Shephearde's
Pipe,* a series of seven eclogues. Two years afterwards,
in 1616, the second part of the pastorals appeared, and
the reputation of the author rose in proportion to the
increasing excellence discovered in this more matured
production. The few particulars of his life which have
descended to us are so very scanty, that we are enabled
to trace only two or three leading incidents; but from
these it may be gathered that he was a man fond of
retirement and study, a lover of the country (which is
sufficiently attested in his poems), and so fondly devoted to tranquil and rural pursuits, that he felt no disposition to take any part in those fierce controversies
which disturbed the repose of nearly every one of his
literary contemporaries. It is to be presumed that
Browne was a puritan, although no very clear evidence
of the fact can be discovered in his writings; and in the
absence of more direct proof, his association with Withers,
who addresses two of his most remarkable pieces to him,
may be admitted as a collateral testimony of the colour
and tendency of his opinions. But, whatever may have
been Browne's political or religious tenets, he kept clear
of the turmoil, and while his friend was suffering imprisonment and confiscation for his daring pasquinades
and satires, Browne appears to have been calmly occupied in the service of the muses.

In 1624, probably actuated by a desire to escape the

tumult of the town, he returned to Exeter College, where he became tutor to Robert Dormer, earl of Caernarvon, who was afterwards killed at the battle of Newbury. At this time he was created M.A., and shortly after leaving the university, he was taken into the family of the earl of Pembroke, but how long he remained in that situation, or what ultimately became of him, is not known with certainty. All that has been further ascertained concerning him is, that he acquired some money, apparently through those channels of noble patronage to which his private character and scholastic attainments originally recommended him; that he purchased an estate; and that the latter part of his life was passed in tranquillity and ease at Ottery St. Mary's, in his native county, where he is conjectured to have died somewhere about 1645.

: The only work ascribed to him, in addition to the poems already referred to, is a series of lives of the English poets, from Joseph of Exeter down to his own time, which he is said to have undertaken and nearly completed ; but this work has never been traced, and its loss is justly regarded as the greatest our poetical biography has sustained. Several of his MS. poems were in the collection of the luckless Mr. Warburton, the herald, who has acquired so unfortunate a notoriety in our literary history, through the Ephesian misdemeanour of a careless servant ; but as they were not included in the papers burned in that memorable process of lighting the fire, having disappeared only on the dispersion of that gentleman's library after his death, there is yet some hope that they may be recovered. Whoever possesses them, if they be still in existence, is bound to give them to the world.

Browne's principal merit as a pastoral poet lies in his originality. He did not imitate any of the poets who preceded him ; he created his own form of pastoral, and derived his illustrations from nature herself. Wither evidently caught an occasional inspiration from his friend, which may be detected in some of the most

felicitous passages of the *Shepheard's Hunting.* *   Mr.
Southey is inclined to think that even Milton may be
traced to him ; but with the closer examples of Spenser
and Shakspeare, it may be doubted whether this conjecture is entitled to much consideration.   Browne's pastorals are singularly unequal, frequently deformed by
those allegorical conceits which the fashion of the time
can hardly be allowed to excuse in poems that were expressly designed to celebrate the simplest subjects, and
sometimes so weakened by the expansion and accumulation of images, that they would become tedious and
fatiguing, were it not for the predominant charm of manner that prevails throughout them all.   The faults of his
poems are to be referred to his want of skill, and not to his
want of sympathy, taste, or feeling. He possessed strong
sensibility, but did not always know how to render it sub-
servient to his purposes ; and hence, carried away by his
enthusiasm, he frequently extended his descriptions to
such a length, that, as we see in an overcrowded picture,
distinctness and identity are sacrificed to minuteness and
variety.   His streams, valleys, groves, mountains, and
plains, are brought before us with the accuracy of a survey, or the special fidelity of a catalogue raisonné ; and
instead of massing off the general effects, he gives us all
the particulars, with a conscientiousness that discovers
the fulness of his love of nature, at the cost of betraying
his deficiency in the art of poetry.   Thus, on arriving
at a grove to which his lovers repair for coolness, he
enumerates the different kinds of trees of which it was
composed, the elm, cypress, alder, plane, oak, ebony,
cedar, box, olive, vine, pine, yew, tamarisk, birch, wal-
nut, mulberry, maple, ash, laurel, myrtle, ivy, date, fir,
beech, adding, as if he apprehended that this plantation
was not sufficiently rich and variegated for his purpose,
that there were a thousand more besides.†   Now, without stopping to observe that a grove, embracing such a

---

* This poem has been reprinted entire in Mr. Southey's *Select Works of*
the British Poets, 1831.
† Britannia's Pastorals, first part, second song.

curious collection of different genera, is not very likely
to have been of spontaneous growth, and that it is more
suggestive of a nursery than a wild retreat in a remote
woodland dell, the very heaping up of the details dis-
tracts the attention of the reader, who, instead of being
led into the cool shade, as he expects from the induction, is stopped at the entrance, and required to perform
a sort of botanical pilgrimage before he is permitted to
rejoin the nymph and her lover who had tempted him
into this arboretical maze. Such passages are frequent
in these pastorals, and ultimately prolong them much
beyond the limits usually assigned to such compositions.
But it must be granted to Browne, that there is always
great truth and beauty in his delineations of nature; that
exquisite specimens of the purest poetry may be culled
from his works; and that, if they are never likely to become popular as a whole, they contain a multitude of
passages which have rarely been excelled in sweetness
and simplicity. With the exception of the incidental
intrusion of quaint ornaments, his figures are almost
invariably just and appropriate, his language fresh and
picturesque, and his versification varied and melodious.
That Thomson is indebted to this poet for some of the
more striking characteristics of his *Seasons*, might be
shown, I suspect, by a critical comparison of the two
works.

The popularity of Browne's poetry did not last long.
It was too delicate to flourish in the rough atmosphere
of those boisterous times, and soon drooped into oblivion *, in which it was buried until 1772, when a new
edition of his works was published by Davies the bookseller Since that time he has been occasionally recalled-

---

* So completely did Browne's poems fall into obscurity, that very few
passing allusions are made to him even by his contemporaries, and shortly
after his death his name seems to have been forgotten altogether. In a
collection of poems, chiefly pastoral, published in 1739 by Mr. Moses
Browne, a very tolerable versifier, I find a somewhat elaborate essay on
pastoral poetry, in which the writer, speaking of those English writers who
had preceded him, mentions the names of Milton, Congreve, Phineas
Fletcher, and others, but does not appear to be aware of the existence of
William Browne, who had certainly written the most remarkable pastorals
then existing in the language,

in fugitive criticisms and miscellaneous collections, and'
Mr. Southey has rendered his principal work, *Britannia's Pastorals*, generally accessible, by introducing·
it entire in his select works of the *British Poets*.

SIR JOHN STRADLING.

1563—1625.

JOHN STRADLING was the son of Francis Stradling,
who belonged to an ancient family residing at Saint
Donat's, in Glamorganshire. He was born in 1563,
in Gloucestershire, near Bristol, and was educated under
Edward Green, the learned prebendary of the cathedral
church of that city. At fifteen years of age he became a
commoner of Brasen-nose College, Oxford, and in 1583
took a degree in arts as a member of Magdalen Hall.·
At that time we are told that he was considered a
miracle for his "forwardness in learning, and pregnancy
of parts." He studied at one of the inns of court for
some time, and afterwards travelled on the Continent.
On his return, so great was his reputation for learning,.
that his society was courted by the celebrated Cambden,
sir John Harrington, and others. In 1597 he published three books, *De Vita et Morte contemnenda*,
which he dedicated to his uncle of St. Donat's Castle.
In 1607 he published four books of epigrams. Two
years afterwards he succeeded to his uncle's property,
settled at Saint Donat's, and in 1611 was made a baronet
in the general batch then created by James.
· Devoting himself to secular business, he wrote nothing·
more till the close of James's reign, when he published
*Beati Pacifici, a Divine Poem, written to the King's
most Excellent Majesty*. This was perused by James
before it went to press, and was printed by authority..
It came out in 1623. Two years afterwards he published *Divine Poems in Seven several Classes, written
to K. Charles I.* The subsequent fortunes of this gentleman are not known ; but we may safely conjecture, that

he employed "the even tenour of his way" between Parnassus and his Glamorganshire castle. A Mr. Harrington states, in a preface to Dr. George Stradling's *Sermons*, that there was scarce a gentleman of that age who
gained such universal esteem and respect by his writings
as sir John Stradling. This, however, is not probable,
nor like probability. Stradling was a mere rhymer,
pious, loyal, and lazy. He had neither the feelings nor
the energy of a poet. His *Divine Poems* have been
described by the bishop of Landaff, to whom he submitted a copy of them for his approbation of their orthodoxy in the following terms :

> " This booke's a sustæme theologicall,
> A paraphrase upon the Holy Bible;
> I wish, who stand upon their gentries, all
> Such poets were; instructed thus to scribble.
> No man could write the theory so well,
> Who did not in the practick part excell."

No one except this worthy prelate, and James I., and
Mr. Harrington, seems to have expressed any approbation
of Stradling's productions. His epigrams and essay on
Contempt of Life and Death do not appear to have attracted the slightest notice. Even Wood does not say
a word in their favour. The poem about Peace-
makers must have been as acceptable an offering to
James I., as the Paraphrase on the Bible to the bishop of
Lanaaff.

JOHN HOSKYNS.

1566—1638.

JOHN HOSKYNS was born at Mownton, in the parish
of Lauwarne, in Herefordshire, of a very humble family.
When he was a child, his father intended to put him to
a trade ; but he was so importunate with him to be made
a scholar, that he was at length sent to school at ten years
of age. So great was his progress, that before the lapse
of twelve months from the time he had commenced the

English alphabet, he began to learn the Greek grammar. After spending a year at Westminster school, he was sent, while still very young, to Wykeham's school at Winchester. At that time he was remarkable for extraordinary strength of body and a very powerful memory. In illustration of the latter faculty, an anecdote is recorded of him to the following effect. Having an exercise of verses to make one day, he neglected it through idleness, and, apprehensive of punishment, he read those of one of his schoolfellows over his shoulder just as he was finishing them. The master coming in immediately and demanding the exercises, called upon Hoskyns first. He at once said that he had lost his, but that he would repeat them if that would be sufficient. The master consenting, he repeated from sixteen to twenty verses of the other boy's composition ; who, when he presented them in writing, was condemned as the thief who had stolen from Hoskyns, and was severely punished for his misconduct. The anecdote is not creditable to his integrity or good feelings, but it is conclusive as to the powers of his memory. Hoskyns made such proficiency in the Winchester school, that he was elected probationary fellow of New College, Oxford, in 1584, and *verus socius* in 1586. In February, 1591, being then *terræ filius* *, he was so bitterly satirical in performing the exercises for the degree of M. A,. that he was not only refused the degree, but expelled from the university. Going into Somersetshire, he taught a school at Ilchester for a year or more, and compiled a Greek lexicon as far as the letter M. ; but marrying a rich widow, he abandoned the school, became a student in the Middle Temple, and was called to the bar. In 1614 he sat in the commons, and was committed to the Tower on the 7th June, for an allusion to the Sicilian vespers. There were four other members of the commons committed about the same time for misconduct in the house. Hoskyns was kept in prison for

* Wood.

a year, was then released, and subsequently held in high estimation for this martyrdom. He was chosen Lent reader to the Middle Temple in the 17th year of James's reign, made a serjeant-at-law four years after, and, finally, a justice itinerant for Wales and one of the council of the Marches. He was a person of very extensive acquirements ; an admirable Greek and Latin scholar, well read in divinity, a tolerable lawyer, a good poet, and a first-rate critic. All his friends were in the habit of submitting their compositions to him before they sent them to the press. We are told that it "was he who polished Ben Jonson the poet, and made him speak clean ; whereupon he ever after called our author father Hoskyns." Sir Walter Raleigh's *History of the World* was examined and reviewed by him before it was published ; and he reckoned amongst his immediate friends such men as Camden, Selden, Daniel, Donne, and Wotton. His opinions were always eagerly sought for by his contemporaries ; and he was so agreeable in company, that his society was generally courted. He fought a duel with Benjamin Rudyard, and wounded him in the knee ; but they were afterwards reconciled, and maintained the strictest friendship to the close of their lives. His works have never been published ; they are in manuscript, and in the custody of his descendants. They consist of a Greek Lexicon, imperfect ; epigrams and epitaphs, in Latin and English ; a law tract, and another on *The Art of Memory.* His own memory was said to have been—whether it was acquired or natural — the best in that age. Besides those works which are still in the possession of his descendants, Wood states that " he had a book of poems neatly written, bigger than those of Dr. Donne, which were lent by his son sir Benedick ('who was a man that ran with the usurping times') to a certain person in 1653, but he could never retrieve it." When he was imprisoned in the Tower, he wrote some verses which his wife presented to James. From these it appears that she had had three children by her former marriage, and one by him up to that time. A few of the first lines may convey some idea of his style.

" Meethought I walked, in a dreame,
Betwixt a cave's mouth, and a streame,
Upon whose bankes sate, full of ruth,
Three, as they seemed,—but foure, in truth ;
For, drawinge neare, I did behould
A widowe fourscore winters old,
A wife with child, a litell sonne
But foure years old, — all foure vndon.
Out of cave's mouth, cut in stone,
A prisoner lookt, whome they did mone;
Hee smiled, they sigh'd, then smoate his breaste,
As if he meant,— God knowes the rest !
The widdowe cry'd, lookinge to heaven,
Oh Phœbus, I thought I had seven ;
Like Niobe doe nowe contest,
Lend this thy light, this sonne, my best.
Taught for to speake and live in light,
Nowe bound to sylence and to night,
Why is hee closed in this cave,
Not basely bred, nor borne a slave?
Alas, this cave hath tane away
My staff and all the brother's stay.
Let that be least, that my grey haires
Goe to the grave, alas, with teares.
I greeve for thee, daughter, quoth shee
Thee and that boy, that babe unborne,
Hee lov'd as his, but nowe forlorne.
'T is not the rule of sacred 'hest
To kill the old one in the nest :
As good be kild as from them hydd ;
The dye with greefe : — O God, forbydd!
❋   ❋   ❋   ❋   ❋   ❋
If kings are men, if kings have wives,
And knowe one's death may coste two lives,
Then were it noe unkingly parte,
To save two lives in me, poore harte,
What if my husband once have err'd,
Men more to blame are more preferr'd.
Hee that offends not doth not live :
Hee err'd but once; — once, king, forgive !
Cæsar, to thee I will resorte,—
Longe be thy life, thy wroth but shorte

This praier goode successe may take,
If all do pray for whom he spake.
With that they wept, the waters swell'd,
The sune grewe darke, the darke caves yeld;
It brake my sleepe, I did awake,
And thought it was my harte that brake.
Thus I my wofull dreame declare,
Hopinge that no such persons are.
I hope none are ; but if there be,
God helpe them, pray ; — pray God with me. ”

Hoskyns died at his house at Morehampton in Herefordshire, on the 20th of August, 1638, at the age of
seventy-two, and was buried at the south side of the
choir of Dour Abbey, in that county.

Sir John Davies.

1570—1626.

John Davies, who is almost better known as a lawyer
than a poet, was born in 1570, at Chisgrove, in the
parish of Tysbury, in Wilts. He is said, by some, to
have been the son of a wealthy tanner of that place,
though in the books recording his admission to the
Middle Temple, his father is described as " late of New
Inn, gentlemen." He became a commoner of Queen's
College, Oxford, in 1585, and, by the aid of a good
tutor and his own natural abilities, soon acquired a
sound classical education. Though his genius was
calculated more for literature than law, he removed to
the Middle Temple as soon as he had become a bachelor of arts, and in July, 1595, was called to the bar.
He seems to have been selected by fortune as a particular favourite. Being of an ardent and hasty temper,
and happening to receive some slight provocation, he
flogged a Mr. Richard Martin — who was afterwards
recorder of London — in the common hall of the
Middle Temple, while he was at dinner. For this

offence he was expelled the society; upon which he
retired to Oxford, and there, ruminating upon his condition, composed the philosophical poem *Nosce Teipsum.*
This was the corner stone of his subsequent prosperity.
Procuring his re-admission to the society in Trinity
term, 1601, through the influence of lord Ellesmore,
the lord keeper of the great seal, he practised at his
profession, and was returned to the parliament which
was held at Westminster in 1601. On the death of
Elizabeth, he went with lord Hunsdon to Scotland to
congratulate James on his accession. His majesty,
inquiring of that nobleman about the names of the
gentlemen in his company, and hearing the name of John
Davies, immediately asked was he *Nosce Teipsum,* and
receiving an answer in the affirmative, most graciously
embraced him, and from thenceforth exhibited such a
regard for him, that in that year (1603) he made him
solicitor general for Ireland, and subsequently attorney
general, with a knighthood. Davies soon afterwards
was elected member for Fermanagh, and, upon a warm
contest between the protestants and the Roman catholics,
was chosen speaker of the first Irish house of commons
formed by a general representation. He returned to
England in 1616, sat in parliament for Newcastle under
Lyne, was made serjeant-at-law, frequently went
circuit as judge of assize, and was at length constituted
chief justice of the King's Bench; but, before he was
installed into the office, he died suddenly, of apoplexy,
on the 7th December, 1626. The robes for the new
office had been made for him; he went to bed quite
well at night, and was found dead in the morning. It
was rumoured at the time, that his wife, whose pro-
phetical character has been celebrated, had foretold
his death on the preceding Sunday. While they sat at
dinner (so the story goes) she suddenly burst into tears.
He asked what was the matter, and she answered,
" Husband, these are your funeral tears;" and he replied, " Pray, therefore, spare your tears now, and I
will be content that you shall laugh when I am dead."

By this mad lady * he had a son, who was an idiot, and a daughter, named Lucy. The son dying young, and Lucy consequently becoming his sole heiress, Ferdinando lord Hastings (afterwards earl of Huntingdon) sought her in marriage, on which occasion her father made this admirable anagrammatic epigram.

" LUCIDA VIS oculos teneri perstrinxit amantis,
    Nec tamen erravit nam VIA DULCIS erat. "

It is unnecessary to observe, that " LUCIDA VIS " form as close an approximation to Lucy Davies as the nature of the two languages will allow.

After his body had lain in state for some days, it was solemnly interred in the south aisle of the church of St. Martin in the Fields, and a slab was fastened in a pillar near his grave with an inscription commemorating his worth.

Davies was pronounced, by all his contemporaries, to have been more a scholar than a lawyer. By Selden Camden, Ben Jonson, and others, he was much esteemed for his sharp and ready wit, bold and active spirit, and very extensive literary acquirements. Nature and study had designed and prepared him for a poet and a man of letters, which he would have been, did not the lucky accident of having a royal pedant to admire his first essay open to him a brighter career. The very titles of the only works he published prior to his being made solicitor and attorney general of Ireland, prove clearly the tendency of his genius. These were—*Nosce Teipsum: This Oracle expounded in two Elegies;*—1. *Of Humane Knowledge;* 2. *Of the Soul of Man and the Immortality thereof. Hymns of Astræa in Acrostic Verse. Orchestra ; or, a Poem expressing the Antiquity and Excellency of Dancing, in a Dialogue between Penelope and one of her Wooers.* All these were published together in 1599, and were much admired, particularly the first,

* She was the lady Eleanor Touchet, daughter of George lord Audley earl of Castlehaven. Sir Archibald Douglas was her second husband, and she is said to have made them both miserable. But there appears to be no doubt that her intellects were deranged.

which has since gone, in a separate form, through several editions.   The following acrostic to Elizabeth, from the *Hymns of Astræa,* leaves a favourable impression of his talents in this department of fantastic and exploded composition.

" E arth now is greene, and heaven is blew,
L ively Spring, which makes all new,
I olly Spring doth enter,
S weet young sun-beams doe subdue
A ngry, aged Winter.

" B lasts are mild and seas are calme,
E very meadowe flowes with balme,
T he earth weares all her riches;
H armonious birds sing such a psalme,
A s ear and heart bewitches.

" R eserve (sweet Spring) this nymph of ours,
E ternall garlands of thy flowers,
G reene garlands, never wasting;
I n her shall last our state's faire Spring,
N ow and for ever flourishing,
A s long as heaven is lasting."

BARNABE BARNES.

1571— ——.

BARNABE BARNES was a younger son of Richard Barnes, bishop of Durham, and was born in Yorkshire about 1571.   At the age of seventeen he became a student of Brazenose College, Oxford, but left the university without a degree.   In 1591 he accompanied the earl of Essex in a military capacity into France, and remained there till 1594.   After his return, he wrote a few pieces, the latest of which was in 1607, but what finally became of him is unknown.   Wood says that " one Barnabe Barnes of the city of Coventry died " about 1644; " but what relation there was between this and the former Barnabe, or whether the same, I cannot tell." His character has been severely attacked, but with what truth or justice it is now impossible to determine. If we may rely upon Nash, he was accused of running away from the enemy in France, and of stealing a " nobleman's steward's chayne, at his lord's installing at Windsore." The veracity of Nash, however, is very equivocal in this case, as Barnes had sided with his antagonist, Gabriel Harvey, — which may have excited his spleen to the propagation of this calumny.

Barnes wrote a great number of songs, sonnets, madrigals, odes, and elegies ; besides a tragedy, and " four books of offices." A very small portion only of them now remain, and from these he appears to have been a writer of some simplicity and grace, and not destitute of refinement, although chargeable with the common defects which deformed the vernacular poetry of the age. Mr. Beloe, in his *Anecdotes of Literature,* gives an account of his *Parthenophil and Parthenope,* a collection of sonnets and madrigals, and a few specimens of the former may be seen in the *Censura Literaria.*

John Sandsbury.

1576—1609.

John Sandsbury was an ingenious Latin poet, of whom little more is known than that he was born in London in 1576, educated at Merchant-Tailors' School, made a scholar of St. John's College, Oxford, in 1593, that he graduated there, became vicar of the church of St. Giles, in the north suburb of that city, in 1607, was admitted to the degree of bachelor of divinity in 1608, and died in 1609. He wrote some Latin tragedies, and a poem, the most remarkable feature of which was that it contained sets of verses explanatory of the arms of each of the colleges of Oxford, and that each set conveyed some compliment to James I.

JOHN OWEN.

15— —1622.

JOHN OWEN* has been so celebrated as a Latin epigrammatist that his name cannot be omitted from the list of
the poets of his time. His epigrams were so universally
admired that they were explained in schools to children.
— that some of them were translated by " a puritanical
poet," who was usher of Christ Church Hospital,— that
a gentleman of the Inner Temple translated 600 of
them into English verse, which were published in 1569,
— that they have been all translated since, — and that
they were so eagerly sought after by all men of letters as
to procure a very extensive and rapid circulation, not
only in England, but on the continent.   Even so lately
as 1794, a neat edition of them was published in
Paris.

John Owen was the third son of Thomas Owen of
Plâdu in Llanarmon, in Cærnarvonshire, where he was
born. He was educated in Wykeham's school, entered
New College, Oxford, in 1582, and after two years'
probation, was made a perpetual fellow.   In 1590 he
took the degree of bachelor of civil law, and leaving his
fellowship the year after, taught school at Trylegh, near
Monmouth, and afterwards at Warwick, about the year
1594.   He published the first three books of his epigrams in 1606.   These went through two editions in
that year. The remaining seven books came out as successive additions to the several editions of the three first
books.   The whole had an extensive sale, and although
they brought the author an enviable fame, yet it appears
that he was " always troubled with the disease that
attends poets (indigence)." †

* He has been called *Audoenus* by some.   † Wood.

If history be "philosophy teaching by example," biography may be regarded as common sense giving instructions in a similar manner. Owen had an uncle from whom he expected legacies. This uncle was a catholic; and Owen, if he had possessed ordinary prudence, ought to have taken care to avoid offence in his epigrams, unless they were so very good that he might reasonably calculate upon deriving as much profit from his book as would compensate him for risking the loss of the legacies. But he was an epigrammatist, and despised calculations. In one of his satirical distichs he scoffed at the Catholic religion, which so much incensed his uncle that he struck his name out of his will; "which was the reason," says the chronicler already quoted, "that he ever after lived in a poor condition." *
The lines which produced this catastrophe are said to have given quite as much offence to the Roman inquisitors, who put the book in which they were contained into the *Index Expurgatorius*. The offending distich may be quoted as a curiosity, considering the price which the author paid for his joke:—

"An Petrus fuerit Romæ, sub judice lis est,
  Simonem Romæ nemo fuisse negat."†

He was not, however, totally neglected by his contemporaries. Dr. Williams, bishop of Lincoln, and, for a time, lord keeper of the great seal, who was his kinsman and countryman, extended his patronage to him, and "for several years exhibited to his wants." ‡ He died in 1622, and was buried in St. Paul's cathedral, Dr. Williams bearing the expenses of his funeral, and erecting a monument to his memory, next to the consistory stairs, with his effigy crowned with laurel, and six verses engraved under it. The two first of these belong pro-

* Wood.
†   "Whether at Rome Peter e'er was or no,
  Is much disputed still, I trow;
  But Simon's being there, on neither side
  Was ever doubted or denied."
Wood.

perly to his history, as being descriptive of the relative
bulk of his book, person, and property —

" Parva tibi statua est, quia parva statura, supellex
Parva volat parvus magna per ora liber."

JOHN DAVIES.

15— —1618.

JOHN DAVIES, who was almost equally distinguished
as a writing master and a poet, was a native of the city
of Hereford. Of his early life few traces have been preserved. Wood says that he studied in Oxford, but that
he did not take out a degree.. It would seem, however,
that he went there only for the purpose of giving instructions in penmanship. He obtained the reputation
of a good poet at an early age, and even while teaching
caligraphy at Oxford, he was known by the title of
Oxoniæ Vates. He attempted to make out a subsistence
by his poetical talents, and published some songs, elegies,
and eclogues, and a volume of religious pieces; but, fail-
ing in this ambitious line, he was obliged to set up as a
writing master, first in Herefordshire, and afterwards
in London, in which latter place we are told that he was
at length esteemed the greatest master of his pen that
England, or, as some of his admirers said, the world, in
his age beheld ; "first, for fast writing ; fair writing,
which looked as if it had been printed ; close writing ;
and various writing, as secretary, Roman, court, and
text-hand."* His eulogists have raised a question
amongst themselves as to whether he occasionally visited
Oxford after he settled in London ; but it is certain
that he praised the university at all times, and in the
following verses especially, as a liberal and " beloved
patronesse."

* Wood.

" For, like a lady full of royaltie,
She gives me *crownes* for my *characterie,*
Her pupils crowne me for directing them,
Where like a king I live without a realme.

     *   *   *   *

But, in a word, to say how much I like thee,—
For place, for grace, and for sweet companee,
Oxford is heaven, if heaven on earth there be."

The members of Magdalen College appear to have
been his particular patrons. Why he should not have
spent his days where he was so singularly favoured, instead of enduring the worst sort of privations in London,
the scanty fragments collected of his biography do not
state ; but, perhaps, he liked to be in the close neighbourhood of the booksellers, to whom he was a most indefatigable contributor. Some opinion of the fecundity
of his genius may be formed from the catalogue of his
publications, which comprises no fewer than twenty-four
volumes, many of them containing several pieces, and
written on every variety of subject, from an *Anatomy
of Fair Writing,* up to religious hymns and essays, elegies, songs, satires, and sonnets. Yet, although he was
considered a good poet, and was singularly industrious in plying his faculties, and was also the first pen-
man of his day, it appears that he did not escape the
common lot of penury. His distresses came early
and heavily upon him, for he tells us that he was made
grey by poverty and suffering before he was five and
thirty.

He died about the year 1618, and was buried within
the precincts of the church of St. Giles in the Fields,
according to Fuller. Wood says that he finds " one
John Davies, gent., to have lived in the parish of St.
Martin in the Fields, who, dying in the beginning of
July, or thereabouts, in 1618, was buried near to the
body of Mary, his sometimes wife, in the church of St.
Dunstan in the West. Whether the same with the poet,"
he adds, " I cannot tell." His contemporary brethren

differed in their estimates of his abilities. One says that he wrote

> " The rascall'st rimes were ever read;"

but by the great majority he seems to have been re-garded as a "good poet," and one of them goes so far as to declare that he was " another Martial."

.THOMAS LODGE.

———— —1625.

THOMAS LODGE was of a respectable Lincolnshire fa-mily. According to Wood he entered Oxford about 1573, where his talents for poetical compositions soon came to be noticed; but Langbaine and Jacob, and after them Wincop and Chetwood, refer his education to Cambridge. When he took his degree of A.B. he left the university, became a soldier, and made a voyage to the Canaries with a captain Clarke. Returning to England, he de-voted himself to poetry, and published some sarcastic compositions, which at once secured him a pre-eminence amongst the satirists of that day; but, probably, find-ing that poetry was not likely to be a very lucrative pro-fession, he turned to the study of medicine about the year 1584, went to Avignon, where he obtained the degree of doctor, and did not return to this country till about the year 1592 or 1593. In that interval he ap-pears to have extended his travels to South America, as he states that " being at sea four years before with M. Cavendish," he found the original of his *Margarite of America* in the Spanish tongue in the library of the je-suits at Sanctum, and that he translated it in the ship passing through the straits of Magellan. *Margarite* was published in 1596, and from that time he continued to compose various pieces, principally songs, sonnets, and satires, till 1610, when the last of his works was printed. He wrote four comedies, *A Treatise in Defence of*

Plays, and *A Treatise on the* P*lague*. Having been in-' corporated in Oxford, according to Wood, or admitted to the same degree which he obtained in Avignon, soon after his return, he practised as a physician in London with great success, which attended him to the close of his career. He was particularly patronised by those of the catholic religion, to which he was suspected by many to belong. He first resided in Warwick Lane, in the beginning of the reign of James, and afterwards. on Lambert Hill, whence he finally removed into Old Fish Street, in the parish of St. Mary Magdalen. There he died, very soon after, in the month of September, 1625, of the plague, as it is generally supposed. He was esteemed by his contemporaries as a man of distinguished abilities. His translations of Josephus and Seneca prove him to have been a good scholar. One of his contemporaries, disposed to be severe on him, and considering him unassailable on other points, censures him particularly for writing too frequently.— or, as he says, putting "his oar in every paper-boat." This charge was no doubt well founded, as Lodge's verses are to be found in nearly all the contemporary gatherings of poetry.

SIR THOMAS OVERBURY,

1581—1613.

THOMAS OVERBURY was born in the parish of Ilmingtou in Warwickshire, in 1581. He was the son of Nicholas Overbury, of Boorton-on-the-Hill in Glocestershire. He became a gentleman commoner of Queen's College, Oxford, in 1595, and, through the aid of a good tutor and severe discipline, made rapid progress in philosophy and logic. In 1598 he, as a "squire's son," took the degree of bachelor of arts, and soon after left the university, and settled in the Middle Temple. He travelled for some time on the continent, and on his return home, had the reputation of being an accomplished person. In 1608, through the influence of Sir Robert Carre, afterwards earl of Somerset, he obtained the honour of knighthood for himself, and a Welch judgeship for his father. Some years after this time, perceiving a familiarity arising between his friend Carre, then viscount Rochester, and lady Frances the wife of Robert earl of Essex, he cautioned him against the danger of such a course. Carre, offended at his honest boldness, disclosed the conversation to lady Essex, who immediately resolved on effecting his ruin. The office of ambassador to Russia or the Netherlands having been subsequently offered to him, be consulted Carre, who recommended him to refuse it. Not doubting the honesty of the motives which produced this insidious advice, he acted on it, refused the service, and was committed to the Tower on the 21st of April, 1613. Such were the liberal views of James and his ministers, with regard to the almost treasonable offence of refusing to take employment under them.

In the following September this victim of an English nobleman was despatched by poison. Two months had scarcely elapsed, however, when suspicions arose; the cause of his death was closely investigated, and several persons were convicted of having been concerned in it. Sir Jervice Elwaies, lieutenant of the Tower, by consenting to it, Richard Weston and James Franklin, by giving him the meats and broths in which the poison was mingled, and Anne Turner, by preparing them, — all these persons were executed; and Carre, then earl of Somerset, and lady Frances, to whom he had been previously married, were soon afterwards tried and found guilty of contriving his death and hiring others to effect it. The capital punishment was remitted by the crown, and they were merely banished from court. The difference in the measure of the punishment awarded to · the plotters and their instruments cannot fail to beget a due respect for his majesty's sense of justice.

Sir Thomas Overbury was much esteemed by Ben Jonson* and the other wits of his day. It has been said that the consideration in which his learning and judgment were generally held made him, while living at court, so excessively proud as to incur the enmity of several persons whom he seemed to undervalue; and, probably, to this foolish vaingloriousness much of his subsequent misfortunes may be traced. He wrote several works in prose and verse, the principal and best of which is, *A Wife; being a most exquisite and singular Poem of the Choice of a Wife.* This piece was so applauded by his contemporaries that it had run through several editions during his lifetime; and after his death, the title being changed to *A Wife, now the Widow of Sir Thomas Overbury; being,"* &c., it went through four or five editions more with this altered title before the close of 1614. It contains several passages of great merit, and affords an abundant justification of the esteem in which his talents were held. Detailed notices of his works will be found in the *Censura* and the *Retrospective Review.*

RICHARD CORBET.

1582—1635.

RICHARD CORBET, better known in his own day as a facetious bishop, than a poet, was the son of Vincent Corbet, who is said to have filled the humble situation of a gardener at Twickenham. He was born in 1582 at Ewell in Surrey, received a good education at Westminster School, was sent, at fifteen years of age, to Broadgate's Hall, Oxford, became a student of Christ Church in the following year, and in 1605 took out the degree of M.A. He appears already to have distinguished himself amongst the wits and roysterers of the university; for at this time, according to Wood, he

* See the epigram to him in the 1st vol. of *Jonson's Works*, Epigr. 113.

was considered one of the most eminent of them all "for poetry, jestings, and romantic exploits and fancies." Entering the church, — which we can hardly suspect to have been the object of his own choice, — he soon acquired celebrity for the quaintness and excellent fancy of his discourses, — qualities which were so highly esteemed by James I., that he made him one of the royal chaplains, and promoted him, shortly afterwards, to the deanery of Christ Church in Oxford, he being then a D.D., a senior student of Christ Church, vicar of Cassington, near Woodstock, in Oxfordshire, and prebendary of Bedminster Secunda in the cathedral of Sarum. Church preferments now flowed rapidly upon him. In 1629, he was made bishop of Oxford, and in 1632 he was translated to the bishopric of Norwich. During the progress of his prosperous fortunes he undertook a journey into France, of which he wrote a lively and amusing narrative; and married a daughter of Leonard Hutton, vicar of Flower in Northamptonshire, by whom he had a son and daughter.

Corbett was a complete personification of that jolly and dare-devil species of ecclesiastic, who flourished in those lax times, when convivial talents promoted a man's progress in the church with greater certainty than the strictest principles and the most decorous conduct. He had extraordinary constitutional vivacity, was a capital boon companion, had great heartiness of temperament, a perpetual flow of animal spirits, a prompt and convivial wit, and a faculty of writing agreeable and lively verses, which were recommended alike by their gracefulness and their pleasantry. A genius so wild and intemperate was not likely to confer much credit upon the sacred office; but it is, perhaps, honourable to him, that he never affected any hypocrisy in his habits or demeanour, and that, even in the midst of his irreverent courses, he acquired much regard by the liberality with which he invariably promoted public designs for the advancement of religion. The anecdotes that are related of his private life are certainly not very favourable to the development either of poetical taste or pious desires. On one occasion, he is said, in a freak of fancy, to have sung ballads at the High' Cross, at Abingdon. He chanced to be carousing at a tavern in that town, when a mendicant ballad singer came into the house, complaining that he could not procure purchasers for his stock; the doctor—for it does not appear that he had then attained the dignity of bishop—exchanged dresses with the itinerant vocalist, and, assuming his leather jacket, went out into the street, where he soon drew around crowds of admirers. At other times, he would shut himself up in his wine-cellar with his chaplain, Dr. Lushington, and, throwing off his gown, exclaim, " There goes the doctor ;" then his episcopal hood, " There goes the bishop;" devote the remainder of the night to ." potations deep and strong." One day, riding out with Dr. Stubbins, who was a very fat man, the coach happened to be overturned, and they were both thrown into a ditch. Describing the adventure afterwards, the bishop used to say that Dr. Stubbins was up to the elbows in mud, and he was up to the elbows in Dr. Stubbins. Such are the characteristic records which have been preserved of this episcopal poet. He never distinguished himself as a divine ; but his sentiments, as far as he took any trouble in giving effect to them, were liberal ;—and he is believed to have inclined to the Arminian party, which was then growing up in the church of England.

The poems of bishop Corbet, principally written in his youth, and never intended by the author to be printed, were not published until 1647,—twelve years after his death. They were issued under the title of *Poetica Stromata*, and were reprinted three times. The last edition, with a short biography by Mr. Octavius Gilchrist, appeared in 1807. They are chiefly remarkable for the easy flow of the measure, sprightliness of fancy, and simplicity of expression.

Bishop Corbet died on the 28th of July, 1635, and was buried at the upper end of the choir in the cathedral church of Norwich. He seems to have con-

sidered himself extremely fortunate in two very essential
particulars; and, in one of his poems, hopes that his son,
to whom the verses are addressed, may inherit his good
luck, as the best blessing he can bestow upon him.

> " I wish thee all thy mother's graces,
> Thy father's fortunes, and his places!"

SIR JOHN BEAUMONT.

1582—1628.

JOHN BEAUMONT was the second son of Francis Beaumont, one of the justices of the Common Pleas in the
reign of Elizabeth, and of an ancient and noble family
living at Grace Dieu, in Leicestershire, where he was
born in 1582.   At the age of fourteen, with his elder
brother Henry and younger brother Francis, the celebrated
dramatic poet, he became a gentleman commoner of
Broadgate's Hall, Oxford, in 1596.   After spending
three years there, he removed to the inns of court. This
period of his life he employed in cultivating letters, in
making translations from the Latin poets, and exercising
his own talents in composition.   He appears to have
been a person of very correct taste, and no inconsiderable ability as a poet; and it is to be regretted that he
did not devote a greater part of his life to an art which
he was so well qualified to adorn.   The following lines,
Concerning the true Forme of English Poetry, afford a
favourable specimen of his discrimination and taste:—

> " He makes sweet musick, whom serious lines,
> Light dancing tunes, and heauy prose declines;
> When verses like a milky torrent flow,
> They equall temper in the poet show.
> He paints true formes, who, with a modest heart,
> Giues lustre to his worke, yet couers art.
> Vneuen swelling is no way to fame,
> But solid ioyning of the perfect frame,
> So that no curious finger there can find
> The former chinkes, or nailes that fastly bind.

Yet most would haue the knots of stiches seene,
And boles where men may thrust their hands between.
On halting feet the ragged poem goes,
With accents neither fitting verse nor prose;
The stile mine eare with more contentment fills
In lawyer's pleadings or physician's bills;
For though in termes of art their skill they close,
And ioy in darksome words as well as those,
They yet haue perfect sense more pure and cleare
Then enuious Muses, which sad garlands weare
Of dusky clouds, their strange conceits to hide
From humane eyes; and (lest they should be spi'd
By some sharpe Œdipus) the English tongue
For this, their poore ambition, suffers wrong.
In eu'ry language now in Europe spoke
By nations which the Roman empire broke,
The rellish of the Muse consists in rime,—
One verse must meete another like a chime.
Our Saxon shortnesse hath peculiar grace
In choise of words, fit for the ending place,
Which leaue impression in the mind, as well
As closing sounds of some delightfull bell.
These must not be with disproportion lame,
Nor should an eccho still repeate the same.
In many changes these may be exprest,
But those that ioyne most simply run the best:
Their forme surpassing farre the fetter'd staues,
Vaine care and needlesse repetition saues.
These outward ashes keepe those inward fires,
Whose heate the Greeke and Roman works inspires:
Pure phrase, fit epithets, a sober care
Of metaphores, descriptions cleare yet rare,
Similitudes contracted, smooth and round,
Not vext by learning, but with nature crown'd:
Strong figures drawne from deepe inuention's springs,
Consisting lesse in words and more in things:
A language not affecting ancient times,
Nor datiue shreds by which the pedant climes;
A noble subject which the mind may lift
To easie vse of that peculiar gift
Which poets in their raptures hold most deare,
When actions by the liuely sound appeare.—
Giue me such helpes, I neuer will dispaire,
But that our heads, which sucke the freezing aire,
As well as hotter braines, may verse adorne.
And be their wonder as we were their scorne."

After spending some time in the inns of court, he retired to Leicestershire, and married Elizabeth, the daughter of John Fortescue, esq., devoted himself to serious pursuits, and was made a baronet in 1626. He died, at the early age of forty-six, in the winter of 1628; and was buried at Belton—and not, as Wood says, in the church at Grace Dieu,—which was not then erected.

He left seven sons and four daughters. John, the eldest, his immediate successor, a man of extraordinary physical powers, was killed at the siege of Gloucester, and was succeeded in title and estates by his brother Thomas. Francis, another son, and the author of some verses on his father's memory, is said to have become a Jesuit. Of Gervase, who died young, we have no record except some verses in which his father lamented his death. The works of sir John Beaumont—consisting of translations from Horace, Virgil, Lucan, Persius, Claudian; *Bosworth Field*, the most considerable of his poetical productions; and other pieces—were collected by his son John, and published in 1629, with commendatory verses by himself and his brother Francis, by Hawkins, George Fortescue, Ben Jonson, and Drayton. Sir John was also the author of a poem called *The Crown of Thorns*, mentioned by Wood; but it has escaped the researches of the collectors. None of his poems were published during his lifetime, and only a part of them have been reprinted since. Dryden, alluding to his death, seems to suggest obscurely the cause of it in the following lines:—

" Thy care for that, which was not worth thy breath,
Brought on too soon thy much-lamented death.
But Heaven was kind, and would not let thee see
The plagues that must upon this nation be,
By whom the Muses have neglected been,—
Which shall add weight and measure to their sin."

It is in vain, now, to conjecture to what circumstances in the life of the poet this dark allusion bears reference.

HUGH HOLLAND.

———1633.

HUGH HOLLAND—who is said by Fuller to have been not a bad English, but an excellent Latin poet; and to whom others have assigned no mean rank, even among the best of our earlier writers — was born at Denbigh, and educated at Westminster School, while Camden taught there. He was elected into Trinity College, Cambridge, 1589; and was afterwards made a fellow. He subsequently went to travel; and while he was at Rome, we are informed that " his overfree discourse betrayed his prudence."* But what his discourse was, is not stated. The probability is, that it had a strong political tendeney, as we are subsequently informed that he was always *in animo Catholicus.* We learn, also, that he was so enthusiastic in his religious feelings, that he went to Jerusalem " to pay his devotions to the holy sepulchre;" and that, on his way back, touching at Constantinople, he was reprimanded by the English ambassador for " the former freedom of his tongue." What the language could be, which a devotee of the holy sepulchre should utter, and which should be displeasing alike to the pope and the protestant ambassador, it is very hard to conceive, unless it were of a political character. As to how Holland spent his time, nothing is known, except that, after his return to England, he remained for a few years at Oxford. He does not appear to have ever been subjected to the misfortunes that too frequently befell his contemporaries; nor even, indeed, to have been dependent on his own exertions for his subsistence. His works were not numerous; — *Verses in Description of the Chief Cities of Europe; Chronicle of Queen Elizabeth's Reign; Life of William Camden, Cla-*

Wood.

renceaux King at Arms ; and *A Cypress Garland for
the Sacred Forehead of the late Sovereign King James."*
The last was a poem published in London, in 1625.
The first three have not yet appeared out of manuscript.
From his epitaph written by himself, in which he says
that he is *"miserrimus peccator Musarum et amicitia-
rum cultor sanctissimus,"* as well as from his devotional
visit to the sepulchre, it may be conjectured that he was
a man of a pious turn of mind. As a poet, his claims to
distinction are very slender. He died in July, 1633,
in Westminster; and was buried in the abbey church of
St. Peter.

WILLIAM SLATYER.

1587—1647.

WILLIAM SLATYER matriculated in St. Mary's Hall,
Oxford, in 1600, describing himself at the time to be
the son of a Somersetshire gentleman, and only thirteen
years of age. Removing in 1607 to Brazenose College,
he was entered there as a "plebeian's son of the same
county." The following year he was made fellow of
that house; in 1611, entered into holy orders; obtained
a benefice soon after ; and in 1623 became a D.D. In
1625 he obtained the rectory of Otterden, in Kent, and
a dispensation to hold it with that of Newchurch — to
which it is supposed he had been first presented. He
also held the office of treasurer to the cathedral church
of St. David's. He wrote several elegies and epitaphs
to the memory of queen Anne, to whom he describes
himself to have been " late servant and chaplain."
These consisted of Hebrew, Greek, Latin, and English
verses, printed in several forms — some like pillars, some
circular, and some chronogrammatically. In 1621 he
published his *Palæ-Albion ; or, the History of Great
Britain, from the first Peopling of the Island to the Reign
of King James.* This was written in Latin and En·

glish verses, with the Latin on one side and the English on the other. The former, strangely enough, are immeasurably superior to the latter, of which the subjoined lines are a very fair specimen : —

" Faine would I visit Phœbus shrine,
And Dodon oracles diuine,
Parnassus hill, and Phocis fields,
That sacred cells, and solace yeelds;
Pierian sisters, honored nymphs,
Lau'd and ador'd by learning's imps,
Pallas, faire Sol, and Memnosine,
O gently fauour my designes,
And shew me out of stories old
The warlike acts of Britons bold;
Or guide me to the towre of fame.
To find their first birth, ere heauen's frame,
Or earth, or sea was, Chaos was;
And out of that confused masse,
Nature's commander did produce
Bright stars from heauen, heauen for earth's vse ;
The flow'ry vales, the hills and woods,
Fresh riuerets, and salt swelling floods;
And earth, and aire, and sea, brought forth
Their wond'rous creatures, sundrie sorts l
The golden sunne appeares in skie,
And dainty showres in clouds on hie,
Whiles Atlas on his shoulders beares
The burden of the starry spheares."

As a poet, his fame was not very great ; yet he appears to have possessed ability enough to have achieved success, if he had possessed courage to persevere ; but neglect, probably, chilled his efforts, and induced him to avail himself of a more accessible road to fortune. Accordingly, we find him publishing, in 1630, the *Genethliacon, sive, Stemma,* in which he traced the genealogy of James I. up to Adam. What effect this production produced, either on his reputation or his temporal prosperity, we are not informed ; for the next and last notice we find of him is, that he died in October or November, 1647, at Otterden, where he was buried.

RICHARD BRATHWAYTE.

1588—1673.

RICHARD BRATHWAYTE was the second son of Thomas Brathwayte, of Warcop, near Appleby, in Westmore-
land. He entered Oriel College, Oxford, in 1604,
being then sixteen years of age, describing himself at
his matriculation as a native of Northumberland. While
he remained at Oxford, he studied history and poetry,
and eschewed the more difficult and unpleasant paths of
crabbed logic and philosophy. After spending three
years there, he went to Cambridge; and having remained
there some time, returned to the North, where his father
presented him with an estate. His life was that of an
independent country gentleman, refined by tranquil enjoyment of his literary tastes. But his rank in the
county forced him to take a personal interest in public
affairs, and he became captain of a foot company in the
trained bands, and a deputy lieutenant of Westmore-
land. On marrying a second wife (of his first there
is no record), he removed to Appleton, near Richmond,
in Yorkshire, where he died on the 4th of May, 1673,
carrying with him the universal respect of his friends.

Brathwayte was a voluminous writer of essays on
general and moral subjects, and of epigrams, satires,
odes, elegies, and sonnets. Some of these were highly
esteemed by his contemporaries, although none of them
have survived the age in which they were written. Their
titles — *A Strappado for the Divel; The Poet's Willow, or
the Passionate Shepherd; Odes, or Philomel's Tears; Love's
Labyrinth; A Congratulatory Poem to his Majesty upon
his happy Arrival in our late discomposed Albion; Time's
Curtaine drawne on the Anatomie of Vanitie, with other
choice Poems, entituled, Health from Helicon* — may sufficiently indicate the character of his productions, and the

justice of the sentence which consigned them to oblivion. In addition to the charge of poverty of invention, and a most fantastic turn of language, apparently employed to conceal it, Brathwayte is vulnerable to the charge of having indulged in a vein of coarse licentiousness, which, even in his own age, must have been offensive to the more educated portion of his readers.

GEORGE SANDYS.

1588—1643.

GEORGE SANDYS was a younger son of Edwin Sandys, archbishop of York. He was born at Bishop's Thorpe, in Yorkshire; and was educated at Oxford, where he matriculated in 1589, at the very early age of eleven. The interval to 1610 is a blank; but, in the August of that year, he proceeded to the Continent on his travels, according to the custom of the age. During an absence of two years from England, he visited the greater part of the Turkish dominions in Europe and Asia, and the remote parts of Italy, up to that time not much frequented by travellers. To Greece, Rome, Venice, Egypt, and the Holy Land, he directed particular attention; and upon his return home he published an account of his travels in a folio volume, which ran through seven editions, with a title-page as full of matter as an index. This work was not less novel, but a great deal more sensible, than the *Crudities* of Tom Coryate; became very popular; and continued to be read long after the death of the author. Sandys afterwards published a translation of the first five books of Ovid's *Metamorphoses*, and of the first book of the *Æneid* of Virgil, in 1626. In a second edition, he published a translation of all the *Metamorphoses*, and inscribed it to the king and queen in two poetical addresses. The following charming and fanciful lines, from the address to the queen, are characteristic of his general style: —

" The Muses, by your fauour blest,
Fairie queene inuite you to their feast;
The Graces will reioyce, and sue,
Since so excel'd, to waite on you.
Ambrosia tast, which frees from death,
And nectar, fragrant as your breath,
By Hebe fill'd, who states the prime
Of youth, and brailes the winges of time.
Here, in Adonis' gardens grow
What neither age nor winter know :
The boy, with whom Love seemed to dy,
Bleeds in this pale anemony.
Selfe-loued Narcissus, in the myrror
Of your faire eyes, now sees his error,
And from the flattering fountaine turnes.
The hyacinth no longer mournes,
This heliotrope, which did pursue
Th' ador'd sun, converts to you.
These statues touch, and they agen
Will from cold marble change to men.
Chast Daphne bends her virgin boughs,
And turnes to imbrace your sacred browes :
Their tops the Paphian myrtles moue,
Saluting you their Queene of Love."

This translation was so highly esteemed, that an eighth edition was called for in 1690. Sandys published, in 1636, a poetical paraphrase of the Psalms of David, and the hymns dispersed through the Old and New Testaments : and in 1638 a second edition, with Ecclesiastes, Job, and the Lamentations of Jeremiah. This book was so very ably executed, that it became one of the favourite volumes of Charles I., which he delighted in reading while he was confined in Carisbrooke. In 1676, some, if not all, of this version of Psalms were set to music by Henry and William Lawes, celebrated by their connection with the immortal lyrics of Milton.

The metrical correctness of Sandys's versification, and the advance he made beyond the majority of the minor poets of his time, in the music of his rhythm, may be exemplified by a passage from his *Hymn to the Deity*.

" How infinite thy mercy ! which exceeds
The world thou mad'st, as well as our misdeeds !

Which greater reverence thy iustice wins,
And still augments thy honour by our sins.
O! who hath tasted of thy clemency
In greater measure, or more oft, than I!
My gratefull verse thy goodnes shall display,
O thou, who went'st along in all my way
To where the morning with perfumed wings
From the high mountaines of Panchæa springs,
To that new-found-out world, where sober night
Takes from th' antipodes her silent flight;
To those darke seas, where horrid winter reignes,
And binds the stubborne flouds in icie chaines:
To Libyan wastes, whose thirste no showres asswage,
And where swolne Nilus cools the lion's rage.
Thy wonders in the deepe have I beheld,
Yet all by those on Judah's hills excell'd;
There, where the Virgin's son his doctrine taught,
His miracles, and our redemption wrought;
Where I, by Thee inspir'd, his praises sung,
And on his sepulchre my offering hung;
Which way so e're I turne my face or feet,
I see thy glory, and thy mercy meet.
Met on the Thracian shores; when in the strife
Of frantick Simoans thou preserv'dst my life.
So when Arabian thieves belaid vs round,
And when, by all abandon'd, Thee I found.
That false Sidonian wolfe, whose craft put on
A sheepes soft fleece, and me Bellerophon
To ruine by his cruell letter sent,
Thou did'st by thy protecting hand prevent.
Thou sav'dst me from the bloody massacres
Of faith-les Indians; from their treacherous wars;
From raging feavers; from the sultry breath
Of tainted aire, which cloy'd the jawes of death.
Preserv'd from swallowing seas, when towring waves
Mixt the clouds, and open'd their deepe graves.
From barbarous pirats ransom'd; by those taught,
Successfully with Salian Moores we fought:
Then brought'st me home in safety, that this earth
Might bury me, which fed me from my birth:
Blest with a healthfull age, a quiet mind,
Content with little; to this worke design'd;
Which I at length have finisht by thy aid,
And now my vowes have at thy altar paid."

Sandys was considered a very accomplished gentleman, and a great linguist. As a poet, he ranked deservedly high. Dryden, with more justice than has ever since been conceded to his memory. pronounced him to be the first versifier of his age ; Pope confessed that he had read him with delight,—observing, in his notes to the *Iliad,* that English owed some of its beauty to his translations; and Warton was of opinion that he did more to polish English versification, than either Denham or Waller. Nor is his prose less entitled to distinguished praise. Whittaker observes, that " the expressive energy of his prose will entitle him to a place amongst English classics, when his verses — some of which are beautiful — shall be forgotten."

Of the incidents of Sandys's life, after his return from the Continent, few particulars have been preserved. A great part of his time is supposed to have been spent with sir Francis Wenman, of Caswell, near Witney, in Oxfordshire, who was married to his sister ;—a situation which he may have chosen in consequence of its proximity to the residence of his friend lord Falkland. From an elegy written to him by Drayton, after the publication of the five books of Ovid's *Metamorphoses,* it would appear that he was then in Virginia, or that he was connected, as treasurer, with that colony. At the time of his death, which occurred in March, 1643, at the house of his niece, Lady Margaret Wyat, at Boxley Abbey, in Kent, he was—or a short time previously had been—one of the gentlemen of the privy chamber to Charles I. He was buried in the neighbouring parish church,· but no memorial was raised over his grave, although he is described in the parish register as " *poetarum Anglorum sive sæculi facile princeps.*"

SIR FRANCIS WORTLEY.

1591— ——.

FRANCIS WORTLEY, born in 1591, was the son of sir Richard Wortley, of Wortley, in Yorkshire, by

Elizabeth, daughter of Edward Boughton, of Canston, in Warwickshire, esq., and who, after the death of sir Richard, married William Cavendish, earl of Devonshire. At seventeen years of age he became a commoner of Magdalen Hall, Oxford. In 1610 he was made a knight; and, in the following year, a baronet. After retiring from Oxford, he settled on his estate in the North, and was esteemed particularly for his hospitable, charitable, and social qualities. In the retirement of the country, he sedulously cultivated his taste for literature; and, in 1641, published a poem entitled *His Duty delineated in his pious Pity and Christian Commiseration of the Sorrows amd Sufferings of the most virtuous yet misfortunate Lady Elizabeth Queen of Bohemia,*— commencing with the following lines, which may be quoted not only as a fair exemplar of his manner, but of the Christian toleration of his sentiments.

> " If all the vertues which the critticks call
> Virtues divine, and vertues cardinall,
> If these together mixed with royall blood,
> Can scarcely make a claim to merit good;
> If her great merits could not impetrate
> So much, as not to bee unfortunate,
> And in misfortunes to exceed so farre
> As if the worst of all her sexe shee were :
> How light would be our best works in Heauen's skale,
> If shee thus farre in point of merit faile.
> Had shee beene Rome's, her supprerogation
> Had beene sufficient for the Brittish nation;
> And would have made the papall sea as great
> As Rome was, when it was Augustus' seate."

When the civil war broke out, sir Francis Wortley joined the royalists, raised a troop, and fortified his own house, Wortley Hall, in the service of the king. For his exertions in the royal cause he was raised to the rank of colonel; but when the republicans triumphed, be was committed to the Tower, and confined there for several years. During his imprisonment, he endeavoured to alleviate his solitude by writing some pieces, which afterwards appeared, in 1646, under the title of *Characters and Elegies*. The latter were written mostly on those loyalists who had fallen in the course of the rebellion. In the following year he published *A Loyal Song of a Royal Feast kept by the Prisoners in the Tower*. He was at length released, but deprived of nearly the whole of his estate, and obliged to compound for the remainder. The precise period of his release is not known : it has been ascertained, however, that applications respecting the disposal of his estate were made in parliament in the month of March, 1656,—though he had compounded for part of it previously. The loss of his property involved him deeply in debt, and he retired for security to the White Friars, near Fleet Street: but whether he lived to see the monarchy restored, cannot now be determined. From Granger's account of a rare head of him, by A. Hertocks, it might be supposed that he died in 1652 ; but it is conceived by a later authority, who appears to have seen the inscription attached to this head, that it meant " only that he was prisoner in the Tower in that year."* He was succeeded in his estates by his son sir Francis Wortley, the last baronet of the family.

As a poet, sir Francis attained little eminence. He is entitled to be recorded amongst the poets, chiefly because he was noted amongst the writers of his party, and because subsequent commentators have occasionally considered it necessary to refer to him.

DAVID LLOYD.

1598—1663.

DAVID LLOYD, the author of *The Legend of Captain Jones*, a poetical romance which appeared in 1648, was the descendant of an ancient family settled in the parish of Llanidloes, in Montgomeryshire. At the age of four-

* Bliss.

teen he became a clerk or chorister of All Souls College, Oxford, in 1612; was elected probationer fellow in 1615; perpetual fellow, in 1616; and took the degrees in civil law in 1628. He afterwards became chaplain to the earl of Derby, and controller of his house, according to the statements of some writers. From December, 1641, to December, 1642, he was promoted to no fewer than three livings in Wales. The wardenship of Ruthyn, in Denbighshire, he obtained, probably, about the same period; though this is not very certain. During the civil wars, he exerted himself strenuously for the royalists, and suffered a long imprisonment for his devotion to the monarchy. After the restoration he was not forgotten, and was rewarded by the deanery of St. Asaph, a prebendship of Chester; and another ecclesiastical appointment, the title of which has escaped record. Notwithstanding all this good fortune, he ran himself, by his generosity, so much into debt, as to expose himself to the malicious ribaldry of some wag, who wrote the following epitaph on him : —

> " This is the epitaph
> Of the dean of St. Asaph,
> Who, by keeping a table
> Better than he was able,
> Run into debt
> Which is not paid yet."

These lines, it is but fair to observe, were, by some people, suspected to have been written by himself. He died in the winter of 1663; but when, or where, the chronicles do not state.

Besides his legend of *Captain Jones*, he wrote several songs, sonnets, elegies, &c.—which, however, have not been published in a separate form. The legend of *Captain Jones* was a burlesque in imitation of a Welsh poem. From the following address to the reader, a very favourable impression is left of his facility as a versifier : —

> " Reader, y' have here the mirrour of the times,
> Old Jones wrapt in his colours and my rimes.

Receive him fairly, pray—nor censure how
Or what he tells; the matter hee'l avow;
And for the forme he speaks in, I 'll maintain it,
It comes as neere his veine as I could straine it.
For 't were improper to set forth an asse
Capparison'd, and trammell a great horse.
My tract claims no invention's praise, for (know it)
His last deeds, here epitomized, intreat
Some thundering pen to set them forth compleat.
Let him whose lofty Muse will deign to doe it,
Drinke sack and gunpowder, and so fall to it."

SIR JOHN MENNES.

1598—1670.

JOHN MENNES, who wrote the greater part of the book
called the *Musarum Deliciæ*, was the third son of An-
drew Mennes, esq. of the parish of St. Peter in Sandwich, Kent, where he was born on the 1st March,
1598. He was educated at the free grammar school in
that place, until he reached the age of seventeen, when
he entered Corpus Christi College, Oxford, as a commoner. After remaining there for some years, and
attaining a considerable acquaintance with poetry, history, and the lighter parts of a university education, he
became a great traveller, and devoted himself with so much
success to the study of naval architecture and maritime
affairs, that he was considered to be more skilful in the
construction, navigation, and the fighting of vessels,
than any person of that age. In the reign of James 1.
he had a place in the Navy Office; and was made comptroller of it in the reign of Charles I. It appears that
it was not then deemed inconsistent for the same individual to hold appointments both in the army and the
navy; and accordingly we find this shipbuilder and sailor
enjoying also a command as militia captain in 1631, and
as a captain of a troop of horse, in the expedition against
the Scots, in 1639. When the civil war broke out, he
continued faithful to the royal cause. In 1641 he was

knighted at Dover, holding at that time the rank of vice-admiral. In 1642 he commanded the Rainbow while the earl of Warwick was vice-admiral; and when the royal cause declined on shore, he adhered to prince Rupert on the seas, till the latter also was unsuccessful, when he joined Charles II. in exile. He was always of a warm, gay, and lively temperament, and was enabled, by his florid spirits, and the practical philosophy of cheerfulness, to bear up more easily against the troubles and privations of exile. In person he was stout and vigorous; in disposition honest, sincere, and generous; well skilled in physic and chemistry, and endowed with considerable talent in poetry. He wrote, besides his contributions to the *Musarum Deliciæ*, a poem entitled *Epsom Wells*, a mock poem on sir William Davenant, and a variety of ballads and other temporary pieces. On the restoration he was made governor of Dover Castle, and chief comptroller of the navy. He died in the Navy Office, in Seething Lane, on the 18th of February, 1670, and was buried at the upper end of the chancel of the church of St. Olave's in Hart Street, where a neat monument was erected over his grave.

The *Musarum Deliciæ* was written in conjunction with Dr. James Smith, and consisted of a collection of verses, entitled by the authors "pieces of poetique wit." There were also scattered through the volumes a few stray poems of bishop Corbet and sir John Suckling. Dr. Smith was the son of the rector of Merston in Bedfordshire, was born about 1604, and educated at Oxford. He was afterwards chaplain to the earl of Holland (admiral of the squadron), and to the earl of Cleveland. Through the interest of these noblemen he obtained a benefice in Lincolnshire, from whence he was removed to the living of Kingshimpton in Devonshire, which he subsequently changed for that of Alphington in the same county, where he died in 1667. Amongst a variety of poetical productions, he was the author of certain anthems, which, in Wood's time, continued to be sung in the cathedral at Exeter. Smith is said to have been much esteemed by Massinger, Davenant, and the wits of the day.

The *Musarum* is a very indifferent collection of fugitive poetry, and, with the exception of some half dozen pieces, could hardly have conferred much credit upon its authors. But sir John Menues obtained considerable notoriety by the celebrated ballad on sir John Suckling's preparations for the Scottish war, beginning—

" Sir John got him an ambling nag," &c.—

which is the principal, if not the only, performance by which he is now remembered. It is a little curious that this ballad was printed in the *Musarum Deliciæ,* which also contained some contributions from the very poet it criticised. A brief account of it is given in the *Censura Literaria,* and in *Ellis's Specimens.*

WYE SALTONSTALL.

16—— ——.

WYE SALTONSTALL's poetical works are few and rare. They are — *Picturæ Loquentes, or Pictures drawne forth in Characters ; A Poem of a Maid,* which was published in 1631 ; and *Funerall Elegies, in English, Latin, and Greek, upon the Death of his Father, Sir Samuel Saltonstall, Knight.* These elegies are only three in number, one in each language. · The English elegy extends to 370 lines. In this publication he betrays more of the characteristics of a pedant than a poet, summoning to his aid " the encyclopaid of arts,". as grammar, logic, rhetoric, &c., in order " to expresse their severall parts" in eulogising his father. The following lines, from that portion where history is introduced, will exemplify his manner of treating these singular topics.

" By death his spanne of life now measur'd is,
Hee seated in the high degrees of blisse.
But Historie, that life vnto death brings,
And registers the famous acts of kings,
Whoe is both witnesse and the lyght of tymes,
That shewes how states, and men, and all declines;
Let her with angell's quills sett downe his storye,
And write a legend to his lasting glorye;
And, as the etymon of her name defines,
Write chronicles which onely honour tymes,
And from obliuion doth preserue the dust
Of worthy men, deposited in trust;
In him a various subject shee shall finde;
In younger dayes the sunn of fortune shin'd
Upon his vertues, and did find her eyes
To crown him with her choice felicityes."

He does not appear to have acquired much celebrity
as a poet, though his translations of some of the Latin
classics, and his *Clavis ad Portam; or a Key fitted to
open the Gate of Tongues, wherein you may readily
find the Latin and French for any English Word,*
printed at Oxford in 1633, and dedicated to all schoolmasters and ushers, procured him a considerable reputation among the scholars of his age. He was born in
Essex, of a highly honourable and ancient family, and
educated as a commoner in Queen's College, Oxford.
There his progress in letters, combined with his respectable descent, tempted him to indulge in flattering
anticipations of literary success which he never realised.
Leaving Oxford without a degree, he studied the common
law in Gray's Inn for some time, and, going afterwards
to travel, became a perfect master of the French language. On his return to England, he retired to the
university in 1625, and remained there for several
years. He afterwards published the *Clavis ad Portam,*
besides poems and translations, at different intervals.
In 1640, he was living in London as a tutor in the
French and Latin languages; but of when or where he
closed his days, no record has been preserved. His
translations of *Ovid's Heroical Epistles* appeared in

1677 ; but it was, probably, a posthumous publication.
That his fortunes were not very prosperous, may be inferred from a slight observation of Wood, who, alluding
to his translation of *Ovid's Tristia*, adds, that his life
was " all *Tristia.*"

ROBERT GOMERSALL.

1600—1646.

ROBERT GOMERSALL was the eldest son of a gentleman of the rank of an esquire, and was born in
London about the year 1600. At the age of fourteen,
he entered Christ Church, Oxford, was shortly afterwards elected a student on the royal foundation, took
the degree of M. A., entered holy orders, and became ¦
known as a very florid preacher in the university. In ᵛ
1628, he was admitted to the reading of the sentences.
His publications consist of a tragedy, sundry sermons,
Poetical Meditations on the 19*th and* 20*th Chapters of
Judges,* and a volume of miscellaneous poems. These
appeared successively from 1628 to 1638. His poems
were reprinted twice. Gomersall is claimed as a dramatist in the *Biographia Dramatica,* and as a divine of
some celebrity in most of the general biographical miscellanies. His talents as a poet are agreeably exhibited
in the following very graceful lines : —

> " How we dally out our dayes,
> How we seeke a thousand wayes
> To find death ! the which, if none
> We sought out, would shew vs one.
> Why then doe we iniure fate,
> When we will impute the date
> And expiring of our time
> To be her's, which is our crime?
> Wish we not our end ? and, worse,
> Mak't a pray'r which is a curse?
> Does there not in each breast lye
> Both our soule and enemy ?

" Neuer was there morning yet,
(Sweet as is the violet,)
Which man's folly did not soone
Wish to be expir'd in noone;
As though such an hast did tend
To our blisse, and not our end.
Nay, the young ones in the nest
Sucke this folly from the breast,
And no stammering ape but can
Spoyle a prayer to be a man. "

No account remains of what was his final fortune.
It is probable that the star of the preacher culminated
over that of the poet, and that he retired in his latter
days to the serene enjoyments of some rural cure of
souls.   During the time of the plague at Oxford, he
resided at Flower in Northamptonshire, and was afterwards vicar of Thorncombe in Devonshire, where it is
presumed he died in 1646.

ROBERT WILD.

16— —1679.

ROBERT WILD is entitled to a place amongst the
poets, chiefly on account of the celebrity he enjoyed as a
" wicked versifier " during the later years of the commonwealth, and subsequently. He was one of the most
distinguished of that extravagant rout of poets who were
annihilated by the severer and loftier style of Dryden.
According to Wood, he was created bachelor of divinity
at Oxford in November 1642, and afterwards became a
covenanter and rector of Aynoe in Northamptonshire.
An anecdote is recorded of him during his residence in
that place to the following effect: — " Mr. Robert
Wild," says the narrator, " parson of Aynce, preaching
before the judges, March 4. 1654, and using many witty
and tart expressions, reflecting partly on the times and
partly on the persons there present, Dr. Owen, the vice
chancellor, gave this character of him : — that he knew

not the man ; but, by his preaching, he guessed him to
have been begotten by Hugh Peters in his younger years.
Wild used to relate this story of himself." Such was
the character of the man all throughout his life—hot-
tempered and misjudging. His publications were very
numerous, consisting of sermons, *Letters on Liberty of
Conscience,* a comedy, tracts, and several poems. The
most remarkable of his poetical productions was the
Iter Boreale, described in the title-page as an attempt at
something upon the successful and matchless march of the
lieutenant general George Monk from Scotland to London.
It was originally printed in 1660, and ran through numerous editions, having acquired extraordinary popularity amongst the citizens of London. Some of his
pieces were published, together with a few of Rochester's,
in a collection entitled *Rome Rhym'd to Death* — the
genuineness of which, however, has been doubted.

The characteristics of Wild's poetry are, pungent humour, coarseness, and metaphorical profusion. Dryden,
in his *Essay on Dramatic Poetry,* describes the popular
fashion of that day, by which the meaning of words was
so wantonly tortured, a *catachresis,* or Clevelandism, and
he speaks of Wild as *un mauvais buffon.* " He is the
very Withers," observes that acute critic, " of the city ;
they have bought more editions of his works than would
serve to lay under all their pies at the lord mayor's
Christmas. When his famous poem first came out, in
the year 1660, I have seen them reading it in the midst
of 'Change time ; nay, so vehement they were at it, that
they lost their bargain by the candles' ends. But what
will you say, if he has been received amongst great
persons ? I can assure you he is this day the envy of
one who is lord in the art of quibbling, and who does
not take it well that any man should intrude so far into
his province." Probably Dryden here alluded to Rochester, against whom he had sufficient cause of jealousy
when his lordship took his most inveterate antagonist
under his special protection.

Wild, was distinguished on the presbyterian side for

the same sort of qualities, but with a very inferior genius, which obtained so much reputation for Clieveland on the other side. He is described to have been a fat, jolly, and boon presbyterian. He died at Oundle in Northamptonshire, in the winter of 1679. Two poems were written on his death, the one entitled *A Pillar on the Grave of Dr. Wild;* the other, *A Dialogue between Death and Dr. Wild.* Whether they were intended to be serious or satirical, can now hardly be determined.

Thomas Randolphe.

1605—1634.

Thomas Randolphe was one of the choicest spirits of the age, a man who into the compass of a short life appears to have crowded all the delights of a long experience, who sprang to the maturity of his powers while he was yet a minor, and who was highly estimated for his brilliant talents in society by the most distinguished wits of his time. The outlines of his career are brief, and but a few facts concerning him have been preserved, although his name is to be frequently found in all the miscellaneous collections of the seventeenth century. He was born at Newnham in Northamptonshire, on the 15th of June, 1605, was educated at Westminster School, where he was a king's scholar, entered Trinity College, Cambridge, in 1623, of which he afterwards became a fellow, and was subsequently incorporated at Oxford with the degree of master of arts. His whole life was a passage of pleasure; the greater part of his time was spent in London, in the company of Ben Jonson and his circle of poets, dramatists, and critics; he was one of the most constant frequenters of those immortal hostelries, the Sun, Dog, and Triple Tun, where his joyous and spiritual nature added new lustre to the " lyric feasts" that filled the attic nights of his celebrated contemporaries; and he acquired so distinguished a reputation amongst them that he was joined with Cartwright as the adopted son, in the Muses, of "rare Ben,"—a distinction which alone is sufficient evidence of the estimation in which he stood with that rich "clustre" of genius. Doubtless these intoxicating excitements, early entered into, and earnestly enjoyed, contributed to terminate his bright career, while he was yet meditating some great work to justify his fame with posterity. He was "untimely killed" by his own quick soul, which prematurely wasted his powers ; and at twenty-nine years of age he died at the house of William Stafford, esq., of Blatherwyke in Northamptonshire, and was buried in the parish church, where a beautiful white marble monument, wreathed with laurel, and inscribed with a Latin and English epitaph, was erected to his memory by sir Christopher (afterwards lord) Hatton.

Randolphe did not publish any of his poems, nor does he appear to have written any with that view. But the greater part of them were collected into a volume by his brother, and published after his death. It consists of *The Muse's Looking-Glass*, a comedy ; *Amyntas, or the impossible Dowry*, a pastoral drama ; *Jealous Lovers; Aristippus, or the Jovial Philosopher;* and *The Conceited Pedlar*, with a variety of minor poems. In addition to these he wrote *Hey for Honesty, down with Knavery*, which was published subsequently. All these poems exhibit evidences of a sprightly fancy, of rapid invention, a shrewd knowledge of character, and no inconsiderable erudition. They are, no doubt, much deformed by a prurient imagination, and it may be presumed that many of them were never designed by the author for any more extended circulation than they obtained in the first instance amongst his admiring, roystering companions, in the night clubs of London. Of all the writers of that age who have been allowed to fall into oblivion, it may be confidently affirmed that he produced the most exquisite poetry; and, although his entire works are not calculated for popularity, an expurgated edition of them would be a grateful undertaking. If the objectionable passages were carefully excluded, the remainder would be likely to survive as long as the works of the seventeenth century should continne to be read. At nine years of age his genius discovered itself in an elaborate poem called the *History of the Incarnation of our Saviour*, and such was his facility in composition, that Owen Feltham tells us he could write faster than others could think.

> " Such was his genius, like the quick eye's wink,
> He could write sooner than another think ;
> His play was fancy's flame, a lightning wit,
> So shot, that it could sooner pierce than hit."

It is supposed that he acted at one period as moderator in Cambridge ; and the following testimony is borne to the effect he produced upon the logicians and philosophers of the university : —

> " The grave divines stood gazing, as if there
> In words was color, or in the eye an ear ;
> To hear him they would penetrate each other,
> Embrace a throng, and love a noisome smother."

It would appear also that he was received at court, — a circumstance which Feltham obviously alludes to in the following lines, —

> " Was he at court ? his compliments would be
> Rich wrought with fancy's best embroidery ;
> Which the spruce gallants, echo-like, would speak
> So oft, as they 'd be threadbare in a week ;
> They lov'd even his abuses, the same jeer,
> So witty 't was, would sting and please the ear."

The variety of styles in which Randolphe wrote exhibits a very rare command of the humorous, pathetic, and descriptive ; and he seemed to be quite as much at his ease on a playful and sportive theme, as when he was moralising upon the passions, or painting some piece of divine beauty. On one occasion, happening to fall into a quarrel in a tavern, he lost the little finger of his

left hand, which was unfortunately cut off in the affray;
but instead of grieving over this calamity, he consoled
himself in the following snatch of lively conceits :—

" Arithmetique nine digits, and no more
Admits of, then I still have all my store :
For, what mischance hath ta'ne from my left hand,
It seems did only for a cypher stand.
But this I 'll say for thee, departed joynt,
Thou wert not given to steal, nor pick, nor point
At any in disgrace, but thou did'st go
Untimely to thy death, only to show
The other members what they once must do :
Hand, arm, leg, thigh, and all must follow too.
Oft didst thou scan my verse, where if I miss,
Henceforth, I will impute the cause to this.
A finger's losse (I speak it not in sporte)
Will make a verse sometimes a foot too short.
Farewell, dear finger, much I grieve to see
How soon mischance hath made a hand of thee."

As a different specimen of his powers, a fragment from
a "platonick elegy" may be selected.

" Here, give me leave to serve thee, and be wise
To keep thy torch in, but restore blind eyes.
I will a flame unto thy bosom take,
That martyrs court when they embrace the stake ;
Not dull and smoky fires, but heat divine,
That burns not to consume, but to refine.
I have a mistress for perfection rare
In every eye, but in my thoughts most fair.
And wheresoe'er my fancy would begin,
Still her perfection lets religion in.
I touch her like my beads, with devout care,
And come into my courtships, like my prayer.
We sit and talk, and kiss away the hours,
As chastely as the morning dews kiss flowers."

Frequently, through his poems, some fine moral lessons
are extracted from trite and ordinary topics, as in some
lines upon his picture, which are not less remarkable for
their truth than for the vigour and beauty of the versification.

" When age hath made me what I am not now,
And every wrinkle tells me where the plough
Of time hath furrowed ; when an ice shall flow
Through every vein, and all my head be snow ;
When death displays his coldness in my cheek,
And I myself in my own picture seek,
Not finding what I am, but what I was;
In doubt which to believe, this or my glass ::
Yet, though I alter, this remains the same
As it was drawn, retains the primitive frame,
And first complexion ; here will still be seen
Blood in the cheek, and down upon the chin ;
Here the smooth brow will stay, the lively eye,
The ruddy lip, and hair of youthful dye.
Behold what frailty we in man may see,
Whose shadow is less given to change than he."

The dialogue of his plays sometimes reaches the boldness of Massinger, and not unfrequently anticipated the delicacy and sweetness of a later age. His character of the epicure has been justly compared to the sir Epicure Mammon of Ben Jonson, and, as a complete picture of a strange species of accomplished and refined sensuality, may be, perhaps, considered to transcend even that memorable portrait. A few broken passages from this picture will suffice to exhibit Randolphe in an aspect which he needed only years and leisure to cultivate with as much success as even his poetical godfather achieved.

" O now for an eternity of eating !
Fool was he that wished but a crane's short neck ;
Give me one, Nature, long as is a cable,
Or sounding line, and all the way a palate,
To taste my meat the longer. I would have
My senses fast together ; Nature envied us
In giving single pleasures ; let me have
My ears, eyes, palate, nose, and touch, at once
Enjoy their happiness ; lay me in a bed
Made of a summer's cloud ——
　　　＊　　＊　　＊　　＊　　＊
Nor cease I here. Give me the seven orbs
To charm my ears with their celestial lutes,
To which the angels, that do move those spheres,

Shall sing some amorous ditty : nor yet here
Fix I my bounds ; the sun himself shall fire
The phœnix' nest to make me a perfume,
While I do eat the bird, and eternally
Quaff off eternal nectar. These, single, are
But torments ; but together, oh, together !
Each is a paradise. Having got these objects
To please the senses, give me senses too
Fit to receive those objects ; give me, therefore,
An eagle's eye, a bloodhound's curious smell,
A stag's quick hearing ; let my feeling be
As subtle as the spider's, and my taste
Sharp as a squirrel's ; then I 'll read the Alcoran,
And what delights that promises in future,
I 'll practise in the present."

The poet who wrote such lines as these is assuredly
deserving of being rescued from the obscurity in which
he has been suffered to lie amongst the almost forgotten
versifiers of his day.

JOHN CLIEVELAND.[*]

1613—1658.

THROUGHOUT the stormy period of the civil war, John
Clieveland was the most popular poet in England —
enthusiastically admired by one party, feared and read by
the other : his verses were received and circulated with
enthusiasm, and such was the popularity he enjoyed,
that his lines were coined off into familiar epigrams,
and constantly used in reference to the public men and
events of the time. One couplet of his, from the most
celebrated of his works, still survives, and is occasionally repeated ; it seems to have been preserved by the
salt of national prejudice : —

" Had Cain been Scot, God would have changed his doom,
Not forced him wander, but confined him home."

[*] The name is variously spelt by different writers ; sometimes Cleveland,
sometimes Clievelande, and so on. Wood has it Cleaveland.

A more elliptical or rugged couplet than this has rarely found its way into popular favour. Verses that grow into " household words " are usually fluent and obvious; but in Clieveland's case, his worst passages were generally the most frequently quoted, because they were generally the most venomous and satirical.

John Clieveland was the son of the Rev. Thomas Clieveland, vicar of Hinckley, and rector of Stoke, in Leicestershire, and was born, in 1613, at Loughborough. The family originally came from the North Riding of Yorkshire, and derived their name from a large tract of country which is still called Clieveland.* He received the rudiments of a good education at Hinckley, under Mr. Vines, a schoolmaster. On the 4th September, 1627, he was entered at Christ's College, Cambridge, where he took his degree of bachelor of arts in 1631. He subsequently removed to St. John's College, of which he became a fellow at twenty-one years of age, and there took his degree of master of arts, in 1635. This was the most useful and tranquil part of his career. His talents had attracted so much notice, especially his skill in Latin prose composition, in which he excelled, and of which some very remarkable specimens are still extant, that he was appointed rhetoric reader; an appointment which imposed upon him the duty of preparing speeches and addresses for public occasions — a duty which he performed with great credit to himself and the university. His time was chiefly occupied by tuition, and he had the honour of educating several pupils of distinguished ecclesiastical rank and literary celebrity. Amongst these were Dr. Lake, bishop of Man, Bristol, and Chichester, and Dr. Drake, vicar of Pontefract, who conjointly edited an edition of his poems in 1667, entitled *The Clievelandi Vindiciæ*, and dedicated to Dr. Turner, bishop of Rochester and Ely, another of his pupils. Clieveland seems to have been originally intended for the church, but to have subsequently changed

* The pedigree of the family is amply detailed in Nash's *History of Worcestershire*, and in Nichol's *History of Hinckley*.

his mind. He was admitted on the law register in November, 1640, and in January, 1642, took a degree in physic, but never practised either of these professions, his office of reader occupying the whole of his time. Bishop Lake speaks of him during this period in terms of the highest eulogy. " He lived," says the bishop, " about nine years, the delight and ornament of that society. To the service he did it the library oweth much of its learning, the chapel much of its pious decency, and the college much of its renown.'   ?

He did not manifest any disposition to take a promi‑ nent part in the contentions that were then undermining the peace of society, until Cromwell became a candidate, in 1641, to represent the town of Cambridge in parlia‑ ment, after having been elected by stratagem in the previous year. On that occasion, Clieveland at once took his stand on the side of the royalists, from which cause, amidst surrounding dangers and defection, he never afterwards swerved. His opposition to Cromwell was so strenuous and powerful as to draw upon him a large share of that persecution which, in the heat of the subsequent struggle, fell heavily on the king's friends ; although it must be allowed that Cromwell treated him with great generosity at a moment when he might have crushed the stubborn poet, with ample justification of precedent and circumstances.

When the election was over, and Cromwell's return was secured, Clieveland is said to have predicted the couse‑ quences, exclaiming. with passionate and prophetic fer‑ vour, "That single vote has ruined both church and state." Upon this occasion, Dr. Lake observes of Clieveland, that " no man had more sagacious prognostics." But it has been acutely noted of Clieveland's prediction that, like many others, it was not published till after the event.

The zeal of Clieveland was no sooner inspired by the contest at Cambridge, than he seems to have reso‑ lutely committed his fortunes to the desperate cause he had thus chivalrously espoused. He is said to have been the first poetical champion of the monarchy at the breaking out of the civil war ; and never had monarchy a champion so fierce, so heedless of consequences, so bold, and so self-sacrificing. The main characteristic of the poems in which he celebrated his devotion to the king, is rampant scurrility. They exhibit a temper of mind. so coarse and vindictive, that it is only surprising the courtly friends of the falling Stuart did not repudiate so vulgar an ally. Had he appeared on the opposite side, he would doubtless have been run down as the poet of the kennels, and his whole party would have been implicated in his offensive ribaldry. But the king's side had ceased to be a tower of strength — the success of the parliament had driven his majesty to the last expedients — men of vigour and original genius were wanted to work upon the public mind — any kind of help was welcome to the retreating royalists — and when Clieveland was compelled to abandon his cloisters by the advance of the triumphant puritans, and to take refuge at the king's head quarters at Oxford, he was received with as much distinction as if he had. brought a legion of mounted soldiers in his train. It is evident, from the estimation in which he was held, that his pungent and abusive verses produced an extraordinary effect upon the public. They were admirably adapted to the purposes they were meant to serve ; and although it is utterly impossible to discover anything in them worthy of praise at this distance of time, yet it is easy to detect those qualities which at the instant of publication made such a vivid and universal impression. He seized with singular felicity upon all the watchwords of party— the traits of personal and sectarian peculiarity — the accidents that every now and then befell the leaders of the parliamentary forces — and, distorting every thing he touched into the most ridiculous shapes, contrived to bring into contempt some of the most sacred and honoured emblems, doctrines, and apostles of the mighty movement against which he combatted. These pieces had something of the effect of broad caricatures, in which the likenesses are faithfully preserved, but ludicrously exaggerated ; yet they were by no means humorous, for Clieveland had scarcely a particle of humour in his nature ; they were filled with scoffing venom, were animated by a most riotous spirit, and their edge, wanting the fine keenness of the Damascene blade, hacked and mangled their victims like a blunt but weighty axe.

His principal poem was a satire called *The Rebel Scot*, to which national antipathies and angry party animosities gave great vogue. He hit the tender points with such certainty, and with so little compunction, that his blow always struck deep. Even his opponents could not help admitting that they would rather have had so unscrupulous a satirist with them than against them, however much they might have disliked so uncongenial an associate. *The Rebel Scot* was esteemed to be a work of so much interest and power that it ran through many editions, and was translated into Latin by one Gawen, a protestant clergyman who embraced the church of Rome. The reader of the present day, however, would be perplexed to find out its claims to such distinction, and would be more likely to condemn its bad taste and vicious tendency than to applaud its wit or its poetry. It continued for a long time to have a great sale, and to be reprinted very frequently, up to the middle of the seventeenth century. Its popularity survived the death of the author by nearly twenty years, the last edition bearing the date of 1687. Such was the reputation it acquired for Clieveland, that Edward Phillips says he was esteemed by some grave men of his time, " in regard that his conceits were out of the common road, and wittily far-fetched, to be the best of English poets ; " and Anthony à Wood tells us that he was " the most noted poet of his time." If far-fetched conceits constitute the excellence of poetry, this award was unquestionably just, for Clieveland's conceits transcended even the most extravagant flights of Donne and his imitators. But the whole of that class of poetry has perished by the gangrene of those very elements in which contemporary criticism declared its greatest merits to reside. The worst productions of Clieveland — those which were most deformed by metaphysical conundrums and florid excesses — were the most popular of all his works; while the few pieces he wrote in a better and purer style, which alone redeemed and vindicated his genius, and which alone are worthy of being revived by posterity, hardly excited any notice amongst his contemporaries, and rapidly passed away into oblivion. It has been said, with great truth, of Clieveland, that he was one of those, who have at one time been too much praised, and at another been too much neglected.

The subsequent life of this eccentric poet was as wayward and luckless as the fortunes of the party he served. During his absence at Oxford, the parliament very properly ejected him from his fellowship at Cambridge, for it was scarcely to be expected that a man who occupied so conspicuous a position at the head quarters of the king, could be suffered to retain his emoluments by the favour of the king's enemies. In this strait, his friends endeavoured to make some compensation to him for the loss he suffered by his loyalty, and accordingly conferred upon him the office of judge-advocate in the fortress of Newark. But such favours were of little value. The king could only confer offices — he could not insure their permanency. Shortly afterwards the garrison of Newark surrendered to the army of the parliament, and Clieveland was driven forth upon the world, without any regular means of support, and reduced to the utmost difficulties to sustain existence.

After wandering about the country for some time in great distress and obscurity, subsisting upon the incidental bounty of his brother loyalists, he was at last apprehended in 1655, at Norwich, by some over-zealous and officious persons, as one whose ability rendered him dangerous to the state. This act of severity appears to have been altogether gratuitous on the part of those who captured him, for, notwithstanding the steadiness of his known attachment to the royal family, whose cause was

now considered to be hopeless, and the rashness with
which he always avowed it, the unfortunate poet committed no fresh transgressions against the dominant party ·
at this period, but, on the contrary, conducted himself
with a temperance and discretion that could not have
been anticipated from so reckless and vehement a partisan. He was condemned, however, to expiate his former offences in prison, at Yarmouth, where he remained
until an opportunity presented itself of appealing to
Oliver Cromwell for his liberation, The petition he
drew up on this occasion exhibits such remarkable skill
in the treatment of the topics upon which it bears, that
it is well worthy of a place in his biography. The
adroitness with which he developes all the points likely
to excite the commiseration and deprecate the anger of
the protector, and the integrity which he manifests at
the same time in the assertion and defence of his principles, confer a permanent interest upon this curious document.

"MAY IT PLEASE YOUR HIGHNESS.— Rulers, within
the circle of their government, have a claim to that which
is said of the Deity — they have their centre everywhere,
and their circumference nowhere. It is in this confidence that I address to your highness, as knowing no
place in the nation is so remote, as not to share in the
ubiquity of your care ; no prison so close, as to shut me
up from partaking of your influence. My lord, it is
my misfortune, that after ten years of retirement from
being engaged in the difference of the state, having
wound myself up in a private recess, and my comport-
ment to the public being so inoffensive, that in all this
time, neither fears nor jealousies have scrupled at my
actions. Being about three months since at Norwich, I
was fetched with a guard before the commissioners, and
sent prisoner to Yarmouth ; and if it be not a new offence to make inquiry where I offended (for hitherto
my faults are kept as close as my person), I am induced
to believe, that, next to the adherence to the royal party,

the cause of my confinement is the narrowness of my
estate; for none stand committed whose estate can bail
them : I only am the prisoner, who have no acres to be
my hostage. Now, if my poverty be criminal (with
reverence be it spoken), I must implead your highness,
whose victorious arms have reduced me to it, as acces-
sory to my guilt. Let it suffice, my lord, that the
calamity of the war hath made me poor : do not punish
us for it. Who ever did penance for being ravished?
Is it not enough that we are stript so bare, but it must
be made in order to a severe lash? Must our scars be
engraven with new wounds? Must we first be made
cripples, then beaten with our own crutches? Poverty,
if it be a fault, it is its own punishment; who suffers
for it more, pays use upon use. I beseech your highness, put some bounds to our overthrow, and do not
pursue the chase to the other world. Can your thunder
be levelled so low as our grovelling conditions? Can
that towering spirit, that hath quarried upon our king-
doms, make a stoop at us, who are the rubbish of those
ruins? Methinks I hear your former achievements
interceding with you not to sully your glories with
trampling on the prostrate, nor clog the wheels of your
chariot with so degenerous a triumph. The most renowned heroes have ever with such tenderness cherished
their captives, that their swords did but cut out work
for their courtesy. Those that fell by their prowess
sprung up by their favours, as if they had struck them
down, only to make them rebound the higher. I hope
your highness, as you are the rival of their fame, will
be no less of their virtues ; the noblest trophy that you
can erect to your honour, is to raise the afflicted. And,
since you have subdued all opposition, it now remains
that you attack yourself, and with acts of mildness
vanquish your victory. It is not long since, my lord,
that you knocked off the shackles from most of our
party, and by a grand release did spread your clemency
as large as your territories. Let not new proscriptions
interrupt our jubilee. Let not that your lenity be slan-

dered as the ambush of your further rigour.   For the
service of his majesty (if it be objected), I am so far
from excusing it, that I am ready to allege it in my.
vindication. I cannot conceive fidelity to my prince
should taint me in your opinion; I should rather expect
it should recommend me to your favour ; had not we
been faithful to our king, we could not have given ourselves to be so to your highness ; you had then trusted
us gratis, whereas, now, we have our former loyalty to
vouch us. You see, my lord, how much I presume
upon the greatness of your spirit, that dare prevent my
indictment with so frank a confession, especially in this,
which I may so justly deny, that it is almost arrogance
in me to own it ; for the truth is, I was not qualified
enough to serve him ; all that I could do, was to bear
a part in his sufferings, and give myself up to be cherished with his fall : thus my charge is double (my obedience to my sovereign, and, what is the result of that.
my want of a fortune). Now, whatever reflections I
have on the former, I am a true penitent for the latter.
My lord, you see my crimes.   As to my defence, you
bear it about you. I shall plead nothing in my justification, but your highness's clemency, which, as it is
the constant inmate of a valiant breast (if you graciously please to extend it to your supplicant, in taking me
out of this withering durance), your highness will find
that mercy will establish you more than power ; though
all the days of your life were as pregnant with victories
as your twice auspicious third of Sep[r]. — Your highness's humble and submissive petitioner,

J. C. CLIEVELAND.

This petition prevailed ; Cromwell immediately ordered the release of the ingenious prisoner, who, making
his way to London, took up his residence there amongst
the few surviving loyalists who were permitted to remain in the metropolis.*   His social talents soon drew

* The *Biographia Britannica* has another version of Clieveland's seizure
by the republicans, which, however, cannot be the true one. According to

ound him the relics of his party, and he became a constant frequenter of their convivial clubs. Nor was he at a loss for a patron rich enough to enable him to sustain the expenses of this new way of life with ease and credit. The close of his career was, in this respect, more brilliant than any previous part of his chequered existence; but he did not live long to enjoy his good fortune. He died of an intermittent fever, on the 29th of April, 1658, in his chambers at Gray's Inn; and was interred in the church of St. Michael Royal, commouly called College Hill, with a degree of splendour which fully testified the high estimation in which he was held. Bishop Pearson honoured his public cousisteney and private virtues, in a funeral sermon*, and numerous poetical elegies were contributed by different writers to the posthumous editions of his works. One of the most ingenious of these was an anagram, in which his genius was apostrophised and characterised.

> « John Clieveland —
> Heliconian dew ! »

Of the general character of Clieveland's poetry, it is perhaps scarcely necessary to add anything to the observations already made in passing through the scanty incidents of his life. The *Rebel Scot* was esteemed to

---

that statement, Clieveland was apprehended, having a bundle of poems and satirical songs in his possession. He appeared before the generai of the parliamentary forces prepared to suffer for his principles, and assuming the dignified air of a martyr. But the military judge only treated him with contempt, and after looking over his papers, exclaimed, " Is this all you have against him? go, let the poor knave sell his ballads!" This scornful acquittal is said, on the same authority, to have affected the pride of the poet so deeply that he broke his heart in consequence. There may be some foundation for the anecdote to a certain extent; but it cannot be correct in the main, since the petition of Clievelanu, above quoted, shows that he had endured imprisonment at the hands of his accusers for three months at all events, and that he was compelled at last to solicit mercy. In additiou to this evidence, we have the particulars of Clieveland's examination, which are preserved in Thurlow's *State Papers*. He was apprehended by general Hayes as comprised in the second class of persons disaffected to the government, and amongst other reasons of judgment against him sent up to the protector and council are, " That Mr. Clieveland liveth in a genteel garb; yet he confesseth that he hath no estate but 20*l*. per annum allowed by two gentlemen, and 30*l*. per annum by Mr. Cooke; and that Mr. Clieveland is a person of great abilities, and so able to do the greater disservice; all of which we humbly submit," &c.
'* Lloyd's Mem. Fuller's Worthies.

be his greatest performance; but it certainly owed its celebrity to the fierceness of its assault upon the kirk and the Scottish covenanters rather than to any qualities of a higher kind. In Fuller's portrait of Clieveland, taken at Oxford, the poet is represented as holding a paper in his hand inscribed " The Rebel Scot," and an engraving from this portrait was prefixed, in 1781, to Nichol's *Select Collection of Miscellaneous Poetry.* The whole gist of the poem, which does not extend to more than 150 lines, may be estimated from one or two specimens.

" Come, keen iambicks, with your badger's feet,
And, badger like, bite till your teeth do meet;
Help, ye tart satirists, to imp my rage,
With all the scorpions that should whip this age.
Scotts are like witches; do but whet your pen,
Scratch till the blood come, they 'll not hurt you then.
Now as the martyrs were inforced to take
The shapes of beasts, like hypocrites at stake,
I 'll bait my Scott so, yet not cheat your eyes;
A Scott within a beast is no disguise."

The following passage will probably recal some of the short bitter lines on the Dutch, which occur in Buller's *Miscellaneous Thoughts.*

" Like Jews they spread, and as infection fly —
As if the devil had ubiquity.
Hence 't is they live at Rover's, and defy
This or that place; rags of geography.
They 're citizens o' the world; they 're all in all;
Scotland 's a nation epidemical.
And yet they ramble, not to learn the mode
How to be drest, or how to lisp abroad;
To return knowing in the Spanish shrug,
Or which of the Dutch states a double jug
Resembles most, in belly or in beard:
(The card by which the mariners are steered.)
No, the Scott's-errant fight, and fight to eat;
Their ostrich stomachs make their swords their meat.
Nature with Scotts as tooth-drawers hath dealt,
Who use to hang their teeth upon their belt."

This poem was followed by another called *The Scot's Apostasy,* in which he returned to the attack with renewed vigour. One of his contemporaries says of him that "he prosecuted this subject with such satirical fury that the whole nation fares the worse for it, laying under the most grievous poetical censure."* He carried his love of satire so far that he even satirised himself; and amongst his poems we find a parody on an ode entitled *Marc Anthony*, which he wrote by way of ridiculing his own verses. This might be forgiven; but his parodies on the church service are not likely to amuse any class of readers in the same degree as they are sure to offend others. Occasionally he committed himself to some gross and immoral compositions, which appear in the late editions of his works, and which, probably, he was too much ashamed of to give to the world during his lifetime. Clieveland succeeded best as a satirist, when he ridiculed the salient and vulnerable eccentricities of the puritans, their platonic love, their gospel semplars with scraps from the Bible wrought in needlework, their ghastly heads, sallow features, and ludicrous expression of farcical gravity. These points he delineated with great force and living truth. His definition of a protector may be cited as an example amongst his smaller pieces.

"What's a protector? He's a stately thing,
That apes it in the nonage of a king;
A tragic actor, Cæsar in a clown;
He's a brass farthing, stamped with a crown;
A bladder blown, with others' breath puft full;
Not the Perillus, but Perillus' bull;
Æsop's proud ass veil'd in the lion's skin;
An outward saint, lin'd with a devil within;
An echo whence the royal sound doth come,
But just as a barrel-head sounds like a drum;
Fantastic image of the royal head,
The brewer's, with the king's arms, quartered;
He is a counterfeited piece, that shows
Charles his effigies with a copper nose:
In fine, he's one we must protector call, —
From whom the King of kings protect us all!

Protector ⎱
Anagram. ⎰   O Portet C. R.

* Philips's *Theatrum Poetarum*, 1675.

But it was not in such exercises as these that the true genius of Clieveland really lay, and it is to be lamented that one who possessed so fine a sympathy for nature, and so large a capacity to extend the domain of poetry, should have sacrificed his powers to such unworthy topics, and should have so utterly " given up to party what was meant for mankind." In two at least of his poems, called *The Senses' Festival*, and *Fuscara, or the Bee Errant,* he appears in a wholly different character. These productions are highly polished, chaste, and tender. Having asserted that Clieveland was gifted with a refined taste, — seldom as he allowed it to influence him, — it may be considered necessary to vindicate the eulogy by an example. The following is the poem called *Fuscara, or the Bee Errant :.*

> " Nature's confectioner, the bee,
> Whose suckets are moist alchymy,
> The still of his refining mould,
> Minting the garden into gold ;
> Having rifled all the fields
> Of what dainties Flora yields,
> Ambitious now to take excise
> Of a more fragrant paradise,
> At my Fuscara's sleeve arrived,
> Where all delicious sweets are hiv'd,
> The airy freebooter distrains
> First on the violet of her veins,
> Whose tincture, could it be more pure,
> His ravenous kiss had made it bluer ;
> Here did he sit and essence quaff,
> Till her coy pulse had beat him off ;
> That pulse, which he that feels may know
> Whether the world's long-liv'd or no.
> The next he preys on is her palm,
> That alm'ner of transpiring balm ;
> So soft 't is air but once removed,
> Tender as 't were a jelly glov'd.
> Here, while his canting drone-pipe scann'd
> The mystic figures of her hand,
> He tipples palmestry, and dives
> On all her fortunes-telling lives :
> He bathes in bliss, and finds no odds
> Betwixt her nectar and the gods' ;

He perches now upon her wrist, —
A proper hawk for such a fist, —
Making that flesh his bill of fare,
Which hungry cannibals would spare.
Where lilies, in a lovely brown,
Inoculate carnation.
Her argent skin with or so stream'd,
As if the milky way were cream'd;
From hence he to the woodbine bends
That quivers at her fingers' ends,
That runs divisions on the three,
Like a thick branching pedigree.
So 't is not her the bee devours,
It is a pretty maze of flowers;
It is the rose that bleeds, when he
Nibbles his nice phlebotomy.
About her finger he doth cling,
I' th' fashion of a wedding ring,
And bids his comrades of the swarm
Crawl on a bracelet 'bout her arm.
Thus, when the hovering publican
Had suck'd the toll of all her span,
Turning his draughts, with drowsy hums,
As Danes carouse by kettle drums,
It was decreed, that posy glean'd,
The small familiar should be wean'd.
At this the errant's courage quails;
Yet, aided by his native sails,
The bold Columbus still designs
To find her undiscovered mines:
To th' Indies of her arm he flies,
Fraught both with east and western prize;
Which, when he had in vain essay'd,
Arm'd like a dapper lance presade,
With Spanish pike he broached a pore,
And so both made and heal'd the sore:
For as in gummy trees there 's found
A salve to issue at the wound,
Of this her breach the like was true,
Hence trickled out a balsam too.
But, oh! what wash was 't that could prove
Ratilias to my Queen of Love?
The king of bees, now jealous grown,
Lest her beams should melt his throne,
And finding that his tribute slacks,
His burgesses and state of wax

Turn'd to an hospital, the combs
Build rank and file like beadsmen's rooms;
And what they bleed, but tart and sour,
Match'd with my Danae's golden shower,
Life-honey all, the envious elf
Stung her, 'cause sweeter than himself.
Sweetness and she are so allied,
The bee committed parricide."

That Clieveland was encouraged by false criticism,
reflecting the vitiated taste of the day, to indulge in
those fantastic images from which even this beautiful
production is not wholly free, cannot be doubted. Almost
all his contemporaries praise his faults, and none of
them seem to have discovered his merits. A learned
writer of his own day describes him as " a general
artist, an eminent poet. His epithets were pregnant
with metaphors, carrying in them a difficult plainness, —
difficult at the hearing, plain at the considering thereof.
His lofty fancy may seem to slide from the top of one
mountain to the top of another, so making to itself a
constant level and champaign of continued elevations."
Had Clieveland been recommended to the notice of
posterity by no other claims than the "slides" of his
fancy, he might be permitted, without much injustice,
to remain in the obscurity in which his name has been
buried for a century and a half; but the better part of
him is worth being rescued from oblivion, and he filled
too large a space in his own age to be wholly omitted,
under any circumstances, from the records of English
poetry.

EDMUND GAYTON.

1609—1666.

EDMUND GAYTON, or, as he styled himself, de Speciosa
Villa, was the son of one George Gayton, of Little Britain, iu London. He was educated at Merchant-Taylors'

School, from which he was elected scholar of St. John's College, Oxford, in the year 1625, at the age of sixteen. He was afterwards chosen a fellow of that house, and in 1636, superior beadle of arts and physic to the university. In 1647, he became a bachelor of physic, and in the following year was deprived of his beadleship by the parliamentary visitors. The loss of this situation forced him, in search of a subsistence, to take up his residence in London, where he lived in a very poor condition, and, as Wood says, " wrote trite things meerly to get bread to sustain him and his wife." It does not appear, however, that his works, at least such as were published with his name, were very voluminous from that period to the restoration. His principal production, *Pleasant Notes upon Don Quixote*, appeared in 1654 ; the *Hymna de Febribus*, and *Will Bagnal's Ghost*, in 1655 ; and in 1659, *The Art of Longevity, or a Diætetical Discourse*, a curious metrical treatise on the choice and use of almost every description of food ; and *Walk, Knaves, Walk*, a satire against rogues in office, written while the luckless author was immured in the Bench. In addition to these writings, he published a quaint piece of invention in 1660, called *Wit Revived*, under the name of Asdryasdust-Tossuffacan.

Gayton evidently had friends amongst the royalists, although in this dreary interval they do not appear to have rendered him much help ; but, immediately after the restoration, he was reinstated in his beadleship, which, being a very lucrative situation, released him from all further necessity for writing. But the love of satire and humour was predominant over all other considerations, and he continued to amuse himself by songs, ballads, and other ephemeral pieces, until he shuffled off this mortal coil at his lodgings in Cat Street, Oxford, on the 12th of December, 1666. Up to the last hour, he employed his thoughts in this way, and the last of his publications was issued from the press only seven days before his death. That he was a spendthrift and a profligate can hardly be doubted. Wood says that he followed "the vices of the poets, of which number he pretended to be one ; and one eminent he might have been, had he not been troubled with the faculty of too much lifting. He hath written some good, others most vain and trashy things." This criticism, however, must be accepted with some reservation, as Wood's choler was doubtless excited against Gayton by those absurd lampoons in which he assailed some of the ancient usages or offices of the university. Of Gayton's extravagant and reckless habits there is proof enough in the fact that when he died he "had but one farthing in his pocket," and he was buried in St. Mary's Church at the expense of the vice-chancellor.

Through the conduct of such men as Gayton, the poets of that troubled period seem to have got into some disgrace in the colleges. Upon the meeting of the convocation to elect his successor to the beadleship, the vice chancellor, in a set speech, exhorted the masters " by all means that they should not elect a poet or any that do *scribere libellos ;* adding therewithal, that the late beadle (Gayton) was such an ill husband and so improvident," &c. &c. But, notwithstanding this very impressive address, the " black pot men, who," exclaims Wood, " (with shame be it spoken,) carry all before them at elections," instead of electing a master of arts, chose a yeoman beadle, who, at a former period of his life, had kept a public house, and who was " good for nothing but eating, drinking, smoking, and punning ;" so that, for the end the vice chancellor gained by his speech, they might as well have elected a poet after all.

Of Gayton's character as a poet, very little remains to be said. The greater part of his compositions were mere verbiage, thrown off upon subjects of local and fleeting interest, and written with just enough of point to catch the immediate humour of the multitude. His longer works evince some metrical skill, and are not deficient in traces of scholarship. His satirical and festive songs were in much request in his own day, and are even now objects of expensive curiosity amongst collectors, who place a factitious value on such things. In a curious MS. on fishing, bearing date about 1750, and published for the first time in the *Censura Lite-raria*, some extracts from Gayton's *Art of Longevity* are given as foot-notes illustrative of particular passages in the text. This shows that, in spite of his mediocrity, he was not entirely forgotten; and although, as a whole, this *Art of Longevity* is a cumbrous and tedious affair, it contains many passages that are worth preservation. The following lines, descriptive of the dietetic properties of certain river fish, will afford a fair exemplar of its plan and treatment : —

> " The fish of lakes, and motes, and stagnant ponds
> (Remote from sea, or where no spring commands,
> And intermingling its refreshing waves
> Is tench unto the mote, and tenches saves
> And keeps them medical), are of all sorts
> Lesse innocent, unless some river courts
> The sullen nymph, and blending waters, she
> Of a foul Mopsa 's made Lencothoë.
> Her inmates, otherwise, like herself, smell,
> Taste of the harbour (that is) scent not well ;
> Slow to digest : alive, they liv'd too close;
> And dead, they can't their native dullness lose.
> Give me a salmon, who with winged fins
> ' Gainst tide and stream firks o'er the fishing-gins
> Of locks and hives, and circling in a gyre
> His vaulting corpse, he leaps the baffled wyre.

SIR JOHN BIRKENHEAD.

1615—1679.

JOHN BIRKENHEAD was the son of a saddler, or, according to a pamphleteering opponent, a poor ale-housekeeper, of Northwich in Cheshire. In the year 1632, at seventeen years of age, he became a servitor or sizar in Oriel College, Oxford, where he continued until he obtained the degree of A. B., and being appointed amanuensis to archbishop Laud, he was elected, through his grace's interest, to a probationer-fellowship in All Souls College in 1640. After the rebellion broke out, and the court had removed to Oxford, he started a sort of weekly paper styled the *Mercurius Aulicus ; communicating the Intelligence and Affairs of the Court at Oxon to the rest of the Kingdom.* In this work, however, he did not confine himself to the simple procedure of "communicating the intelligence," &c., but openly attacked the Roundheads with every species of missile usually employed in party warfare, sparing no species of satire, ridicule, or buffoonery, to bring himself into notice. The first number of his paper appeared on the 1st of January, 1642, and the periodical was carried on with regularity, till about the close of 1645, after which it appeared at uncertain intervals. In a rival publication of that day, it was asserted that the *Mercurius Aulicus* was the work of several persons, and that there was even a regular assessment of wit imposed upon each of the colleges for supplying its columns. But it is tolerably certain that Birkenhead is entitled to whatever credit may be attached to the principal and almost only writer in its columns, except Heylin, who in his absence occasionally supplied his place. The king was so well pleased with the manner in which Birkenhead conducted this publication, that he recommended him to the office of moral philosophy reader ; to which chair he was accordingly elected. But he did not enjoy the scanty profits of the appointment long, for upon the next visitation of the presbyterians, in 1648, he was deprived both of that place and his fellowship. But even this misfortune could not repress his natural tendency for satire, and he immediately published *News from Pembroke qnd Montgomery ; or Oxford Manchester'd, &c.;* in which he gave a mock speech affecting to have been spoken by the earl of Pembroke when he went down as parliamentary visitor to remodel the university : a piece of humour that was very much relished at the time, on account of its close but ludicrous imitation of Pembroke's style. Removing to London,

Birkenhead remained faithful to the royal cause, and published several pieces in prose and verse against the republican party. The principal of his poetic works are, some songs and verses which have been since set to music, a translation of Anacreon's *Ode on the Lute*, a poem on his staying in London after the act of banishment for cavaliers, and another called *The Jolt*, written on the protector's being thrown off the box-seat of his coach in Hyde Park, as he attempted to drive it when drawn by six German horses, which had been sent him as a present by the count of Oldenburgh. His devotion to the royal cause exposed him to much severe suffering and several imprisonments. During the period that elapsed between his dismissal from the college in 1648 and the restoration, we are told that he " lived by his wits, in helping young gentlemen cut at dead lifts in making poems, songs,. and epistles, to and on their respective mistresses, and also in translating and writing several little things, and other petite employments."* But after the restoration, his fidelity was abundantly rewarded. In 1660 he was created a bachelor of civil law, and appointed master of the faculties, by letters patent ; in 1661 elected a burgess for Wilton ; in 1662, knighted by the king; and in 1663 constituted one of the masters of requests. An anonymous pamphleteer says that he had received moreover 3000*l.* in gifts at court †, and adds that it was by his lying and buffooning he obtained those " gifts and places." His ribaldry might be forgiven ; but it is not so easy to palliate the grave offence with which he is charged, of ingratitude, in his prosperity, to those who had assisted him in his misfortunes. This jocular satirist died within the precincts of Whitehall, about the 4th of December, 1679, and was buried near the school door of the church of St. Martin in the Fields.

Sir John Birkenhead possessed the exact qualities

* Wood.
† *A Seasonable Argument to persuade all the Grand Juries to petition for a new Parliament.* 1677.

that would have fitted him for the office of court jester,
— great courage in words, scoffing humour, an unscrupulous conscience, or rather, no conscience at all,
considerable shrewdness, and an inexhaustible fund of
arch and mischievous drollery.   He brought no weight
to the cause he espoused, but his banter was so pert and
bold, and he was so prompt in seizing upon happy occasions for its employment, that he may be regarded as
one of the most expert and successful guerilla partisans
on the side of the royalists.

PAYNE FISHER.

1616—1693.

PAYNE FISHER was the son of one of the captains in
Charles the First's lifeguards, and was born in 1616, at
Warnford in Dorsetshire, in the house of his grandfather, sir Thomas Neale.   Wood tells us that he
became a commoner of Hart Hall, Oxford, at eighteen
years of age, that he continued there for three or four
years under the severe discipline of two tutors, and then
went to Magdalen College, Cambridge, where he took
one degree in arts.   His poetical talents developed
themselves sufficiently at this time to excite the expectations of his contemporaries ; but he preferred a life of
adventure to the seclusion of the muses, and joined the
army of Brabant in the garrison of Bolduc.   He subsequently became wearied of this way of life, and returned to England, where we find him employed as
ensign, together with the celebrated Lovelace, in the
expedition undertaken by Charles I. against the Scots.
He next figured in Ireland under viscount Maserene,
ascending gradually to the rank of captain-lieutenant ;
and subsequently obtained an appointment as major in
a foot regiment, raised by sir Patrick Curwen, in Cumberland.   He afterwards assisted at the relief of York,
and the battle of Marston Moor ; but the victories of the

Scots compelled him to abandon his command; and he retired into London, to live in obscurity by his wits, and sell his pen to the protector, after having so long devoted his sword to the king. Fisher is said to have ingratiated himself so successfully with the men then in power, as to obtain the honour, such as it was, of being appointed poet laureat to Cromwell. The doubtful favour, however, in which poetry was held during the commonwealth, rendered the office a mere idle badge, from which the holder derived scarcely any emolument. Payne Fisher appears to have grown heartily tired of this beggarly service; for the restoration no sooner brought back the royal family, than he hastened to offer up his allegiance, and to describe, in the agonies of rhyme, the great sufferings he had endured for his loyalty. But it was too late; he had committed himself too far to the commonwealth, and was not now to be trusted by the royalists. The consequence was, that poverty came apace upon him, and he was cast upon the most wretched expedients for eking out existence. He lived by what he could get for dedications, epitaphs, epithalamiums, and other pieces of a personal and occasional kind. When any person of distinction happened to marry, or die, Fisher immediately presented himself with a string of suitable verses. His flattery of the great was gross, and deservedly brought him into ridicule and contempt. Falling deeply into debt, he was arrested, and imprisoned in the Fleet, where he was detained for several years; and, after his liberation, he died in great distress, in a coffee-house in the Old Bailey, on the 2d of April, 1693, and was buried in St. Sepulchre's churchyard. Notwithstanding the poverty of his career, and his want of principles, Fisher (or, as he used to call himself, Paganus Piscator) was a man of considerable attainments, and excellent talent for poetry. He was esteemed, by competent judges, as a good Latin poet; and the catalogue of his productions exhibits a numerous list of works on a variety of subjects.

RICHARD LOVELACE.

1618—1658.

RICHARD LOVELACE was, in many respects, one of the most remarkable men of his day, and must have achieved a distinguished figure, had he not fallen upon times for which his genius was altogether unfitted.   A little later, or a little earlier, Lovelace would have occupied a proud niche amongst the poets ; — there would have been an ample field open to him, either under Elizabeth or Charles II.; and, perhaps, the latter reign would have been more favourable to the development of his rich and passionate imagination ; — but the civil war overwhelmed him with troubles ; checked him in the cultivation of that art, in which, as far as the few specimens he has left enable us to judge, none of his contemporaries excelled him ; and turned his whole thoughts and feelings into channels repugnant to the real tendencies of his nature.   He was the eldest son of sir William Lovelace, of Woolwich, in Kent, where he was born in 1618.   He received the rudiments of his education in a grammar school near London, and became a gentleman commoner of Gloucester Hall, Oxford, in 1634; at which time, says Wood, he was " accounted the most amiable and beautiful person that ever eye beheld ; a person, also, of innate modesty, virtue, and courtly deportment, which made him then — but especially after, when he retired to the great city — much admired and adored by the female sex." The singular beauty of his appearance, and the exquisite graces of his manners and conversation, appear to have captivated every body who knew him.   While the king and queen were on a visit at the university, in 1636, he was created a master of arts, at the intercession of a great lady belonging to her majesty, although he was then of but two years' standing ; and upon leaving the university, and after living at court for some time in

great splendour, he was commissioned by the earl of
Norwich, in the expedition against the Scotch, in 1639.
In the second expedition, he was made captain of a
regiment ; and found leisure, during that busy and dis-
astrous period, to write a tragedy, called *The Soldier,*
— which, however, never was performed, the stage being
shortly afterwards suppressed by the puritans. When all
hopes were at an end for the king's party, Lovelace
retired to his estate in Kent, which was at that time
worth at least 500*l.* per annum ; and, although the
prospect of effecting the recal of the Stuarts became
every day more and more desperate, this devoted adhe-
rent continued to struggle on their behalf in the face of
the most appalling dangers. The gallantry exhibited by
Lovelace, throughout the perilous interval that ensued,
is in the highest degree honourable to his character ;
and in him, at least, the integrity of the poet's mission
was preserved with purity to the last. His constant
efforts to awaken the people to a sense of the duty which
he honestly believed they owed to the banished monarch, succeeded in producing, from the inhabitants of
Kent, an energetic petition to the house of commons,
praying for the settlement of the government, and the
restoration of the king to his rights. This petition was
presented by Lovelace, at the unanimous request of its
subscribers : and for this bold and hazardous service, the
chivalric cavalier was committed to the Gate House, at
Westminster — where he was kept in strict confinement
for nearly four months. The exquisite song —

" When Loue, with vnconfined winges," &c. —

was written during this imprisonment. Several spurious
copies of this beautiful composition have, from time to
time, found their way into print ; yet, although occasionally maimed and deformed in the transcription, there
is scarcely any single production of the seventeenth century which enjoys such extensive popularity. Lovelace
was at length released from prison, on condition (en-

forced by bail to the amount of 40,000l.) that he should not move beyond the lines of communication without a pass from the speaker. He was consequently limited to a close residence in London, — a trial which his proud spirit could ill brook; and the effect it had upon him was, to plunge him into expenses beyond his means, and finally to involve him in more serious difficulties than any he had previously encountered. His whole fortune was spent in the king's cause, — in secretly supporting its friends — in furnishing men with arms and provisions — and in otherwise rendering honour to his master. The turn which affairs took in 1646 developed to him — unfortunately, when it was too late — the desperate circumstances of the king; and Lovelace, as if his sanguine temperament saw nothing more to rest upon, raised a regiment for the service of the king of France, taking the command of it himself at Dunkirk, where he was wounded. The heaviest misfortunes of his unlucky life now began to set in thickly upon him. Shortly before he left England, he had formed an attachment for Lucy Sacheverel, a lady of great beauty and fortune, to whom he subsequently addressed the collection of poems entitled *Lucasta:* and the entire course of his fortunes might probably have been changed, through her influence over his mind, had it not so happened that a false report of his death reached her at this juncture; and she was thus no sooner liberated from her engagement, than she bestowed her hand on some other suitor. Returning to England soon afterwards, Lovelace found himself a bankrupt on all sides. Hardly a vestige of his former resources remained; and the failure of his party was now demonstrated so clearly, that even the agitation of doubt had given way to blank despair. But the puritans were still afraid of this adventurous man; and, to make secure of him, they cast him, and his brother, and a captain who had served under him, into prison, where they kept him until after the king's execution,—when, reduced to a condition of naked destitution, they once more permitted him to go at large. His poems, entitled *Lucasta*, and

consisting of epodes, odes, sonnets, and songs, were produced during this dreary interval. But the star of the
fascinating Lovelace was now set for ever. Instead of
the cloth of gold and silver, which he was wont to wear
in the days of his prosperity, he now went about in
rags, and was•become an object of common charity, fre-
quenting the most obscure dens of the metropolis, and
living, of necessity, with the humblest and most wretched
mendicants. Aubrey says that Mr. Edmund Wyld made
several collections of money for him ; and that George
Petty, a haberdasher in Fleet Street, used to carry him
20s. every Monday morning for many months. To this
account of his destitution, Aubrey adds, that " he was an
extraordinarily handsome man, but prowd." According
to the same authority, he died in a cellar in Long Acre,
a little before the restoration ; but, according to Wood,
he died in a mean lodging in Gunpowder Alley, near
Shoe Lane, and was buried at the west end of the church
of St. Bride, in 1658. But all accounts agree in repre-
senting his death to have taken place under circumstances of the most painful distress.

His works are not numerous, and principally consist
of lyrics full of tenderness and grace. A second part of
the *Lucasta* was published by his brother, after his death,
in which, with the former volume, all his printed productions are comprised. The tragedy of *The Soldier*, and
a comedy called *The Scholar*, written at sixteen years of
age, and acted with applause in Salisbury Court, were
never printed. He was highly esteemed by his contemporaries, for the generosity of his disposition, and the constancy with which he maintained his friendships. He
was well versed in the Greek and Latin poets, was an
accomplished musician, and a witty speaker. The combination of qualities which his biographers represent
him to have possessed, must have rendered him one of
the most popular men of his time, had that time been
more favourable to their developement.

Thomas Flatman.

1633—1688.

Thomas Flatman, who was eminent in his day for his skill in law, poetry, and painting, was the son of a clerk in Chancery, and was born in Aldersgate Street, in the city of London, about the year 1633. After having been instructed in Wykeham's school, near Winchester, he was elected a fellow of New College, Oxford, in 1654,—but went to the Inner Temple before he had taken a degree. It appears that he subsequently procured his degree of B.A.; and that, in 1666, he was made M.A. of Cambridge, by the king's letters patent. He wrote several odes, which were very highly esteemed by his contemporaries. One of these — a *Pindarique Ode on the Death of Thomas Earl of Ossory*, the son of James duke of Ormond—made such an impression on the duke, that he sent Flatman a mourning ring, with a diamond in it, worth 100*l.* Flatman's principal compositions were pindaric odes on the death of the duke of Albemarle, prince Rupert, Charles II., &c. He published a volume of songs and poems in 1674, which were again printed in 1676, and again in 1682. In his younger days, he is said to have entertained an aversion to matrimony; but in maturer life he renounced that graceless heresy, — for, " being afterwards smitten with a fair virgin, and more with her fortune *," he married her on the 26th of November, 1672. He died in his house in Fleet Street, on the 8th of December, 1688, being then about fifty-five years of age, and was buried in the church of St. Bride.

He is said, by some of his critics, to have been the author of *Heraclitus Ridens.* An extract from his acknowledged works will be sufficient to indicate the character of his style.

* Wood.

" When on my sick bed I languish,
Full of sorrow, full of anguish,
Fainting, gasping, trembling, crying,
My soul, just now about to take her flight
Into the regions of eternal night —
  Oh tell me yo,
That have been long below,
  What shall I do?
What shall I think, when cruel death appears,
  What may extenuate my fears?
Methinks I hear some gentle spirit say,
  Be not fearful, come away !
Think with thyself that now thou shalt be free,
And find thy long expected liberty !
Better thou mayest, but worse thou canst not, be,
Than in this vale of tears and misery.
Like Cæsar, with assurance then come on,
And, unamazed, attempt the laurel crown
That lies on t' other side death's Rubicon."

Such is a fair specimen of that pindaric poetry, which, two centuries ago, enjoyed the highest popularity in England. It is not surprising that Granger should declare of this Flatman, that one of his portraits (for he enjoyed a good reputation as a painter) was worth a ream of his pindarics.

MATHEW MORGAN.

1652 — ——.

MATHEW MORGAN, the author of *A Poem to the Queen on the King's Victory in Ireland and his Voyage to Holland,* and an *Elegy on the Death of the Honourable Robert Boyle* — both published in 1691; and of *A Poem upon the late Victory over the French Fleet at Sea,* published in 1692; was born in 1652, in the parish of St. Nicholas, in Bristol, of which city his father had been alderman and mayor. In 1667, he became a commoner of St. John's College, Oxford; and, after going through the several gradations, took the degree of doctor

of law in 1685.   In 1688 he was presented to a good
living in Somersetshire; but lost it by neglecting to read
the Articles in time.   He was afterwards in great misery.   He appears to have been a man of very little
moral or religious principle.   In 1683 he published a
translation of some of *Plutarch's Morals;* and a passage
in the preface to the first volume having been complained of to the vice-chancellor, and his expulsion
threatened in consequence, he disowned the authorship,
although it was subscribed with his initials, and the
bookseller, to screen him, took it upon himself.   This
preface was unfortunate, also, in other respects; as another passage declaring " the image of the Deity to be
so closely impressed upon him (*Charles II.*), that the
idea comes very near the original," was considered
almost blasphemous ; and a third was objected to, for
implying that Plutarch and other pagan philosophers
might, in a future world, attain the same state of happiness as Christians, — a suggestion which was regarded
as being, if possible, still more impious.   To compare
the king to the Creator was justly denounced as irreverent, but to call into question the doctrine of exclusive
salvation was a crime beyond discussion or forgiveness.

Morgan published translations of some of Plutarch's
Lives, and portions of Cornelius Nepos and Suetonius.
After a long and severe struggle with fortune, he was
at last placed at his ease in a small cure near Bristol, to
which he was appointed in 1692, and where it may be
hoped he expiated his errors in tranquillity during the
remainder of his life.

SIR RICHARD BLACKMORE.

16— —1729.

RICHARD BLACKMORE was the son of Robert Blackmore, an attorney, of Corsham, in the county of Wilts.
After completing his education in the country, he re-

moved to Edmund Hall, Oxford, in 1668, — where he remained for thirteen years, and subsequently followed the profession of a schoolmaster. During this period, he devoted his leisure to the study of medicine. Having graduated at the university, he went upon the Continent, took out the degree of M.D. at Padua, and, returning to England, was admitted a fellow of the College of Physicians. He rapidly acquired eminence in his profession, of which he was a distinguished and laborious member; and, in 1697, was appointed physician to king William — receiving at the same time the honour of knighthood. His literary career dates from the previous year, when he published an epic poem called *Prince Arthur;* which was quickly followed by another epic, entitled *King Arthur;* and, in 1700, by a paraphrase in folio of the Book of Job.

These poems would hardly entitle the author of them to any more lengthened notice than a slight outline of his life, and an enumeration of his works, were it not that they form rather a remarkable feature in the literature of the times, which sir Richard Blackmore, with the very best intentions, but with the most inadequate means, proposed to correct and improve through their influence. Dryden was at the height of his reputation; he had ceased to write for the stage, but his plays were occasionally acted, and the vicious taste they had inspired was still predominant amongst the dramatists; the useful effects of the revolution, in reproving the licentiousness that had descended upon the people from the profligate example of Charles II., were beginning to be felt; and sir Richard Blackmore, a sedate physician, moving with pious gravity in the circles of the court, and observing, with unaffected regret, the base uses to which the theatre was converted, thought that the moment had arrived when these excesses might be profitably exposed. That he was right in his view of the subject is unquestionable; and, however indifferently he executed his design, he had, at least, the merit of being the first to assail the corruptions that had eaten into the heart of almost every form of popular poetry. If he did not triumph over the distinguished writers he attacked, his cause did; and the work of reform, which he commenced, was afterwards completed by the vehement eloquence, the subtle wit, and invincible courage of Jeremy Collier.

In the preface to *Prince Arthur,* he openly avowed his object, — declaring that his contemporaries employed their talents " in opposition to religion, and to the destruction of virtue and good manners in the world; " and that it was his design to rescue the Muses, and " restore them to their sweet and chaste mansions, and to engage them in an employment suited to their dignity." The subject of the poem was, in itself, dangerous ground for such a writer to tread. It had been contemplated by Milton, and actually appropriated in two lyrical dramas by Dryden, who, in his celebrated *Essay on Satire,* had laid down rules for the conduct of an epic poem, which rules, Blackmore, without acknowledgment, implicitly followed in this very work, that was to demolish Dryden and the whole fraternity of living poets.   But he was so infatuated by his project, that he could not see the quicksands that lay before him ; and he even went so far as to assail Dryden in his preface, — taunting him with the plea of poverty, by which he had excused himself for continuing to write for the vitiated appetite of his audiences, — and recommending all such starving poets to abandon their profession, and take up with some more creditable calling. The passage in which this assault is contained, belongs to the literary history of the age; and is not less remarkable for its truth, than for the feeble periods through which the honest purpose of the writer is diluted. This was not the tone likely to bring Dryden into contempt.

" Some of these poets, to excuse their guilt, allege for themselves, that the degeneracy of the age makes their lewd way of writing necessary : they pretend the auditors will not be pleased, unless they are thus entertained from the stage ; and to please, they say, is the chief business of the poet. But this is by no means a just apology: it is not true, as was said before, that the poet's chief business is to please. His chief business is to instruct, to make mankind wiser and better; and in order to this, his care should be to please and entertain the audience with all the wit and art he is master of. Aristotle and Horace, and all their critics and commentators, all men of wit and sense, agree, that this is the end of poetry. But they say, it is their profession to write for the stage; and that poets must starve, if they will not in this way humour their audience: the theatre will be as unfrequented as the churches, and the poet and the parson equally neglected. Let the poet then abandon his profession, and take up with some honest lawful calling, where, joining industry to his great wit, he may soon get above the complaints of poverty, so common among these ingenious men, and lie under no necessity of prostituting his wit to any such vile purposes as are here censured. This will be a course of life more profitable and honourable to himself, and more useful to others. And there are among these writers some, who think they might have risen to the highest dignities in other professions, had they employed their wit in those ways. It is a mighty dishonour and reproach to any man that is capable of being useful to the world in any liberal and virtuous profession, to lavish out his life and wit in propagating vice and corruption of manners, and in battering from the stage the strongest entrenchments and best works of religion and virtues. Whoever makes this his choice, when the other was in his power, may he go off the stage unpitied, complaining of neglect and poverty, the just punishment of his irreligion and folly."

The poem to which this preface was attached, and that by which it was succeeded, can scarcely be commended for any higher qualities than regularity and commonplace. Blackmore was totally deficient in all the higher attributes of a poet—in imagination, invention, strength. He was merely a versifier, and never advanced

beyond the narrow confines of respectable mediocrity.
It is very probable that Dryden would never have condescended to notice him, and would have left him to the
minor wits who mercilessly attacked him at all his vulnerable points, immediately after the publication of these
pieces, had he not returned to the charge in a poem
which he designed to be very smart and caustic, entitled
A Satire on Wit. In this production, Blackmore made
a more lively attempt at severity, suggesting that a bank
of wit should be established, and that all the base coin
that had previously obtained currency should be called
in, melted down, freed from alloy, and re-issued. By
this process, he believed, very little real gold would be
left for circulation.

> " 'T is true, that when the coarse and worthless dross
> Is purged away, there will be mighty loss.
> E'en Congreve, Southerne, manly Wycherly,
> When thus refined, will grievous sufferers be.
> Into the melting pot when Dryden comes,
> What horrid stench will rise ! what noisome fumes !
> How will he shrink, when all his lewd allay,
> And wicked mixture, shall be purged away ?
> When once his boasted heaps are melted down,
> A chest-full scarce will yield one sterling crown.
> Those who will D——n's melt, and think to find
> A goodly mass of bullion left behind,
> Do, as the Hibernian wit, who, as 't is told,
> Burnt his gilt feather, to collect his gold."

This contemptuous—but, it must be allowed, in reference to Dryden's plays, very just—satire roused the
anger of the dethroned laureat, who, in his old age, was
not disposed to see his glory obscured by a writer of
Blackmore's stamp. He accordingly retorted upon him
in his *Fables**, charging him with stealing the hint of
King Arthur from the preface to Juvenal, and then
with having " the baseness not to acknowledge his bene-
factor, but, instead of it, to traduce him in a libel."
Under the name of " Maurus," he effectually disposed of

---

* Mr. Malone, misled by the dates on the titlepages, says that the *Fables*
were published before the *Satire on Wit.*

poor Blackmore, in his double capacity of poet and physician. Referring to the *Fables*, which are accessible to all readers, for the whole passage, the following incidental lines will be sufficient to render our episode complete : —

> " Quack Maurus, though he never took degrees
> In either of our universities *,
> Yet to be shown by some kind wit he looks,
> Because he play'd the fool, and writ three books.
>
>   *   *   *
>
> " At leisure hours in epic song he deals,
> Writes to the rumbling of his coach's wheels ;
> Prescribes in haste, and seldom kills by rule,
> But rides triumphant between stool and stool.
>
>   *   *   *
>
> " We know not by what name we should arraign him,
> For no one category can contain him.
> A pedant, — canting preacher, — and a quack,
> Are load enough to break an ass's back."

Notwithstanding these withering invectives, however, and the ridicule of nearly all the writers of the day, Blackmore had his admirers, and continued to write on. Good intentions are always sure to command an audience amongst well-disposed people; and Blackmore had sufficient self-complacency to be satisfied with the applause of his own sober unpoetical friends, and to persevere against the raillery and unsparing mockery of his literary contemporaries. His strict Whig principles drew down upon him the resentment of Arbuthnot, Pope, and Swift; while his solemn, dry, and pedantic morality stood out in such absurd contrast with his pretensions as a writer of English epics, that he became the common butt of his day. Never was mediocrity so confident or so fruitful. And to render his position still more preposterous, he seemed to be quite unconscious of the snares that were spread for his unsuspicious egotism, and readily fell into any trap that was laid for him by his mischievous critics. The quantity of his works, considering

---

* This is not correct. Wood says that he graduated in arts at Oxford.'

that he enjoyed a very large practice in his profession, is almost incredible.   In addition to the epics already mentioned, he wrote *The Redeemer,* in six books ; *The Nature of Man,* in three books ; *Eliza,* in ten books ; *King Alfred,* in twelve books; and *The Creation,*. in seven books.   These performances he had the simplicity to avow were written " by such catches and starts, and in such occasional uncertain hours, as his profession afforded; and for the greater part in coffee-houses, or in passing up and down the streets ;" so that Dryden's accusation of writing " to the rumbling of his coach's wheels" was not a mere figure of speech.   It is not easy to account for the delusion under which that individual must have laboured, who supposed that epics could be thus produced ; but, nevertheless, some of these poems enjoyed a very extraordinary, but temporary, celebrity. *Prince Arthur* ran through three editions in two years; and *The Creation* produced, from Addison, a panegyric which it is extremely difficult to reconcile to the usual sagacity of that accomplished critic.   It is, he observed in *The Spectator,* " a philosophical poem, which has equalled that of Lucretius in the beauty of its versification, and infinitely surpassed it in the beauty and strength of its reasoning." Whoever may be tempted to read *The Creation* on Addison's recommendation, will probably look in vain for these excellences ; but, should he find them, he may be disposed to refer them to the fact stated by Draper, on the authority of Ambrose Philips, that, during the progress of the narrative, Blackmore submitted it from time to time to a club of wits, who contributed so largely to its improvement or correction, that, said Philips, " there are, perhaps, nowhere in the book, thirty lines together that now stand as they were originally written." Even with all these contributions and suggestions, it is very doubtful whether posterity will be inclined to admit the justice of Addison's eulogy, or of the still higher praise of Johnson, who observes, that if Blackmore had written nothing else than this poem (of which it appears he had really written so little), it would have transmitted his name amongst the first favourites of the English Muse.

This genius, that was so fertile of epics, occasionally descended to the lower kinds of poetry,—producing such pieces as *The Kit-kat Club*, *A New Version of the Psalms of David*, *Advice to the Poets how to celebrate the Duke of Marlborough*, and *Advice to a Weaver of Tapestry*,— a piece that was hardly worth the ridicule cast upon it by Steele in *The Tatler*. Blackmore was equally productive in prose, and tried all descriptions of composition, from the humblest essay to the loftiest history, — ranging through all fields of study which the human mind can be supposed capable of surveying. He wrote *A true and impartial History of the Conspiracy against King William ;* and, embarking in theology with the same facility he had exhibited in his epics, astonished the world with two books against the Arians, called *Modern Arians unmasked*, and *Just Prejudices against the Arian Hypothesis ;* also a work entitled *Natural Theology ;* and another, with the curious title of *The Accomplished Preacher, or, an Essay on Divine Eloquence*. When Addison dropped *The Spectator*, he took up the design in a series of periodical papers, called *The Lay Monastery*, which, appearing three times every week, extended to forty numbers ; and, when this project was exhausted, he issued two volumes of essays, that have been described, by a competent judge of style, as " languid, sluggish, and lifeless." In reference to medical subjects, his publications were equally voluminous, and equally un-readable. Of these productions, Dr. Johnson, who would have praised him if he could, out of his admiration of his unspotted private life, says, " I know not whether I can enumerate all the treatises by which he has endea-voured to diffuse the art of healing ; for there is scarcely any distemper, of dreadful name, which he has not taught the reader how to oppose. He has written on the small-pox, with a vehement invective against inocu-lation ; on consumption, the spleen, the gout, the rheu-matism, the king's evil, the dropsy, the jaundice, the

stone, the diabetes, and the plague." Such a catalogue
of medical treatises proceeding from a fellow of the
College of Physicians in the present day, with our increased knowledge, and our multiplied facilities for procuring it, would be regarded with astonishment; but
what would be thought of it, if the same author were
the prolific parent of epics, hymns, essays, histories,
controversies, and satires, enough to fill up the average
term of human life ? A practitioner of pretensions so
varied, and industry so singularly distributed, would be
very likely to incur the distrust which attaches to men,
who, possessing a certain adroitness in all trades, are
supposed to be masters of none.

Some such opinion seems to have grown up, at last,
respecting sir Richard Blackmore. His practice, at one
period considerable, began gradually to fall away, and
finally retreating from him, like receding waves, left
him in his green age stranded on the beach. There is so
little known of his private life, that we have no means of
ascertaining in what circumstances he died ; but it may
be presumed that he received some allowance from the
court, or that he was enabled to spare something for
the winter of his life from the profits of a long and apparently successful career. He died on the 8th of October,
1729, at a very advanced age ; and Mr. White, the
minister who attended him at his death, has not failed
to testify the piety of his last hours. His life, throughout all his relations, was irreproachable ; — his poetry,
alone, exposed him to ridicule and censure.

Having brought these sketches of the minor poets of
the sixteenth and seventeenth centuries to a conclusion,
it is necessary to say a few words upon one or two points
that may, probably, have already suggested themselves
to the mind of the reader.

These outlines present merely a selection from the
crowd of writers who enjoyed various degrees of cele-

brity and popularity throughout that long period, but who afterwards fell into oblivion. It would have answered no very useful purpose to introduce the names of all the small poets turned up in the course of these researches ; nor, indeed, would the limits of this work have enabled me to embrace them. If enough has been done to indicate the existence of a mass of poetry which in its own time occupied by no means an insignificant space in public attention, but which, from a variety of causes, has been subsequently neglected or forgotten, the main object of these brief notices will have been fully accomplished.

But all such selections are exposed to the charge of omissions on the one hand, and, on the other, of yielding to inferior claims some space that might have been more profitably occupied. Criticisms of this kind cannot, perhaps, be appeased by any explanations ; yet it must be allowed that the conduct of every undertaking which includes the responsibilities of choice and rejection, becomes ultimately resolved into a matter of opinion, upon which it is impossible to obtain the sanction of universal assent. It may be hoped, however, that the reader who misses a few names he expected to find, will discover others with which he was not familiar before ; while he who may be disposed to think that some authors are brought in who might have been advantageously dispensed with, need only be reminded, that the catalogue of names gathered in the progress of this collection, and omitted from an apprehension of extending it to an inconvenient bulk, is nearly as numerous as the whole series selected.

Notices of some of the more prominent of the minor poets — such as Crashaw, Suckling, Herrick, Carew, will be found distributed through the former volume ; and for others, not included in the preceding sketches, it may be enough to observe, that none of them are of much individual importance. Examples of almost every class are given, and might have been considerably increased, if any corresponding advantage could have been gained by the accumulation of illustrative instances. The number of poets who flourished from the time of Elizabeth to the revolution, is much greater than may be generally supposed ; and even the time of the commonwealth, unfavourable as the events and the temper of that period were to polite literature, produced more poets than any of its historians seem to have been aware of. Necessity appears to have driven many highly educated persons to the employment of their talents in this way, as a last alternative to eke out subsistence ; and in this category may be included nearly all those fellows and students of the universities who were expelled for their attachment to the royal cause, upon the visitation of the parliamentary commissioners. These individuals, cast out of their tranquil cloisters without the means of living, were forced to turn their learning to the best account they could ; and accordingly we find crowds of such scholars hurrying to the metropolis in the hope of obtaining occupation from the booksellers. Many of them were engaged in translations ; others distinguished themselves as Latin poets ; some wrote love verses for the use of rich young gentlemen who could afford to buy panegyrics for their mistresses ; and not a few, as a last resource, endeavoured to subsist upon political pasquinades, scurrilous lampoons, satires, and doggerel ballads. Thus, in various ways, a population of poets — good, bad, and indifferent — were called into existence ; and after flickering for a season in their different phases of temporary notoriety, went out, one by one, into total darkness. If it be objected that it is a waste of time to revive the recollection of such ephemeral versifiers, all that can be said is, that if they were never to be noticed, we should lose, not only the instruction which the knowledge of their failure and its causes affords, but also a very curious chapter in the history of our national poetry.

Of the names that are excluded from our series, some were set aside on account of the scantiness of the materials, and others, because they presented no distinct points of individual interest, being more like the shadows of their cóntemporaries, than men of original powers. An enumeration of a few of the omitted poetasters will show, at least, that enough remains behind to tempt those collectors who may wish to carry the investigation farther, although it is very doubtful whether they would be rewarded in proportion to the drudgery which such an inquiry would impose upon them. With this enumeration — in itself a selection from a heap of notes — these outlines of the minor poets may be considered to be as complete as it need be rendered for all general purposes.

GEORGE CORYAT, a divine, who flourished about the middle of the sixteenth century, and author of several Latin poems: he died in his parsonage-house at Odcombe, in Somersetshire, and, for some inexplicable reason, was preserved above ground for six weeks, by his son. WILLIAM WYRLEY (1566—1617), an industrious collector of ancient arms and inscriptions, who was created Rouge Croix, a pursuivant of arms, and who is claimed as a poet by Bliss, on the ground that there were two copies of verses affixed to a book of his, called the *Use of Armory;* but as it was the custom of that day to prefix such tributes from friendly writers, the proofs of the claim are not very satisfactory. THOMAS FREEMAN (1591— ——), who graduated in Oxford, and is said to have been highly esteemed for his poetry by Shakspeare, Chapman, Heywood, Owen the epigrammatist, and others; but he appears to have published only two books of epigrams, and some miscellaneous pieces, the best of which was a poem in praise of Cromwell. RICHARD ARGALL, of whom nothing is known, except that he was a noted divine in the reign of James I., and that he wrote and published several sacred poems, a funeral elegy on the bishop of London, and sundry pious meditations. HENRY HUTTON, equally obscure, but in his own day he enjoyed some celebrity as an autaor of satirical epigrams, and a curious book called *A compendious History of Ixion's Wheel.* JOHN HEATH (1585—1619), a pupil in Wyckham's school, who wrote a multitude of epigrams, and translated De Moulin's defence of James against Bellarmine. RICHARD NICHOLES (1584—1616), of whom we have no particulars, except that he wrote some poetry, for which Wood says, he was " esteemed eminent in his time," and of whom Park declares that he was " a melodious versifier, if not a first-rate poet:" all that remains of him is this breath of incense. RICHARD BARNFIELD (1594 — ——), chiefly celebrated as a writer of sonnets; Phillips ranks him with Lodge, Green, and Breton; Beloe observes, that much cannot be said in favour of his poetry; and Warton praises him for tenderness and purity. ROBERT ROCHE (1577—1629), wrote one poem called *Eustathia, or the Constancy of Susanna*, which had become so rare, that Wood gives a long extract from it in the *Athenæ Oxoniensis*. ROBERT HAYMAN (1583—1632), in his youth an associate of Ben Jonson and Drayton, in his maturity, governor of a plantation in Newfoundland, where he wrote some *Quodlibets, Epigrams*, and other small parcels, both moral and divine; he is said to have had, " though fantastical, (as most poets are!) the general vogue of a poet." JOHN LLOYD, remarkable only for having written a paraphrase on the *Canticles* of Solomon. MARTIN LLEWELIN, or Llvelyn (1616—1681), one of the ejected of the parliamentary commissioners, who had sense enough to devote himself to the study of physic, in which he succeeded, and folly enough to write some mad verses against a rival practitioner, in which he failed. THOMAS WEAVER (1616—1662), another poet turned out of the university of Oxford by the presbyterians, and author of a collection of songs, in which he ridiculed the puritans so effectually, that the book was denounced as a seditious libel against the government, and a capital indictment founded upon it; the author escaped with his life, in consequence of a very humane charge from the judge; he afterwards sunk into the office of an exciseman at Liverpool, where we are told he was called captain Weaver, and where he died in inglorious obscurity. Wood attributes his.

death to having "prosecuted too much the crimes of poets, which brought him to his grave in the church there:" but as Wood seems to have been impressed with a general notion that all poets were, more or less, depraved, and especially as he does not particularise which of the multifarious iniquities of the poets produced the catastrophe, the reader is left to his own conjectures concerning captain Weaver's offences. HENRY BOLD, a "macaronique," "heroique," and "lyrique" poet, who was attached to the law about the middle of the seventeenth century, and who died in one of the last places in the world where one would look for a poet — Chancery-lane. JOHN SPEED, about the same date, was one of the victims of the university visitors, turned physician, and wrote some poetical satires of local and personal application, which had the good luck to run through two or three editions. ROBERT WHITEHALL (16— —1685), another scholar ejected by the visitors, but with good reason; for, in answer to their usual interrogatory, whether he would submit to their authority, he made this pert reply—

"My name's Whitehall, God bless the poet;
If I submit, the king shall know it."

But he repented this indiscretion; and, through the intercession of the Ingoldsbies, was afterwards restored, and became a physician. He was a bad poet, and was utterly destitute of principle, devoting what little skill he possessed to time-serving applauses of Cromwell and the presbyterians. RICHARD HEAD (—— —1678), an Irishman of exuberant spirits, bound to a Latin bookseller in London, a trade which he soon abandoned to write humorous poems, comedies, and novels; he was unfortunate through life, and was at length relieved of his troubles by being drowned at sea on his way to the Isle of Wight. SAMUEL AUSTIN (1636—1665), a conceited fellow, who fancied himself a poet, and published a volume not inappropriately called *Naps upon*

Parnassus; a sleepy Muse nipt and pincht, though not awakened." HENRY LOTE, described as a divine poet, because he versified Solomon, and produced divers sonnets addressed to persons of quality. HENRY VAUGHAN, who was called the Silurist, because he happened to come from that part of Wales which was formerly inhabited by the Silures. He was a physician of some eminence, and acquired no inconsiderable celebrity as an author of devotional poetry. RICHARD REEVE (1642—1693), a Latin poet of celebrity, who was appointed usher to the school which stood near the great gate of Magdalen college, Oxford; but, embracing the catholic religion, he went to Douay, and became a Benedictine monk, and taught poetry, rhetoric, and Greek. He afterwards went to a little monastery called La Cell, in the diocese of Meaux, but was recalled to England as head master of the Gloucester hospital, which he was obliged to abandon at the revolution, taking refuge in the house of the catholic recorder, where he was discovered, seized, and confined in Gloucester castle, as a priest and jesuit, although he was neither. He ultimately died in Berkeley-street, Piccadilly. He was celebrated as a teacher, and is said to have educated no fewer than 60 clergymen of the established church, and forty Roman catholic priests. JAMES SCUDAMORE (1642—1666), a bachelor of arts, who wrote *Homer a-la-mode*, a mock poem on the first and second books of the Iliad, and who was drowned in the river near Hereford, where he was swimming for his amusement. ABRAHAM MARKLAND (1645— ——), a clergyman, and prebendary of Winchester, who published, in 1667, a collection of poems on the birth and restoration of Charles II., on prince Rupert's victories, the plague, and the fire of London. THOMAS WOOD (1661— ——), a barrister, patronised by sir John Holt, who translated the first satire of Juvenal, which, in his own words, he " taught to speak plain English," and some of the odes of Anacreon, and wrote a rambling pindaric on the death of Charles II. FRANCIS WILLIS (1663— ——), a physician, who was associated with Wood in the translation of Anacreon, and published also various miscellaneous poems. SAMUEL WESLEY (1666— ——), a clergyman, remarkable only for having written a life of our Saviour in the form of an heroic poem, and sundry other things not very creditable to his profession.

MATTHEW PRIOR.

1664—1721.

Matthew Prior was born on the 21st of July, 1664. So far all authorities agree; but concerning his parentage, and the place of his birth, it is almost impossible to come to any very confident conclusion. On his admission into St. John's college, Cambridge, he was registered by the president as Matthew Prior of Winburn in Middlesex; and by himself, on the following day, as Matthew Prior of Dorsetshire, in which county, and not in Middlesex, Winburn, or Winborne, as it stands in the *Villare*, is to be found. Five years afterwards, when he was a candidate for a fellowship, he registered himself as of Middlesex, which, whether it was correct or not, he was in a measure compelled to do for the sake of consistency. " The last record," says Johnson, " ought to be preferred because it was made upon oath." But the grounds of this preference, which ought to be decisive even upon more important subjects than the birthplace of a poet, are so sensibly shaken by suspicious circumstances, that a doubt must always linger over the statement. It has been said in his extenuation, that he was obliged to conceal his county in order to entitle himself to the fellowship. *   Again, it has not escaped observation that, as a native of Winborne, he is styled *Filius Georgii Prior, generosi,* which is altogether irreconcilable with the assertion that his father was a citizen and joiner, and lived in London in good repute.† Johnson remarks upon this uncertainty about his origin, that " he was, perhaps, willing enough to leave his birth unsettled, in hope, like Don Quixote, that the historian of his actions might find him some illustrious alliance." If Prior entertained so silly a prospect of being smuggled into renown, he was egregiously mistaken in his calculations; for, although a great deal of industry has been thrown away to ascertain his father's rank in society, no difficulty whatever has existed in tracing the other branches of his family.

Upon the death of his father, whatever he may have been, Prior was committed at a very early age to the care of his uncle, Samuel Prior, who kept the Rummer tavern at Charing-cross.* By this uncle he was treated with marked affection and tenderness, which he afterwards gratefully acknowledged.† He was sent at a proper age to Westminster school, of which he was admitted a scholar in 1681. We are told that Dr. Busby, who then presided over that school, had no sooner furnished him with the means of displaying his genius, than he rapidly distinguished himself above his form-fellows. But, before he had remained there long, his uncle took him home, in order to give him a practical knowledge of his own business, which he naturally considered of greater consequence to his future prospects than all the Latin, Greek, and philosophy, Westminster was able to bestow upon him. In this unpropitious situation the embryo poet remained, until he was rescued from it by a fortunate accident, which his own good sense and industry enabled him to profit by to the utmost.

After his removal from Westminster school, he had continued to indulge his inclination for classical studies, whenever he could spare time from his new employment; and acquirements so rare in such circumstances soon drew upon him the notice of the polite company that used to resort to his uncle's tavern. It happened one day that a party of gentlemen, conversing on a pas-

---

* At his house the annual feast of the nobility and gentry of the parish of St. Martin-in-the-Fields wa. celebrated on Oct. 14. 1685.

† See *Memoirs of Prior*, by Humphries, prefixed to the third volume of his poems, in 1733, third edition, p. 1.

sage of one of the odes of Horace, were divided in their opinion respecting it, and one of them said, "I find we are not likely to agree in our criticisms; but, if I am not mistaken, there is a young fellow in the house who is able to set us right," and thereon named Prior, who was immediately sent for, and desired to give his version of the disputed passage, which he did, with such ingenuous modesty, and so much to the satisfaction of the company, that the earl of Dorset, who was present, resolved from that moment to remove him from the business of the tavern to a mode of life more adapted to his genius and talents. Under the countenance and at the cost of that nobleman, he was accordingly sent to Cambridge, and supported, while he remained there, in a manner worthy of the generosity of his patron. Such is the account given in the *Memoirs of his own Times,* and in those by Humphries; but Burnet gives a slightly different account of this part of Prior's history. " Prior," he observes, " had been taken a boy out of a tavern by the earl of Dorset, who accidentally found him reading Horace; and he, being very generous, gave him an education in literature."* Yet it would appear that his greatest friend in early life, the man whom he considered responsible for diverting him from his original destination, was Fleetwood Sheppard, esq. To him, on his coming from Cambridge to London, in 1689, he addressed an epistle, from which the following passage may be extracted for the sake of its autobiographical interest. It contains a plain recital of his juvenile condition, and of what had been done to remove him from it, with a sort of reproach to his patrons for not having done more: —

" My business, sir, you'll quickly guess,
  Is to desire some little place;
  And fair pretensions I have for 't,
  Much need and very small desert.
  Whene'er I writ to you, I wanted;
  I always begg'd, you always granted.

* History of his own Times, vol. ii. p. 584.

Now, as you took me up when little,
Gave me my learning and my vittle ;
Ask'd for me from my Lord things fitting,
Kind as I'd been of your begetting ;
Confirm what formerly you've given,
Nor leave me now at six and sevens,
As Sunderland has left Mun-Stephens.
No family, that takes a whelp,
When first he laps, and scarce can yelp,
Neglects, and turns him out of gate,
When he's grown up to dog's estate ;
Nor parish, if they once adopt
The spurious brats by strollers dropt,
Leave them, when grown up lusty fellows,
To the wide world, that is the gallows ;
No thank them for their love, that's worse
Than if they'd throttled them at nurse.
    " My uncle, rest his soul, when living,
Might have contriv'd me ways of thriving ;
Taught me with cider to replenish
My vats or ebbing tide of rhenish ;
So when for hock I drew prickt white wine,
Swear 't had the flavour, and was right wine ;
Or sent me with ten pounds to Furni-
val's Inn, to some good rogue-attorney ;
Where now by forging deeds, and cheating,
I 'ad found some handsome ways of getting.
    " All this you made me quit to follow
That sneaking whey-faced god Apollo ;
Sent me among a fiddling crew
Of folks, I 'ad never seen or knew ;
Calliope, and God knows who.
To add no more invectives to it,
You spoil'd a youth to make a poet."

Sheppard, however, seems to have been only the medium through whom the earl of Dorset patronised the
young poet, and was probably almoner, or private secretary, to that nobleman.

Prior was admitted to St. John's College, Cambridge,
in 1682, became bachelor of arts in 1686, and was soon
afterwards made a fellow. During his residence at the
university, he formed an acquaintance with Crashaw
Montague, subsequently earl of Halifax, and, in conjunc-

tion with him, wrote and published, in 1687 *, *The*
Country and City Mouse, in ridicule of Dryden's *Hind
and Panther*. This piece, which was well calculated to
bring the writer into notice, led to the immediate advancement of Montague, of which Prior, with great
justice, and some asperity, complained in the epistle to
Sheppard already cited.† From the effect which this
poem is said to have produced upon Dryden, and an
observation he made in reference to its authors ‡, it must
he inferred that Prior was at that time an occasional
frequenter of Wills's coffee-house, and that he was known
personally to the author of the *Hind and Panther*, as
well as to the other wits who used to assemble there.

In 1688 he wrote his poem on *The Deity*, as an exercise for his college, which had been in the practice of
sending every year to the earl of Exeter some poems
upon sacred subjects, in acknowledgment of a benefaction
conferred on them by the bounty of one of his ancestors.
This poem is supposed by Johnson to have recommended him to some notice; " for his praise of the
countess's music, and his lines on the famous picture of
Seneca, afford reason for imagining that he was more or
less conversant with that family." According to the
Biographia Britannica, it procured him so much fame
at Cambridge, and raised him so high in his own estimation, as to induce him to leave his college, and, spe-
culating on the strength of his reputation, to push his
own fortune in the world.

His political expectations, however, were attributable
to his share of the celebrity arising from *The Country
and City Mouse;* to the fact, that his associate in that
poem was rewarded by a place under the government;
and to the still more cheering circumstance, the accession
of the whigs to the administration of affairs by the revolution. Feeling a college to be too limited a sphere
for the exercise of his talents, and urged on by high

---

* Johnson assigns the date of 1688 to this publication, and makes it second
in order of time to *The Deity*, a mistake easily rectified by examination.
† See antè, p. 66..   ‡ See antè, ibid.

hopes of success in a political career, he went to London in 1689, and immediately applied to Fleetwood Sheppard, through the poetical epistle to which reference has already been made. At the solicitation of that gentleman he was introduced by the earl of Dorset to the court, and appointed, in 1690, secretary to the English embassy deputed to the congress at the Hague.* The ambassadors and plenipotentiaries were, the earls of Pembroke and Portland, and lord Dursley (afterwards earl of Berkeley). Oldmixon has very unfairly misrepresented him as secretary only to the latter; whereas he was secretary to all, and derived his appointment directly from William and Mary.† When it is remembered that the congress at the Hague was the most splendid assembly of princes and nobles which Europe had witnessed for many years, and that it met for no less an object than the formation of the grand alliance against Louis XIV., it may fairly become a matter of surprise that a post of such importance should have been conferred on a young man just come from college, of obscure birth, inexperienced in public business, and who had no higher claims to recommend him than a share in the authorship of a political squib. But, although some of Prior's critics denied to him the possession of political abilities at any period of his life, his selection by the king for this responsible office must be admitted as a proof that very favourable anticipations were formed of his talents, and his conduct certainly shows that he did not disappoint them.

Looking back upon his early years, and tracing his progress from boyhood to the sudden turn of good fortune that raised him to this influential and lucrative position, it is obvious enough that Prior's success in the pursuit of political distinction, gave a new direction to his thoughts, which nearly marred his literary tendencies. The poet was sunk in the diplomatist. It is true he

---

· * It is thus expressed in his epitaph : " Serenysimis Regi Gulielmo Regi-· naque Mariæ in Congressione Federatorum Hagæ, 1690, celebrata Secretarius.

† Oldmixon, History of Englana, p. 150, ediion, 1735, fol.

acquired distinction as a poet notwithstanding; but that
distinction was acquired in spite of circumstances. How
much greater he might have become — how much he
might enriched our national stores, had literature become
the business, instead of the amusement of his life, may
be presumed from the fact that, like Pope, he "lisped
in numbers," and that even in the midst of the harass-
ing labours of his maturity, he always yearned secretly
towards those delights of poetry which he could no
longer enjoy except in incidental snatches. In a MS. in
his own handwriting, entitled, *Heads of a Treatise upon
Learning,* which was formerly in the possession of the
duchess dowager of Portland, he makes a sort of confession, to the following effect, of these early tastes and vain
regrets: — " As to my own part, I felt this (poetical)
impulse very soon, and shall still continue to feel it as
long as I can think. I remember nothing farther in life,
than that I made verses. I chose Guy of Warwick for
my first hero, and killed Colborne, the giant, before I
was big enough for Westminster. But I had two accidents in youth which hindered me from being quite
possessed with the muse. I was bred in a college where
prose was more in fashion than verse; and as soon as
I had taken my first degree, was sent the king's secretary to the Hague. There I had enough to do in studying my French and Dutch, and altering my Terentian
and original style into that of articles and conventions."
     In this task of self-subjugation he effectually succeeded,
and carried himself throughout the negotiation with so
much discretion, that immediately upon his return his
majesty conferred special marks of favour upon him, and
appointed him one of the gentlemen of the bedchamber,
for the sake of keeping him near his person. This
situation enabled him to enjoy independence and leisure
for a few years, during which he divided this golden
time between the muses and Mrs. Elizabeth Singer,
afterwards the celebrated Mrs. Rowe *, to whom he is

---

* See her life, prefixed to his *Miscellaneous Works,* 1739.

said to have paid his addresses. Like other court poets,: he produced several small pieces on the events of the, war, and various public occurrences, but was too much favoured by fortune to be tempted into the depths of any more elaborate subjects. On the death of queen Mary, in 1695, he wrote a long ode, which was presented to the king, " by whom," says Johnson, " it was not likely to be ever read." The retaking of Namur, in the same year, by William, gave him a more agreeable opportunity of displaying his poetical abilities. Louis having taken it in 1697, in sight of the allies, who were unable to rescue it, Boileau, the French poet, wrote a pindaric hymn on the occasion, in which he elevated his royal master above all the heroes of Greece. Prior burlesqued this extravagant effusion in an English ballad, and caused both to be reprinted and circulated together. This burlesque was considered a very successful sally, and, in consequence of the great fame of his adversary, procured him more general notice than any of his preceding compositions, with the single exception of the lucky parody with which he entered life. He now accompanied William to Holland as gentleman of the bedchamber in 1696, and presented him, on the discovery of the conspiracy, with a copy of verses addressed to the guardian angels of mankind, in which he apostrophises Louis as if he really suspected him to be privy to that plot, peremptorily requiring him, at the same time,

" To be at once a Heroe and a Foe."

On the first overtures of peace he was again employed in the way which appeared to be best suited to his abilities, and obtained the post of secretary to the embassy, at the treaty of Ryswick in 1697.* After his return, the same year, he was made principal secretary of state in Ireland. In 1698 he went to Paris as secretary to the embassy there, in which post he con-

* He received a present of 200 guineas from the lords justices for his trouble in bringing over this treaty.

tinned till July or August, 1699, during the successive
embassies of the earls of Portland and Jersey. While
one of the officers of the royal household was showing
him the apartments and curiosities of Versailles, particularly the victories of Louis, which had been painted
by Le Brun in a very ostentatious manner, with inscriptions so arrogant that even Boileau and Racine
deemed it necessary to make them more simple, Prior
was asked whether the king of England had such de-
corations in his palace. " The monuments of my
master's actions are to be seen every where but in his
own house," was his reply. Notwithstanding this
indisposition to flatter *le grand monarque,* his personal
qualities rendered him a great favourite with Louis,
and gave him so much influence at the French court,
that, although the powers of his commission were superseded, on the appointment of the earl of Manchester to
the embassy, in 6199, he did not leave Paris for some
time after the arrival of that nobleman ; and, while he
remained there, was enabled to render him considerable
service.

On the 20th of August, 1699, he left Paris for Lee, in
Holland, whence, after he had a long and particular audience of William, he returned to England towards the end
of October, and became, on his arrival, under-secretary
in the office of the earl of Jersey. He had not been more
than a few days in his new employment, when he was
sent back to Paris to assist the ambassador in the affair of
the partition treaty by his interest with the French court.
The very great credit which he possessed at that period,
both in England and in France, is evident from the
letters which passed between the earl of Jersey and the
earl of Manchester.* The former, in a letter dated at
Whitehall, October 23, 1699, O. S. says — " It is his
majesty's desire that you discourse the business of the
partition treaty with Mr. Prior ; and according to the
account your lordship gives next of it, you shall receive

* See the earl of Manchester's letters, in Prior's *History of his own
Times,* p. 105–6. 113–4.

his majesty's further direction." The earl of Manchester, in one of his letters, says, " Mr. Prior's coming here, and the private audience I had of the king, the day of my entry, occasioned much discourse, and did me service with the ministers, for now they see that the king does not rely on monsieur de Tallard. King James, upon Mr. Prior's coming hither, believed I was to be recalled, and he to be left here, which for some time gave him great satisfaction." Prior arranged the business of the treaty to the entire satisfaction of both courts; and leaving Paris on the 18th of November, reached London with the speed of a courier * ; bringing with him a letter from the earl of Manchester to the earl of Jersey, in which the writer says that he did not trouble the latter with an account of what he had done in obedience to his majesty's commands, "since Mr. Prior is informed of all proceedings and what passed in my private audience. I shall always discharge his majesty's orders with all the secrecy and care imaginable. I am apt to think this occasion will make monsieur De Tallard take care how he behaves himself, for he was not very easy when he found Mr. Prior had come."

During the Christmas holidays of this year, he published his celebrated *Carmen Seculare*, a poem purely panegyrical, and of no value beyond the immediate interest of the king whose actions and virtues it celebrated.

In 1700 the university of Cambridge applied to him to do them some service with the learned on the other side of the channel, which he most readily performed ; and was, in return, with equal alacrity, created a master of arts, upon the king's mandate.

The earl of Jersey accepting the post of lord chamberlain, about the midsummer of this year, Prior's place of under secretary became vacant; but Locke being soon after compelled to resign his seat at the board of trade†;

---

* Prior, in a letter to the earl of Manchester, says, " I arrived here on Friday night, and every body confesses that only Roger is fitter than I to be sent express." This Roger was a servant usually employed on such occasions.

† As one of the commissioners.

on account of ill health, Prior was appointed to succeed him. This was considered to be in many respects a better place than the former, as he had less work and more profit, and the business to be transacted was generally thought more adapted to his capacity and mental acquirements. Towards the close of that year, he entertained a notion of setting up for Cambridge, and applied to the earl of Manchester for his interest. In a letter dated December 10th, 1700, O.S., he writes thus to that nobleman : — "As to my own affairs, I have a great many friends who would set me up at Cambridge; I know I shall find great opposition from Mr. Hammond's party there; and great trouble, in case I should throw him out, from those men, who will never be satisfied, let me act as I will or can. If your lordship thinks it convenient, I know you will not refuse me your letter to the university." This design, however, he seems to have abandoned, as we find him sitting in the new parliament, which met in February, 1701, as representative for East Grimstead, in Sussex, and voting for the impeachment of the several lords who were charged with advising the partition treaty. This has been justly considered one of the blackest acts of his political life; but, perhaps, it is only fair to observe, that while he obeyed the orders of his sovereign, in carrying on the negotiations respecting that treaty, he never approved of it himself. On the contrary, he seems all throughout to have condemned the measure, notwithstanding that he participated in the proceedings connected with it. He thus betrays his feelings in the letter to the earl of Manchester already quoted: " I take it to be happy for the king," he observes, " that the *will* is preferred by the French at a time when every body was peevish against the court, though with reason (God knows), about the treaty ; " and in his *Conversation, a Tale,* we find the following passage : —

" Matthew, who knew the whole intrigue,
Ne'er much approved that mystic league."

Lord Jersey is also said to have acted in a similar manner with regard to that treaty; but, however Prior may be extenuated by the necessity of his position for acting against his judgment, in submission to the commands of his sovereign, it is impossible to find any excuse for his subsequent vote in parliament. After he had violated his conscience to please the king, the least that could have been expected was, that he should give it a little repose where he was no longer under similar obligations to violate it over again. But the whole of his conduct on this occasion is inexplicable; nor is it rendered much more clear or satisfactory by the following remarks on the impeachments, which he makes in his history of his own times :—

"It seems to have been agreed," says he, "both by the lords and commons, in this dispute, that the partition treaty was of pernicious consequence; and that the transacting it in private, without communicating it to the council, was a high misdemeanor in those that advised and transacted it. But whether the commons suspected that the lords, who were generally in the interest of the old ministry, would not pass any censure on the impeached lords, or for what other reason, is uncertain, the commons seem to have been a little dilatory in their proceedings, and might design the lords should have lain under an impeachment during the recess of the parliament. There might possibly be something of party also in the case : the impeached lords were the chiefs of the whigs, and had long reigned at court without control; and the tories, who succeeded them, had a view, perhaps, of preventing their returning to their posts, as well as of bringing them to justice for negotiating the partition treaty, and for the other misdemeanors mentioned in the articles. There are few prosecutions of this kind; but there is a great deal of private pique, interest, and resentment mixed with views of the public good."

It is generally supposed that it was at this period Prior went over to the tories ; but as he did not become an open opponent of his old friends the whigs until some years later, any observations suggested by his ter- giversation may be advantageously postponed.

Upon the accession of Anne, a war with France break- ing out again, Prior once more invoked his muse to cele- brate the glories of his country. " When," says Johnson, " the battle of Blenheim called forth all the versemen, Prior, among the rest, took care to show his delight in the increasing honour of his country by *An Epistle to Boileau*." If he were really a tory at this time, he adopted rather a strange method of avowing his creed, unless it is to be understood that his admiration of Marlborough the hero absorbed his hostility to Marl- borough the politician. In the epistle on this battle he demands, with all the exultation of an excited patriot,—

" And is there not a sound in Marlborough's name,
Which thou and all thy brethren ought to claim,
Sacred to verse, and sure of endless fame?"

About this period he published a volume of his poems, together with an encomium on his first patron, the earl of Dorset. This collection opened with the college exercise, and ended with *The Nut-brown Maid*.

In 1706 the battle of Ramilies inspired him with another poem, and he published his ode *On the glorious Success of her Majesty's Arms*. Of this production Johnson observes, that " it would not be easy to name any other composition produced by that event which is now remembered." This was true in Johnson's time, but it is no longer so. Prior's ode is now forgotten, a ong with the others.

It has been supposed that the speech put into the mouth of the royal treaty breaker, in this ode, had pro- bably some foundation in fact, for presently after that battle Louis made overtures for peace, as appears from a letter written by the duke of Bavaria to the duke of Marlborough, dated from *Mons*, October 21.1706, which begins thus: —" The most christian king, sir, finding that some overtúres of peace which he had caused to be made by *private ways* *," &c.

The next character in which Prior appears is that of a contributor to the *Examiner*, a tory paper, set up under the influence of Mr. Harley and St. John, and chiefly supported by the writings of Prior and Swift, Mr. Oldsworth, Dr. Freind, and Mrs. Manley. In this publication he abused all his political opponents — and especially the duke of Marlborough, against whom he is generally thought to have written (at least in conjunction with Swift) a very satirical fable, entitled *The Widow and her Cat*, which concludes with these lines : —

> " So glaring is thine insolence, —
> So vile thy breach of trust is, —
> That longer with thee to dispense
> Were want of power, or want of sense.
> There, Towzer, do him justice —— "

For this complete renunciation of his former views there is not a shadow of excuse or justification to be found, except his own statement before the secret committee, that when he thought Marlborough too much influenced by private designs in prolonging the war, he concurred with the queen's inclination for peace. But in justice to him, it must be observed that he had never been a violent partisan of the whigs ; for, although he entered life with them, he did not conspicuously identify himself with their party. In 1699 he writes to the earl of Manchester, that " whig and tory are, as of old, implacable ; " and in 1700 he addresses the same nobleman as follows : —

" Whig and tory are railing on both sides, so violent, that the government may be easily overturned by the madness of either faction. We take it to be our play to do nothing against common sense or common law — and to be for those who will support the crown, rather than oblige either party." Thus it would appear,

---

* Salmon's Modern History, vol. xxv. p. 340.

that instead of lending himself to either party, his real
desire was to support, on all occasions, the interests of
the crown. This conduct is perfectly reconcilable with
his answer before the select committee, that when the
queen wished for peace, he deemed it his duty to
coincide in her inclination ; — and throws a further
light upon his proceedings in the affair of the partition
treaty. The divine right of monarchs was his rule of
faith, and he does not seem to have committed any
more flagrant inconsistencies than. that doctrine inevitably imposed upon him. If it be remembered also,
that about that period the most singular notions were
entertained in both our universities respecting the rights
of sovereigns, it will not appear surprising that Prior
should have been infected by the same sentiments which
prevailed amongst nine-tenths of his contemporary
scholars and gownsmen in these realms. He does not
appear to have been very obnoxious to the partisans of
the exiled family ; but, on the contrary, to have been
considered rather more inclined to favour their interests
than any of his whig colleagues. How else can we
account for the satisfaction which the expectation of his
replacing the earl of Manchester in the embassy at
Paris afforded to James, as appears by the extract .
previously cited from that nobleman's letter.* While
he was acting with the whigs, we have seen that he
scarcely called himself a whig, and was exceedingly
temperate in his political feelings ; but as soon as he
became a tory, his zeal knew no limits, and he carried
his new enthusiasm so far, that he even exhibited reluctance to mix in society with persons of different
opinions. He was one of the sixteen tories who met
weekly, and agreed to address each other by the title of
brother. To the earl of Oxford and his family he
seems to have been extremely attached, not only by
political feelings, but also by private and social relations.
He made that nobleman, together with a Mr. Adrian
Drift his literary and pecuniary executors, as being

* See antè, p. 241.

" the noblest and kindest men I shall leave behind me
in the world." When personal feelings of so powerful
a nature, combined with the other circumstances of the
times, laid siege to his political principles, we cannot be
surprised at the latter having been compelled to sur-
render.

The steadfastness of his adherence to this party
might almost be allowed to counterbalance his error or
his guilt in forsaking the other. The panegyrist or
defender of Prior might safely rest here; but the
historian of his life is bound to lay before the reader all
the facts and circumstances by which an impartial
judgment may be formed of the character of the man.
In his *Heads of a Treatise upon Learning*, to which
reference has already been made, he sets forth his
reasons for abstaining from satire, in the following
terms, after telling us that the love of verse was his
earliest passion : —" So that poetry which, by the bent
of my mind, might have become the business of my
life, was, by the happiness of my education, only the
amusement of it ; and in this too, from the prospect of
some little fortune to be made, and friendship to be
cultivated with the great men, I did not launch much
into satire ; which, however agreeable at the present to
the writers or encouragers of it, does in time do neither
of them good : considering the uncertainty of fortune,
and the various changes of mnistry, and that every man,
as he resents, may punish in his turn of greatness ; and
that in England a man is less safe as to politics, than
he is in a bark upon the coast in regard to the change
of the wind and the danger of shipwreck." Is it not very
possible that he was influenced by the same prudential
considerations in his political as in his poetical career ?

In 1711 Prior was made a commissioner of customs
by the tory ministry ; and shortly after, when it was
determined to treat with France, he was appointed
minister plenipotentiary to that court. He proceeded
privately to France with propositions of peace, arranged
his business with all possible despatch, and returned to

London in a few weeks, bringing with him the abbè
Gaultier, and the French minister Mesnager, invested
with full powers to settle all preliminaries.* The
transaction not being at that period fully avowed, all
three had been seized at Canterbury by a Mr. Mackay,
the master of the Dover packet-boats, but had been also
immediately released by orders from the queen.

The first meeting in this negotiation was held on the
20th of September, 1711, at Mr. Prior's house, where
Mr. St. John, the earl of Dartmouth, lord treasurer
Harley, and the earl of Shrewsbury, having assembled
to confer with Monsieur Mesnager, looked on Prior as
a person of so much importance in the diplomatic
arrangements as to adopt the following minute for the
approbation of the queen —:

" My lord treasurer moved, and all my lords were of
the same opinion, that Mr. Prior should be added to
those who are empowered to sign ; the reason for which
is, because he, having personally treated with Monsieur
de Torcy, is the best witness we can produce of the
sense in which the general preliminary engagements are
entered into : besides which, as he is the best versed in
matters of trade of all your majesty's servants who have
been trusted in this secret, if you should think fit to
employ him in the future treaty of commerce, it will be
of consequence that he has been a party concerned in
concluding that convention which must be the rule of
this treaty."

In accordance with this minute, it was intended to
associate him with the two other ministers who were
to take care of our commercial interests at the treaty of
Utrecht ; but the earl of Strafford, refusing to be joined
in a commission with a person of such lowly origin,
threatened to lay down his employment, and the cabinet
were compelled to abandon the appointment.

The meeting on the 20th September with M. Mesnager was in some measure clandestine, as the intention

* Upon Prior's arrival in Paris, De Torcy writes to Mr. St. John to acknowledge with pleasure the return of Mr. Prior, and that he wished that
he had greater liberty to employ those talents which he was persuaded he
would have made good use of.

of treating was not then avowed ; and was, therefore,
made the ground of a charge of high treason afterwards,
when the whigs came into office. To this charge Prior
replies, in his answer to the report of the committee of
secrecy, that no treaty was ever made without private
interviews and preliminary discussions ; — a defence so
very obvious, that it is only surprising his enemies gave
him the opportunity of making it.

Though Prior did not go to Utretcht, yet, in conse-
sequence of matters proceeding so slowly there, Bolingbroke went to Paris in August, 1712, in order to ac-
commodate the differences which had remained unsettled at the congress, and Prior accompanied or followed him ; and, after his return, had the appointments and authority of an ambassador, though no
public character. By some mistake of the instructions
from home, the court of France had been disgusted;
and Bolingbroke thus implores Prior to repair the blunders of others: " Dear Mat , hide the nakedness of
thy country, and give the best turn thy fertile brain will
furnish thee with to the blunders of thy countrymen,
who are not much better politicians than the French are
Poets."

The duke of Shrewsbury went shortly after on a
formal embassy to Paris. It was the intention of the
ministry to have joined Prior in the commission ; but
Shrewsbury, like Strafford, refused to be associated with
a man of such humble birth. Prior, however, continued to act without a title during the duke's stay, who
transacted very little business of the embassy, but merely,
by his high rank and public character, gave a sanction to
the negotiations conducted by the more gifted individual
whom " the accident of an accident " had afforded him
a pretence for despising. But though he had no regular
commission, he was received at both courts, and was
sent in October, 1712, by Louis, with a letter to the
queen, to interest her in favour of the elector of Bavaria.
In this he says, " Madame, my Sister — You having
acquainted me that you have an entire confidence in

Mr. Prior, I thought he would be more capable than any body to inform you of the new proofs that I am ready to give you of the particular regard I have for you ; as also my desire to terminate without any delay, in concert with you, the negotiations of peace. He goes into England to give you an account of the further advances that I am willing to make to facilitate an entire conclu.. sion of this work. . . . . . I expect with impatience the return of Mr. Prior, whose conduct is very agree- able to me." Prior returned to Paris about the middle of November with a conciliatory answer from the queen. During the time that Shrewsbury was still at Paris, even Bolingbroke applied to Prior in the following terms : " Monsieur de Torcy has a confidence in you ; make use of it, once for all, upon this occasion, and con- vince him thoroughly that we must give a different turn to our parliament and our people, according to their resolution at this crisis."

It was only in August, 1713, that Prior's official dignity as ambassador commenced, from which time it continued until the death of queen Anne. Even after that event he exercised the functions of public minister to the December following, and was paid the allowance of a plenipotentiary up to that date. But it is supposed that he did not enjoy all the advantages of his station : something was cut off in consideration of his low birth. He did not receive as much as was usually given to ambassadors ; he had not a service of plate, and his remittances were not punctually paid. An ambassador of so mean an origin was expected to labour at a reduced rate of payment.

It has been stated that his recall and degradation followed immediately on the accession of George I. in August 1714.* But he remained in a public capacity in France for several months subsequently. His suc- cessor, the earl of Stair, was not appointed till the 4th of October, and did not take on himself the title of am- bassador for some time after. Prior presented a me-

* See letter of lord Halifax, Dec. 2. 1714.—*Hist. of his own Times.*

morial to the king of France on the 3d of October, requiring him to demolish the canal and new works at Mardyke; and was allowed all the expenses of a plenipotentiary from the 1st of August (the accession of George) up to the 1st of December, amounting to 1176 guineas. This was a sum which it may be presumed that ministry would not have allowed him to earn, if they had thought him incompetent to his duties, or could have easily found a person to supply his place. Even after he was deprived of his office, he was treated with almost ostentatious courtesy until he arrived in England. The ministry declared that they felt "pleasure in informing him that his pecuniary demands were complied with." The earl of Halifax, in February, 1715, felt "great pleasure" in telling him that the king had directed them to pay him 2408l., which, together with whatever else was due to him, should "be despatched with all the favour and civility we can show you. It will be a great pleasure to me, in particular," he added, "to hasten your return from an unhappy station to your own country and friends, in which number I desire you will rank me." Surely this ex-ambassador must have been a man of some consideration and worth, when his victorious opponents thought it necessary to treat him — a renegade from their own ranks — with such respect.

The earl of Stair, on succeeding to Prior, took possession of all his papers, according to instructions from home. Prior, having received his arrears, and paid off his debts, early in March, 1715, arrived in England on the 25th of that month, and was immediately taken up by an order from the house of commons, and confined to his own house, under the custody of a messenger. On the 1st of April following, he was examined before a committee of the privy council, and then laid under stricter confinement, in the house of the messenger. The subject of his examination was the share which he and the other ministers had in the treaty of Utrecht. Walpole was chairman of the committee, and lord Coningsby, Mr. Stanhope, and Mr. Lechmere were the

principal interrogators.   Prior represents them as acting
with all the imperious boisterousness of men elated by
the recent and unexpected enjoyment of authority, and
forcing him by their bullying turbulence to sign a paper
which, if he had ever come before a legal tribunal, he
would have explained away or contradicted.   They were
particularly anxious to obtain a pretext for some accusation against the earl of Oxford, and asked him with
great earnestness who were present when the preliminary
articles were discussed and signed at his house.   He
replied, that either the earl of Oxford or the duke of
Shrewsbury was absent, but he could not tell which.
This perplexed them, as it afforded no grounds of a
charge against either.   On this attempt to entrap him
into the betrayal of his friends, he says, " Could any
thing be more absurd, or more inhuman, than to propose
to me a question, by the answering of which I might,
according to them, prove myself a traitor ?   And, notwithstanding their solemn promise, that nothing which
I could say should hurt myself, I had no reason to
trust them, for they violated that promise about five
hours after.   However, I owned I was there present.
Whether this was wisely done or no, I leave to my
friends to determine."   It seems that this committee
had already printed their report, and that in this examination they were endeavouring to eke out proofs to
support it.   Prior gives the following account of the
close of this singular proceeding.   " When I had thus
signed the paper, the chairman (Robert Walpole, esq.),
told me that the committee were not at all satisfied with
my behaviour, nor could give such an account of it to
the house that might merit their favour on my behalf ;
that at present they thought fit to lay me under stricter
confinement than in my own house."   He was accordingly confined to the house of the messenger, who was
told that he " must secure this prisoner, — it is for the
safety of the nation : if he escapes, you must answer
for it."
On the 10th of June following, Walpole moved his
impeachment, for holding clandestine conferences with

the French plenipotentiary. On the 17th of that month
he was committed to close custody, with orders that no
one should be admitted to see him without leave from
the speaker. Notwithstanding, however, all these seve-
rities, and his special exception from an act of grace
which was passed in 1717, he was soon afterwards discharged, without having even been brought to trial.
During his imprisonment he wrote his *Alma,* the only
piece among his works of which Pope said that he
should wish to be the author.

He had been through life remarkable for his judgment and forethought. Of this the retention of his fellowship, notwithstanding his numerous appointments, is
a remarkable proof. In reference to this part of his
conduct, the following story is related. After he became
a minister of state, he was often told that a fellowship
was too trifling an affair for him to keep ; and when he
was made an ambassador, it was particularly intimated
to him that a fellowship was scarcely consistent with
that dignity. But his reply was, " that every thing he
had besides was precarious, and when all failed, that
would be bread and cheese at last."

On being now discharged from prison, he felt the advantage of this prudential foresight ; for having always
spent whatever he received from his employments, he
was now, at the age of 53, without any security against
want, but the fellowship which he had been so frequently urged to resign. In this state, however, he did
not long remain ; for being encouraged to add other
poems to those which he had already printed, and to
publish them by subscription. the expedient succeeded,
by the exertions, care, and liberality of his friends.
The price of the volume was two guineas ; the sum
thus collected, 4000*l.* This circumstance proves how
sincerely and generally he was esteemed. To the above
sum lord Harley, the son of the earl of Oxford, added
4000*l.* more, to purchase Downhall, a small villa in Essex,
on condition that it should revert to him after Prior's
death.

" He had now," says Johnson, " what wits and philosophers have often wished, the power of passing the
day in contemplative tranquillity. But it seems that
busy men seldom live long in a state of quiet. It is not
unlikely his health declined. He complains of deafness,
" for " says he, " I took little care of my ears, while I
was not sure that my head was my own."

That he had retired to his fellowship before he published his poems, seems extremely probable. In a letter
to Swift, he says, " I have treated Lady Harriet at
Cambridge, (a fellow of a college treat!) and spoke
verses to her in a gown and cap ! (What, the plenipotentiary, so far concerned in the damned peace at
Utrecht — the man that makes up half the volume of
terse prose, that makes up the report of the committee,
speaking verses !) *Sic est homo sum.*"

But he left the college as soon as the villa was secured
for him, and in that retreat he spent the greater part of
the remainder of his life. There he employed his lei-
ture in preparing a defence of himself and the ministry
in the four last years of the reign of Anne, in answer to
the charge alleged against them in the report of the
secret committee, and also in writing a history of his
own times. But he had not completed the first, or proceeded far with the second, before he was taken off by a
lingering fever, on the 18th of September, 1721, at
Wimpole, the seat of the earl of Oxford. His body
was buried, according to his own directions, in Westminster abbey, where a stately monument was erected to
his memory, for which, as the " last piece of human
vanity," as he himself termed it, he had set apart 500*l.*
by his will. His bust stands at the top of this monument, exquisitely sculptured by Coriveaux. Beneath is
engraven a long Latin epitaph, written by Dr. Robert
Freind, then head master of Westminster school.

After his death, another small collection of his poems
was published ; and in 1740, a work appeared under
the title — *The History of his own Times, compiled from
the original Manuscripts of his late Excellency Matthew
Prior, esq.* Though this Publication is stated in the

title-page to have been revised and signed by himself, it is reasonably suspected that it contains very little of his own composition.

To his college he made amends for retaining his fellowship, by bequeathing to it a set of books to the value of 200*l.*, to be chosen by themselves out of his library; a picture of the earl of Jersey; and another of himself, at full length, in a sitting posture, and in his rich ambassador's robes, which had been painted by La Belle, and presented to him by Louis XIV.* The books which are all in magnificent bindings, are placed in the college library, in one case, which they fill, with his own picture over it, and the earl of Jersey's close by.

The remainder of his property he left in equal shares between Mr. Adrian Drift, one of his executors, and Mrs. Elizabeth Cox, his *chère amie.* This woman, who was not very remarkable for beauty or intellectual acquirements, had grown so imperious before his death, that several of his friends could not forbear to notice it to him. To these he is said to have made the same answer as Moliere, who had been in exactly the same circumstances — " that he was sensible of the truth of their remarks, as well as the friendliness of their advice; but he had been so long used to her humours, that they were become familiar to him, and by that means tolerable: whereas a new mistress would bring a new temper, which would create a very sensible trouble to conform with."

Prior's public and private character has been almost uniformly assailed by all his biographers and critics. Pope thought him less qualified for business than Addison. But the multitudinous proofs which we have offered of his success as a diplomatist should silence this charge. In the minute drawn up at his house on the 20th Sept., 1711, the ministers present declared him to have a greater knowledge of commercial affairs than any other " of all her majesty's servants who have been trusted in this secret." We have seen Bolingbroke en-

---

* Lewis gave La Belle 100 pistoles for it.

gaging him to arrange the difficulties which could not
be settled at Utrecht, and to repair the blunders of the
government. We have seen him taken in his boyhood
from a'tavern—without family, or fortune, or parliamentary influence — and employed successively by whigs
and tories as their chief diplomatic agent at the first
court in Europe, and on the most important affairs.
After these evidences of the trusts to which he was promoted, and the confidence of those he served, it would
be a gratuitous slander, at this distance of time, to
call his qualifications into question.

Johnson defends him from this splenetic attack of
Pope; but, to balance the account, assails him on other
points. " His opinions," he says, " so far as the means
of judging are left us, seem to have been right; but his
life was, it seems, irregular, negligent, and sensual."
Where Johnson obtained this information it is impossible to determine, for there is not extant any where
a single particle of evidence to favour even the supposition that Prior's life was irregular or negligent. Of
his industry there cannot exist any doubt whatever; and
that he should not have made a fortune by his employments, is by no means a proof of improvidence; for it
may with truth be asserted, that no man ever yet made
a fortune by such employments, while many have been
plunged into difficulties by the expenditure they entailed.
That he should have lived to the age of fifty-seven without complaining of any illness except a deafness contracted in prison, and that at last, instead of betraying
any symptoms of corporeal decay, he should have been
carried off by a fever, may be allowed as a proof that he
could not have lived a very sensual or irregular life.
Johnson himself says, that " he lived at a time when the
rage of party detected all which it was any man's interest to hide; and, as little is heard of Prior, it is certain
that much was not known. He was not afraid of provoking censure." Now, under these circumstances. it
may be fairly assumed, that, as little is known concerning
his habits, there was little in them to censure. If there

had been, the malevolence of party, on Johnson's own showing, would have found it out. The subscription of 4000 guineas among his friends and admirers, under the delicate pretext of purchasing his work, but really for the purpose of securing him an independence in his old age, proves that his character must have been held in great respect by his contemporaries. Even the anta-gonist administration complimented him upon his talents, and treated him with courtesy; and his own sovereign and the king of France did not hesitate to express the esteem with which his whole conduct had inspired them. Had he been " irregular, negligent, and sensual," it is not very likely that we should be able to cite such testi-monies in defence of his reputation.

Having committed himself to an ornate sentence of depreciation, Johnson endeavours to support it by an epigram. " A survey of the life and writings of Prior," he observes, " may exemplify a sentence which he doubtless understood well, when he read Horace at his uncle's; ' The vessel long retains the scent which it first receives.' In his private relaxation he revived the ta-vern, and in his amorous pedantry he exhibited the col-lege." The pedantry may be dismissed as an impu-tatiou which applies to Prior in a much less degree than to Johnson himself; but the revival of the tavern habits is a more serious affair, and appears to be founded on the following statements, given by the same writer, in a previous page:—

" Tradition represents him as willing to descend from the dignity of the poet and statesman to the low delights of mean company. His Chloe probably was sometimes ideal: but the woman with whom he cohabited was a despicable drab * of the lowest species. One of his wenches, perhaps Chloe, while he was absent from his house, stole his plate, and ran away; as was related by a woman who had been his servant. Of this propensity to sordid converse I have seen an account so se-riously ridiculous, that it seems to deserve insertion.†

" I have been assured that Prior, after having spent the

---

* Spence; and see Gent. Mag. vol. 57. p. 1039.
† Richardsoniana.

evening with Oxford, Bolingbroke, Pope, and Swift, would go
and smoke a pipe, and drink a bottle of ale, with a common
soldier and his wife, in Long Acre, before he went to bed; not
from any remains of the lowness of his original, as one said,
but, I suppose, that his faculties,

'—— strained to the height,
In that celestial colloquy sublime,
Dazzled and spent, sunk down, and sought repair.'

" Poor Prior, why was he so strained, and in such want of
repair, after a conversation with men, not, in the opinion of the
world, much wiser than himself? But such are the conceits
of speculatists, who strain their faculties to find in a mine what
lies upon the surface."

Of the three tales or insinuations on which it is sought
to degrade Prior's character, it is only fair to observe,
that Johnson did not consider the authority of Spence,
who is referred to for one of them, to have been infal-
lible, as he questions the correctness of his anecdote
about Dryden shedding tears on account of the parody on
the *Hind and Panther*; and that, as he doubted Spence
in one instance, he could not refuse to tolerate a similar
doubt in another. But having quoted Spence, he was
bound to quote him correctly. Spence, or rather Pope,
who communicated the statement, gives the following
brief description of Chloe, who, it seems, was the iden-
tical " drab " of Johnson, although he endeavours to make
it appear that there were two " drabs," or at least one
Chloe, and a " drab " in addition.

" Prior left most of his effects to the good woman he
kept company with, his Chloe ; every body knows what
a wretch she was. *I think she had been a little alehouse-
keepers wife.*" *

Now as nobody can undertake to answer for the
actual meaning intended to be assigned by Pope to the
expression, " what a wretch she was," it is not easy to
determine, from this vague and vulgar exclamation, the
exact extent of Chloe's depravity. Perhaps Pope meant
that she must have been a wretch because she had been
a little alehouse-keeper's wife, a circumsatnce which
was quite enough to render her odious to him, and

* Spence, p. 49.

which seems to have made so deep an impression on
Spence, that he continues the history of this illustrious
outcast in a note, where he solemnly informs us that she
was afterwards " married to a cobbler at * * * *! " But
it is certain, at all events, that neither Spence nor Pope
called her a "despicable drab;" that Spence, in the biographical note alluded to, (which consists of a single line,)
designates her as " this celebrated lady;" and that she
is distinguished also as a " lady " in various works of
authority. Whatever she was, she was unworthy of a
controversy, and it would have been better taste to have
left her, without discussion, in that obscurity which even
Pope, who had a natural relish for such tales, could
only faintly illuminate. It is quite clear that, manifest as Prior's general indiscretion was in reference
to her, he must have exhibited at least a courteous
respect for public opinion, since even his jealous contemporaries were unable to furnish any further particulars about the affair than a very unsatisfactory speculation.

The second story, of what one " woman, who had been
his servant," related of another, who had stolen his plate,
is composed of still more fragile materials. If the character of a man who passed thirty years of his life
before the public without a blemish is to be whispered
away by the scandal of thieves and discharged servants,
then there is very little protection in a good name. The
last story is palpably an invention. Had the author of
Richardsoniana been " assured " of it by any one worthy
of credit, or fit, from his name and station, to be referred
as witness of such a scene, why did he not give his authority? These anonymous assurances have been the
vehicles in all ages for conveying unfounded slan-
ders which the slanderers themselves were afraid to
circulate on their own testimony. It is only necessary,
for the vindication of Prior's fame, to bear in recollection that he lived in a period when, according to
Dr. Johnson, " the rage of party detected all which it
was any man's interest to hide," and that these three

equivocal and obscure statements constitute the whole of the charges that have been brought against his private life.

Prior appears to have been as sedate in society as he was formal in poetry. He made no pretensions to the character of a wit. There are only two instances of liveliness in repartee recorded of him; and as they are to be found in the majority of his biographies, they cannot be refused a place here.

During his embassy at Paris, he sat at the opera by a man who in his rapture accompanied the principal singer with his own voice. Prior fell to railing at the performer, till the Frenchman, ceasing from his song, began to expostulate with him for condemning a man who was confessedly the ornament of the stage. " I know all that," replied the ambassador, " Mais il chante si haut, que je ne saurais vous entendre."

In a gay French company, where every one sung a little song or a stanza, of which the burden was " Banissons la Melancholie," when it came to his turn to sing after a young lady who sat next him, he produced these extemporary lines:

> " Mais cette voix et ces beaux yeux,
> Font Cupidon trop dangereux;
> Et je suis triste quand je crie
> Banissons la melancholie."

It must be accorded to Prior, that if did not display a very high order of imagination in his poetry, he at least exhibited considerable skill in versification. His lines are generally remarkable for their melodious regularity, and the diction is so carefully selected, and so judiciously employed, that Pope, who does not seem to have been a very warm admirer of his genius, included him with Spenser, Shakspeare, Fletcher, Waller, Butler, Milton, Dryden, and Swift, in a list of English authorities for poetical language. There is some reason to believe that he corrected his compositions with unusual pains, frequently letting them remain until he had nearly for-

gòtten them, that he might return to their revision in a
more fresh and critical spirit. He was in the habit of
preserving all his manuscripts, even to his school exercises; and we are told that there was a large collection
of this kind in the hands of his servant Drift, which
contained at least half as much as his published works.
Pope saw this collection, and thought that there were
several things in it of greater value than any of those
chosen for publication by Prior himself, especially a
dialogue, of about two hundred lines, between Apollo
and Daphne.

Of Prior's longer poems — those to which he chiefly
trusted for a durable reputation — it must be said, that
while their polished refinement is always likely to keep
them in the memory of numerous readers, their tedious-
ness will for ever prevent them from being popular.
They present no points of interest calculated to engage
and reward the attention, and the utmost pleasure they
are capable of imparting, is that sort of pleasure which
is always communicated by well regulated numbers, and
choice phraseology. His tales are of a more agreeable
character, and, with less pretensions to poetical excellence, possess the rare merit of a familiar style,
always fluent and appropriate, and rarely mean. In
the art of relating a metrical narrative in the language
of common life, without descending to flippancy or
vulgar idioms, Prior has never been excelled. His songs
and love poems are like small carved images wrought
with exquisite taste, highly embellished with classical
accessories, but cold and lifeless. There is no true
passion in any of these pieces. His mistress, real or
imaginary, never assumed the complexion of a living
woman in these premeditated addresses, but takes the
attributes of a goddess or a statue. She is either a
fantastic creation, like Venus, to whom he assigns all
the miraculous gifts of the mythology, or a marble
figure like the Niobe, whom he approaches to study and
describe with a kind of mincing and retreating reverence,
rather than to propitiate and woo. It may be reasons

ably doubted whether all the poems of this kind which he produced, instead of being what they profess to be, were not mere imitations, daintily masked in his own style, of his metaphorical predecessors. But of all Prior's poems, that which is most generally known, and which has been most generally admired, is the dialogue of *Henry and Emma*, modelled upon an old ballad, called the *Nut-brown Maid*. When Prior wrote this piece, it may be taken for granted that the *Nut-brown Maid* was not in much request amongst his readers ; or, unless he was greatly deceived in his judgment of his own work, he would scarcely have ventured upon so monstrous a heresy in taste. The only way in which it is possible to account for the popularity of this production, is by the supposition, that its admirers detected in it the beauties borrowed by the author from the old ballad, and which even his lumbering heroics could not entirely deform ; and that, for the sake of these straggling charms, they were content to compromise the heaviness of the treatment, the inordinate length to which the subject is drawn out, and the lethargic structure which Prior contrived to raise over one of the simplest and most touching specimens of the early English poetry. But since that period, the *Nut-brown Maid* has been rescued from oblivion, and is now to be met with in most of our anthologies ; and those who have an opportunity of comparing the original with the monotonous imitation, will have some reason for wondering how this piece could have acquired the reputation which successive generations have indolently allowed it to retain. Not only is the form of verse adopted by Prior wholly unfitted to bring out the character of the story, but it is so prolonged by idle reiterations, and the arguments on both sides are made so minute, special, and ingenious, that the sweet spirit of the ballad, like some fine and delicate essence, evaporates in the lingering process. The melancholy expression of this trial of love is thus utterly lost, and throughout the whole performance there is not a single trace of that pathos which in the ballad melts the reader into tears. It is impossible to recognise the *Nut-brown Maid* in such lines as the following, when, after informing us that Emma was christened after the name of her mother, he goes on to add, that her father used frequently in sport to call her his nut-brown maid : —

> " Usage confirmed what fancy had begun;
> The mutual terms around the land were known;
> And Emma and the nut-brown maid were one."

It would be difficult to imagine any worse desecration of the simple quatrain of the original ; but he who could turn it into heroics, was able to devise a still greater deformity, and, as if he had not already done enough to spoil the gentle contention of the lovers, he completed the sacrilege by tagging an alexandrine at the end of each speech.

ALEXANDER POPE.

1688—1744.

THE materials from which the biography of Alexander Pope is drawn are ample, but the actual incidents of his life are few. It has been justly observed, however, by Mr. Roscoe, that "nothing which relates to a favourite author, or his writings, can be indifferent to us ; that though he be dead, he yet speaketh ; we feel him breathing in his works; and our minds are formed, and our characters modified, by a master spirit that survives alike the attacks of envy and the efforts of time." Pope has been the subject of innumerable critical essays, controversies, and speculations ; and almost every one of his biographers have buried the immediate details of the poet's life under a heap of commentaries and contemporaneous notices and illustrations, which, though of great value in the general history of English literature, yet have more or less the effect of interrupting the direct progress of the personal narrative. The importance of such biographical inquiries is sufficiently obvious ; executed with industry, and displaying considerable acumen, applied frequently, no doubt, to minute and trivial points, but often to questions of permanent interest, they supply, perhaps, all that research can discover, or the severest judgment suggest in reference to the particular subject of which they treat. There is a large class of readers, however, who want both the leisure and inclination for the investigation of works of this elaborate description, and to whom a briefer and simpler estimate of the poet's history, character, and produc · tions, would be more acceptable. It is for the use of such readers that the following memoir has been prepared. The principal, if not the only merit to which it can assert any pretension, is that of exhibiting, in a short compass, a complete view of all the facts that have been gathered into scattered publications concerning the life and writings of Pope, and of the speculations and literary controversies that have arisen out of them.*

The inquiry into Pope's birth and descent introduces us at once to a vulgar controversy, which is very commonly forced upon men of genius by that impatience of self-achieved distinctions which men of birth sometimes so unworthily betray. He who rises out of the middle ranks of life to a place of honour amongst the most famous persons of his time, must expect to be reminded occasionally of his origin. The circles of hereditary nobility are seldom willing to allow any patents but those that are attested by the herald's office. The life-peers of nature are not recognised in the tables of precedence. Pope might have despised the scornful allusions that were made to the meanness of his birth by some of his more lucky contemporaries; but he seems to have had an uneasy feeling about rank,

* The chief authorities from which this biography has been compiled may be recited here, to save the necessity of encumbering the narrative with frequent foot notes. The first biography of Pope, which appeared in 1744, the year of his death—a short, scanty, and ill-digested memoir, drawn up evidently in a hurry to satisfy the curiosity of the public. *Memoirs of the Life and Writings of Alexander Pope*, by William Ayre, Esq., 2 vols. This was published in the following year, and contains many particulars not to be found in the previous tract, with much matter wholly irrelevant to the subject. *The Life of Alexander Pope, &c.*, by W. H. Dilworth, 1759; a compilation from the preceding. *The Life of Alexander Pope, compiled from Original Manuscripts*, by Owen Ruffhead, Esq., 1769.—The author of this work, a barrister, announced it as " the fruit of a leisure vacation," and as having been founded on materials furnished by Dr. Warburton, bishop of Gloucester, the intimate friend of Pope, who had contemplated the undertaking himself, but from some motive, perhaps want of leisure, relinquished his intention. Ruffhead's life was the most full and authentic that had then appeared. Johnson's life is the next in order, adding nothing to the statement of facts, but darkening, by the strangest malignity, the moral and social character of the poet. The next are the Life published by Mr. Bowles, in 1806; and the Life, by Mr. Roscoe, in 1824, the ablest, most impartial, authentic, and complete of them all. In addition to these sources, many miscellaneous publications have been consulted; amongst the rest, Warton's *Life and Essay on the Genius and Writings of Pope*—Spence's *Anecdotes*—Lord Wharncliffe's edition of the *Letters and Works of Lady Mary Wortley Montague*—the controversies between Bowles, and Gilchrist, and Byron—Campbell's *Essay on English Poetry*—Hazlitt's *Lectures*; and a variety of other publications, in which notices of Pope are incidentally introduced, including the annotations to the numerous editions of his Works.

which tempted him to claim a remote and indefinite
relationship to a noble family, for which there is no
evidence on record except his own assertion.   If any
thing could bring genius into contempt, it is this species
of wretched vanity that will not suffer it to stand erect in
its natural dignity, but seeks to give it an artificial grandeur in the shadowy folds of a disputed pedigree.

· In a note to his *Epistle to Dr. Arbuthnot*, Pope in-·
forms us that his father was of a gentleman's family in
Oxfordshire, the head of which was the earl of Downe,
whose sole heiress married the earl of Lindsay, and that
his mother was the daughter of William Turner, Esq.
of York.   Upon this statement, Mr. Pottinger, a relation of Pope's, observed that he did not know where
his cousin could have got such a pedigree ; that, for his
part, he had never heard of it before ; that he had an
old maiden aunt who was a great genealogist, and who
was always talking of her family, but that she had
never mentioned the circumstance ; and that the earl of
Guildford had examined the Downe pedigree, and was
sure that there were none then living of the name of
Pope who could be descended from that family.*   In
addition to this, it is stated by Mr. Bowles, that a
search had been made at the herald's office, and that no
such pedigree as that claimed by Pope, could be traced. †
The assertion, therefore, seems to have been wholly
unfounded; and it is only charitable to suppose that
Pope was misled into the supposition that he was
related to an extinguished title, by the coincidence of
the family name, and his belief that his father derived
his lineage (and even that must have referred to a remote
period) from the same county where the earls of
Downe had been formerly seated.   But how much more
worthy of the poet was the following vindication of
his birth, in his admirable rejoinder to the sarcasms of
lord Hervey: — " I think it enough that my parents,
such as they were, never cost me a blush, and that

* Note by Wharton on the *Epistle to Arbuthnot*.
† Bowles's *Life of Pope*.

their son, such as he is, never cost them a tear."* He sinned against the true nobility of his parentage when he endeavoured to quarter it upon the lords of Wroxton.

The grandfather of Alexander Pope was a clergyman of the church of England, settled in Hampshire, whose younger son, Alexander, was sent, for the purpose of acquiring a knowledge of mercantile affairs, to Lisbon, where he embraced the Roman catholic religion. Returning to England, he engaged·in business on his own account, and married the daughter of William Turner, Esq., of York, also a Roman catholic. This lady was then the widow of a Mr. Rackett, by whom she had a son, named Charles, whose wife was the sister Rackett celebrated by the poet. Mrs. Rackett had three brothers, one of whom was killed, and another died in the service of Charles I.; the third became a general officer in Spain. She inherited the property of the whole family, which probably was not much, after it was reduced by the sequestrations and forfeitures incurred under the commonwealth. Of this union between Alexander Pope and Mrs. Rackett, the poet was the only offspring. His father settled as a linen-draper in Lombard Street, where he made an independent fortune, upon which he retired, first to Kensington, afterwards to a small estate of twenty acres which he purchased at Binfield, in Windsor, and lastly to his son's house at Twickenham, where he died.

Alexander Pope, the subject of this notice, was born in Lombard Street, on the 21st of May, 1688. In his infancy, as through his life, which he describes as " a long disease," he was of a weak and fragile constitution, having some spinal deformity, which compelled him constantly to wear stays †, and which he is said to have inherited from his father, and being troubled with incessant headaches, an infirmity which, in a prologue to one of his satires, he traces to his mother. Not-

* Letter to a Noble Lord.
† A waterman at Twickenham, who was accustomed to lift Pope into his boat, often felt his stays. When he took the water, he used to sit in a sedan chair in the boat with the glasses down.

withstanding the delicacy of his health, he was remarkable for the beauty of his features in his youth, and for
the sweetness of his disposition ; and such was the
melody of his voice, that he was fondly called " the little
nightingale."

His first lesson in reading was given to him by his
aunt ; and at the early age of seven or eight years, he
exhibited an extraordinary passion for books. He seems
to have taught himself to write by the mechanical process of imitating print, an exercise of ingenuity in which
he attained great excellence, which communicated even
to his ordinary handwriting a character of remarkable
neatness and precision. His first regular tutor was
Banister, a priest, who taught him the rudiments of
Greek and Latin together, a customary method in the
schools of the Jesuits. He was afterwards removed to a
Catholic seminary at Twyford, near Winchester, where
he read Ogilby's *Homer*, a work which he afterwards
condemned, and Sandy's *Translation of Ovid*, the exquisite versification of which made a deep impression
upon his mind.* At Twyford, Pope ridiculed his
schoolmaster in a lampoon, for which he was visited
with a severe corporeal punishment, which led to his
removal to another school, kept by a Mr. Deane, at
Marylebone, and afterwards at Hyde Park Corner. The
proximity of this establishment to the amusements of
the town procured him the occasional pleasure of a visit
to the theatres, where he quickly imbibed a taste for the
drama, the result of which was the production of a play
made up of speeches from Ogilby's *Homer*, linked
together with occasional verses of his own ; which piece
of curious juvenile patchwork was acted by his schoolfellows, with the help of the gardener, who is immor-
talised in all the biographies as the representative of
Ajax.

The system pursued in these schools was inimical to
the young poet's progress. His extreme sensibility resented compulsion and discipline of all kinds. So long

* See ante, p. 172.

as he was permitted to prosecute his studies as a voluntary enjoyment, and to select his own paths of inquiry, he was indefatigable; but he pined and grew indifferent under the slow and regular course prescribed by his masters. Speaking of these schools afterwards, he says that he never learned any thing at them, and adds, that he never should have followed any thing that he could not learn with pleasure. His disinclination to submit to enforced drudgery is sufficiently exhibited in the fact, that although, during this period, he made no further advance in his classical tasks than enabled him to construe a little of Tully's *Offices*, his natural powers were displayed in a lampoon on one of his teachers, in the compilation of a rude drama from the English *Homer*, and in the *Ode to Solitude*, which, from its date, must have been written while he was located with Mr. Deane. But he was soon relieved from his irksome situation, and taken home to Binfield when he was little more than twelve years of age. He was now placed under the care of another priest, who seems to have had no better success than the rest, and who was discarded after a few months, the youthful scholar having now resolved literally to educate himself. The scanty tuition included within these broken terms of schooling, spreading altogether over about four years and a half, constituted, to use his own words, " all the teaching he ever had." That the future translator of Homer should have commenced with so small a stock of instruction is no less marvellous in itself, than valuable as an illustration of what may be done by zeal and perseverance.

From the time he had taken up this resolution until he reached nineteen or twenty, he devoted himself, with untiring energy, in the solitude of Windsor Forest, to a variety of studies. In the pursuit of the particular objects which from day to day fascinated his attention, he ran through the works of numerous authors, and thus, by hunting after his own delights, he gradually acquired a considerable knowledge of Greek, Latin, French, and Italian. " I followed every where," he tells us, " as

my fancy led me, and was like a boy gathering flowers
in the woods and fields, just as they fell in my way, and
those five or six years I still look upon as the happiest
part of my life." Nor did he confine himself to these
pursuits. He was already acquainted with the principal
works of the English poets, and was so especially charmed
with the versification of Dryden, (a part of poetical excellence which from his childhood seems to have exercised a permanent influence over his feelings,) that he
entreated a friend to carry him to Will's coffee-house,
and introduce him to the distinguished author whose
productions he had read with so much enthusiasm. At
that time Pope was only twelve years of age. It was
not surprising that one who manifested so much ardour
at such an age should also endeavour to emulate even the
loftiest forms of that poetry by which it was excited.
Accordingly we find him, in the midst of his multifarious studies, throwing off an endless profusion of
verses, grave, gay, heroic, and satirical, abundantly real-
ising that picture of his prolific youth which he has
drawn in the well-known lines—

" As yet a child, and all unknown to fame,
    I lisp'd in numbers, for the numbers came;"

or, as Dr. Johnson, with still greater felicity of expression,
has observed, that "it might have been said of him, as
of Pindar, that when he lay in his cradle, ' the bees
swarmed about his mouth.'"

During this interval he wrote a comedy, of which no
account has been preserved ; a tragedy, founded on
the legend of St. Geneviève ; an epic poem, in four
books, consisting of a thousand lines each, entitled
Alcander, which he afterwards burnt on the suggestion, it is said, of Atterbury, who lamented that he
had not saved the first page to retain it among his
curiosities ; several imitations of the English poets,
which were afterwards published ; the *Pastorals,*
written at sixteen ; and the first part of *Windsor Fo-*

rest *; and translations of the treatises of Cicero, *De Senectute,* and of a part of the *Metamorphoses,* and of Statius. " I believe," was the remark of Mrs. Rackett, "nobody ever studied so hard as my brother did in his youth. He did nothing but write and read." Speaking of that early and happy time of self-imposed labour, Pope said, " I had made an epic poem, and panegyrics on all the princes of Europe, and I thought myself the greatest genius that ever was. I cannot but regret these delightful visions of my childhood, which, like the fine colours we see when our eyes are shut, are vanished for ever."

At about fifteen years of age, he visited London for the purpose of completing his acquisition of the French and Italian languages; in the latter of which he never appears to have made much proficiency.† The assiduity with which he applied himself to these pursuits impaired his health so seriously that his life was despaired of, and under this impression of approaching death he took a solemn leave of his more intimate friends in farewell letters; but the relaxation of his studies under medical advice, and air and exercise in the country, speedily restored him. His earliest friend — the first whose cultivated judgment discovered and encouraged the germ of his genius — was sir William Trumbull, who had formerly been ambassador to the Ottoman Porte, and subsequently one of the secretaries of state to king William, and who, in the decline of his life, went to reside at West Hampstead, near Binfield, where Pope was so fortunate as to make his acquaintance. Sir William was an

---

* According to the tradition which has descended with this poem, Pope is said to have written it under a beech tree in the forest, which, being decayed, lady Gower had an inscription carved on another tree near it, " Here Pope sang." A similar story is related concerning a tree in the Vale of Avoca, where Moore is said to have written one of the Irish Melodies. The former anecdote has probably as little truth in it as the latter.

† Voltaire says, that Pope could hardly read French, and that he could not speak one syllable of the language. The latter assertion may be true without rendering the former necessarily so, the correctness of which is sufficiently disproved by numerous passages in Pope's Works. Some of his critics have even supposed that he owed more to the *Lutrin* of Boileau than he cared to acknowledge.

excellent scholar, and finding in Pope a companion entirely adapted to bis refined tastes, an intimacy rapidly sprang up between them, which lasted as long as Sir William lived. They continually rode out together, and when circumstances prevented them from meeting, they maintained their intercourse by a correspondence which is still preserved in the complete edition of Pope's miscellaneous works. Sir William introduced Pope to Wycherly, then nearly seventy years old, and just released from the Fleet prison through the liberal interposition of the king, who, happening to be present at the representation of the Plain Dealer, was so delighted with it, that he ordered the debts of the author to be paid, and settled a pension on him of 200*l.* per annum.* The disparity between the ages of the veteran dramatist and the yet undeveloped poet, did not prevent them from forming a close and confidential friendship. " I know," says Pope in one of his letters to Wycherly, "it is the general opinion that friendship is best contrasted between persons of equal age; but I have so much interest to be of another mind, that you must pardon me if I cannot forbear telling you a few notions of mine in opposition to that opinion. In the first place, it is observable that the love we bear to our friends is generally caused by our finding the same dispositions in them which we feel in ourselves. *This is but self-love at the bottom;* whereas the affections between persons of different ages cannot well be so, the inclinations of such being commonly various. The friendship of two young men is often occasioned by love, or pleasure, or voluptuousness ; each being desirous, for his own sake, of one to assist or encourage him in the course he pursues; as that of two old men is frequently on the score of some profit, lucre, or design upon others. Now, as a young man, who is less acquainted with the ways of the world, has, in all probability, less of interest; and an old man, who may

* Lives of the most Eminent Literary and Scientific Men of Great Britain, Vol. III. p. 206.

be weary of himself, has, or should have, less of self-love; so the friendship between them is more likely to be true, and unmixed with too much self-regard. One may add to this, that such a friendship is of greater use and advantage to both; for the old man will grow gay and agreeable to please the young one, and the young man more discreet and prudent by the help of the old one; so it may prove a cure of those epidemical diseases of age and youth, sourness and madness." Although this argument is not entirely free from sophistry, yet it affords a remarkable evidence of shrewdness and sagacity for the period of life at which it was written. It is in such qualities that Dr. Johnson finds the largest ground for admiration of Pope's genius. His versification, melodious as it was, formed, according to Johnson, but a small part of his merits. "He discovers," says the critic, "such acquaintance both with human life and public affairs, as is not easily conceived to have been attainable by a boy of fourteen, in Windsor Forest." The observation is just and obvious; but the union of such a fine poetical faculty, and so much clear worldly sense at fourteen, is even more remarkable than his precocious knowledge of mankind.

In the beginning of their acquaintance, Wycherly introduced Pope to Mr. Walsh, who was considered one of the most accomplished critics of the time, and who had previously read the *Pastorals,* upon which be pronounced a very favourable judgment. This gentleman's friendship proved of great value to Pope, who gladly availed himself of an invitation to spend a part of the summer of 1705 with him, at his seat at Abberley. Mr. Walsh was so impressed with the talent exhibited in the *Pastorals,* that he urged Pope to attempt something in the form of a pastoral comedy on the model of the Italian schools. But this suggestion Pope judiciously declined, observing that the taste of the age would not relish a poem of that sort, as people sought for what they called wit, on all subjects and in all places, not considering that nature loves truth so well that it hardly ever admits of flourishing. The critical acumen of Pope was frequently drawn out in occasional remarks of this description, when, rejecting the suggestions of more experienced writers, he felt it necessary to assign the reasons that induced him to differ from them, in which he rarely failed to exhibit a judgment far in advance of his contemporaries. Of all his advisers, Walsh, himself an excellent poet, appears to have been the most discriminating. He earnestly counselled him to cultivate correctness beyond every thing else, as the element which had been chiefly neglected by his predecessors, and as presenting the surest basis for a superstructure of fame. How closely Pope followed an injunction that accorded entirely with his own views, need not be pointed out. But while he was forming his mind for those severe exercises of poetical skill by which he afterwards illustrated the importance of such maxims, he lost his friend Walsh, who died in 1708. Pope rendered a grateful and affecting tribute to his memory in some lines at the close of the *Essay on Criticism.*

This calamity was rendered the more poignant by the gradual estrangement of Wycherley, the companion of both. Wycherley had been in the habit of submitting his poems for revision to his young friend, who, at his special request, made such alterations in them as they appeared to him to require ; but it may be readily imagined that a censorship of that kind could not be long carried on without giving offence to the author, and in the end Wycherley declined his services in a tone that too visibly betrayed his irritation at the liberty that had been taken with his verses. " I would not have you give yourself more trouble about them," he observed in a letter to Pope, " which may prevent the pleasure you have, and may give the world, in writing upon new subjects of your own ; whereby you will much better entertain yourself and others." That it would have been impossible for Pope to have discharged so invidious an office to the satisfaction of the writer whose labours he undertook to criticise, must be freely admitted; yet it is not improbable that, in the heat of a youthful temperament, heightened by a natural turn for sarcasm, he may have exceeded the fair limits of a task which ought to have been executed with the utmost delicacy and forbearance. But it is greatly to his credit that he bore Wycherley's ill-concealed anger with patient submission, and always spoke of him with the greatest kindness, paying him a visit of reconciliation shortly before his death. " Be assured," says Pope in a letter to one of his friends, " that gentleman (Wycherley) shall never, by any alteration in me, discover any knowledge of his mistake; the hearty forgiving of which is the only kind of return I can possibly make him for so many favours." There is more real goodness in all this than the world has generally given Pope credit for, and certainly more than the predominant character and tenor of his works would justify any one in attributing to him.

The interview with Dryden at Will's coffee-house left, doubtless, a strong image in the memory of Pope, presenting to him a picture of that sort of intellectual society which a mind like his might be supposed to yearn after when the fatigues of the day were ended in the silent woods of Binfield. At seventeen years of age he is said to have mixed freely in that company of wits, and even then may probably have aspired to fill the vacant chair of Dryden. It was here he made the acquaintance of Mr. Henry Cromwell, a gentleman who afterwards became one of his constant correspondents, and whose judgment in poetry was so highly prized by him, that he put a juvenile version of Statius into his hands for correction. This Mr. Cromwell had some turn for poetry and criticism, as his letters to Pope evince; but his principal claims to distinction seem to have consisted in his ludicrous affectation of the airs of a gallant, and in a tie-wig, in which Johnson says he used to go out a hunting. Mr. Cromwell, who is alluded to in *The Tatler*, was evidently an eccentric person

in his dress and habits, equally vain of his conquests, or
pretended conquests, over the ladies, and of his literary
talents, and probably with no better reason in one case
than the other. " Pope," says one of the poet's biographers, " early caught the manners of his tutor, and
something of his affectation, particularly in regard to
the ladies, of whose acquaintance Cromwell was super-
latively vain."* If this were the case, never was there
a more unpropitious conjunction of stars ; and it may be
presumed that Pope, " who was not formed to court an
amorous looking-glass " must have very soon discovered
that nature had never designed him to become the imitator of Mr. Cromwell, either in his toilet or his gallantry. He may possibly have languished and fluttered
in his train while the glare of fashion was fresh upon
him, for Pope was not wholly free from the weakness of
egotistical display ; but the fascination could not have
lasted long. Nobler impulses called him to a higher
sphere of action. He was about to appear before the
public in the character of a poet.

Through the introductions of Sir William Trumbull,
and the acquaintance of Cromwell and the wits of
Will's coffee-house, Pope's circle of friends and admirers now included some of the most distinguished
persons in the country. His *Pastorals* had been
long known and applauded, and he was frequently
urged to give them to the world. The lord Lansdowne,
lord Somers, lord Halifax, Congreve, Garth, and Main-
waring, were amongst the crowd of critics who urged
him to a step which his modesty, or timidity, withheld
him from adopting, until their repeated persuasions at
last inspired him with confidence. Tonson, the bookseller, was then preparing a Miscellany, and the reputation of the *Pastorals* was so high in those coteries
where their worth was most likely to be truly appreciated, that he applied to the poet for permission to
insert them in his collection.† This was a mode of

* Bowles's *Life of Pope.*
† Tonson's application to Pope is 'a curiosity in its way. It runs as follows :— " Sir, I have lately seen a pastoral of yours in Mr. Walsh's and

publication which precisely suited an inexperienced author, who, fearful of criticism, was glad to come out in a book along with several others, who would carry off a portion of public attention from himself. Accordingly the *Pastorals* appeared in the sixth volume of the *Miscellanies* in 1709, closing an anthology which opened with the *Pastorals* of Philips. The test was a severe one for so young a poet, but the result was flattering beyond his most sanguine hopes, — Wycherley encouraged him by the kindest expressions of approbation ; and even the professional critics, of whom Pope entertained a sort of nervous dread, were, according to his authority, " only displeased by being pleased too well."

The success of the *Pastorals* gave him courage to proceed; and, in 1711, he published the *Essay on Criticism*. It has not been ascertained with certainty when this poem was written. One of his biographers says that it was composed before the author had attained his twentieth year * ; Pope, in one place, declares that he showed it to Mr. Walsh in 1706, when he was only eighteen years of age † ; and in another, that it was written in 1709 ‡, the date assigned to it in the title of the printed copies. But, taking even the latter of these years as the correct date, he could have been only twenty-one when he wrote an essay which is not less remarkable for the singular beauty of the versification, than for the solidity of the matter and the perspicuity of the style. In any case, there can be no doubt that it was meditated some time before, as we are told that he originally laid down the plan and arranged the whole argument in prose in the first instance, and then turned it with facility into verse. His usual practice was to write rapidly, and to retain his compositions in ma-

Congreve's hands, which is extremely fine, and is approved by the best judges in poetry. I remember I have formerly seen you in my shop, and am sorry I did not improve my acquaintance with you. If you design your poem for the press, no one shall be more careful in printing it, nor no one give greater encouragement for it than, sir," &c.
   * Ruffhead.   † Spence's *Anecdotes*.   ‡ Ibid.

nuscript for the purpose of deliberate correction, for a long time before he ventured to publish them. The *Essay on Criticism* underwent a careful revision of two years, " which," he tells us, " is as little a time as ever I let any thing of mine lie by me." They who attempt to emulate the metrical excellence of Pope, ought to bear in mind the laborious process through which it was attained.

Pope appears to have anticipated the feuds to which the publication of this piece was destined to expose him. He observes, in a letter to Wycherley, that " if his verses should meet with a few flying commendations, Virgil had taught him that a young author has not too much reason to be pleased with them, when he considers that the natural consequence of praise is envy and calumny : —

> ' Si ultra placitum laudarit, baccare frontem
> Cingite, ne vati noceat mala lingua futuro.' "

But it may be suspected that he discovered other reasons than the envy and calumny consequent upon success for these well-grounded apprehensions. The Essay not only touched upon some points in reference to the imputed intolerance of the Roman catholics, from which he must have anticipated a controversy, but assailed the critics of the time in a spirit which they could not be expected to pass over in silence. That a clamour was raised against the poem on account of the freedom with which it spoke of the monks, in reference to the suppression of literature in the dark ages, is attested by Pope himself ; and the quarrel with Dennis, arising from the assault on the critics, is immortalized in the *Dunciad.* The history of this quarrel is comprised in the fact that Pope attacked Dennis without provocation, and that Dennis, exasperated by what he was quite justified in regarding as a wanton insult, replied with a degree of asperity that led to prolonged and bitter hostility between them.

Dennis's attention was drawn to the offensive lines

by a mere accident. He happened to be in the shop of
Lintot, the bookseller, and seeing the *Essay on Criticism*
lying on the counter, he read a page or two of it with
evident vexation, when, coming to the lines,

> " *Some* have at first for wits, then poets pass'd,
> Turned critics next, and proved plain fools at last,"

he threw down the book in a burst of passion, exclaiming, " He means me, by G— ! " There was
another passage in the poem which pointed at him still
more directly, and which could not be mistaken by the
public, as it appears that his violent temperament was a
matter of common notoriety :

> " But Appius reddens at each word you speak,
> And stares, tremendous, with a threat'ning eye,
> Like some fierce tyrant in old tapestry."

The consequence was the publication of a pamphlet full
of the most scurrilous invectives, but containing amidst
its exaggerations some objections to the poem, the justice
of which Pope had the magnanimity to acknowledge.*
Before this pamphlet was issued to the public, Dennis
communicated a copy of it to Lintot, who transmitted it
to Pope. The only use Pope seems to have made of it
was to insert some notes in the margin, observing, in a
private letter to his friend Craggs, that he could not conceive what ground Dennis had for so excessive a resentment, nor imagine how three lines could be called a reflection on his person, which only described him subject
to a little anger on some occasions ; but allowing, at the
same time, that if he had known before what Dennis
stated in his preface, that he was at that time persecuted
by fortune, he would have spared his name for that only

* The following line was altered by Pope, in consequence of the animad-
versions of Dennis:
  " What is this wit? —
  Where *wanted* scorned, and envied where *acquired*."
Dennis asked how wit could be scorned where it did not exist, observing,
that the figure was Hibernian, and that the person who wants wit may be
scorned, but the scorn shows the horror which the contemner has for wit.
Pope judiciously altered the line in the second edition to
  " The more we give, the more is still required."

reason.   That the allusion to the angry critic did not
warrant so fierce a rejoinder, and that Dennis descended
to the coarsest abuse under the mask of criticism, must
be admitted ; but he had at least one good argument in
in his defence, which he did not fail to enforce, namely,
that "he found himself attacked, without any manner
of provocation on his side, and attacked in his person,
instead of his writings, by one who was wholly a stranger
to him, at a time when all the world knew he was persecuted by fortune ; and not only saw that this was attempted in a clandestine manner, with the utmost falsehood and calumny, but found that all this was done by
a little affected hypocrite, who had nothing in his mouth at
the same time but truth, candour, friendship, good nature,
humanity, and magnanimity." How Pope could persuade himself that it was not a personal reflection to describe a man reddening in the face, and staring tremen-
dously with a threatening eye, like an old tyrant, cannot
be very easily understood, except by people whose sensi-
bilities are dull by nature, or obliterated by the rudest
uses of satire.

    But the censures of Dennis were more than counter-
balanced by the applauses of Addison in *The Spectator*,
and the commentaries of Warburton, who is believed to
have discovered merits in the poem of which the author
himself was unconscious.   The popularity of the work
was further established by three translations into the
French — one by Hamilton, the author of the *Comte de
Grammont*, another by Robotham, Hanoverian secretary
to the king, and a third by Resnel.

    The *Essay on Criticism* was followed in the same year
by *The Rape of the Lock*, which appeared in a volume of
the Miscellanies.   Pope did not acknowledge the authorship on its first publication, perhaps because the persons
referred to in it, and who really quarrelled about the theft
of a lock of hair, which sir George Brown had stolen from
Miss Bell Fermor, were not yet reconciled.   The first
draught of the poem, which was all that was published in
the Miscellanies, contained nothing more than the simple

narrative: the introduction of the machinery, skilfully adopted from the Rosicrucian system, was an afterthought. When this additional source of interest cccurred to Pope, he communicated it to Addison, with whom he had been for some time on terms of intimacy ; but Addison received it coldly, and strongly advised him not to make any alteration, observing that the poem in its original state was a delicious little thing, and, as he expressed it, *merum sal.** This is said to have been the first indication of Addison's jealousy of Pope's growing reputation, a feeling which, under all the circumstances, cannot be very satisfactorily accounted for, and which, even those who bear testimony to it, do not attempt to explain. Mr. Pope, says Warburton, was " shocked for his friend," upon the communication of his objections to the use of machinery, by which the delicate trifle was to be advanced to the dignity of a mock epic poem, and " then first began to open his eyes to his character." There surely must have been something more in this interview than the mere expression of a speculative critical opinion to " shock " the feelings of the poet, and open his eyes to the character of his friend. Nor was Addison's judgment in the matter so much at fault after all; for although the interest of the poem was greatly increased by subsequent revision and extension, it was quite impossible to have foreseen the extraordinary felicity with which Pope managed an undertaking so replete with difficulties of an uncommon kind, and the critic might be reasonably excused for doubting the prudence of venturing upon any change in a poem, which, in its original form, had been already received with universal approbation. The anecdote must, therefore, be admitted with some distrust, and certainly cannot be accepted as a proof of Addison's duplicity, which Pope himself does not appear to have suspected until other circumstances produced an open breach between them.

The poem in its improved form was allowed, on all

* Warburton

hands, to be the most exquisite example of that kind of ludricous invention cast in the finest mould of verse that had ever appeared in the language ; and even Addison must have acknowledged that Pope, " who," says Johnson, " foresaw the future efflorescence of imagery then budding in his mind," was right. Dennis was so enraged by this fresh triumph of his satirist, that he prepared a trenchant criticism upon it, in which he compared it in contemptuous terms with the satires of Boileau ; but he did not hazard the publication of his commentaries for several years afterwards, and probably would not have printed them even then had he not been attacked afresh in the *Dunciad.* But the panegyric of Berkeley made ample amends for the caustic censures of Dennis. Some foolish persons supposed that *The Rape of the Lock* was only a veil for deep designs, political and religious; a notion which Pope ridiculed with considerable humour in a pamphlet, entitled *A Key to the Lock,* in which, under the feigned name of Esdras Barnivelt, Apoth., he affected to discover that Great Britain was typified in Belinda, that sir Plume was intended for prince Eugene, Clarissa for Mrs. Masham, Thalestris for the duchess of Marlborough, and the baron who cuts off the lock the earl of Oxford. This essay completely silenced the absurd suspicions that were entertained concerning the veiled intention of the poem.

The intimacy that existed between Pope and Steele appears to have led to the composition of several of those smaller pieces which are familiar to all readers of poetry, and which, of their kind, may be regarded amongst the most successful of Pope's productions. At Steele's suggestion, he wrote the pathetic lines entitled *The Dying Christian to his Soul,* and *The Ode for Music,* which with all humility he declared was not designed as " rivalling Dryden," and also translated the celebrated verses which the emperor Adrian is said to have repeated on his death-bed. About this period, 1712, he also completed *The Messiah,* and wrote the *Elegy to the*

Memory of the Unfortunate Lady, upon the subject and history of which his biographers have wasted in vain a great deal of ingenious speculation and minute research. There is, in fact, nothing more known concerning the lady than the poem itself reveals, that she was a woman of rank and fortune, that she was beautiful and sensitive, that she was crossed in love, and that she died by her own hand. Warton says that her name was Wainsbury; that she was deformed, like Pope; and that she hanged herself. But these are no better than idle conjectures. Whatever her name was, it never transpired; and Pope must have been the coarsest of all flatterers if he celebrated in such rapturous terms the beauty of a misshaped figure. As to the supposition that she died by a halter, the poem itself may be allowed to set it at rest, since it is there plainly indicated that she died by a sword. After a careful examination of all the particulars that have been put together concerning it, the conclusion that seems to be most reasonable is that the whole affair was purely imaginary. If it were otherwise, why did Pope persist in observing such a mystery about it? How did it happen that his closest friends could never discover who the lady was, and some of them must be presumed to have known her, if such a person really existed? And, if she did exist, and silence respecting her was considered necessary, why did Pope draw the outlines of her history in a poem which was certain to attract attention and provoke enquiry?

The Temple of Fame, written two years before, was now submitted to Addison and Steele, the latter of whom says of it (12th Nov. 1712), that he " cannot find any thing amiss of weight enough to call a fault, but that he sees in it a thousand, thousand beauties." Pope, notwithstanding his great success, seems to have still entertained considerable distrust of his own powers. " You speak of the poem," he observes, in his reply to Steele, " in a style I neither merit, nor expect; but I assure you, if you freely mark or dash out, I shall look upon your blots to be its greatest beauties; I mean, if Mr. Addison and yourself should like it on the whole, otherwise the trouble of correction is what I would not take, for I really was so diffident of it as to let it lie by me these two years, just as you see it. I am afraid of nothing so much as to impose any thing on the world which is unworthy of its acceptance." The true interpretation of the last sentence is probably this — that he was afraid of nothing so much as imposing any thing upon the world which was likely to diminish his reputation. The nervousness he exhibited about his writings is quite as likely to have sprung from an anxiety to render whatever he produced worthy of himself, as from a desire that it should be worthy of the public. Such an anxiety was natural enough, and is inseparable from the circumstances of an author who has acquired, by his first essay, that extended popularity which, in other cases, grows only upon the labours of years.

The next publication was *Windsor Forest*, which appeared in 1713. The greater part of it was written so far back as 1704, when Pope was only sixteen years of age; but as the concluding lines upon the peace of Utrecht testify that additions were subsequently made to it, and as it may be taken for granted that it received numerous and important corrections during the five years it lay upon the author's hands, we are justified in referring the work, as a whole, to a more mature period, although the plan was laid, and the poem, as it originally stood, completed in the boyhood of the poet, and in the solitudes it describes with such surpassing beauty.*

- * One of the most interesting objects in Windsor Forest and Park, the reader need not be reminded, is Herne's Oak, and as a controversy which has recently taken place concerning it has established, beyond all doubt, the fact that the ancient tree celebrated by Shakspeare is still standing, it may not be out of place here to give such particulars as have been preserved in reference to it. Mr. Jesse, in his popular work, entitled *Gleanings in Natural History*, identified this oak, and gave a description of it, which Mr. Loudon adopted into his *Arboretum Britannicum;* but the *Quarterly Review*, in an article upon the latter publication, expressed some surprise that Mr. Loudon should have admitted what the writer called an apocryphal story, adding, that it was well known that the tree in question had been cut down one morning by order of George III.

Windsor Forest was dedicated to lord Lansdowne, a highly influential tory, and one of the most distin-

when in a state of great excitement. In reply to this statement, Mr. Jesse published a letter in the newspapers, from which the following passage is extracted, as a matter of too much interest to fall into oblivion in the journals of the day : —" The story to which the *Quarterly* reviewer refers, of a tree having been cut down by order of George III., ' when in a state of great, but transient, excitement,' is well known, and was often repeated by his late majesty George IV., who, however, always added, ' that tree was supposed to have been Herne's Oak, but it was not.' There is no occasion to go into the particulars of this story, as, luckily for my argument, the person is still alive who heard the order given by George III. to fell a tree in the Little Park, about which some angry words had passed with the prince of Wales, and he assures me that the tree was an elm. I do not feel myself at liberty to mention his name, but he informs me that the tree stood near the castle, that it was cut down early one morning, and he points out the spot where it grew. The whole character, however, of George III., would, of itself, be a sufficient guarantee that Herne's Oak was not cut down by his order. He always took a pride and pleasure in pointing it out to his attendants whenever he passed near it, and that tree was the one whose identity I am now advocating. It may also be doubted whether any monarch would venture to incur the odium and unpopularity of felling such a tree as Herne's Oak.

" Soon after the circumstance referred to took place, three large old oak trees were blown down in a gale of wind in the Little Park, and one of them was supposed by persons who probably took little trouble to inquire into the real facts of the case, to have been Herne's Oak. This windfall was cut up into small pieces, and sold to carpenters and cabinet makers in the neighbourhood, who found it very profitable in calling the articles they made a part of Herne's Oak, and disposing of them as Shakspearian *reliquiæ*. These circumstances combined, might probably give rise to a report in the newspapers of the day, that Herne s Oak was no longer in existence. It would, however, have been a kind act, if the reviewer of the *Quarterly* had informed the public in what year, and at what date, the particulars he mentions are to be found in the newspapers he refers to.

" To set the matter at rest, however, I will now repeat the substance of some information given to me relative to Herne's Oak by Mr. Ingalt, the present respectable bailiff and manager of Windsor Home Park. He states that he was appointed to that situation by George III., about forty years ago. On receiving his appointment he was directed to attend upon the king at the castle, and on arriving there he found his majesty with ' the old lord Winchelsea.' After a little delay the king set off to walk in the park, attended by lord Winchelsea, and Mr. Ingalt was desired to follow them. Nothing was said to him until the king stopped opposite an oak tree. He then turned to Mr. Ingalt, and said, ' I brought you here to point out this tree to you. I commit it to your especial charge, and take care that no damage is ever done to it. I had rather that every tree in the park should be cut down than that this tree should be hurt. *This is Herne's Oak.*' Mr. Ingalt added, that this was the tree still standing near Queen Elizabeth's Walk, and is the same tree which I have mentioned and given a sketch of in my *Gleanings in Natural History.* Sapless and leafless it certainly is, and its rugged bark has all disappeared.

' Its boughs are mess'd with age,
And high top bald with grey antiquity ;'—

but there it stands, and long may it do so, an object of interest to every admirer of our immortal bard. In this state it has been, probably long before the recollection of the oldest person living. Its trunk appears, however, sound, like a piece of ship-timber, and it has always been protected by a strong fence round it—a proof of the care which has been taken of the tree, and of the interest which is attached to it.

guished members of the October club.* This dedication, and the concluding lines, referring to the peace
which had been settled by the queen†, gave deep
offence to Addison, who was on the opposite side. The
couplet containing the disagreeable allusion to the treaty
was hardly worth so much anger.

" At length great Anna said, Let discord cease !
— She said — the world obey'd, and all was *peace*."

That Pope should throw himself into the arms of
the tories was to have been expected. He was a
Roman catholic — a moderate and rational one, no doubt
— but, falling under the ban of the restrictive and op-
pressive laws that affected his class, he, of course, sym-
pathised with the party that favoured the Stuarts. This
slight expression of his political feelings, however, was
not the only vexation of which Addison had to complain. When he finished the tragedy of *Cato*, he sub-

---

" Having stated the above fact, I may add, that George III. was perfectly
incapable of the duplicity of having pointed out a tree to Mr. Ingait as
Herne's Oak, if he had previously ordered the real Herne's Oak, ' the
Simon Pure,' to be cut down. I have also the authority of one of the
members of the present royal family for stating, that George III. always
mentioned the tree now standing as Herne's Oak.

" King William III. was a great planter of avenues, and to him we are
indebted for those in Hampton Court and Bushy Park, and also those at
Windsor. All these have been made in a straight line, with the exception
of one in the Home Park, which diverges a little, so as to take in Herne's
Oak as a part of the avenue—a proof, at least, that William III. preferred
distorting his avenue to cutting down the tree in order to make way for it
in a direct line, affording another instance of the care taken of this tree 150
years ago."

A vignette of this venerable tree will be found in the title-page of the
present volume.

* There were two political clubs called into existence at this period, the
Kit-katt, and the October club. The former—so called from a person
named Christopher Katt, a pastrycook, at whose house, in Shire Lane, its
meetings were held — consisted of the whigs, zealously attached to the protestant succession. Amongst the members were the dukes of Marlborough,
Richmond, Grafton, Somerset, and Devonshire; the earls of Manchester,
Wharton, Dorset, Sunderland, and Kingston; lords Halifax and Somers;
Steele, Addison, Garth, &c. Of this society Jacob Tonson was secretary,
and having employed sir Godfrey Kneller to paint the portraits of the members of a size sufficient to admit the introduction of the hands, he occasioned that term in reference to portraits which distinguishes what is called
the Kit-katt size. The October club was so called, from the month in
which the great alteration in the ministry took place. Swift was one of its
founders, and its principal members were Bolingbroke, lord Oxford, Wynd-
ham, Masham, Arbuthnot, &c. This was the society which Prior joined
when he changed sides, and of which the members used to address each
other as brothers.

† This was the treaty in which Prior the poet was concerned, and for
which he was afterwards imprisoned by the house of lords.

mitted it to Pope for his critical opinion, and Pope recommended him not to get it acted, assigning as a reason that it was not "theatrical enough." That this opinion was erroneous the issue proved, as the play was acted for thirty-five successive nights with the greatest applause; but it was not more erroneous than the opinion Addison had formerly pronounced upon the proposed alterations in the *Rape of the Lock*, and, considering the character of the drama, was perfectly justifiable. Indeed, Addison professed to take the same view of the subject himself, and declared that, in suffering Cato to be played, he only yielded to the pressing importunities of his friends. Pope seems to have resigned his own scruples at the same time, and to have testified his desire to assist the success of his friend by contributing a prologue, which, says Roscoe, was no less admired than the tragedy itself. Up to this time their friendship continued. Any dissatisfaction Addison might have felt at Pope's verdict upon *Cato* was removed by the Prologue; but, unluckily, the very tribute which Pope designed as a testimony of his strong regard for Addison, led to consequences painful to them both. When Dennis found Addison associated with Pope, he immediately assailed him. He had a short time before attacked *The Temple of Fame*, in which he discovered one blemish, where the poet makes Sculpture represent Motion; but Pope treated his remarks with silent contempt. To a man of an irritable temper like Dennis, indifference is more galling than the fiercest satire, and Dennis was resolved to try another method of endeavouring to enrage his opponent. He accordingly published an elaborate and scurrilous critique upon *Cato*, and Pope, who had enough of discretion to leave the assault upon himself unanswered, was fired with resentment, and took up his friend's quarrel, which he vindicated in a coarse and ironical pamphlet, entitled *A Narrative of the Frenzy of J. D.* An officious friend is sometimes more dangerous than an open enemy, and Pope's conduct on this occasion, instead of propitiating the favour of Addison, had the contrary effect of giving him much disquietude. He disapproved altogether of the spirit in which Pope attempted to revenge him, and was so anxious to have it known that he had no participation in the work, that he desired Steele to communicate his sentiments fully to Lintot, the bookseller. After stating that Mr. Addison condemned the manner of treating Mr. Dennis, which was adopted in the *Narrative*, Steele adds, " When he thinks fit to take notice of Mr. Dennis's objections to his writings, he will do it in a way Mr. Dennis shall have no just reason to complain of ; but when the papers above-mentioned were offered to be communicated to him, he said he could not, either in honour or con-science, be privy to such a treatment, and was sorry to to hear of it." This very decisive repudiation of Pope's championship did not produce, at the time, any external breach between them. Pope must have been made aware of it, through Lintot, yet he does not appear to have taken any notice of it; but the feelings it gene-rated at both sides, continued to rankle in their minds, and terminated at last in a rupture that produced from the poet some lines equally remarkable for their polished malignity and their obvious exaggeration.

In *The Guardian* of April, 1713, a series of humo-rous essays, written by Tickell, were published under the sanction of Addison, that drew Pope into another literary feud. The object of the essays was to show, that of all the English writers of pastoral poetry, Am-brose Philips, whose pieces were published in the same volume of the *Miscellanies* in which Pope's appeared, was entitled to the precedence. Pope was incensed, and being solicited by Steele to contribute to that journal, be furnished a paper, in which he continued the subject, drawing a direct comparison between his own pastorals and those of Philips, and assigning the superiority to the latter in a vein of artful panegyric, while the reasons he furnished for his opinions were so weak and futile, as to cast the most ingenious ridicule upon Philips, under the mask of extravagant admiration. It was now Philips's turn to seek revenge ; and he is said to have contemplated a species of vengeance which, had he carried it into effect, might have fairly annihilated his opponent. He repaired to Button's coffee-house, which was the rendezvous of all the wits of the day, and which Pope used to frequent almost every night,—and hanging up a great rod in the public room, he avowed his determination to chastise Pope with it, whenever he should meet him there.* Such is the account we find in the biographies ; while Pope, in a letter to a private friend, states that Philips did express himself with much indignation against him one evening at Button's, but that he never opened his lips to him on the subject, although he had frequently met him there, afterwards. It is not improbable, however, that Philips might have declared his resolution to inflict some such punishment upon Pope in the first heat of his passion, and that he might afterwards have been dissuaded from it by personal considerations. At all events, Pope was the aggressor in this case, as in that of Dennis; and Philips would have been justified in any course he might have taken within the limits of appropriate retaliation. But Pope seldom appears to have thought himself in the wrong in affairs of this kind, and to have regarded with a sort of ostentatious contempt the anger of the adversaries his unwarrantable severity provoked. Thus, in the letter above quoted, after saying that Philips had accused him of entering into a cabal to write against the whigs, he goes on to observe, that " Philips did all he could secretly to continue the report with the Hanover Club, and kept in his hands the subscriptions paid for me to him, as secretary to that club. The heads of it have since given him to understand that they take it ill; but (*upon the terms I ought to be with such a man*) I would not ask him for this money; but commissioned one of the players, *his equal*, to receive it." The social morality of all this is infinitely entertaining. Pope, in the first instance, attacks Philips (who had given him no offence) in a very

* Ayre's *Life of Pope.*

insidious way; and then, because Philips resents it, he disdains to hold any direct communication with him; but, agreeably to the only terms he could keep with *such* a man (that is, a man who takes the liberty of being angry at a very wanton outrage), he sends one of the players, *his equal*, to transact a matter of business with him. Intercourse with lords and ministers of state had, by this time, quite spoiled Pope; and in the artificial estimate he put upon rank, and his habitual struggle to maintain himself in the good favour of the aristo-cracy, he seems to have wholly lost sight of his original position. He was so accustomed to mix with lords, that he at length came to talk and to write like a lord. When he sent the player to Philips, *as his equal*, he must have been labouring under a fit of profound vanity, which rendered him forgetful of the fact, that he was the son of a linendraper. Such a circumstance could never have been discreditable to him, if he had not assumed the airs of a superior to one who really inherited a higher rank in society than himself. Philips was descended from an ancient family in Leicestershire, was educated at Cam-bridge, and possessed affluent means throughout his life. We have already seen that neither Pope's birth nor edu-cation exhibited any special grounds of exultation; and of his fortune, it may be enough to observe, that about the very period of this controversy, when Gay suggested a journey with Pope to the continent, it was arranged that the former was to bear the chief part of the expenses in consideration of the narrow resources of the latter!

The affectation of Pope is abundantly testified in his correspondence. He imagined that he had a taste for painting, and took lessons from Mr. Jervas; but disco-vering his incapacity or inaptitude for the art, he gave it up. In one of his letters to Gay he says, " I have thrown away three Dr. Swifts, each of which was once my vanity ; *two lady Bridgewaters, a duchess of Mon-tague, half a dozen earls, and* one *knight of the garter.*" This has been considered elegant banter, especially as he adds, in a playful style, " I have crucified Christ over again in effigy, and made a Madonna as old as her mother, St. Anne. Nay, what is yet more miraculous, I have rivalled St. Luke himself in painting; and as it is said an angel came and finished his piece, so you would swear a devil put the last hand to mine, it is so begrimed and smutted." But the vanity of having painted so many lords and ladies is predominant. Half a dozen earls, and a knight of the garter!—was this a love of finery or a love of art?

We have a sort of commentary upon all this in the remarkable fact, that throughout the whole of Pope's works we do not find a single specimen of what Mr. Roscoe designates "love poems." It was suspected by some people, who never penetrated the surface of his character, that he entertained an attachment for the *two* miss Blounts, ladies with whom he was acquainted from infancy, and his passion for whom, he says, in a letter to one of them, full of artificial humour, was divided between both with the most wonderful regularity in the world. But this conjecture, whatever we may think of his connection with *one* of them, is set aside by a multitude of passing allusions in his poems, and by the whole tenor of his correspondence with the sisters. The only circumstance in his life which had a colouring of love in it, was his intercourse with lady Mary Wortley Montagu; an affair we shall have occasion to notice at some length in its proper place. Upon the whole survey of his conduct and his writings, it does not appear that he ever was seriously moved in his affections. He was too much absorbed in himself. His ill health, perhaps, repressed any disposition to form an alliance for domestic happiness; but if he were susceptible of such impressions, it must have found some shape of expression in his poetry, where we look in vain for such evidence, and find, in its stead, sententious scandal, formal compliments, and cold maxims.

The translation of the *Iliad*, the greatest undertaking of his life, was at last commenced, in the year 1714. He had often contemplated some such work as this; but the magnitude of the enterprise had as often deterred

him from beginning. Even when he did begin, he
sometimes felt as if he would sink under the task,
dreaming of it at night, and ready to abandon it in the
morning. But, encouraged by Addison and lord Lansdowne, he persevered, and at last accomplished his vast
labour. The poems he had hitherto published produced
him very little profit, although their diffusion laid the
foundation of his fame. In these circumstances, his
means were so straightened, having but a small allowance
from his father, who could not afford more, and being
incapacitated by his religion from holding any civil
employment, that he even complained of wanting money
to buy books. To remedy this state of things, it was
proposed to print the *Iliad* by subscription, a project
which was considerably aided by the active assistance of
such friends as lord Oxford, Swift, and Addison.

Pope has not failed to satisfy the curiosity of posterity about his mode of proceeding through this laborious undertaking. " In translating both the *Iliad*
and the *Odyssey*," he says, " my usual method was to
take advantage of the first heat, and then to correct
each book, first by the original text, then by other translations ; and lastly, to give it a reading for the versification only." In another place he observes, that " the
things he wrote fastest always pleased the most," and
that, " he wrote most of the *Iliad* fast ; a great deal
of it on journeys, from a little pocket *Homer ;* and
often forty or fifty verses in a morning in bed." It is
well known that nearly the whole translation was written
on the backs or covers of letters, from which he acquired the designation of *paper-sparing Pope.* These
manuscripts originally belonged to lord Bolingbroke,
afterwards to Mallet, and are now deposited in the
British Museum.

The plan on which the work was issued, was similar
to that which had been previously adopted with so much
success by Dryden.* Pope obtained through his friends,

---

* The same plan was adopted, with equal success, when the *Tatlers* were
collected into volumes.

' list of 575 subscribers; but, as many subscribed for more than one copy, the number actually issued was 654. A contest is said to have arisen amongst the booksellers about the purchase of the copyright; but Lintot offered the highest terms, and was of course preferred. Indeed, he offered so much, that Pope had some scruples in accepting his proposal, lest he might seriously injure his fortune. As it turned out, however, Lintot's sagacity was fully vindicated by the result. The work was to be printed in six volumes, quarto, at the price of six guineas; and Lintot agreed to supply, at his own expense, all the copies for the subscribers, to furnish Pope with surplus copies for friends, and to pay him, in addition, 200l. per volume. Upon the total account, Pope cleared by the *Iliad* the enormous sum of 5,320l. 4s.

It was stipulated that quarto copies should be printed only for the original subscribers; but Lintot, says Johnson, impressed the same pages upon a small folio, and sold, exactly at half the price, for half a guinea each volume, books so little inferior to the quartos, that, by a fraud of trade, these folios, being afterwards shortened by cutting away the top and bottom, were sold as copies printed for the subscribers. Lintot also issued an impression of 250 copies on royal paper folio, at two guineas a volume. To what extent he might have carried the sale at a high price, may be conjectured from the fact, that the work attained such popularity as to tempt a piratical bookseller in Holland to print an edition in duodecimo, which he imported clandestinely into England, and which had so rapid a circulation as to compel Lintot to contract his folio at once into a duodecimo, in order to compete in the market with his fraudulent rival. Of this edition upwards of 7000 copies were disposed of in a few weeks; and the very circumstance which appeared to threaten him with a serious loss, led fortunately to a greater amount of profit than he might otherwise have secured, by forcing

him to bring out a cheap edition while the work was in
the zenith of demand. The consequence was, that
Lintot became suddenly enriched, purchased estates,
and grew to the honour of high sheriff of his county.

In the course of his labours, Pope encountered many
difficulties that increased the trepidation which affected
him even to the close. Several invidious reports were
spread to his prejudice; amongst the rest, that he was
incompetent to the task he had undertaken, an insinuation which derived some plausibility from the irre-
gularity and insufficiency of his education; nor were
there wanting enemies on the one side, who denounced
him as a whig, and, on the other, who accused him of
being a tory. The most serious of all these charges
was, his want of classical learning, for which there
was perhaps, some foundation. But his assiduity had
long before supplied the want of masters, and enabled
him to conquer for himself those fields of erudition
which a legitimate collegiate course had enabled his
more fortunate contemporaries to traverse with ease.
Besides, he had the assistance of Broome, who furnished
a portion of the notes, and of Parnell, who wrote the
Life of Homer (which, however, Pope was obliged to
revise), and may be supposed to have received occasional suggestions from his more intimate literary
friends, who were abundantly qualified to counsel him
whenever he might have required their help. His own
fears of the issue of the undertaking appear to have
been greater than even his envious rivals affected to
entertain. In one of his letters he says, he is " ready
to hang himself" with apprehension; " but this misery," observes Dr. Johnson, " was not of long con-
tinuance; he grew by degrees more acquainted with
Homer's images and expressions, and practice increased
his facilities of versification, and in a short time he
was enabled to despatch as many as fifty verses a day."
He was not always, however, in the mood for such a
swift progress, and the work occupied him, from the
date of its commencement to its termination, a period

of six years. He began in 1712, when he was only twenty-five years of age, and ended in 1718, in his thirtieth year.

The work was published volume by volume, as the translation proceeded, the first four books appearing in 1715. The profits of the whole completely relieved Pope from the pecuniary difficulties under which, from the narrowness of his income, he had been previously labouring. He secured himself from all such dangers for the future, by the judicious purchase of life annuities, one of which, for 500*l.* per annum, was chargeable upon the estates of the duke of Buckingham. Nor did he lack friends to sustain him in the progress of his toils, who were prompt at least with offers of service, if they did not actually bestow upon him any substantial proofs of their friendship. Lord Oxford expressed his regret that Pope's religion excluded him from public employment, and Mr. secretary Craggs proposed to use his influence to procure him a pension, a species of independence which Pope declined; observing, however, that if he should require any occasional help, he would not hesitate to apply to him for it; but it does not appear that he ever made any such application to his friendly patron, who shortly after retired from office. Lord Halifax also volunteered some acts of generosity which Pope seems to have been unwilling to accept. In a letter to his lordship, he speaks as if he had already received some favours, but was not very anxious to increase the burthen of obligations. " If I ever become troublesome or solicitous," he says, " it must not be out of expectation, but out of gratitude. Your lordship may cause me to live agreeably in the town, or contentedly in the country, which is really all the difference I set between an easy fortune and a small one. It is, indeed, a high strain of generosity in you to think of making me easy all my life, only because I have been so happy as to divert you some few hours," &c. The spirit in which this is conceived, evinces a feeling of ill-suppressed irritation, which is irreconcilable with the magnificence of the acknowledgment that his lordship had thought of making him easy all his life, and clearly points at some unexplained vexation which was rankling in the mind of the writer. Spence relates an anecdote, on Pope's authority, which in some measure accounts. for this disinclination to be obliged by his lordship.

Lord Halifax, it appears, according to Pope's report, was a pretender to taste, rather than really possessed of it; and when the first two or three books of the *Iliad* were translated, he wished to have them read at his house, when Addison, Garth, and Congreve were present. In the course of the reading, he stopped Pope three or four times, in a very civil tone, suggesting that there was " something" in the passage that did not quite please him, and requesting Pope to mark it, and consider it at his leisure. " I am sure," said his lordship, " you can give it a little turn." Upon returning home with Dr. Garth in his chariot, Pope declared himself to be placed in a perplexity by the looseness of his lordship's criticisms, observing that he could not guess what were the actual blemishes at which his lordship was offended. Garth laughed heartily, and said that Pope was not long enough acquainted with lord Halifax to know his way yet. " All you need do," said he, " is to leave them just as they are; call on lord Halifax a month or two hence, thank him for his kind observations on those passages, and then read them to him as altered. I have known him much longer than you have, and will be answerable for the event." Pope followed his advice, waited on lord Halifax, hoped he would find his objections removed, read the passages exactly as they were at first, and his lordship, extremely pleased with them, cried out, " Ay, now they are perfectly right; nothing can be better."

Of the truth of this anecdote we are not permitted to entertain any doubt, since it is related by Pope himself (if Spence's authority may be relied upon); yet Mr. Roscoe does not think it probable that Pope had ever read this work to lord Halifax; because he finds, by a letter to Addison, that the translation of the first and second books were left in his lordship's hands for the purpose of obtaining his deliberate remarks upon them. The two circumstances, however, are not so irreconcilable as Mr. Roscoe seems to think. Pope might have read portions of the work as it proceeded, and afterwards left the manuscript with his lordship: at all events, until some more conclusive reason can be assigned for throwing distrust upon the story, we are bound to accept it upon the attestation of Spence, to whom we are indebted for so many minute particulars concerning the life and opinions of the poet. The origin, then, of Pope's ill-will to Halifax, was the freedom with which his lordship pretended to criticise his translation, for which it appears Pope took his revenge in a way that reflects very little credit on his candour or independence. If Halifax earns our pity by his affectation of literary taste, Pope exposes himself to contempt by the cheat he practised upon his patron. That the translator of Homer should have degraded himself by so mean a subterfuge, was more humiliating to him than the detection of false pretensions could be to lord Halifax. In reference to this affair, Dr. Johnson observes, that " the great or wise seldom suspect they are despised or cheated; and that Halifax, thinking this a lucky opportunity of securing immortality, made some advances of favour, and some overtures of advantage to Pope, which he seems to have received with sullen coldness." The same writer closes his remarks by saying, " It is not likely that Halifax had any personal benevolence to Pope; it is evident that Pope looked on Halifax with scorn and hatred." Mr. Roscoe dissents strongly from this view, observing, that " these harsh and supercilious remarks on this transaction, and the supposed traffic between fame and money, seem scarcely justifiable from what appears upon the subject;" adding, that no proof exists that Pope's " manly and independent" letter gave offence to his lordship; or that Pope, in return, looked upon Halifax

with scorn and hatred.* As it rarely happens that a
dispassionate reader finds himself agreeing with Dr.
Johnson in his severe estimates of the motives and conduct of the poets whose biographies he wrote, it is the
more desirable to mark those passages emphatically where
his censures are sustained by evidence, as they appear to

---

* The strictures which I felt it necessary to make in the first volume of
these biographies upon certain parts of Dr. Johnson's *Lives of the Poets*,
especially his *Life of Milton*, have elicited observations in quarters where a
blind reverence for Johnson seems to regard all impartial criticism that
touches upon his errors as an act of sacrilege. In appealing from such
prejudices to the common sense of the public, I am quite confident of the
result; nor do I entertain the least apprehension that, in exposing the malevolence and bigotry by which *The Lives of the Poets* are sullied, I shall be
suspected of a disinclination to render honest homage to the genius of their
celebrated author. Dr. Johnson is one of the few writers whose fame can
suffer to be treated with candour; and, for my own part, desiring nothing
so heartily as the vindication of truth, I have neither hesitated to differ
from him where I believed him to be wrong, or where he allowed splenetic
resentments to usurp the awards of justice, nor refused to adopt his opinions where I found them to be right. That I am not alone in my view of
the unworthy spirit that characterses his poetical biographies, the following
passage from the preface to Mr. Roscoe's *Life of Pope* will satisfactorily
testify. " *The Life of Pope* by Dr. Johnson has been considered," says Mr.
Roscoe, " as one of the best of that series which, unfortunately for the memory of our national poets, and the character of our national poetry, he was
induced to undertake. Throughout the whole of those lives there appears
an assumption of superiority in the biographer over the subjects of his
labours, which diminishes the idea of their talents, and leaves an unfavourable impression on their moral character. It could only be from the representations of Johnson, that so amiable a man as Cowper could thus close
his remarks on reading *The Lives of the British Poets :* "After all, it is a
melancholy observation, which it is impossible not to make, after having
run through this series of poetical lives, that where there were such shin-
ing talents, there should be so little virtue. These luminaries of our country seem to have been kindled into a brighter blaze than others, only that
their spots might be more noticed ; so much can nature do for our intellectual part, and so little for our moral. What vanity, what petulance in
Pope! how painfully sensible of censure, and yet how restless in provocation! To what mean artifices could Addison stoop, in hopes of injuring
the reputation of his friend! Savage, how sordidly vicious! and the more
condemned for the pains that are taken to palliate his vices! offensive as
they appear through a veil, how would they disgust without one. What a
sycophant to the public taste was Dryden! sinning against his feelings, lewd
in his writings, though chaste in his conversation. *I know not but one might
search these eight volumes with a candle, as the prophet says, to find a* MAN,
and not find ONE, *unless, perhaps, Arbuthnot were he.*" Can this have been
said in the country of Spenser, of Shakspeare, of Sidney, and of Milton ? of
Donne, of Corbet, of Hale, of Marvel, and of Cowley ? of Roscommon, of
Garth, of Congreve, of Parnell, of Rowe, and of Gay ? of Thomson, of
Lyttelton, and of Young ? of Shenstone, of Akenside, of Collins, of Gold-
smith, of Mason, and of Gray ?

" Unspotted names ! and memorable long,
    If there be force in virtue or in song ! ' "

The lustre of which, as well as of many others that might be adduced, can
never be obscured, either by the most morbid malignity or by the darkest
fanaticism '

be in this instance. Of the authenticity of Pope's letter to lord Halifax, in allusion to his lordship's desire to improve his circumstances, no doubt exists.

Mr. Roscoe, whose good feelings betrayed him into panegyrics that cannot be always defended, describes that letter as being " manly and independent ; " while Dr. Johnson speaks of its " frigid gratitude" and "sullen coldness." Whatever reluctance may be felt in disallowing the generous interpretation of Mr. Roscoe, it is very difficult to refuse assent to the obvious truth or Dr. Johnson's view of an epistle which admits benefits conferred, and endeavours to evade the expression of a becoming acknowledgment. Pope either looked for more favours before he would commit himself to any profuse terms of gratitude, or he conceived that lord Halifax's criticism had obliterated the obligation. Mr. Roscoe endeavours to show that they continued to maintain mutual sentiments of attachment as long as lord Halifax lived, and refers, in proof of that supposition, to a stanza written after his lordship's death, in which the poet bewails the loss the arts had suffered by his decease, — a passage in the preface to the *Iliad*, where he speaks of his lordship as one of the first who had favoured him, — and some lines in the epilogue to the *Satires*, written twenty years afterwards, where he cites the name of Halifax as one of his friends. Believing these testimonies of Pope's attachment for his lordship to be conclusive, Mr. Roscoe asks, " How is it possible to reconcile this gratuitous effusion of disinterested regard with Johnson's assertion, that Pope looked on Halifax with scorn and hatred ? " The only answer that can be made to this question is, that it is not possible to reconcile them ; but as Johnson's assertion is founded upon Pope's explicit betrayal of scorn and hatred, the irreconcilable elements are not Pope's effusions of regard on the one hand, and the biographer's imputation on the other, but Pope's own expression of contradictory sentiments. It is not Pope and Johnson who are irreconcilable, but Pope alone, who cannot be reconciled with himself. The simple solution of the dilemma is this, — that Halifax offended Pope by affecting to find fault with his translation, and that Pope never forgave him, although he had no objection to let the world know that he enjoyed his lordship's friendship.

"The life of a wit," says Pope, in the preface to an edition of his poems, "is a warfare upon earth ; and the present spirit of the learned world is such, that to attempt to serve it (any way) one must have the constancy of a martyr, and a resolution to suffer for its sake." His own life was a remarkable illustration of this pugnacious condition of the wits. While he maintained some close and valuable friendships through a stormy literary career, he came into collision with others, whose good opinion had been useful to him in the beginning, and could not at any time have been forfeited without injury. The most memorable instance of alienation between Pope and his friends, was that which separated him from Addison. It is always difficult to trace the origin of such quarrels, which generally take root in trifles, and expand into serious differences almost imperceptibly. But there is sufficient reason to believe that Pope's intimacy with the heads of the tory party, who took an active interest in promoting the subscription for his translation of Homer, gave offence to Addison in the first instance ; and that Pope, recoiling from what he regarded as an injustice, widened the breach by the manifestation of a proud resentment, too sensitive and hasty, perhaps, in its utterance. Addison may also have favoured Philips, who was politically connected with him, in the feud about the pastorals, and have thus furnished Pope with an additional ground of complaint. On such occasions the interference of well-intentioned people usually exasperates existing distrusts, and throws in the way of reconciliation a thousand new obstacles. Mr. Jervas, the painter, in the hope of restoring amity between Pope and Addison, attempted to make them both think better of each other, and produced the inevitable result of increasing their mutual animosity. In a letter to the former, he tells him that he had seen Mr. Addison, and then goes on to repeat the kind things Mr. Addison had said of him. "He assured me," says Jervas, "that he would make use not only of his interest, but of his art, to do you some service." He did not mean his art of poetry, but his art at court ; and he is sensible that nothing can have a better air for himself than moving in your favour, especially since insinuations were spread that he did not care you should not prosper as a poet. He protests that it shall not be his fault if there is not the best intelligence in the world, and the most hearty friendship," &c. The allusion to the insinuations refers to a suspicion that was entertained that Addison was jealous of Pope's reputation, which might have had some foundation, although it appears not a little unreasonable. To this letter Pope returned an answer that shows reluctance to advance towards Addison, but that asserts with a becoming dignity his right to be grateful to his friends, whether they were tories or whigs, without caring who might be dissatisfied with him. "As for any affairs of real kindness or service," he observes, "which it is in his (Addison's) power to do me, I should be ashamed to receive them from any man who had no better opinion of my morals, than to think me a party man. * * For all that passed between Dr. Swift and me, you know the whole (without reserve) of our correspondence. The engagements I had to him were such as the actual services he had done me in relation to the subscription for Homer obliged me to. I must have leave to be grateful to him, and to any one who serves me, let him be never so obnoxious to any party. Nor did the tory party ever put me to the hardship of asking their leave, which is the greatest obligation I owe to it ; and I expect no greater from the whig party than the same liberty.—A curse on the word ' party ' !—which I have been obliged to use so often in this period." Soon after this, Pope wrote to Addison, asserting that the real friendship of one who asks no real service, ought not to be questioned ; and then, as a proof that he believed him to be sincere in his expressions of good will, requesting him to look over two books of the translation, which were at that time in the hands of lord Halifax, and oblige him with his opinion of them.   This request placed Addison in a situation of some embarrassment. He had previously been privy to a translation of the first book of Homer, which his friend Tickell had made at college, and which he now intended to publish, and he apprehended that it would look like double dealing were he to read both manuscripts.   The course he adopted was frank and honourable.   Meeting Pope at Button's coffee-house, he asked him to adjourn with him to a tavern to dinner, and there disclosed to him very candidly the perplexity in which he was involved. Pope was perfectly satisfied, observed that Mr. Tickell' had as much right to translate any author as himself, and added that he would not desire Mr. Addison to read the first book, but could wish to have the benefit of his advice on the second, which was then finished, and which Tickell had not touched.   This interview' averted the threatened breach for a time ; but mutual suspicions had set in, and the acquaintance was carried on by an exchange of civilities, which was more danger-ous than an open rupture.

Pope, notwithstanding that he declared himself to Addison satisfied about Tickell's version, was secretly chagrined that such a publication should appear at all, especially under the patronage of the most distinguished critic of the day ; and when the book was printed, he resolved to expose its errors by a severe critique.   For this purpose he prepared a variety of notes in the margin of a copy which afterwards fell into the hands of Warburton, in which he classified the several faults committed by his rival, and even went so far as to state that the appearance of such a work, at so critical a juncture, by a " creature of Addison's," was another shaft from the same quiver ; and that, putting

together many odd circumstances, he was fully convinced
that it was published, not only with Addison's participation, but was indeed his own performance. This
statement is copied by Warburton from the notes in
Pope's own hand-writing; and, startling as the assertion
is, not an atom of evidence of any kind has ever been
discovered to justify it; nor can the utmost ingenuity of
Pope's defenders furnish any thing better than a few
vague conjectures in its support. Pope had confessedly
been galled by the reception which was given in some
quarters to Tickell's translation. Gay had written to
him, to tell him that Addison had said that it was the
best that had ever appeared in any language ; that both
Pope's and Tickell's were very well done, but that the
latter had more of Homer in it. To balance this, he
had plaudits — qualified, no doubt, by small scraps of
objective criticism—from Arbuthnot, Swift, Parnell, and
Berkeley. But the single sting from Addison struck
deeper than the panegyrics of the crowd, and was never
forgotten or appeased. The only circumstance that
gives the slightest colour of probability to his suspicion
that the translation was made by Addison, and published
to annoy him, was an observation made by Young,
whom he met accidentally in the street, to this effect,
that he and Tickell used to communicate to each other
whatever verses they wrote, that he had never heard of
this translation before, and that he thought there must
be a mistake in the matter. Hence Pope concluded, to
use his own words, "that there was some underhand
dealing in the business."*

With such feelings existing at one side, and a perfect
knowledge of them at the other, the dissolution of their
friendship became inevitable. Steele and Gay, in the
hope of making up the breach, contrived an interview
between them, the issue of which terminated all prospect of reconcilement. In the beginning of the evening,
Addison was all reserve and silence, but as wine and

* Spence.

conversation circulated, he became more familiar. Then
Steele opened the business, by expressing a desire that
amity should be restored between him and Mr. Pope.
Pope begged that he would waive all ceremonious
forms, and freely state the grounds of offence. To
these requests Addison made a calm and formal answer,
advising Pope to divest himself of part of his vanity,
reminding him that he had not yet arrived at that pitch
of excellence he might imagine, and that when he and'
Steele had corrected his verses they had a different air ;
then, after citing the mistakes and inaccuracies pointed
out by different critics, he observed that Pope was
not wrong to get a large sum of money for his translation,
but that it was an ill executed thing, and inferior to
Tickell's : for himself, he added, that he had quitted the
muses for public life, and that all he spoke was through
friendship, and from a desire that Mr. Pope, as he
would do if he were much humbler, might look better
to the world. Gay made some cautious remarks, having
expectations from court that checked him from in-
terfering too boldly ; and then Pope broke out, appealing
from Addison's judgment, telling him that he was not
able to correct him, that he knew him too well to
expect any thing from his friendship, that he (Addison)
was a pensioner from his youth, and had always endeavoured to cast down new-fledged merit. This burst of
passion terminated the meeting, and they separated
abruptly.* The result was, that vindictive satire, in
which, under the name of Atticus, the enraged poet
took vengeance upon the critic. It is necessary, however,
to observe, that an attack made upon Pope by Gildon,
and which was said to have been instigated by Addison,
is urged as an additional provocation, crowning all the
other circumstances. But the testimony on which it
rests is so feeble, and the fact itself is so improbable, that,
although such an impression might have been made
upon Pope's mind, his belief in it only affords a further

proof of that natural irritability of temperament which appears to have prevented him from judging dispassionately, even where his most important interests were at stake.

Upon the whole, it must be allowed that there were faults on both sides; that Addison was displeased with Pope for defending him with such coarse weapons from the assaults of Dennis; that he was further displeased with him (which he certainly had no right to be) for his connection with the Tories; and that having assisted him by his countenance in the commencement of his literary labours, he was afterwards offended at the vanity which sprouted out of his great and rapid success. All this displeasure betrayed a foolish weakness of character, which was unworthy alike of his genius and his position. On the other hand, Pope imagined injuries that never were committed; was ready to start into arms at every breath of suspicion; was prompt to accuse and slow to retract his accusations; petulant, waspish, and filled with a swelling sentiment of self-importance that would have deserved to be designated as pride, did it not so frequently exhibit the littlenesses of a paltry egotism. It is impossible to decide where the balance of error lay; but it may be presumed in this case, as in most others where mere faults of character intervene to prevent a seasonable adjustment of differences, that judicious mediation might have re-united friends who, left to themselves, discovered nothing at either side but the salient antagonist points.

During the progress of the translation Pope made frequent visits to London; and although (when he consulted his own inclinations) a man of abstemious habits, he fell into the dangerous excesses to which the clubs and convivial parties to which he was invited exposed him. Perhaps a desire to keep on good terms with men of all parties may have drawn him more largely into company than was consistent with his tastes or his physical powers; and, unluckily, he formed an acquaintance with the young earl of Warwick, Addison's son-in-law, and Colley

Cibber, who led him night after night into a course of dissipation that at last seriously affected his health. In a letter to Congreve, written at this time, he says, " I sit up till two o'clock over burgundy and champaigne, and am become so much a rake that I shall be ashamed, in a short time to be thought to do any kind of business." He carried his revelling to such a height that his vene- rable friend, sir William Turnbull, ultimately interfered, entreating of him to " get out of all tavern-company, and fly away, *tanquam ex incendio.* What a misery is it for you," he adds, " to be destroyed by the foolish kindness (it is all one, real or pretended) of those who are able to bear the poison of bad wine, and to engage you in so unequal a combat." Pope was, indeed, so unfit for such perilous pleasures, that the preservation of his life depended upon the caution he exercised even in the matter of diet. Some years afterwards Swift was so anxious upon this point that he observed to him in one of his letters, " I had rather live in forty Irelands, than under the frequent disquiets of hearing you are out of order. I always apprehend it most after a great din- ner ; for the least transgression of yours, if it be only two bits and one sup more than your stint, is a great debauch, for which you certainly pay more than those sots who are carried dead drunk to bed."

The great success of the *Iliad* fortunately enabled Pope to retire from the town ; and prevailing upon his father to dispose of his estates at Binfield, he purchased the lease of a house and grounds at Twickenham, to which, with his father and mother, he retired in March 1715-16. His father did not long survive this re- moval. After enjoying an excellent constitution through- out his life, he died suddenly in November 1717, in the seventy-fifth year of his age. The event deeply affected Pope, and he sought to alleviate his grief by occasional visits to his friends and the university of Oxford. His father's fortune descended to him unincumbered, and added to what he had secured by his publications enabled him to live not only in affluence, but to engage in the improvement of his grounds, which now occupied a considerable share of his attention. In his correspondence at this period, he gives ample accounts of his "drafts, elevations, profiles, perspectives," &c.; and his fantastic gardening obtained so much celebrity, that the prince of Wales made him a munificent present of urns and vases to decorate his walks and grottoes, to which he afterwards added a series of busts of the poets. Of his celebrated grotto formed by an excavation under the public highway, which he devised to connect his two gardens separated by the road, he has left an animated and picturesque description familiar to .all the readers of his Letters. His pleasant schemes, however, of an elegant retirement on the banks of the Thames, were nearly frustrated by an unfortunate purchase in South Sea bonds, in which he was induced to speculate upon the extravagant promise of profit which, in the rage of the day, they seemed to hold out. The stock had risen to upwards of 1000 per cent.; and it is not very surprising that a poet should be deceived by golden dreams that deluded so many persons of quality, tradesmen, and merchants. The extent of Pope's actual loss was never ascertained, and he appears to have preserved a studious silence upon the subject; but it is believed that the world is indebted to the injury his fortune sustained on that occasion for the project of the *Odyssey*, which is said to have been undertaken for the purpose of retrieving it.

In the course of his visits to Oxford, Pope formed an intimacy with Dr. Clarke, a man distinguished for his erudition, who was led by frequent conversations with the poet to attempt his conversion to the reformed faith. A similar effort was made in a more formal way by the celebrated Atterbury, bishop of Rochester; but Pope remained firm, and begged of his friends to allow him to enjoy their acquaintance without entering upon religious discussions, which could produce no other result than that of confirming both in their previous convictions. On one occasion, Pope declared to the bishop

that though he was but a bad advocate for his religion, its
orthodoxy and strength would give him sufficient power
to venture an argument with any heretic either with or
without a mitre.   Atterbury accepted the challenge in
good humour; and after an exchange of general assertions,
the dispute ended by Pope declaring that if it were possible for any man to raise the dead in proof of any other
religion than that acknowledged by the Roman catholic
church, it would not shake his creed.   After such a declaration it was idle to persevere; yet Atterbury did not
wholly relinquish his design, and frequently renewed the
subject afterwards in his letters to Pope, but with no
better effect.   Notwithstanding this fundamental difference between them, Atterbury and Pope continued to
maintain the closest personal attachment; and when the
former was impeached for secretly favouring the Pretender (which was a strange offence for so strenuous an
advocate of the church of England), Pope appeared as
a witness on his trial, to bear testimony to his manner
of passing his time, with a view to show that he had no
leisure for plots.   The novelty of his situation covered
him with confusion; and although he had but little to
say, he acknowledges that he blundered in its utterance.
When Atterbury was sentenced to banishment, Pope
attended him to the last, and received a Bible at his
hands as a parting gift.   Lord Chesterfield relates a
story, for which he assigns the authority of Pope himself, that, with all this show of sincerity in his religious
professions, Atterbury was a free-thinker.   Such a story
might be fairly rejected on its intrinsic improbability,
were it not even most fully disproved by the numerous
proofs contained in Pope's correspondence with Atterbury, covering a long space of years, in reference to that
prelate's zealous and repeated efforts to draw his friend
over to the doctrines of the established church.   It is
needless to observe, that if Atterbury were an infidel,
and Pope knew the fact, such a correspondence could
not have taken place.

Before the death of his father, Pope published, in

1716, the first general edition of his Miscellaneous Poems; and the next labours in which he appeared before the public were a selection from the poems of Parnell, which he undertook as a duty of friendship, and an edition of Shakspeare, both of which were issued in 1721. The high reputation of Pope induced Tonson to offer him a sum of 217*l.* 12*s.* to undertake a new edition of Shakspeare's Plays, the text of which had become deteriorated and corrupted in the hands of successive interpolators and incompetent critics. To this edition Pope annexed a preface which was creditable to his judgment; but did little for the text, which he seems to have passed over with almost as much negligence as any of his predecessors. Theobald, who brought to the task hardly any other qualifications than persevering industry, exposed his defects in a subsequent edition which so completely reduced the value of Pope's publication that, of 750 copies which were originally issued at the costly charge of six guineas, no less than 140 copies were sold at sixteen shillings each. Pope's vexation, inflamed by the complaints of the bookseller, may be inferred from the castigation he afterwards inflicted upon Theobald in the *Dunciad.*

He now issued proposals for a translation of the *Odyssey,* which he undertook in conjunction with Fenton and Browne. The terms were five guineas for five volumes; three of which, introduced by a general view of the epic poem, and of the *Iliad* and *Odyssey* translated from Bossu, were published in 1725. Of this work 819 copies were printed, and subscriptions were obtained for 574. Pope sold the whole copyright to Lintot for 600*l.*; but as the sale did not equal the expectations that were formed of it, Lintot complained that he had been imposed upon, and threatened legal proceedings. The ground of this assertion was, that having undertaken the translation, and secured a numerous subscription, Pope employed some underling to perform what should have come from his own hand. But a reference to the original proposals of Pope showed explicitly that he had stipulated for the assistance of two friends. An ingenious criticism upon this translation by Spence led to an acquaintance with that accomplished person, whose affection for Pope induced him to collect so many valuable anecdotes concerning his habits and opinions.

One of the most remarkable passages in the life of Pope was his connection with lady Mary Wortley Montagu, which may be properly adverted to in this place. It is not known exactly when their friendship commenced; but from the dates of their earliest correspondence, it is evident that they were personally acquainted before lady Mary left England for Turkey. Distinguished alike by her wit and her beauty, lady Mary Wortley Montagu was one of the most remarkable women of her age. She was the eldest daughter of the earl of Kingston, afterwards marquis of Dorchester and duke of Kingston: she came of the races of Pierrepoint and Fielding, both of whom won laurels in the civil war; the blood of poets as well as knights coursed in her veins; she was related on one side to Beaumont the dramatist, and on the other to Henry Fielding, who was her second cousin; and she appeared to unite in her own person all the graces and spirit of her proud descent. Even in her childhood she became so conspicuous for her charms and vivacity, that her father at a meeting of the Kit-kat club to choose toasts for the year, proposed her as a candidate, though she was then only eight years of age. The members demurred, as it was contrary to the rules to elect a beauty they had never seen. "Then you shall see her," cried the earl; and in the gaiety of the moment sent orders home to have her finely dressed, and brought to him to the tavern. She was received with acclamations, her health rapturously drank, and her name engraved in due form on a drinking glass. Some of the most eminent men in England were present; and she went from the lap of one poet or statesman to the arms of another, was overwhelmed with caresses, and feasted with sweetmeats

and panegyrics on her wit and beauty.*   It was a scene
of ecstasy which left a deep impression on her mind,
and probably gave a predominant tinge to the rest of
her life.   Her education was irregular and miscellaneous; but it had the advantage of embracing a vast
course of reading that is rarely traversed by her sex.
She early became a proficient in classical learning, after
having absorbed all the romances and poetry she could
procure.   In the height and mellow development of her
beauty and accomplishments, she was seen by Mr. Montagu, the grandson of the earl of Sandwich, who was so
fascinated by her talents that he made proposals for her
hand, which in due time were accepted.   A difference
arose, however, about the marriage settlements.   Her
father required that Mr. Montagu's estates should be
entailed upon the eldest son ; a proposal which the latter
rejected, offering to make the best provision he could
for lady Mary, but refusing to settle his property upon
a son, who might, for aught he knew, prove a spendthrift or an idiot.   Lord Kingston could not consent
that *his* grandchildren should run the risk of being left
beggars ; and both parties being firm, the negotiations
were broken off.   But lady Mary had a will, which was
not to be coerced by aristocratic theories of property.   She
kept up her correspondence in private with Mr. Montagu,
while her father commanded her to accept the offers of
another suitor.   Exerting to the full his parental authority, and not doubting that his threats of banishing her
to the country, and cutting her off with a small annuity,
would have the desired result, he ordered the settlements
to be drawn up, the wedding clothes to be bought, and
appointed the day for the ceremony.   Lady Mary was
in a flutter of excitement, as any lady might be under
such circumstances.   She was at no loss for an alternative, for she had a vast number of offers ; but the difficulty was who to choose, for it seems, after all, that her
choice of Mr. Montagu was only an accident, determined

---

* The Letters and Works of Lady Mary Montagu, edited by Lord
Wharncliffe. 1837.

x 4

by her resolution to oppose the arbitrary demands of her father. The appointed morning brought her indecision to a close ; and while the husband selected by her father was buying the wedding ring, she, in another part of the town, became the wife of Mr. Montagu.*

. This union was as ill assorted as it was hastily entered into. Mr. Montagu was too staid, dull, and ceremonious in his views of life, for a woman of so much spirit; and they were not long married until her superior sense and brilliancy became evident, and his cold and exacting disposition took umbrage at her wit and her supremacy. Detained by parliamentary and official duties in London, he would leave her, even for months together, alone in the country. Her temper, perhaps, which was no doubt over-ruling, may have helped to sunder her more widely from her husband ; and it is not unlikely that his treatment contributed to increase the evil he wanted to avoid. An appointment at the Treasury obliged him to bring her to town, and present her at court ; but the universal admiration she attracted so completely eclipsed his consequence, that it may be presumed he was now less inclined than ever to attempt to reconcile himself to her character. The next change of scene was not more propitious. Mr. Montagu was appointed, in 1716, minister at Constantinople, and took her along with him. But every where they went she drew all eyes, and her husband fell into deeper shadow than before. She was surrounded by gallants, and painters, and poets ; and her correspondents addressed her in the most passionate language, to which her sprightliness and willingness to please and be pleased gave a kind of encouragement ; and throughout all these scenes of enchantment nobody seemed to think of Mr. Montagu, or even to observe such a bearing to the lady as if they were conscious there was such a person in existence. He may have sullenly exaggerated these incidents to his imagination, and given fresh occasion to their repetition by affecting indifference

* Spence.

or public neglect. The faults on both sides expanded into graver shapes: mutual aversion, concealed under the most hopeless forms of external respect, worked deeper and wider channels in their hearts; and some years after her return to England, she went to the Continent *alone*. The cause of her departure from England has never been explained, and conjecture has in vain attempted to supply the place of information. In a letter to lady Pomfret, written at Venice in the first year of her absence, she says that she had been long endeavouring to persuade her husband to go abroad; and at last, tired of delay, had set out alone, he promising to follow her, which as yet business had prevented him from doing. All this was possible; and the fact that they parted on friendly terms, is exhibited in the intimation of her intention to travel for several months before she carried it into effect; and when she did go, she wrote to her husband from Dartford, the first stage, again from Dover, and again on landing at Calais, and during the whole of her residence on the Continent they continued to correspond. But they never met again. Lady Mary remained abroad for a period of twenty-two years, until the death of her husband; and then, but not until then, returned home. It has been surmised from all these circumstances that their separation was a matter of private arrangement between themselves — perhaps to avoid scandal ; that a show of correspondence should be observed, to mislead curiosity; and that, with an ample allowance on her side, and independence of action on his, she should remain abroad during his life-time. To whatever weight such surmises may be entitled, they present an explanation of the circumstances which is perfectly compatible with the characters and probable motives of the decorous minister and his witty but prudent wife.

Such was the fascinating woman for whom Pope professed the most passionate regard. His acquaintance with her may possibly have commenced about the time he went to reside at Twickenham. Some of his letters to her are dated previously to her departure for Con-

stantinople; and throughout the whole term of her absence there, and afterwards during her long residence in
Italy, he continued to correspond with her. His letters are
for the most part full of the most laboured compliments
and careful criticism on men, manners, and literature;
sometimes he employed language that, under other circumstances, would have been regarded as the solicitations or remonstrances of a lover; and in more instances
than one he appears to have run into excesses which
betrayed a freedom unbecoming both of the writer and
his correspondent. Lady Mary prized his genius, and
was perhaps proud of his admiration; and, so long as it
was kept within regulated limits, did not care to let him
indulge his vanity with any idle expressions that satisfied his poetical nature — as far as his nature was poetical in that sense. The times were favourable to this
species of gallantry; and Pope was surrounded by people
who were not scrupulous about mock-heroic tenderness,
or even bolder familiarities. Congreve's devotion to the
duchess of Marlborough, Swift's affair with Stella, the
freaks of the second lady Walpole before her marriage,
lady Sandwich's scandals, and other illustrations of the
influence of a licentious court, might easily be cited to
show that appearances at least were not very anxiously
consulted, even in some cases where there was much solid
virtue behind. But it may be observed, that a woman
of so much wit and beauty as lady Mary might give an
unconscious licence to the advances of such a man as
Pope, without dreaming that he would presume any
further, or without entertaining a suspicion that his own
thoughts were taking advantage of the occasion. And
such seems to have been the case.

When she arrived in London, Pope prevailed upon
her to take up her residence in Twickenham; negotiated
a house for her; and had the happiness to find his wishes
crowned in having the woman he so ardently admired
living close in his neighbourhood. This object was no
sooner accomplished than he asked permission to have
her portrait painted by sir Godfrey Kneller; and in the
progress of the work he wrote to her, saying, amongst

other things, " The picture dwells really at my heart,
and I have made a perfect passion of preferring your
present face to your past.   *   *   *   Still give me
cause to say you are good to me, and allow me as much
of your person as sir Godfrey can help me to." Such
language as this in ordinary life would be considered
abundantly explicit, but lady Mary seems to have regarded it with perfect indifference ; indeed so much so,
as to have hardly troubled herself to put any construction upon it whatever, accepting it as mere words of
course, without any definite object or meaning. She
shortly afterwards, however, became sensibly awakened
to a passion, the existence of which she evidently never
suspected before.

In reply to a congratulatory letter addressed to him
by Gay, Pope wrote some verses lamenting the temporary absence of lady Mary in a strain of despondency,
and in terms of avowed devotion that could not be
mistaken. It is not known whether Pope sent a copy
of these lines to lady Mary, or whether she procured
them from some other quarter ; but it is certain that
after perusing them, she treated the writer with à degree
of reserve that gave a new turn to their intercourse,
which from that time began to decline. Some speculations were hazarded as to the cause of this estrangement ; and it was supposed that the publication of lady
Mary's Four Eclogues, which Pope was known to have
revised, had created his jealousy. But more serious
feelings than so ridiculous a sentiment lay at the bottom
of their quarrel ; and until the recent publication by
lord Wharncliffe of the works of lady Mary, the real
cause that turned so much love into such bitter and
unrelenting hate as Pope exhibited in his subsequent
conduct to her ladyship, was variously and erroneously
conjectured. Mr. Bowles supposed that Pope had
" presumed too far, and was repulsed ;" a supposition
which was interpreted by Mr. Gilchrist to mean a gross
assault, which Mr. Bowles indignantly denied, but
which Mr. Roscoe, notwithstanding this disclaimer, reasserted. It appears, however, that Mr. Bowles was

not very wide of the truth in referring the immediate cause of their disagreement to some direct overture, the precise nature of which had not transpired when he wrote. Lady Mary's own statement, as recorded in the work to which we have referred, sets the question at rest. It is this—" that at some ill-chosen time, when she least expected what romances call *a declaration*, he made such passionate love to her, as, in spite of her utmost endeavours to be angry and look grave, provoked an immediate fit of laughter: *from which moment he became her implacable enemy.*"

What followed was the consequence of this untimely, and, all things considered, cruel levity. That Pope had no right to make such a declaration may be true ; but lady Mary had admitted him to an intimacy which her knowledge of the world ought to have warned her to discourage. His resentment lasted as long as his life. The humiliation he suffered was overwhelming, and reminded him painfully of his personal defects, which, perhaps, more than any other consideration, embittered his disappointment by exposing to him his real insignificance in the estimation of her to whom he had offered up the passionate homage of his genius. In such a situation, whatever satirical pieces he wrote that could be applied to lady Mary were seized upon by her friends, and treated as an affront. He did enough to immortalise his wrong, but not all that he was charged with. Some lines in one of his imitations of Horace, where, under the name of Sappho, he stigmatized one of the profligate female writers of the day, were hastily believed to have been designed for lady Mary. But when called upon for an explanation, he earnestly denied the imputation ; and it is only charitable to give him credit for the entire sincerity of the disclaimer.

The whole of this curious narrative, reaching such a climax, and terminating in such a catastrophe of wounded pride, becomes the more strange if it be reviewed in reference to other circumstances in the life of Pope, indicated rather than developed in his poems and correspondence. During a part of the time when he was engaged upon the translation of the *Odyssey*, he appears to have indulged in some tender feelings for a lady whose name remains a blank in his letters, but who is celebrated in his verses under the appellation of Erinna. This lady, whoever she may have been, was the author of some poems which she entrusted to Pope for correction, and in his letters to her he speaks in flattering terms of her talents. That she shook his allegiance, for a time at least, to lady Mary may be gathered from the following lines: —

" Though sprightly Sappho force our love and praise,
A softer wonder my pleased soul surveys—
The mild Erinna, blushing in her bays.
So, while the sun's broad beam yet strikes the sight,
All mild appears the moon's more sober light ; .
Serene in virgin majesty she shines,
And, unobserved, the glaring sun declines."

Without charging Pope with designing to designate lady Mary by the name of Sappho in the scurrilous lines in the imitation of Horace, it may be observed that he frequently applied that title to her, and even used it in some of the letters he addressed to her after she came to reside at Twickenham. The application in this instance is clear enough ; and the tendency of the verses is obviously to insinuate that Erinna was gaining a gradual ascendency over lady Mary, although, hearing no more about Erinna, we are compelled to conclude that she did not maintain her ascendancy long. The passion, therefore, might have been intense enough while it lasted ; but its duration was brief. We cannot so easily, however, explain away the mystery of his attachment for the " fair-haired " Martha Blount, which, of whatever kind it may have been, appears to have subsisted to the end, and to have continued even when he was involved in the progress of his unfortunate addresses to lady Mary. The nature of that attachment, or connection, cannot now be ascertained ; but Martha Blount is spoken of by some of his contemporaries, as a lady who was either privately married to him, or who ought to have been so. That the former could not have been true, his declaration to lady Mary places beyond doubt; and the truth or falsehood of the latter insinuation rests upon circumstantial evidence, which is by no means conclusive either way.

It would be useless to investigate the subject at much length; but a few particulars may be collected from which the reader may draw his own inferences. Upon the death of his father, Pope wrote in the following terms to Martha Blount:—" My poor father died last night. Believe, since I do not forget you this moment, I never shall.—A. POPE." Again, after the death of his mother he writes thus:—" It is a real truth, that to the last of my moments, the thought of you, and the best of my wishes for you, will attend you, told or untold. I could wish you had once the constancy and resolution to act for yourself; whether before or after I leave you (in the only way I shall ever leave you) you must determine: but reflect that the first would make me as well as yourself happier, the latter could make you only so." These passages, and many others of a similar nature which occur in his correspondence with this lady, have been supposed to convey the expression of his wishes that she would quit her friends to reside with him altogether; but Mr. Roscoe is of opinion that they meant nothing more than a recommendation to avail herself of some respectable offer *, forgetting that he had previously shown, by a copy of verses quoted from the " love poems," that Pope had strenuously urged her never to marry. †

These speculations about Martha Blount are strengthened by an observation in a letter from Pope to Atterbury, written on the eve of Atterbury's banishment. " The greatest comfort I had," he says, " was an intention (which I would have made practicable) to have attended you in your journey, to which I had brought that per-

* Roscoe's Life of Pope, p. 373.
† Ibid. p. 107

son to consent who only could have hindered me by a tie, which, though it may be more tender, I do not think more strong than that of friendship." Who was the *person* here alluded to ? Could he have so designated his mother ? And what was the *tie* which he thus draws into a direct comparison with the bonds of friendship ?

That Pope's attachment to Martha Blount was known to all his friends, and recognised by them — although it does not appear in what light they regarded it, — is exhibited in a variety of instances, of which the following is in many respects the most remarkable. About a year before Pope's death, Martha, at the desire of Pope and Mr. Allen, paid a visit to the latter at Prior Park, either in company with Pope, or when he was there. According to one authority * she deported herself with so much arrogance as to give great offence to Mrs. Allen. Being of the Romish persuasion, she desired the use of Mr. Allen's chariot to take her to chapel ; but he being mayor of the city was compelled to decline her request, as he could not, in his magisterial capacity, appear to sanction that place of worship. Mrs. Blount resented his refusal, related the matter to Pope, and they both abruptly left the house. By her own account of the matter, it appears that they did not leave the house together, but that she remained there after Mr. Pope's departure ; that she observed a strangeness of behaviour on the part of the Allens; that they treated Pope very rudely, and used her oddly in a stiff and over-civil manner; that she communicated her feelings to Pope, who said they had got " some odd thing or other in their heads;" and that she afterwards urged him to inquire into the matter, employing the word *satisfaction*, by which, however, she declares she did not mean that Pope should fight Mr. Allen. Pope did endeavour to obtain an explanation, and urged upon Allen that his wife " must have had some very unjust or bad thing suggested to her against Mrs. Blount ;" but all the satisfaction he obtained was a declaration that it all rested upon a " mutual misunderstanding."

* Ruffhead.

between the ladies, which he spoke to his wife about, but " could not make her at all easy in." The way in which Pope interfered in this remarkable misunder- standing—the difficulty in satisfying Mrs. Allen—the evasion on the part of Allen of an explanation, which in ordinary circumstances might either have been refused at once or given with frankness—and the amnesty that was effected afterwards between Pope and the Allens, from which Martha was excluded, throw doubts upon their connection which it is now impossible to remove or to confirm.

The loss of Atterbury, which was severely felt by Pope, was compensated by the society of Bolingbroke, who was now permitted to return to England, after an exile in the service of the Pretender. Swift also vi- sited him in 1726, and helped to dissipate his regrets. Pope at this time contemplated an answer to the *Maxims* of Rochefoucault; designing to show that instead of our virtues being vices, our vices are virtues ; neither position being true, but the latter being the more agreeable doctrine. He wisely reserved all such moralities, however, for his ethical poems. In the following year Swift returned, when the *Miscellanies*, which had been planned by them both, were published. This work was speedily assailed by a variety of essays and critiques, which were afterwards collected as anno- tations on the *Miscellanies* of " Pope and Company." But the success of the publication was not affected by these attacks. The profit of the three volumes is said to have amounted to 150*l*., which Swift, with his ac- customed liberality, relinquished to Pope.

One of the contributions to the *Miscellanies*, called the *Art of Sinking in Poetry*, in which Pope had the largest share, gave great offence to the tribe of small wits who were satirized in it. A number of authors were designated by initials, and the result was that Pope became immediately engaged in a fiercer warfare than ever he had encountered before. Upwards of sixty separate pamphlets and publications appeared, in which he was personally attacked; and a book called the *Popiad* was printed, in which the poetasters joined their forces to expose the multifarious errors of his *Homer*. Threats of violence were even resorted to; and an absurd story was circulated, that he had been seized in the dusk of the evening in Ham-walks, and whipped naked with rods. Thus driven to extremities, he replied in the *Dunciad*, which included all enemies and pretenders, in one comprehensive and scourging satire.

Pope did not escape with triumph out of all the controversies into which this business plunged him. Amongst the initials affixed to the *Art of Sinking in Poetry*, were those of A. H., which Aaron Hill naturally took to himself, and resented in a satirical poem. A correspondence ensued, by which it appeared that Pope had attacked Hill on mistaken grounds, and which ended, after some evasions and doublings, in a graceful acknowledgment of his error, and a flattering compliment to his opponent.

The death of Gay, followed shortly by the death of Mrs. Pope, in 1733, in the ninety-third year of her age, brought fresh griefs upon the poet, which his numerous friends endeavoured to alleviate by redoubled attentions. He had previously published, in 1731, his *Epistle on Taste*, subsequently called *Of False Taste*, and afterwards *Of the Use of Riches*, and which ran through three editions in a year; and, in 1732, he had given to the world, anonymously, his celebrated *Essay on Man*, which he was accused of having versified from a prose manuscript of Bolingbroke, a charge of which Mr. Roscoe has fully and unanswerably disposed. He contemplated about this time a grand design in a series of ethical epistles, of which, however, he executed only some fragments that were afterwards published in folio, and collected into the general edition of his works. Connected with one of these, the *Epistle on the Characters of Women*, understood to be addressed to Martha Blount, a strange story is related by Warton, who says

that the character of Atossa, intended for the portrait
of the duchess of Marlborough, was shown to her
under the pretence that it was designed for the duchess
of Buckingham, but that her grace soon tracing her
own resemblance, abused Pope heartily, but afterwards gave him 1000*l.* to suppress the character, which
consequently did not appear until after her death.
This bribe, which he is said to have accepted on the
persuasion of Martha Blount, is in itself so derogatory
and dishonourable, that none of the biographies believe
the circumstance to be true ; yet not one of them furnish
us with the means of proving it to be false.

 Pope appears to have employed himself for some
time after the death of his mother, chiefly in gardening
and paying visits to his friends, meditating, perhaps,
new literary projects, but executing none.   In 1736,
he began to collect his *Letters* for publication, a proceeding which was treated with considerable severity by
his enemies, as an evidence of his self-love and over-
weening vanity.   His defence of that step, however, if
it may be strictly relied upon, shows that he was forced
into the publication in his own defence, a spurious
copy of several of his private letters having got into the
hands of Curll, a disreputable bookseller, who, without
consulting the feelings of any of the parties concerned,
announced them for publication.   The advertisement of
the work containing the names of several noblemen, induced a suspicion that the book was likely to involve
a breach of privilege, and Curll was cited to the bar of
the house of lords; but, when the case was investigated,
it appeared that there was no infringement of the rights
of parliament, and Curll was dismissed.   His statement
was, that a man in a clergyman's gown, but with a
lawyer's band, came to his house one evening, and
offered for sale a number of volumes containing Pope's
correspondence ; that he bought them without inquiry,
and thought himself justified in using them to his own
advantage.   At another time, he stated that they were
given to him at the door of a tavern by a man on

horseback ; and, at another, that they were given to his
wife. The variations in his story are not surprising,
when the surreptitious character of the whole affair is
borne in mind. A man who is committing an un-
justifiable act, will not scruple about the means of
screening himself against consequences, and may be expected to confound himself in the invention of excuses.
According to Dr. Johnson, another copy was sent to
Lintot at the same time, for which no price was demanded ; but Lintot did not make any use of it. These
circumstances, which formed the cause of the legitimate
collection undertaken by Pope, were turned into an
accusation against him, and he was charged with
having sent the copies to Curll privately, in order to
make an excuse for bringing out the entire work
afterwards himself. Mr. Roscoe enters into a minute
statement of particulars, to show that Pope did not
contemplate such a publication until after a volume of
his correspondence had been printed under similar circumstances in Dublin, nor until Curll had issued five
volumes of his *Epistles*, in the preface to one of which
he charged him with having attempted to poison him ;
when Pope's friends interfered, and intreated him to sanction a correct edition of the whole. Upon a review of
the statements at both sides, it seems much more likely
that Pope was glad of the pretext for publishing his
letters, and that he seized on it with avidity, rather
than that he laid so clumsy and perplexing a plot to
bring about the necessity.

The *Imitations of Horace,* published in 1737, and
Dialogues in Verse, which were afterwards used as the
Epilogue to the Satires, published in 1738, were his next
productions. His health now began to decline, and he
was induced to leave Twickenham for change of air, and
visit his friend Allen at Bath. It was during his short
residence here that he wrote to Warburton, whom he had
never seen, inviting him to come to visit him, a request
with which Warburton promptly complied, laying the
foundation ef a friendship which terminated only with

the death of Pope. In the following year, 1740, his labours were limited to editing a collection of Latin poems by Italian writers, under the title of *Selecta Poemata Italorum.* He planned also a comprehensive history of English poetry, but never carried it beyond the first outlines of the project. Warburton had now paid him a second visit at Twickenham, and prevailed on him to accompany him to Oxford. While they remained in that neighbourhood, the heads of the university announced their intention of presenting a degree in divinity to Warburton, and another in civil law to Pope ; but when the former came to be discussed, it was overruled, and Pope indignantly refused the latter, and satirised the university in the fourth book of the *Dunciad,* which was published in 1742, with notes by Pope and Warburton.

In this publication, Colley Cibber, formerly the boon companion of Pope, was coarsely ridiculed, and justly complained of the injustice with which he was treated. But the effect of all such remonstrances was to increase the mischief, and Pope retaliated in a new edition on the *Dunciad,* 1743, in which he dethroned Theobald, and elevated Cibber in his place. This edition was accompanied by a long discourse of *Richardus Aristarchus* on the hero of the poem, written by Warburton, and intended as a reply to the various attacks on Pope contained in the letters and memoirs of Cibber. The patience of the dramatist was now fairly exhausted, and he replied in an angry rejoinder, which, had, it come from a man of greater influence with the public, must have seriously affected the popularity of his opponent.

Pope's strength was now visibly declining. He was not old, but his constitution was wasting and breaking up. His mind had worn out his body: and at length the spirit alone remained to struggle for life. His last days were painfully embittered by the disabilities under which he suffered on account of his religion. A report of the approach of the pretender had created such alarm, that a proclamation was issued prohibiting all Roman

catholics from appearing within ten miles of the metropolis. Pope complied with the law, but it pressed
heavily upon his thoughts. " I may slide along the
Surrey side (where no Middlesex justice can pretend
any cognizance)," he says in a letter to Mr. Allen, " to
Battersea, and thence across the water for an hour or
two, in a close chair, to dine with you, or so. But to
be in town, I fear, will be imprudent, and thought in-
solent. At least, hitherto, all comply with the proclamation." He had been ill for many weeks before he
died, but occasionally rallied, and preserved a wonderful
elasticity and composure to the last. On the 6th of May,
1774, he was delirious all day, and spoke of it afterwards as a humiliation of human vanity. He afterwards complained of seeing things through a curtain,
and asked what was the arm which he saw protruded
from the wall. His greatest inconvenience, he observed,
was inability to think. A few days before his death, he
rose at four o'clock in the morning, and went into his
library, where he was found busy writing on the immortality of the soul. Martha Blount is said to have treated
him with " shameful unkindness " in his last illness ;
and coming up the terrace one day while he was sitting
in the air with lord Bolingbroke, she asked lord March-
mont, " What, is he not dead yet? " — a story which
it is revolting even to repeat, and which, for the honour
of our common humanity, one would be disposed to
think untrue. But, in spite of all Pope's commendations
of his " favourite," it is difficult to entertain a cordial
feeling of a woman who exercised so strong an influence
over his mind, and who seems to have seldom exercised
it for any very useful or benevolent purpose. The conduct of lord Bolingbroke, on the contrary, exhibited the
affection of true friendship. He constantly attended
Pope in his last illness, and, says Roscoe, sometimes
wept over him in his state of helpless decay.

Pope maintained his resolution to sustain himself with
all the energy he could summon to the end. One day,
seated at table, when others in like circumstances would

have remained in bed, he was so ill that every body
believed him to be dying, when Mrs. Arbuthnot made a
sort of melancholy epigram, exclaiming, " Mercy upon
us ! this is quite an Egyptian feast !" Two days before
he died he sat in a sedan in his garden for three hours,
and the following day took an airing in Bushy Park.
He was aware that his case was hopeless, and beheld
his approaching dissolution with magnanimity. On the
morning of his death, his physician observed that his
pulse was good, and noticed other favourable circumstances. Pope replied, " Here am I, dying of a hundred
good symptoms !" Shortly before his death, he fell into
frequent slumbers, and he expired so gently, that his
attendants could not discover the moment when he
breathed his last.

He died on the 30th of May, 1744, about eleven
o'clock at night.

EDWARD YOUNG.

1681—1765.

EDWARD YOUNG was born at Upham, near Winchester, in June, 1681. His father, Edward Young, was at that time fellow of Winchester college, and rector of Upham ; and we are somewhat ostentatiously reminded by all the poet's biographers, that his grandfather, John Young, of Woodley, in Berkshire, was styled *gentleman* by Wood. In September, 1682, bishop Ward promoted Edward Young, the father, to the prebendal stall of Gillingham Minor, in the church of Sarum ; and at bishop Sprat's visitation, in 1686, Young preached a Latin sermon of such excellence, that the prelate expressed his regret at finding so meritorious a preacher occupying one of the worst prebends in the church. Perhaps the approbation of the bishop may have assisted his advancement; for, through the interest of lord Bradford, to whom, in 1702, he dedicated two volumes of sermons, he was afterwards appointed chaplain to William and Mary, and preferred to the deanery of Sarum. Jacob, who wrote in 1720, says that he was chaplain and clerk of the closet to the late queen, who honoured him by standing godmother to the poet. He had an only daughter, who married a gentleman of the name of Harris, in whose favour he resigned his Winchester fellowship. He died at Sarum, after a short illness, in 1705, in the 63d year of his life.

The poet was placed upon the foundation of Winchester college, where he remained till the election after his eighteenth birthday — the period at which those on the foundation are superannuated. On the 13th of October, 1703, he was entered as an independent member of New college, that he might live at little expense in the warden's lodgings, who was a particular friend of his father's, till he should be qualified to stand for a fellowship in All Souls. Some of his biographers have indulged in certain speculations as to why he was not elected from Winchester college to a fellowship in New college, on the foundation of William of Wykeham ; but there could have been only one of two reasons for it — either a vacancy did not occur in his .time, or he was not considered the most deserving candidate. The warden of New college dying a few months after he had settled there, he was invited to Corpus college by the president, from regard also for his father, in order still farther to lessen his expenses ; and in 1708 he was nominated to a law fellowship at All Souls, by archbishop Tennison. From these instances of patronage, it may be inferred that his father died in indifferent circumstances, but that he bequeathed to his son a richer inheritance than wealth — an unspotted reputation. On the 23d of April, 1714, Young took the degree of bachelor of civil law, and on the 10th June, 1719, that of doctor.

It has been said that his conduct for some time after he had obtained his fellowship was not marked by the same regard for religion and morality which he afterwards displayed ; an imputation which friendly critics have attempted, without much success, to controvert. Tindal, the atheist, admits his ingenuity in arguing against his doctrines ; a fact, however, which affords no proof whatever as to his practice. Tindal's words are — " The other boys I can always answer, because I know whence they have their arguments, which I have read a hundred times ; but that fellow Young is continually pestering me with something of his own." It should be remembered that Young does not appear to have had any particular vocation for the church in the commencement of his career, and that therefore no more should be expected from him than from any other young layman at the university, who is drawn either by accident

or the force of circumstances into the priesthood. It is
unjust and cruel to condemn the aged clergyman and
stern moralist, for the idle freaks of his boyhood, or to
expect from youth the same evidences of a christian
life which grave examination and slow conviction produce in maturer years. But whatever may have been
the trivial offences of his early days, they ought to be
forgotten in the decorum of his manhood and decline.
What Pope is said by Ruffhead to have told Warburton respecting him appears probable and just — that
Young "had much of a sublime genius, though without
common sense ; so that his genius having no guide, was
perpetually liable to degenerate into bombast. This
made him pass a *foolish youth*, the sport of peers and
poets ; but his having a very good heart, enabled him to
support the clerical character when he assumed it, first
with decency, and afterwards with honour." This is so
just in reference to the poet, that it is probably equally
so in reference to the man ; but it must be acknowledged,
after all, that a strict investigation into the career of
Edward Young is not calculated to impress the dispassionate inquirer with a very high opinion either of
his morality or his piety. Perhaps the most appropriate
definition of his "fair behaviour" is comprised in a
single word—prudence ; not the prudence of the common
sense, which Pope denies him to have possessed, but the
prudence of self-protecting cunning. He seems to have
set out in life with a firm resolution to attain rank,
wealth, and eminence, without being over-fastidious as
to the means ; — to get them, like Murphy's citizen,
honourably if he could, but to get them at all events.
Poetry, politics, and piety were only different modifi-
cations of the expedients by which he sought to ac-
complish his ends. With this preliminary clue to his
guiding principles, it is easy to unravel the otherwise
inexplicable mystery of his conduct.

Throughout the whole range of English authors it
would be impossible to discover one who wrote so many
encomiastic pieces, of which he himself felt afterwards

so thoroughly ashamed. Young flattered every one
from whom he expected to gain any thing to such an
excess, and with such bad taste and judgment, that he
found his eulogies not only drew down the ridicule of
his literary contemporaries, but were treated with contempt by the very persons whose patronage they were
designed to entrap. His whole life is little more, with
a few slight exceptions, than a history of fulsome
panegyrics, published to allure the friendship of those
who were, or were likely to be, able to serve him; and
withdrawn or disclaimed when they had failed of their
intended purpose. Of the pieces which he admitted
into the last edition of his works he says, " I think the
following pieces, in four volumes, to be the most excusable
of all that I have written : and I wish less apology was
needful for these. As there is no recalling what is got
abroad, the pieces here republished I have revised and
corrected, and rendered them as pardonable as it was in
my power to do." When we consider that he had
never offended against morals or religion, and that the
principal object of this revision was to remove the traces
of superfluous, profitless, and slavish adulation, we may
form some notion of the extent to which he carried that
unmanly and derogatory vice.

Young's first poetical essay was in reference to the
" batch " of twelve peers created in 1772. In order
to reconcile the nation to one at least of the new peers, he
wrote *An Epistle to the Right Honourable George Lord
Lansdowne ;* endeavouring, at the same time, to excuse
the recent peace, on the very conclusive and original
ground, that in war men are slain, but that in peace
" harvests wave, and commerce swells her sail." He
speaks of the patronage of the noble lord ; displays the
exuberance of his laudatory faculties ; and finally omits
the piece from his subsequent collection.

In 1713 he prefixed a copy of recommendatory verses
to Addison's *Cato ;* and, in the same spirit of recantation,
afterwards omitted them in his collected works.

About the same period his poem *On the Last Day*

was printed at Oxford, though it had been written in 1710. This piece was inscribed to the queen, in a dedication in which he acknowledges some obligation formerly received from her royal indulgence, which is supposed to refer to the honour her majesty conferred upon him at his baptism 1 He was suspected, but it is difficult to determine whether truly or falsely, of having been employed, at that time, at a settled stipend, as a writer for the court ; — a circumstance to which Swift appears to refer in his *Rhapsody on Poetry*, where, alluding to the court, he says —

> " Whence Gay was banish'd in disgrace,
> Where Pope will never show his face—
> Where Y—— must torture his invention
> To flatter knaves, or lose his pension."

" The dedication was clearly political," observes Herbert Croft, " notwithstanding the subject of the poem, and may be regarded as a curiosity in its way. It speaks in raptures of the peace ; applauds her majesty for her victories ; but says that the author is even still more delighted to see her rise from the lower world, soaring above the clouds, passing the first and second heavens, and leaving the fixed stars behind her ; nor does he lose sight of her majesty in those misty altitudes, but continues to keep her in view through boundless spaces on the other side of creation in her journey towards eternal bliss ; until, at last, he beholds the heaven of heavens open, and sees angels receiving and conveying her still onward from the stretch of his imagination, till it becomes jaded in her pursuit, and falls back again to earth.

This dedication was also omitted by the author from his subsequent collection.

The Force of Religion, or Vanquished Love, appeared before the death of the queen. This piece was founded on the execution of lady Jane Grey, and her husband lord Guilford. It was dedicated to the countess of Salisbury. In this dedication he hopes that it may be some excuse for his presumption, that the story could not have been read without thoughts of the countess of Salisbury, even though it should have been dedicated to another. " To behold," he proceeds, " a person *only* virtuous, stirs in us a prudent regret ; to behold a person *only* amiable to the sight, warms us with a religious indignation ; but to turn our eyes to a countess of Salisbury, gives us pleasure and improvement — it works a sort of miracle, occasions the bias of our nature to fall off from sin, and makes our very senses and affections converts to our religion, and promoters of our duty." This dedication was also omitted.

In 1714 he published a poem, inscribed to Addison, on the death of Anne, and the accession of George I., in which he eulogised " the rising sun " to " extravagant excess," and discovered that the gods blessed his new subjects in such a king.   This was also omitted.

When the foundation of the Codrington library was laid, in 1716, Young was appointed to speak the Latin oration, which was afterwards dedicated, in English, to the "ladies of the Codrington family;" but both oration and dedication were dropt out of the subsequent edition of his works.

Young's connection with the Wharton family forms so important a feature in his life, that it is necessary to notice it in as much detail as the materials will allow, although the particulars are for the most part rather obscure. His father, it appears, had been well acquainted with lady Anne Wharton, the first wife of sir Thomas Wharton, a lady who was celebrated for her poetical talents by Burnet and Waller ; and who, in testimony of her regard for him, wrote some verses on the visitation sermon already referred to, which were printed in the English translation. This friendship steadily descended to the son, and when sir Thomas was ennobled, he continued to the poet the same consideration he had always shown to the father. His dissolute successor, the " infamous duke," also extended his patronage to him in a very substantial way ; and when that notorious

nobleman went to Ireland, in 1717, it is generally supposed that Young accompanied him. It is certain, however, that Young was in Ireland at some period of his
life, as, in his letter to Richardson, he relates the following anecdote of Swift as having occurred there. " I
remember," he observes, " as I and others were taking
with him an evening walk about a mile out of Dublin,
he stopped short ; we passed on ; but perceiving he did
not follow us, I went back, and found him gazing upwards at a noble elm, which in its uppermost branches
was withered and decayed. Pointing at it, he said,
' I shall be like that tree ; I shall die at the top.' "* (It
is needless to remind the reader, parenthetically, how
remarkably this strange prophecy was fulfilled.) From
a letter of Wharton's to Swift, dated 1717, there seems
to be no doubt that Young was at that time with him
in Ireland.

In 1719 he entered the Exeter family as tutor to lord
Burleigh ; but although he was offered an annuity of
100*l.* if he would continue his services to that young
nobleman, he shortly afterwards resigned his engagement, on the pressing solicitations of the duke of Wharton, and his grace's promises to provide for him in a
much more ample manner. About this period the duke
granted him two annuities, one of which, dated the 24th
March, 1719, contained the following *consideration*
clause : " Considering that the public good is advanced
by the encouragement of learning and polite arts, and
being pleased therein with the attempts of Dr. Young,
in consideration thereof, and the love I bear him," &c.
The other annuity was dated the 10th July, 1722.
He obtained, beside, from his grace, a bond for 600*l.*,
dated the 15th March, 1721, in *consideration* of his
taking several journeys, and being at great expenses, in
order to be chosen member of the house of commons, at
the duke's desire ; and in *consideration* of his not taking
two livings, of 200*l.* and 400*l.*, in the gift of All Souls
college, on his grace's promises to advance him in the

* Conjectures on Original Composition.

world. Young stood a contested election at Cirencester
— an odd preparation for an excessively devout minister
of the gospel ; but he does not appear to have repeated the experiment, there or elsewhere.

Busiris was brought out at Drury-lane, in 1719, and
received with some favour. It was dedicated to the duke
of Newcastle, " because the later instances he had received of his grace's undeserved and uncommon favour
in an affair of some consequence, foreign to the theatre,
had taken from him the privilege of choosing a patron."
This dedication was afterwards suppressed.

From *The Englishman* it appears that a tragedy by
Young was in the theatre so early as 1713 ; but *Busiris*
was the first publicly performed.

In 1721 his best tragedy, *The Revenge*, came out.
It was dedicated to the duke of Wharton. " Your
grace has been pleased," says Young, in the dedication,
" to make yourself accessary to the following scenes, not
only by suggesting the most beautiful incident in them,
but by making all possible provision for the success of
the whole." After some other passages, it concludes
thus : " My present fortune is your bounty; my future,
your care ; which, I will venture to say, will be always
remembered to your honour; since you, I know, intended your generosity as an encouragement to merit,
though, through your very pardonable partiality to one
who bears you so sincere a duty and respect, I happen
to receive the benefit of it."

This dedication was also suppressed ; and Young employed every other means in his power to conceal the
fact that he had ever been patronised by such a man as
Wharton —

" —— the scorn and wonder of our days."

But in vain — a chancery suit revealed all in 1740,
when lord Hardwicke had to determine, among other
things, whether the annuities to the future melancholy
moralist had been granted on legal considerations.

Upon the merits of this remarkable case, it is now

impossible to throw any further light than the report
in the law-books affords. Young deposed upon oath
to all the circumstances recited in this narrative: to
the duke's promises, to the *considerations* for which
the annuities had been granted, and to his abandonment
of his employment in the Exeter family at the duke's
special instance. We have, therefore, no other testimony, either way, than that of the poet himself, which,
whatever it may be worth, leaves the whole affair in
darkness. There can be no difficulty, however, in de-
ciding Young's ingratitude in suppressing, in the subsequent edition of *The Revenge*, the acknowledgment
which he originally made, that he was indebted to
Wharton for the suggestion of its most beautiful incident. The obligations of the poet, at least, ought to
have been avowed, apart from all pecuniary and personal
circumstances.

In the year following this trial, Young commenced
his *Night Thoughts*. It would seem that at that time
his thoughts were gloomy enough for such an undertaking.

Herbert Croft directs attention to some lines contained
in a letter from Young to Tickell, on the death of
Addison, 1719, and observes, " for the secret history of
the following lines, if they contain any, it is now vain
to seek: —

" *In joy once join'd*, in sorrow, now, for years —
Partner in grief, and brother of my tears,
Tickell, accept this verse, thy mournful due. "

And Johnson states that Tickell and Young were in the
habit of communicating to each other whatever verses
they wrote, even to the least things. The " secret history" is obvious enough — the poets were close friends.

In the same year, Young published a *Paraphrase on
Part of the Book of Job*, and dedicated it in an extravagant strain of flattery to lord chancellor Parker, of
whom it is evident that he had no kind of knowledge
beyond the circumstance of his having extensive patron-

age at his disposal. This dedication was omitted like all the rest.

His satires published under the title of *The Love of Fame, or the Universal Passion*, appeared in succession, from 1725 to 1728; each of the six being dedicated to a different personage, in the hope of securing a corresponding variety of patronage. The precise dates of their composition, or of the publication of the earlier numbers, cannot be fixed; but they are supposed to have appeared within the above years.

The fifth satire, *On Women*, was not published till 1727, and the sixth not till 1728, though, according to Croft, it was certainly finished in the beginning of 1726; for, says he, " In December, 1725, the king, in his passage from Helvoetsluys, escaped with great difficulty from a storm, by landing at Rye; and the conclusion of the satire turns the escape into a miracle, in such an encomiastic strain of compliment as poetry too often seeks to pay to royalty." In this satire we have a characteristic illustration of contemptible flattery and gross egotism. Always bearing in mind that her majesty was his godmother, he tells us —

> " Midst empire's charms, how Carolina's heart
> Glow'd with the love of virtue and of art; "

for this special reason, because —

> " Her favour is diffus'd to that degree,
> Excess of goodness it has dawn'd on me!"

These pieces he collected and published in 1728, in one volume, with a preface, in which he advocates, in the following fashion, the philosophy of laughing at the vices and follies of mankind, instead of mourning over them. " No man can converse much in the world, but at what he meets with, he must be either insensible or grieve, or be angry or smile. Now to smile at it, and turn it into ridicule, I think most eligible, as it hurts ourselves least, and gives vice and folly the greatest offence. Laughing at the misconduct of the world will in a great measure ease us of any more disagreeable passion about it. One passion is more effectually driven out by another, than by reason, whatever some may teach." This very preface he afterwards printed with his melancholy *Night Thoughts.* Towards the close of the preface, he applied Plato's fable of *The Birth of Love,* to modern poetry, with this addition, that " Poetry, like Love, is a little subject to blindness, which makes her mistake her way to preferments and honours, and that she retains a dutiful admiration of her father's family ; but divides her favours and generally lives with her mother's relations." This was evidently intended to bear some mythological relation to himself — as, though he was well paid in ready cash, he was singularly unsuccessful in obtaining honours or preferments.

These satires became popular, and brought him in no less than 3000*l.* Spence, on the authority of Rawlinson, relates, that, upon their publication, Young received 2000*l.* from the duke of Grafton ; and that when one of his friends exclaimed, " Two thousand pounds for a poem !" he said it was the best bargain he ever made in his life, for the poem was worth double the money. " This story," says Croft, " seems to have been raised from the two answers of lord Burleigh and sir Philip Sydney, in Spencer's life ;" but there is not much ground for doubting its truth. Young was very likely to take a trader's view of his productions ; and if he never made use of the expression, it is precisely the sort of expression he was very likely to make use of.

It grows tedious at last to follow Young through his hyperbolical panegyrics, and his regular disavowal or withdrawal of them. There was scarcely a single instance in which he praised any individual, in the hope of gain, that he did not afterwards recall his admiration. He seems to have put his flattery up to auction, and, when he could not get a bidder for it, to have bought it in himself. He watched all occasions in public that were susceptible of poetical commemoration, and immediately addressed an ode, or a string of stanzas, to

the person chiefly concerned ; and, like the mendicant
poets at Christmas, who go about from house to house
to present their congratulatory lines, he was always
ready with a seasonable poem to be forwarded on the
instant when it was most likely to be appreciated.
Thus, when the order of the Garter was conferred
on Walpole, Young immediately addressed him in a
piece entitled *The Instalment.* One might naturally
wonder what he could say on such an event ; but poets
like Young are never at a loss, and so we find him
bestowing immortality on the immaculate knight, and
gratefully acknowledging former bounties, not forgetting a hint that future services of a similar kind
would be equally acceptable. But this production
shared the fate of all the preceding panegyrics, and was
suppressed in due course of time.

The first speech of George II. to the parliament,
afforded him another opportunity of exercising his
talent for time-serving in verse, and accordingly he
wrote an ode called *The Ocean,* founded on his majesty's recommendation to invite, rather than to force,
seamen to enter the naval service. In this ode he
designates his majesty, who was a total stranger in
England, who had as yet done nothing for the country,
whatever his inclinations might have been, and who, in
fact, could not even speak the English language, by
the title of *pater patriæ.* Having wrought out the
topic to the utmost, he concluded with the expression
of a tedious wish for retirement, which every body
knew to be insincere, and the hypocrisy of which he
afterwards betrayed by omitting the whole of that
portion from his subsequent edition of the poem.

Young was now fifty years of age ; he had wearied
his stars with prayers for preferment, and had got
none ; but he had succeeded, by one means or another,
in making money, which in some measure helped to
console him. He had, no doubt, cleared a handsome
sum by the Whartons and the rest of his incidental
patrons ; for it may be reasonably conjectured, that out

of such a multitude of addresses, some of them must have succeeded. Besides, a man who could so fashion himself to the servility of hollow adulation, must have been despicable enough in spirit to persecute the great until they purchased his forbearance. Of his positive current resources at this time, nothing more is known than that it is presumed he was in the pay of government for writing against the opposition. There is no proof extant of the fact; but the absence of proof does not weaken its probability, as arrangements of that nature are always secret, and it may be safely conjectured, that if it were true, Young had too much low sagacity not to conceal it. Whether he lost his pension, or believed that the time was now arrived when he could make a bold advance upon the administration for a reward, or whether he had succeeded in obtaining any promise of patronage from the king upon the presentation of his oceanic lyric, does not appear; but soon after the publication of that poem, he entered into orders, and was almost immediately appointed chaplain to George II.

His invariable caution did not forsake him on this occasion. At the time of this appointment, he had a tragedy, *The Brothers*, in rehearsal, and, apprehensive that its production would damage his reputation in his new profession, he suddenly withdrew it, to the great mortification and disappointment of the actors, who had taken the trouble to study their parts. This small incident is a complete key to his character. So long as the theatre was useful to his purposes, he did not scruple to write for it, and to reap all the advantages, in the way of payment and reputation, which the stage could yield; but the moment he was appointed chaplain to the king, a new light broke upon him, his conscience interposed between him and the profane drama, and he affected to regard with sentiments of devout aversion that very occupation which he had only so recently been well content to follow. All this was nothing more than worldly cunning in the mask of piety. Before he entered holy orders, he evidently did not think the stage dishonourable to a christian. While he was performing the necessary preliminaries for ordination, his play was in the hands of the manager, and the parts were distributed amongst the actors, and, according to all precedent, the probability is, that he attended the rehearsals, and marked the readings in the green-room. But he was no sooner made a chaplain at court than he withdrew both the piece and himself, and prepared with equal zeal and address to adapt his external manners to the demands of a severer pursuit. If this proceeding were the result of a sincere conviction, it must be admitted that never was conviction so swift in taking. possession of a dramatist's mind, or so coincident with circumstances that covered it with suspicion.

On taking orders, it is said that he applied to Pope for instructions as to the best mode of acquiring a knowledge of theology ; that the latter, in a sly, malicious humour, recommended the perusal of Thomas Aquinas ; that he, believing Pope serious, retired to an obscure place in the suburbs of London, for the purpose of studying Thomas Aquinas free from interruption ; and that Pope, after the lapse of half a year, having heard nothing of him, sought him out, and found him just in time to prevent what Ruffhead, the recorder of the story, calls " an irretrievable derangement." Now this tale is altogether incredible : in the first place, because Young must have been in some measure prepared in divinity when his college offered him the two livings which he had refused on Wharton's assurances of advancing him in the world ; and in the second, because Pope, to whom he is said to have applied for advice, was a Roman catholic, and not very likely, therefore, to be consulted on such an occasion. Independently of these reasons, the several pieces he published about that time sufficiently prove that he could not have devoted six months to such a ✦ close study of Aquinas as to endanger his reason ; but the existence of the report shows, that, amongst his contemporaries, Young was not suspected of being very well qualified for the profession of a theologian.

In 1728, Young published, in prose, *A Free Estimate of Human Life,* dedicated to the queen ; and, in the following year, a sermon, preached at St. Margaret's, Westminster, before the members of the house of commons, and dedicated to them, called *An Apology for Princes, or the Reverence due to Government.* Both compositions are cumbrous, artificial, and cold. In the *Estimate,* he professes to consider the passions " in a new light ; " and he opens the preface with some observations which would seem to imply that the passions had rarely, in his opinion, been properly considered before. " I knew not well why," says our author, " but the passions are a favourite subject with mankind : the reason may possibly be, because men are much concerned with them, both as to themselves and others ; and where we have a self-concern, we have an attention ; or because they are such powerful and universal springs, that almost all the pleasures, pains, designs, and actions of life are owing to them, and therefore it is our interest to know them well ; or, because every man carrying them in his own breast, he thinks he knows them well already, and is therefore an able judge of such compositions and thus his pride has a fondness for them ; or, because the passions, like the boy at the fountain, fall in love with their own representation ; or, because many are all passion, and if men consider a treatise on the passions as a history of themselves, it is no wonder they read it with pleasure ; or, because what a most celebrated ancient wit said on this subject is lost, to the great regret of the learned and polite world, which is studious of some reparation of that loss ; and the more so, because what other ancients have left on that head is imperfect and short." The general tenor and character of the treatise may be inferred from this curious prologue. A writer who believed he was doing something extraordinary for the world in furnishing so many conjectures as to why the passions are a favourite subject with mankind, who thinks that, because every man has passions himself, his pride must therefore have a fondness for composi- tions which treat of them, and who imagines that the passions fall in love with their own representation, may fairly aspire to the distinction which he claims in his titlepage, of considering the passions " in a new light" As this new light, however, exhibited only one aspect of the inquiry, he announced, at the same time, a counter- part to it, to be called the *Second Course.* From some cause, this piece was never printed. It was said to have been torn in pieces by a lady's monkey — a sort of accidental vindication of poetical justice. Several years afterwards, Dr. Hill attempted to repair the loss; by publishing a second part, called *The New Estimate,* which appeared in 1754 ; but, like the " old " estimate, it seems to have had but few readers.

The *Imperium Pelagi,* a naval lyric, written in avowed imitation of Pindar, was produced in 1730, with a dedi- cation to the duke of Chandos. This piece was ridiculed by Fielding, in *Tom Thumb;* and Young not only omitted it from the subsequent edition of his works, but. actually disavowed its authorship.

Two epistles to Pope, concerning the *Authors of the Age,* followed in the same year. " Of these poems," says Croft, " one occasion seems to have been, an appre- hension lest, from the liveliness of his satires, he should not be deemed sufficiently serious for *promotion* in the church." Here the deferential and prudent chaplain appeared again. But he might have spared himself his fears, for the satires had made no impression, favourable or unfavourable. Swift justly said of them, that they should have been either more merry or more angry.

But all this prudence was necessary to the mainte- nance of his position. He now seemed to be rapidly advancing towards the attainment of the objects he had always kept in view ; and his caution increased as he approached the goal, lest, by some unlucky false step, he might lose his balance. The rectory of Welwyn, in Hertfordshire, in the gift of his college, fell to him just after he had published his apologetical addresses to Pope; and it has been conjectured, not without reason, that he had originally looked forward to this living when he entered the church. Having secured this benefice, every thing around him took the *coleur de rose.* He soon obtained celebrity as a popular preacher ; and it may be taken for granted, that he cultivated with consummate address, for the use of the pulpit, all those arts of delivery and action that he had formerly learned in the theatre. Such was the reputation his oratorical talents acquired for him, that Walpole endeavoured to turn them to account for political purposes ; but in what way does not appear. Like the majority of favourite preachers, who draw large congregations, Young is celebrated in more than one curious anecdote. It is said that, preaching on one occasion at St. James's, and perceiving that it was out of his power to command the attention of the audience, he became so affected, that he sat back in the pulpit and burst into tears. The circumstance is not impossible. This was exactly the sort of way in which Young was likely to be affected — or to appear so, which was all the same.

In May, 1731, he married lady Elizabeth Lee, daughter of the earl of Lichfield, and widow of colonel Lee ; a connection which arose from the intimacy that subsisted between his father and the lady Anne Wharton, who was the heiress of sir Henry Lee of Ditchley, in Oxfordshire. The issue of this marriage was one child, a son, who was born in 1733 ; and so highly was Young estimated at this time, that the prince of Wales stood godfather to the child, and allowed him to be called after himself. This union, and the royal patronage, seemed to have accomplished the measure of his good fortune, although not, perhaps, of his expectations. But all such human calculations are vain. His wife survived her marriage only ten years, and his son lived

to become a cause of bitter grief to his staid and admo-
nishing father.

Lady Elizabeth Lee had a daughter by her former
marriage, to whom both she and Young appear to have
been strongly attached. This young lady was married
to Mr. Temple, the son of lord Palmerston, and, falling
ill, her removal to a southern climate was determined
upon, as the only means left for her restoration. She
was accompanied by her mother, her husband, and
Young. The circumstance is recorded by the poet ,in
the well-known lines —

> " I flew, I snatched her from the rigid North,
>   And bore her nearer to the sun." *

But the balmy airs of Italy were useless to a frame
already worn out, and Mrs. Temple died at Nice, in
1736, and was buried amidst the scenes described with
so much agony of expression in the *Night Thoughts.*
The effect which this circumstance apparently produced
upon Young, is familiar to all the readers of his melancholy poem, — who may gather from the whole account, and the deep misery of the tone throughout, that
the shock was almost beyond his strength. Mr. Temple,
however, seems to have possessed an extraordinary
resiliency of spirit under this great affliction, for he
married the daughter of sir John Barnard shortly afterwards; but, as if such sudden infidelity to the dead
brought a sort of punishment with it, he died himself
in 1740, only four years after the death of his first wife.
In he following year, lady Elizabeth also died.

To these calamities we are 'indebted for the *Night
Thoughts ;* and it is supposed that Young alluded to his
domestic bereavements in the following lines : —

> " Insatiate archer! could not one suffice?
>   Thy shaft flew thrice; and thrice my peace was slain;
>   And thrice, ere thrice yon moon had fill'd her horn."

* This was a favourite figure with Young.   In his *True Estimate,* he says
that " a fly in winter is for nations nearer the sun."

But a glance at the dates, when his wife, and his step-daughter, and her husband died, must be conclusive of the fact, either that the sorrow of the poet is, from beginning to end, a mere fiction, or that the three calamities referred to, must be some calamities which none of his friends were aware of, and could not certainly have been the deaths that took place in his family. In the above lines we are informed that the shaft flew thrice in less than three months: now Mrs. Temple died in 1736, Mr. Temple in 1740, and lady Elizabeth in 1741; so that, instead of undergoing all this woe in three months, it extended over a space of no less than five years. Some allowances must, doubtless, be made for the necessities of poetry; and a religious poet, above all others, must be allowed ample scope for rumination and mourning over the destinies of man; but when such a writer becomes precise and circumstantial, and claims a right to be tender and lugubrious in reference to some particular fact which he thinks proper to indicate or describe, it is the legitimate duty of criticism to ascertain whether the special statement be true, for on its truth depends the whole value of the poem as an expression of real grief. In Young's case, it is so difficult to reconcile the actual events with the poetical allusion to them, that we are left to the painful conjecture, that he merely availed himself of a private sorrow to promote his fame in the religious world, by a poem full of pious meditations. If his grief had been as profound as his poem is doleful, it never could have taken so elaborate a form. But, in any case, the *Night Thoughts* is not calculated to procure sympathy or pity.

He commenced the composition of the work immediately after the death of his wife. The first part appeared in 1742, and the last in 1744. In the preface he stated, that " the occasion of this poem was real, not fictitious; and that the facts mentioned did naturally pour out these moral reflections on the thought of the writer." Hence the characters have been supposed to represent his most intimate friends. All the passages

and circumstances relative to Narcissa have been found
sufficiently applicable to his step-daughter.   Her husband, Mr. Temple, between whom and Young the
strongest friendship constantly subsisted, is supposed to
be delineated in Philander, though some of the passages
respecting the latter do not appear to apply to Mr. Temple,
or any other person with whom Young was known to
be acquainted.   His son, who by some early irregularities had fallen under his displeasure, has been considered
the prototype of Lorenzo ; but all the speculations on
this head must be at once dismissed, when it is recol-
lected that this son was only eight years of age when the
poem was begun, and eleven when it was finished.   Lorenzo is a character completed by travel, by education,
and by familiarity with every vice and iniquity ; and
however precocious a child might be, he could scarcely
have arrived at such perfection at the early age of
eleven.   A few of the passages applying to Lorenzo on
other points, leave no room to doubt that the individual
who sat for this portrait was a person of some rank and
years, and a father.   In one place he says,

> " Lorenzo, Fortune makes her court to thee." —

In another :

> " And burns Lorenzo still for the sublime
> Of life to hang his airy nest on high ? "

Again :

> " So wept Lorenzo fair Clarissa's fate ;
> Who gave that angel boy on whom he dotes,
> And died to give him orphan'd in his birth."

And elsewhere he refers to his travels :

> " In foreign realms (for thou hast travell'd far).'

Croft observes, that many expressions in the *Night
Thoughts* would tend to prove that Lorenzo was a mere
creature of the poet's fancy, did not a passage in Night
Eight appear to show that he had something in his eye

for the groundwork at least of the painting. Lovelace or Lorenzo may be feigned characters; but a writer does not feign a name of which he only gives the initial letter:

> " Tell not Calista: she will laugh thee dead,
>   Or send thee to her hermitage with L———. "

So far we have Croft's surmise, which he leaves to make its own impression. If this were Lorenzo, it is clear that his name was a monosyllable; so that it might not have been difficult to trace him out in the list of Young's acquaintance. But it is not easy to discover any connection between the two characters. It is, on the contrary, extremely probable that this " L ———" was, after all, either a fictitious initial, or not the initial of the real Lorenzo. In the absence of all evidence on the subject, would it be hazarding too much to suggest, that, in this compound of bad qualities, Young may have taken revenge upon Wharton for the annuity deeds? That such a design should have been allowed to enter a religious poem, could not with any propriety be suspected of any other religious poet. Had the *Night Thoughts* been written by Dr. Watts, their piety would have been so clear, that a conjecture of this kind could not be permitted to darken it; but Watts and Young are as far removed from each other, as truth and charity from simulation and intolerance.

Young is popularly supposed to have been a man of a melancholy temperament; but so many instances of his jocose humours are related, in a variety of miscellaneous works, as to warrant the inference, that he put on his suit of sables only to suit the occasion. His jocoseness (if that be the correct term) had no touch of cheerfulness in it, probably; — no elasticity — no heartiness; for none of these attributes belonged to his nature. But he had a certain tact in bringing out the mood that was requisite to the surrounding circumstances, by which he was enabled to pass through the scene with a certain degree of effect. With the religious world he was aus-

tere and scrupulous; with Voltaire he spoke impromptu
epigrams; he mourned over his deceased friends in solemn blank verse; and he burlesqued the enemies of
the government in satirical pindarics. He seems to have
had as little stability of temper, as constancy of style.
He never maintained the same disposition long, and he
never wrote twice in the same way. One obvious consequence of all this was, that he hardly ever made up his
mind about any thing; or if he did, he was sure to discover some reason for changing it again. The uneasy
fidget of one whose grand object is to keep up appearances tormented him everlastingly. He was so anxious
to have a reputable exterior with the world, that he was
constantly twirling round and round like a vane — constantly catching the breeze and turning with it; he was
always with the wind, from whatever point it blew; and
hence sometimes he pointed to the north, and sometimes
to the south, and in the course of his life may be said to
have indicated every point of the compass. Thus, what
he wrote one day, he suppressed, disavowed, or contradicted another day. His true estimate of human life,
which set up laughter as the best scourge of vice, was
balanced by the darker philosophy of his "melancholy
maid" in the *Night Thoughts*. His panegyrics were reduced to pulp by his own hands; and after writing for
the theatre, and abandoning it, he returned to it again,
when he thought the wind sat in that quarter.

The tradition of his habitual sadness, or morbid dull-
ness, is derived partly from the character of his principal
poem, and partly from the circumstance, that Grafton,
when Young was writing a tragedy, is said to have sent
him a human skull with a candle in it for a lamp, which
Young is related to have used. But this anecdote is
not worth much. Probably the donor of the scull may
have intended the gift as a joke, or as a sarcasm upon
the graveyard heaviness of Young's dramas; he might
have supposed, that as Young was not a student of living
passion or real character, he stood in need of some such
artificial help; and that his imagination, which was so

rarely lighted up by existing humanity, might catch a
ray from a lamp borrowed from the dead. That Young
cultivated this humour of melancholy, is likely enough ;
and that the occasions which seemed to produce it, were
as often premeditated as accidental, is not less probable.
But causes of grief, when they did actually occur, were
not suffered to pass away unprofitably. " It is not clear
to me," says Croft, " that his muse was not sitting upon
the watch for the first that happened."

The proofs of his capacity for enjoyment are much
more numerous and direct than the evidences of his
poetical and clerical gravity. While he had sundry wise
inscriptions disposed throughout his garden, he conferred an assembly and a bowling-green upon his parish.
Tscharner, in a letter to count Haller, says that he
had lately spent four days with Young, at Welwyn,
where the author took all the ease and pleasure mankind
can desire. " Every thing about him shows the man,
each individual being placed by rule. All is neat
without art. He is very pleasant in conversation, and
very polite." This, and more, observes his biographer
already referred to, may possibly be true ; but Tscharner's was a first visit, a visit of curiosity and admiration, and a visit which the author expected. He might
have added, that, if Young was so agreeable, during a
visit of curiosity from a foreigner, as to afford his guest
" all the ease and pleasure mankind can desire," it may
be naturally inferred, that with intimate friends he was
even more pleasant and agreeable. But it does not appear that he had many intimates. When he made his
will, he could remember the names of only two friends
to be inserted in it for legacies : — his housekeeper, and
a hatter living at the Temple gate, and this after a long
life spent in solicitation for preferment, and the active
employment of his talents in the flattery of the great.
By some people he was supposed to have been the
original of Fielding's Parson Adams ; but that honour is
claimed by others, with greater reason, for a Mr.
William Young, a clergyman whose principal occupa-

tion appears to have been preparing translations from the Greek for the booksellers. The credence, however, given to this supposition, affords us an insight into the notion his contemporaries entertained of his character. At Mr. Doddington's seat, he enjoyed his retirement in so social a spirit, that Pitt records the fact in an epistle, where he speaks of Young seated with Doddington, and

" Charmed with his flowing Burgundy and wit ; "

and the testimony of Mrs. Montague to the charms of his ordinary conversation, by which

" He drew his audience upward to the sky,"

indicates, that he was not of a very austere and melancholy temperament. His housekeeper, probably, was more freely admitted to a knowledge of his real character than any other person, for with every one else he appears to have been " dressed for company ; " with her alone he was in his " wrapper and slippers." His confidence in this domestic lady, to whom he left 1000*l.* in his will, inscribing himself her deceased *friend*, evidently attracted some notice, and drew down rather a malicious and ill-natured piece of ridicule in a kind of novel published by Kidgell, in 1755, called the *Card*, in which the poet and his useful companion were satirised under the names of Dr. Elves and Mrs. Fushy. Sir Herbert Croft was so anxious to learn some particulars concerning Young from the old lady, that he went expressly into the country to visit her; but she was buried two days before he reached the town where she resided.

The strong worldly tendencies of Young were not less remarkably betrayed in the number and adulation of his addresses to the great, than in the complaints against fortune which are scattered through his *Night Thoughts*, notwithstanding the repeated remonstrances on the vanity of earthly desires which that very poem contains. In one place he says—

" When in his courtiers' ears I pour my plaint,
   They drink it as the Nectar of the Great ;
   And squeeze my hand, and beg me come to-morrow."

And elsewhere he avows that he wasted twenty years in besieging the court : —

" Twice told the period spent on stubborn Troy,
   Court favour, yet untaken, I besiege."

Even in the publication of the *Night Thoughts*, in despite of its religious character, and its renunciation of all the objects of mundane ambition, the same pursuit of favours is visible in the dedication of each Night separately to some individual who was either rising, or had already risen, to eminence and power.   Yet, persevering as he was in the chase, he never succeeded in obtaining any preferment whatever.   Perhaps he wearied the patience of his patrons by reiterated applications before an opportunity occurred for serving him; and he may thus have acquired a reputation for importunity which, descending from one administration to another, for ever closed the avenue to advancement upon him. Or it may have been, that his poetical labours were considered inconsistent with his clerical avocations; or, as some suppose, that he gave offence to the king by attaching himself to the prince of Wales, and preaching an obnoxious sermon at St. James's.   But, to whatever cause it may be ascribed, he was consigned to the living conferred upon him by his college, and left there to the end of his life.   The king always turned off any application that was made to him on behalf of Young, by observing, that he had a pension, alluding to a grant of 200*l.* per annum, which had been procured for him by Walpole in the previous reign ; and it is clear, from a passage in a letter to Young, from Secker, archbishop of Canterbury, dated 1758, that all hopes of assistance from the court were idle; and that Secker, who was anxious to serve him in that way, knew that his interference would not only be hopeless, but feared that it would even have the effect of injuring his own interest.   " I have

long wondered," he writes, " that more suitable notice
of your great merit hath not been taken by persons in
power. But how to remedy the omission I see not. No
encouragement hath ever been given me to mention
things of this nature to his majesty. And therefore, in
all likelihood, the only consequence of doing it would
be, weakening the little influence which else I may possibly have on some other occasions." The perusal of
this letter inevitably suggests the inquiry—why did not
the archbishop himself advance him, if he thought him
worthy of his patronage? Archbishops surely have some
livings at their disposal. But it is tolerably obvious that
the whole letter is merely a diplomatic refusal to take
" more suitable notice" of the poet's " great merit." It
is humiliating to contemplate the spectacle of a man of
genius at fourscore years of age persecuting the bishops,
the nobility, and the government, with fruitless solicitations for higher appointments in the church, especially
as the living he already held, and the careful savings of
a prosperous career of authorship, raised him far above
the reach of necessity. The feeling which this mean
passion inspired, was that of immitigable disgust; and it
was perhaps to relieve the court from his applications,
or the church from the scandal of his clamour, that the
princess dowager appointed him clerk to the closet, when
he was too old to perform any more effective duties than
that of receiving the salary of the office.

 In a moment of despondency, after having been repulsed, perhaps, by a minister or some other influential
person, he resolved to abandon the struggle, and to look
for a patron in heaven, having suffered so many disappointments from treasury secretaries, chancellors of
the exchequer, archbishops, dukes, and lords innumerable. Henceforth, he says—

 " Thy *patron* He, whose diadem has dropt
  Yon gems of Heaven; Eternity thy prize;
  And leave the racers of the world their own."

But he did not long continue in this state of beatitude;

for, soon after the publication of the *Night Thoughts*, he wrote a political poem, entitled *Reflections on the Publick Situation of the Kingdom*, in which he once more joined the " racers " he had thus determined upon abandoning for ever. Whether he was subsequently ashamed of this piece, or of the duke of Newcastle, to whom it was inscribed, cannot now be known; but both were left out of his expurgated collection.

He now turned his attention again to the stage, and allowed *The Brothers*, which he had formerly withdrawn upon entering holy orders, to be acted. He designed to bestow the produce, which he calculated would amount to at least 1000*l.*, upon the Society for the Propagation of the Gospel in Foreign Parts; but the play did not meet much success, and he made up the difference from his own purse, bestowing upon the society the full sum he originally contemplated as the probable profit of the production. This is the only instance of pecuniary generosity that can be traced in his life, and, being connected with the diffusion of Christianity, he is entitled to full credit for it; although it is difficult to avoid a suspicion, that one who was so solicitous for advancement in the church, may have thought that a munificent contribution to church objects would have attracted attention in the right quarter. The motives of sordid men, whenever they appear to act with such unexpected liberality, are always exposed to distrust.

The Centaur not fabulous, a series of six letters to a friend, was Young's next publication. One of the most memorable portions of these letters on the sins and frivolities of the day, which the author treats in his usual lumbering and irregular manner, is the description of the death-bed of an imaginary character, the " gay, young, noble, ingenious, accomplished, and most wretched Altamont." This spirited youth dies with a confession, that " his principles had poisoned his friend, his extravagance had beggared his boy, and his unkindness had murdered his wife." Young was fond of these pictures of revolting crime, and seems to have taken a morbid pleasure in throwing the darkest shadows of despair over them. He supposed he was assisting the cause of virtue by making such hideous representations of vice; but his colouring is so extravagant as to render his figures even more ridiculous than revolting. The reader who has sense enough to be impressed by practical illustrations of guilt, is not very likely to be affected by a portrait in which he detects so much absurd exaggeration. None but the lowest order of imagination can be touched by such coarse and vulgar horrors. Lord Euston was supposed to have been delineated in the depraved and miserable Altamont; but the figure bears a family resemblance to Lorenzo, and may with greater propriety be attributed to the invention of the writer.

A piece called the *Old Man's Relapse* has been attributed to Young, and even published with his name; but Croft doubts that it was written by him, and says that it had appeared in a miscellany thirty years before his death. About this time, 1758, he dedicated a sermon to the king, which he had preached before their majesties ; and in the following year he addressed to Richardson, the author of *Sir Charles Grandison*, a letter, called *Conjectures on Original Composition*, the most entertaining of all his prose writings. Considering that Young was now approaching eighty years of age, the sprightliness and variety of this essay cannot fail to excite admiration. The principal aim of the work is to examine and exhibit the difference between the originality of genius and the weakness of imitation, a theme which he elucidates with a felicity of comparison rarely displayed in his other productions. The occasional points of criticism thrown up in the course of inquiry, are for the most part judiciously treated ; and the personal anecdotes of Swift, Addison, and Pope, with which it is enlivened, give it an increased interest. To the memory of Addison he renders full justice, and, perhaps, may be said to carry panegyric too far in his praises of *Cato ;* but of Pope's translation of Homer, he speaks in terms of unmeasured censure. After observing that Homer is "untranslated still," he says of

Pope's version — " What a fall is it from Homer's numbers, free as air, lofty and harmonious as the spheres into childish shackles and tinkling sounds ! But, in his fall, he is still great —

> ' nor appears
> Less than archangel ruined, and the excess
> Of glory obscured.'— *Milton.*

Had Milton never wrote, Pope had been less to blame : but when, in Milton's genius, Homer as it were personally rose to forbid Britons doing him that ignoble wrong,—it is less pardonable by that effeminate decoration to put Achilles in petticoats a second time." All this is intended as a protest against the adoption of rhyme in the translation of Homer ; and a little further on he enforces this view of the subject still more emphatically. " Blank is a term of diminution," he adds ; " what we mean by blank verse, is verse unfallen, uncurst; verse reclaimed, reinthroned in the true language of the gods, who never thundered, nor suffered their Homer to thunder, in rhyme; and therefore I beg you, my friend, to crown it with some nobler term ; nor let the greatness of the thing lie under the defamation of such a name." This suggestion is ingenious, and might be adopted in some cases with advantage. *Blank* verse is certainly a very unhappy term for the full and rich melody of Milton, although it may be doubted whether it is not sufficiently appropriate to the hollow pomp of the *Night Thoughts.* His criticism on Pope, the general justice of which will probably be admitted by the majority of readers, was written after Pope's death ; and Young lies under a heavy charge of inconsistency, or caprice in thus assailing the reputation of a poet whom he had eulogised in the following lines during his lifetime : —

> " Or Milton, thee. Ah! could I reach your strain ;
> Or his, who made Mæonides our own.
> Man too he sung. Immortal man I sing.
> Oh! had he prest his theme, pursu'd the track,
> Which opens out of darkness into day !

> Oh! had he mounted on his wing of fire,
> Soared where I sink, and sung immortal man,
> How had it blest mankind and rescu'd me."

And again in the following line, which appeared immediately after his death:

> " Pope, who could'st make immortals, art thou dead?"

During the life of Pope, Young had always expressed
the highest admiration of his genius, and had enjoyed
the advantage of his friendship for many years; yet in
1756 he permitted an essay on the writings of Pope to
be dedicated to himself, in which the author attempted
to pluck from him—

> " who made Mæonides our own "—

the whole glory of his name, reducing him with much
show of critical independence to the second rank amongst
English poets. Young assented to this dishonouring
verdict; and ratified his acquiescence in it, by his assault
on the translation of Homer in the letter to Richardson.
His second opinion may have been more correct than
his first, and would have excited little animadversion,
had it been expressed in Pope's lifetime; but, appearing
when Pope was in his grave, it recalls the significant
fable of the Ass and the Dead Lion.

Only three years after this vindication of the majesty
of blank verse, Young appeared in rhyme; for it seems
to have been his strange lot to vibrate perpetually from
one extreme to another, and to have no sooner formed a
resolution, or declared a conviction, than to be compelled
by some inexorable fatuity to renounce it. The poem
was entitled *Resignation*, and was written at the request
of one lady, to console another, who had just lost her
husband. It is composed in quatrains of eight and six
syllables, and appears to have been treated with extraordinary and undeserved severity by the critics of the
day. Portions of it had got abroad, and were printed in
the newspapers; and Young, who did not intend it for
publication, having merely printed a few copies in quarto
for his friends, was forced in self-defence to give an

authentic edition of the whole to the world. While the first part was going through the press, Richardson, the printer, died, a circumstance which is alluded to in a passage of earnest and deep feeling introduced by Young upon the receipt of the melancholy intelligence. *Resignation* was the last of Young's poems, and, for its length, the best. It is sustained more equally throughout, possesses stricter unity of design and execution than any of his former works, and is pervaded by a tone of sincere piety, pathetically reflecting the emotions of a man upon whom the flickering scenes of life were swiftly closing.

His anxiety about his fame increased as he advanced in years; and in the hope of releasing himself from the responsibility of all his inferior and doubtful productions, he prepared an edition of his works, in which he struck out all the pieces he did not care to preserve, and all the dedications which he had no longer any motive for retaining; and collecting the remainder into four volumes, he published them under the title of *The Works of the Author of the Night Thoughts.* His grand ambition was to be known to posterity as the author of the *Night Thoughts;* and lest the reputation which he believed that work must finally establish for his name should suffer any diminution of its lustre by the productions of his old age, he placed a special injunction upon his executors, in his will, dated February, 1760, that they should burn all his manuscripts, books, and writings of every description, except his account-book, adding a codicil in the following September, with a dying request to his housekeeper (and a legacy, already mentioned,) to the same effect. This desire was carefully complied with, and no works by the author of the *Night Thoughts* remain, except those which were published during his lifetime.

Of Young's private life, few particulars have been preserved. He appears to have maintained, in his retreat at Welwyn, the commonplace respectability of a

man of easy circumstances and inoffensive habits, tinged
with a little eccentricity in his domestic arrangements,
in the fashioning of his garden, and other domiciliary
matters that concerned merely his own tastes. He who
became a clergyman at fifty, and who practised poetry
until he was eighty years of age, might be allowed to
indulge in such peculiarities, without provoking much observation ; and accordingly we find that, although he had
painted grottoes with classical inscriptions in his grounds,
and many other things out of the ordinary course of cot-
tage gardening and embellishment, and had the reputation
of being a poet into the bargain, which in the country is
the most dangerous of all reputations for a quiet gentleman, he was no lion in his immediate neighbourhood after
all. Not a single record remains of his parochial intercourse, which, considering that he was the incumbent of a
populous district, may be admitted as a proof that he
held little correspondence with the surrounding gentry ;
a conjecture that is strongly confirmed by that remarkably dearth of friendships which marked his decline.
Of the two persons mentioned in his will, one was his
servant, and the other was a London tradesman ; and a
few years before he wrote an epitaph on his footman, in
which he designates him as his *friend.* These circumstances, not very strange in themselves, are singular in
reference to the career of an aspiring and successful
author, who had been all his life soliciting the acquaintance and patronage of the great. If to this paucity of
personal friends and intimates, we add the equally unexplained neglect with which he was treated by those
who had the disposal of ecclesiastical patronage, we are
forced to arrive at a conclusion not very favourable to
his character, to suspect that there must have been some
cause for this universal desertion of the religious poet,
and to look for that cause, not in a malignant conspiracy
of society against an individual, but in some moral
ground of objection to the individual himself.

 The rectory of Welwyn fell to him by virtue of his
standing in the college, and did not come by choice or

favour. He never got any thing else, except the appointment of chaplain to George II., and clerk of the closet to the princess dowager; yet he was incessant in his applications for preferment, and never ceased to flatter every one who had any to bestow. Secker's letter, which was written in answer to one of Young's perpetual demands, shows to what a late period of life he continued to urge his fruitless solicitations. Nor was this all. Upon the accession of George III., his name was struck out of the list of court chaplains, an indignity to a clergyman of fourscore which would scarcely have been determined upon, had there not existed some strong reason for its adoption. Many causes have been suggested for these accumulated disappointments; but they are all purely conjectural, as none of his contemporaries troubled themselves to furnish any statements concerning him; and sir Herbert Croft, who wrote shortly after his death, seems to have been restrained by personal considerations from following up the inquiry; if, indeed, he possessed the means, which is doubtful. Some of these causes have been already alluded to, and the whole may be gathered from the progress and tenor of this biography. It was said that the court which he paid to the prince of Wales, while his royal highness was at variance with his father, injured his interest with the king; that the union of the poetical and the clerical character was, with George II., a certain bar to his advancement, which is not very credible, as the most objectionable and frivolous of his poems were written just before his majesty appointed him to a chaplaincy at court; that he had the bad taste, and worse policy, to preach an unpalatable sermon at St. James's; that he had a pension, which was deemed a sufficient recognition of his pretensions; that his indiscriminate and hyperbolical flattery of men of rank and title, created more enemies than friends; that he was always meddling indiscreetly in politics, and endeavouring to connect himself with political characters; that, while he affected much external piety, he pub-

lished few sermons; that in his latter years he was·
continually proclaiming his unalterable love of retirement, and at the same time straining and striving for
public employment; and that the systematic recantation of his lavish panegyrics generated an impression
that there was no confidence to be reposed in his professions, nor no reliance to be placed on the permanency
of his opinions. These suggestions present a curious
bead-roll of charges and suspicions; yet they do not
solve the enigma. There must have been some cause,
more powerful than the whole of these, for the uniform
repulses he experienced on all sides. If the court neglected him, and private acquaintances did not choose to
be harassed by his importunities, why did not the pre-
lates of the church raise him out of his obscurity?
Can it be doubted that the author of the *Night Thoughts*
would have conferred honour upon any ecclesiastical
station to which he might have been called, if there
existed no insurmountable obstacle to his advancement?
What the obstacle was, cannot now be discovered; but
it is certain that, as a churchman, he filled an equivocal and unenviable position. There is scarcely a solitary
record of a clergyman of any rank amongst his acquaintances or associates; all his dedications and addresses,
without a single exception, were inscribed to laymen.
Secker commiserated his condition, in a short letter, but
did nothing for him, although he possessed the power
to remedy the neglect he professed to deplore: and
when Young died, it is said that the master and children of a charity school, which Young had founded in
his own parish, neglected to attend his funeral, and that
the church bell was not tolled as frequently as was usual
on such occasions.* How are we to account for this

* This fact is stated in the *Biographia.* Sir Herbert Croft denies its
truth, but does not furnish any circumstantial refutation. The value of
his denial will be best appreciated from his own words : " Much," says
the writer, " which I know not to have been true, of the manner of his
burial, is told in the *Biographia ;* of the master and children of a charity
school, which he founded in his parish, who neglected to attend their bene-
factor's corpse ; and of a bell which was not caused to toll as often as upon
those occasions bells usually toll. Had that humanity, which is here lavished upon things of little consequence either to the living or the dead,

general disrespect and avoidance of the man, unless we refer it to some blot in his life, or some serious defect in his character, which the delicacy or indifference of his contemporaries spared? After the death of his wife, he confided the entire management of his domestic affairs to the housekeeper who was so liberally remembered in his will, and who was said to have obtained an improper ascendancy over him in the decline of his life. But that circumstance, however it may have affected him in the estimation of those who chanced to be aware of it, was too obscure in its nature to wound his public reputation, and occurred, moreover, at too late a period to furnish a clue to the continuous neglect of thirty years. Could the disclosures that were made in 1740, of his connection with the profligate Wharton, and the mysterions affair of the annuity deeds, have produced such an extensive alienation of patrons and admirers, desolating his path to the end, and leaving him to close his eyes without the common consolations of friendship? One false step frequently destroys the fairest prospect of a proud career; and such, perhaps, might prove to be the dark moral of this strange narrative, if any evidences remained by which it could be traced.

Towards the latter part of his life, Young was not wholly free from domestic disquietude. His son Frederick had fallen into dissipated courses, and committed so many youthful irregularities, that, even after he had reformed his habits, his father refused to see him, declining an interview with him even on his death-bed. This parental severity was in some measure balanced by a final expression of forgiveness uttered at the last moment, and the bequest of the residue of his property, after the payment of certain legacies. The character of the son has been drawn in strong colours, but without much accuracy or clearness. That he was charge-

been shown in its proper place to the living, I should have had less to say about Lorenzo. They who lament that these misfortunes happened to Young, forget the praise he bestows upon Socrates, in the preface to 'Night Seven,' for resenting his friend's request about his funeral." — See *Life, in Johnson.*

able with some juvenile indiscretions is certain; but it is equally certain that he was not the paragon of iniquity described by those who identified him with the imaginary Lorenzo. He was said to have been dismissed from his college for misconduct, a story which was subsequently disproved. The harsh conduct of Young to this thoughtless heir may probably have had the effect of heightening the errors that drew down his displeasure; inflaming, instead of checking, the impetuous heat of youth. Croft, who defends the son, but seems always to protect the fame of the father, says, in a very suggestive way, " Young was a poet; and poets, with reverence be it spoken, do not make the best parents. . . . He who is connected with the author of the *Night Thoughts* only by veneration for the poet and the Christian, may be allowed to observe, that Young is one of those concerning whom, as you (Dr. Johnson) remark, in your account of Addison, it is proper rather to say nothing that is false, *than all that is true.*" From the extreme caution with which Croft passes over unnoticed many circumstances in Young's life, which would have had the effect in some slight degree of lowering the character of the poet, it is obvious that he was aware of facts connected with Young's conduct as a father, which he thought it prudent, for many reasons, not to disclose. The application to Young of the remark, that it was better to say " nothing that was false, *than all that was true,*" leaves this opinion in the biography open to much speculation. But the curtain of time has fallen upon these incidents, whatever they were, and cannot now be removed.

For the last three or four years of Young's life, he performed no clerical duties although he retained full possession of his faculties to the hour of his death, which took place in the month of April, 1765. He was buried under the communion table of the parish church of Welwyn; and his son erected a marble slab over the spot, on which he caused an epitaph to be inscribed to the memory of both his parents.

Young's reputation as a poet is fixed. It is not, at all events, likely to acquire any additional glory from the applauses of a remote posterity. The *Night Thoughts* will probably be always acceptable to a certain class of readers, who like to find pious reflections in a garb of metre; and the *Revenge* will, doubtless, long keep possession of the stage as a favourable medium for declamation. But, with these exceptions, his works cannot be said to possess the elements of durability. His versification is singularly irregular and crude; and, although he evidently bestowed great pains upon his more important compositions, he rarely attains true grandeur, and never displays much grace or sweetness. His diction is frequently turgid, his conception almost invariably extravagant, and his general treatment of his subjects florid and unnatural. The scholar and the visionary are more apparent in his productions, than the man of observation and feeling; sympathy with human life is every where deficient in his writings; and, while he often dazzles by the unexpected flights of his imagination, he seldom pleases by the truth or continuous beauty of his lines.

MARK AKENSIDE.

(1721—1770.)

Mark Akenside was born on the 9th of November, 1721, at Newcastle-upon-Tyne, where his father followed the humble business of a butcher. The meanness of his origin is said to have given him so much uneasiness in after life, that he tried every means in his power to conceal it from his friends ; but unfortunately he was perpetually reminded of it himself by an awkward halt in his gait, occasioned by the falling of a cleaver on his foot.

He received the rudiments of his education at the free grammar school of his native town, and was afterwards removed to an academy kept by a Mr. Wilson. His friends and relatives being principally of the Presbyterian persuasion, he was sent at eighteen years of age to the university of Edinburgh, for the purpose of becoming a dissenting clergyman, and the expenses of his collegiate course were discharged from a fund subscribed for such objects by the general body of dissenters. After spending one winter in the requisite preparatory studies, he altered his professional destination, and devoted himself to physic ; conscientiously repaying to the fund at a subsequent period the monies that had been expended upon him with a view to the design he thus voluntarily abandoned. He remained three years at Edinburgh, then removed to Leyden, where he studied for two years more, and obtained the degree of M.D. on the 16th of May, 1744.

In a medical thesis which he was required to write, as one of the exercises at the examination for his degree, he is said to have displayed considerable ability and judgment by attacking some opinions of Leeuwenhoeck and others, at that time generally received, but now discarded by the best physicians and philosophers ; and boldly proposing an hypothesis, which has since been received and confirmed.

His poetical genius was developed at a very early period ; even when he was at the grammar school, and private academy in Newcastle. His *Pleasures of the Imagination*, and several other pieces are said to have been written at Morpeth, while he was upon a visit to some relations before he went to Edinburgh. In the latter place he continued to cultivate his literary taste, and composed the *Ode on the Winter Solstice*, which is dated 1740.

In 1744, the poem called the *Pleasures of the Imagination* was offered to Dodsley the publisher, who, afraid to give precipitately the price demanded for the MS., took it to Pope, who, upon reading it, advised him not to make a niggardly offer, as the author was no every-day writer. Dodsley immediately published the poem, which met with great success, and at once raised Akenside to a high rank in the poetical world. Such was the celebrity of the work, that Warburton, Pope's friend, being offended with a note in the third book, in which Shaftesbury's notion that ridicule is the test of truth was revived and supported, did not deem it beneath him to attack the author, not, however, as a poet, but as a philosopher. Akenside was defended in an anonymous pamphlet by his friend Dyson ; and the immediate result of this polemical duel was to attract considerable attention to the new poet. In the revised edition, however, which he contemplated, but did not live to complete, he adopted Warburton's opinions by leaving out both the lines and the note to which that commentator had objected.

The *Pleasures of the Imagination* was followed immediately by a severe invective in an epistle to *Curio*, against the celebrated Pulteney, earl of Bath, for his political tergiversation. With this production he was afterwards dissatisfied — struck out half the lines, and

changed it to the form of an ode. In 1745 he published
ten odes on several subjects, written, as he states in the
preface, at different intervals, and with a view to different
modes of expression and versification. The chief merit
to which he aspires in these lyrics, is that of endeavouring to be correct, and of carefully attending to the best
models. After this period, his poetical publications
were neither numerous nor important. He appears to
have exhausted his imagination in singing its pleasures,
or to have been fearful of risking, by any very elaborate undertaking, the laurels he had already gained. A political
ode to the earl of Huntingdon, in 1748, an ode to the
country gentlemen of England in 1758, and a third in
1766 to Mr. Edwards, on the late edition of Pope's
works, the main object of which was to assail Warburton, constituted the entire of his poetical productions that
appeared in a separate form during those years. Such
of his other pieces as were published in his life-time
appeared in Dodsley's collection. Of these the most
considerable was a hymn to the Naiads.

As a physician he does not appear to have acquired
much reputation. It is said that in his desire to appear
superior to his birth, he exhibited a species of contemptible *hauteur* and ostentation that rendered him
unpopular with his professional brethren, and offended
his patients. He first attempted to practise at North-
ampton; but either not meeting sufficient encouragement there, or being desirous of entering a more ambitious field, he shortly afterwards removed to Hampstead,
where he resided about two years and a half, and then
finally settled in London. Fortunately, his friend
Mr. Dyson had the will as well as the power to
promote his views, and in order to enable him to sustain the appearance necessary to a favourable introduction to practise in town, he generously allowed him 300*l.*
per annum. Whether he annexed any condition to this
munificent patronage, or exacted any pledge of repay-
ment, has not been stated; but even if he did, his liberality
was not the less worthy of admiration. Under such

encouraging auspices, Akenside appears to have made a steady advance in his profession. He became a member of the London College of Physicians — was admitted by Mandamus to the degree of M D. in Cambridge, and chosen Fellow of the Royal Society, and physician to St. Thomas's Hospital. He read the Gulstonian lectures on anatomy, in the theatre of the College of Physicians, and was appointed Krohnian lecturer; but having chosen for his subject the history of the revival of literature, and delivered three lectures on it, a member of the college expressed an objection against his selection of a subject foreign to the objects of the institution; and Akenside threw up the appointment in disgust.

He also published several papers on medical subjects, as *Observations on the Origin and Use of Lymphatic Vessels in Animals*, being the substance of his Gulstonian lectures. These appeared in the *Philosophical Transactions* for 1757. *An Account of a Blow on the Heart, and its Effects*, published in the *Transactions* for 1763. His principal medical works, *A Treatise on the Epidemic Dysentery of* 1764, written in elegant classic Latin, and *Observations on Cancers, On the Use of Ipecacuanha in Asthmas*, and *On a Method of Treating White Swellings of the Joints*, appeared in the first volume of the *Medical Transactions*. Having thus obtained some reputation, and probably extended his practice, he was appointed, on the settlement of the queen's household, one of her majesty's physicians. For this distinction it is supposed he was principally indebted to Mr. Dyson, who had then become a member of the administration, particularly as his extremely liberal opinions must have been so unpalatable at court, as to require some high ministerial influence to procure him such a mark of favour. He did not live long, however, to enjoy his good fortune, having taken a putrid fever, of which he died on the 23d of June, 1770. He was buried in the parish church of St. James, Westminster. After his death Mr. Dyson took possession of his effects, and particularly of his books and prints, which he had been at much pains to collect. It does not appear in what capacity he acted, whether as friend, creditor, or legatee; but certainly no person was so well intitled to inherit the personal effects of the poet.

Of Akenside's life, private or professional, few memorials remain. He seems to have glided away almost unnoticed, and to have had scarcely a single friend who was interested enough about him to publish any particulars concerning his habits, his studies, or his actions.

He was a great admirer of the literature and philosophy of the ancients, particularly of Plato, Cicero, and their disciples, adherents, and followers; and was suspected to have imbibed a greater respect for their free principles and natural religion than was consistent with a thorough devotion to the monarchy and the faith of a Christian. It has been said that in politics he was a republican, and in theology a deist. The *Pleasures of the Imagination* may be referred to in support of the latter charge. Throughout that work there is not the slightest allusion to the immortality of the soul. To the great fundamental principles of religion he is considered to have been sincerely attached, though the excess of his liberality in favour of the ancients and of natural religion leaves him open to the charge of heterodoxy by all the established churches of the world.* Of the republicanism imputed to him no very clear evidence can be discovered in his works. When he celebrates the cause of freedom with reference to this country, he does so only as a zealous liberal, warmly attached to the cause of civil and religious liberty. For the memory of William III. he always testifies the highest veneration. and for that of the other men by whom the Revolution was

---

* In his *Ode to the Author of the Memoirs of the House of Brandenburg,* he says —

" Ye who made victorious Athens wise,
Ye first of mortals *with the blest inroll'd.*"

For uttering a similar sentiment, admitting the possibility that the pagans of antiquity might be received into Paradise, one of the Oxford poets, referred to in the previous notices of the Minor Poets, was severely censured by the university.

effected. Mr. Dyson is supposed to have shared in the early republican tendencies of his friend, but the enthusiasm of both was gradually cooled in subsequent years.

Two alterations in Akenside's *Odes* have been noticed in reference to this change of sentiment. In the *Ode on leaving Holland* the following lines appeared in the first edition : —

> " I go where *Freedom in the streets is known,*
> And tells a monarch on his throne,
> *Tells him, he reigns, he lives but by her voice.*"

Those lines he modified in the last edition to —

> " I go where *Liberty to all is known,*
> And tells a monarch on his throne,
> *He reigns not but by her preserving voice.*"

In the *Ode to the Earl of Huntingdon* the following lines originally appeared —

> " But here, where Freedom's equal throne
> To all her valiant sons is known,
> *Where all direct the sword she wears,*
> And each the power which rules him shares."

In the last edition the third line is altered to —

> " *Where all are conscious of her cares.*"

Such alterations as these have been quoted in proof of a change of sentiment ; but it is difficult to detect any thing more in them than perhaps a nicer discrimination of truth or euphony. It does not appear that he connected himself with the liberal party of his day. Indeed the only political character, except Mr. Dyson, with whom there are any reasons for supposing him to have been even acquainted, was the right honourable Charles Townshend, to whom he makes such allusions in two of his *Odes* as to leave the impression that they were on terms of intimate friendship.

Notwithstanding the favour with which the *Pleasures of the Imagination* was received, Akenside became sensible that it required revision and correction. This disagreeable labour he accordingly undertook, but so quick was the demand for the several successive editions, that there was not sufficient time to complete all the corrections he considered desirable. He continued for several years to amend the poem at his leisure, until at length, despairing of being ever able to execute it to his own satisfaction, he resolved to write the poem anew upon a somewhat different and enlarged plan. This undertaking, however, he did not live to complete, which, perhaps, the world need not regret, as it appears, from the changes he made, that while the poem was gaining in philosophy it was losing in poetry. He designed at first to comprise the whole of the subject in four books, but afterwards determined to distribute it into a greater number. How far his new plan would have carried him, had he lived to finish it, is uncertain. At his death he had arranged only the first and second books, a considerable part of the third, and the introduction to the fourth.

INDEX.

THE END.

LONDON:
Printed by SPOTTISWOODE & Co.,
New-street-Square.